Cultural Trauma

In this book, Ron Eyerman explores the formation of the African American identity through the theory of cultural trauma. The trauma in question is slavery, not as an institution or as personal experience, but as collective memory: a pervasive remembrance that grounded a people's sense of itself. Combining a broad narrative sweep with more detailed studies of important events and individuals, Eyerman reaches from emancipation through the Harlem Renaissance, the Depression, the New Deal, and the Second World War to the civil rights movement and beyond. He offers insights into the intellectual and generational conflicts of identity-formation which have a truly universal significance, as well as providing a new and compelling account of the birth of African American identity. Anyone interested in questions of assimilation, multiculturalism, and postcolonialism will find this book indispensable.

PROFESSOR RON EYERMAN is the holder of the Segerstedt Chair of Sociology at Uppsala University and Professor of Sociology at the University of Copenhagen, and a fellow of the Center for Advanced Study in the Behavioural Sciences at Stanford University (1999–2000). His recent publications include *Music and Social Movements* (Cambridge, 1998).

Cultural Trauma

Cambridge Cultural Social Studies

Series editors: JEFFREY C. ALEXANDER, *Department of Sociology, Yale University, and* STEVEN SEIDMAN, *Department of Sociology, University at Albany, State University of New York.*

Titles in the series

ILANA FRIEDRICH SILBER, *Virtuosity, Charisma, and Social Order* 0 521 41397 4 hardback

LINDA NICHOLSON AND STEVEN SEIDMAN (eds.), *Social Postmodernism* 0 521 47516 3 hardback 0 521 47571 6 paperback

WILLIAM BOGARD, *The Simulation of Surveillance* 0 521 55081 5 hardback 0 521 55561 2 paperback

SUZANNE R. KIRSCHNER, *The Religious and Romantic Origins of Psychoanalysis* 0 521 44401 2 hardback 0 521 55560 4 paperback

PAUL LICHTERMAN, *The Search for Political Community* 0 521 48286 0 hardback 0 521 48343 3 paperback

ROGER FRIEDLAND AND RICHARD HECHT, *To Rule Jerusalem* 0 521 44046 7 hardback

KENNETH H. TUCKER, JR., *French Revolutionary Syndicalism and the Public Sphere* 0 521 56359 3 hardback

ERIK RINGMAR, *Identity, Interest and Action* 0 521 56314 3 hardback

ALBERTO MELUCCI, *The Playing Self* 0 521 56401 8 hardback 0 521 56482 4 paperback

ALBERTO MELUCCI, *Challenging Codes* 0 521 57051 4 hardback 0 521 57843 4 paperback

SARAH M. CORSE, *Nationalism and Literature* 0 521 57002 6 hardback 0 521 57912 0 paperback

DARNELL M. HUNT, *Screening the Los Angeles 'Riots'* 0 521 57087 5 hardback 0 521 57814 0 paperback

LYNETTE P. SPILLMAN, *Nation and Commemoration* 0 521 57404 8 hardback 0 521 57683 0 paperback

(list continues at end of book)

Cultural Trauma

Slavery and the formation of African American identity

Ron Eyerman

PUBLISHED BY THE PRESS SYNDICATE OF THE UNIVERSITY OF CAMBRIDGE
The Pitt Building, Trumpington Street, Cambridge, United Kingdom

CAMBRIDGE UNIVERSITY PRESS
The Edinburgh Building, Cambridge CB2 2RU, UK
40 West 20th Street, New York, NY 10011-4211, USA
477 Williamstown Road, Port Melbourne, VIC 3207, Australia
Ruiz de Alarcón 13, 28014 Madrid, Spain
Dock House, The Waterfront, Cape Town 8001, South Africa

http://www.cambridge.org

First published 2001

Printed in the United Kingdom at the University Press, Cambridge

Typeface Times (monotype) 10/12.5   *System* LATEX 2_ε [TB]

A catalogue record for this book is available from the British Library.

Library of Congress cataloguing in publication data
Eyerman, Ron.
Cultural trauma: slavery and the formation of African American identity / Ron Eyerman.
    p.   cm.
Includes bibliographical references and index.
ISBN 0 521 80828 6 – ISBN 0 521 00437 3 (pb.)
1. African Americans – Race identity.   2. Slavery – United States – Psychological aspects.
3. African Americans – Psychology.   4. Slaves – United States – Psychology.   I. Title.
E185.625 .E96   2001
305.896′073 – dc21   2001035639

ISBN 0 521 80828 6 hardback
ISBN 0 521 00437 3 paperback

Contents

Acknowledgments

This book would not have been possible without the financial help of the Swedish Research Council for the Humanities and Social Sciences (HSFR) and the inspiration provided by my colleagues at the Center for Advanced Study in the Behavioral Sciences, Stanford University and Uppsala University. It was during my stay at the Center that the ideas which form the basis of this book took shape; special thanks to Jeff Alexander, Nancy Cott, Bernhard Giesen, Neil Smelser, and Piotr Sztompka, as well as the wonderful staff who provided the necessary groundwork that permitted my spirit to range freely. My colleagues at Uppsala University listened patiently to my presentations and provided insightful comments, as did Johanna Esseveld of the University of Lund. Finally, the Cambridge University Press readers and editors were extremely helpful and encouraging in their criticisms and comments. Warm thanks to Birgitta Lindencrona for lending me her African American cookbooks.

1

Cultural trauma and collective memory

What has been lost is the continuity of the past . . . What you then are left with is still the past, but a *fragmented* past, which has lost its certainty of evaluation.

Hannah Arendt

It is memory that counts, that controls the rich mastery of the story, impels it along . . .

Jorge Semprun

Introduction

In this book the formation of an African American identity will be explored through the theory of cultural trauma (Alexander *et al.* 2001). The "trauma" in question is slavery, not as institution or even experience, but as collective memory, a form of remembrance that grounded the identity-formation of a people. There is a difference between trauma as it affects individuals and as a cultural process. As cultural process, trauma is mediated through various forms of representation and linked to the reformation of collective identity and the reworking of collective memory. The notion of a unique African American identity emerged in the post-Civil War period, after slavery had been abolished.[1] The trauma of forced servitude and of nearly complete subordination to the will and whims of another was thus not necessarily something directly experienced by many of the subjects of this study, but came to be central to their attempts to forge a collective identity out of its remembrance. In this sense, slavery was traumatic in retrospect, and formed a "primal scene" which could, potentially, unite all "African Americans" in the United States, whether or not they had themselves been slaves or had any knowledge of or feeling for Africa. Slavery formed the root of an emergent collective identity through an equally emergent collective memory, one that signified and distinguished a race, a people, or a community depending on the level of abstraction and point of view being put

1

forward. It is this discourse on the collective and its representation that is the focus of this book.

That slavery was traumatic may seem obvious, and, for those who experienced it directly, certainly it must have been. In a recent attempt to trace the effects of slavery on contemporary African American behavior patterns, Orlando Patterson (1998:40) writes, "another feature of slave childhood was the added psychological trauma of witnessing the daily degradation of their parents at the hands of slaveholders . . . to the trauma of observing their parents' humiliation was later added that of being sexually exploited by Euro-Americans on and off the estate, as the children grew older." While this may be an appropriate use of the concept of trauma, it is not what I have in mind here. The notion of an African American identity was articulated in the later decades of the nineteenth century by a generation of black intellectuals for whom slavery was a thing of the past, not the present. It was the memory of slavery and its representation through speech and art works that grounded African American identity and permitted its institutionalization in organizations like the National Association for the Advancement of Colored People (NAACP), founded in 1909. If slavery was traumatic for this generation of intellectuals, it was so in retrospect, mediated through recollection and reflection, and, for some, tinged with some strategic, practical, and political interest.

As opposed to psychological or physical trauma, which involves a wound and the experience of great emotional anguish by an individual, cultural trauma refers to a dramatic loss of identity and meaning, a tear in the social fabric, affecting a group of people that has achieved some degree of cohesion. In this sense, the trauma need not necessarily be felt by everyone in a community or experienced directly by any or all. While it may be necessary to establish some event as the significant "cause," its traumatic meaning must be established and accepted, a process which requires time, as well as mediation and representation. Arthur Neal (1998) defines a "national trauma" according to its "enduring effects," and as relating to events "which cannot be easily dismissed, which will be played over again and again in individual consciousness," becoming "ingrained in collective memory." In this account, a national trauma must be understood, explained, and made coherent through public reflection and discourse. Here, mass-mediated representations play a decisive role. This is also the case in what we have called cultural trauma. Neil Smelser (in Alexander *et al.* 2001) offers a more formal definition of cultural trauma that is worth repeating: "a memory accepted and publicly given credence by a relevant membership group and evoking an event or situation which is (a) laden with negative affect, (b) represented as indelible, and (c) regarded as threatening a society's existence or violating one or more of its fundamental cultural presuppositions."

In the current case, the phrase "or group's identity" could be added to the last sentence. It is the collective memory of slavery that defines an individual as a "race member," as Maya Angelou (1976) puts it.

In Cathy Caruth's (1995:17; Caruth 1996) psychoanalytic theory of trauma, it is not the experience itself that produces traumatic effect, but rather the remembrance of it. In her account there is always a time lapse, a period of "latency" in which forgetting is characteristic, between an event and the experience of trauma. As reflective process, trauma links past to present through representations and imagination. In psychological accounts, this can lead to a distorted identity-formation, where "certain subject-positions may become especially prominent or even overwhelming, for example, those of victim or perpetrator . . . wherein one is possessed by the past and tends to repeat it compulsively as if it were fully present" (LaCapra 1994:12).

Allowing for the centrality of mediation and imaginative reconstruction, one should perhaps speak not of traumatic events, but rather of traumatic affects (Sztompka in Alexander *et al.* 2001). While trauma refers necessarily to something experienced in psychoanalytic accounts, calling this experience "traumatic" requires interpretation. National or cultural trauma (the difference is minimal at the theoretical level) is also rooted in an event or series of events, but not necessarily in their direct experience. Such experience is usually mediated, through newspapers, radio, or television, for example, which involves a spatial as well as temporal distance between the event and its experience. Mass-mediated experience always involves selective construction and representation, since what is seen is the result of the actions and decisions of professionals as to what is significant and how it should be presented. Thus, national or cultural trauma always engages a "meaning struggle," a grappling with an event that involves identifying the "nature of the pain, the nature of the victim and the attribution of responsibility" (Alexander *et al.* 2001). Alexander calls this the "trauma process," when the collective experience of massive disruption, and social crises, becomes a crisis of meaning and identity. In this trauma process "carrier groups" are central in articulating the claims, and representing the interests and desires, of the affected to a wider public. In this case, intellectuals, in the term's widest sense (Eyerman 1994), play a significant role. Intellectual here will refer to a socially constructed, historically conditioned role rather than to a structurally determined position or a personality type. Although bound up with particular individuals, the notion will refer more to what they do than to who they are. Generally speaking, intellectuals mediate between the cultural and political spheres that characterize modern societies, not so much representing and giving voice to their own ideas and interests, but rather articulating ideas to and for others. Intellectuals are mediators and translators between spheres of activity and differently situated social groups, including the situatedness in time and space. Intellectuals in this sense can be film directors and singers of songs, as well as college professors. In addition, social movements produce "movement intellectuals" who may lack the formal education usually associated with the term intellectual, but whose role in articulating the aims and values of a movement allow one to call them by that name.

Like physical or psychic trauma, the articulating discourse surrounding cultural trauma is a process of mediation involving alternative strategies and alternative voices. It is a process that aims to reconstitute or reconfigure a collective identity through collective representation, as a way of repairing the tear in the social fabric. A traumatic tear evokes the need to "narrate new foundations" (Hale 1998:6) which includes reinterpreting the past as a means toward reconciling present/future needs. There may be several or many possible responses or paths to resolving cultural trauma that emerge in a specific historical context, but all of them in some way or other involve identity and memory. To anticipate, the appellation "African American," which may seem more or less obvious and natural today, was one of several paths or reactions to the failure of reconstruction to fully integrate former slaves and their offspring as American citizens and to the new consensus concerning the past in the dominant culture in which slavery was depicted as benign and civilizing. The idea of returning to Africa had been a constant theme amongst blacks almost from the first landing of slaves on the American continent.[2] Another alternative, later in its development, also involved emigration, but to Kansas and the North, to Canada or the free states, rather than to Africa. Such a move in the later decades of the 1800s would not necessarily exclude a new identity as, say, an African American, but would not necessarily include it either; it would, however, involve an openness to new forms of identification and the attempt to leave others behind.[3]

Developing what W. E. B. Du Bois would describe as a "double consciousness," both African and American, offered another possibility, one that implied loyalty to a nation but not necessarily to its dominant culture or way of life. In 1897, Du Bois posed the question "What, after all, am I? Am I an American or a Negro? Can I be both? Or is it my duty to cease to be a Negro as soon as possible and be an American?" (Du Bois [1897] 1999:16–17). Being an aspect of the process of cultural trauma, however this dilemma is resolved, interpretation and representation of the past and the constitution of collective memory are central. The meaning of slavery was a focal point of reference. A similar process was under way amongst whites, and black attempts to negotiate cultural trauma were intimately intertwined with this national project. By the mid-1880s the Civil War had become the "civilized war," "a space both for sectional reconciliation and for the creation of modern southern whiteness" (Hale 1998:67ff.). As the nation was re-membered through a new narration of the war, blacks were at once made invisible and punished. Reconstruction, and blacks in general, were made the objects of hate, the Other, against which the two sides in the war could reunite and reconcile. The memory of slavery was recast as benign and civilizing, a white man's project around which North and South could reconcile.

Collective memory

The history of the study of memory is a tale of the search for a faculty, a quest for the way in which the mind-brain codes, stores and retrieves information. Only with the recent interest in language and in cultural aspects of thinking has there emerged the wider view of remembering as something that people do together, reminding themselves of and commemorating experiences which they have jointly undertaken.   (Radley 1990)

Memory is usually conceived as individually based, something that goes on "inside the heads" of individual human beings. "Memory has three meanings: the mental *capacity* to retrieve stored information and to perform learned mental operations, such as long division; the semantic, imagistic, or sensory *content* of recollections; and the *location* where these recollections are stored" (Young 1995). Theories of identity-formation or socialization tend to conceptualize memory as part of the development of the self or personality and to locate that process within an individual, with the aim of understanding human actions and their emotional basis. In such accounts, the past becomes present through the embodied reactions of individuals as they carry out their daily lives. In this way, memory helps to account for human behavior. Notions of collective identity built on this model, such as those within the collective behavior school, theorize a "loss of self" and the formation of new, collectively based, identities as the outcome of participation in forms of collective behavior like social movements. Here memory, as far as it relates to the individual participant's biography, tends to be downplayed, because it is thought to act as a barrier to forms of collective behavior that transcend the normal routines of daily life. The barrier of memory once crossed, the new collective identity is created *sui generis*, with the collective rather than the individual as its basis. The question of whether this collective may develop a memory has, as far as we know, rarely been addressed by this school.[4]

Alongside these individual-focused accounts of memory have existed concerns with collective identity and with "how societies remember" (Connerton 1989), with roots in Durkheim's notion of collective consciousness. Here collective memory is defined as recollections of a shared past "that are retained by members of a group, large or small, that experienced it" (Schuman and Scott

1989:361–62), and passed on either in an ongoing process of what might be called public commemoration, in which officially sanctioned rituals are engaged to establish a shared past, or through discourses more specific to a particular group or collective. This socially constructed, historically rooted collective memory functions to create social solidarity in the present. As developed by followers of Durkheim such as Maurice Halbwachs (1992), memory is collective in that it is supra-individual, and individual memory is conceived in relation to a group, be this geographical, positional, ideological, political, or generationally based. In Halbwachs' classical account, memory is always group memory, both because the individual is derivative of some collectivity, family, and community, and also because a group is solidified and becomes aware of itself through continuous reflection upon and recreation of a distinctive, shared memory. Individual identity is said to be negotiated within this collectively shared past. Thus, while there is always a unique, biographical memory to draw upon, it is described as always rooted in a collective history. This collective memory provides the individual with a cognitive map within which to orient present behavior. From this perspective, collective memory is a social necessity; neither an individual nor a society can do without it. As Bernhard Giesen (in Alexander *et al.* 2001) points out, collective memory provides both individual and society with a temporal map, unifying a nation or community through time as well as space. Collective memory specifies the temporal parameters of past and future, where we came from and where we are going, and also why we are here now. Within the narrative provided by this collective memory individual identities are shaped as experiential frameworks formed out of, as they are embedded within, narratives of past, present and future.[5]

The shift in emphasis in the social sciences and humanities toward language-based, text-oriented analysis has brought new developments to the study of memory. In the field of comparative literature, for example, more attention is being paid to the importance of collective memory in the formation of ethnic identity, and the role of literary works in this reflective process. With the cultural turn focusing on cognitive framing, language, and the emphasis on language and inter-textuality, memory is located not inside the heads of individual actors, but rather "within the discourse of people talking together about the past" (Radley, 1990:46). This is a development which has its roots in linguistic and textual analysis which often is called "post-structuralism," and in feminist theory and practice. In the 1970s feminists developed techniques of "consciousness-raising" which attempted to make the personal political, to theorize the development of the self within a political as well as a symbolically structured social context. Armed with theories of socialization that combined Marx and Freud (and sometimes G. H. Mead), feminists developed techniques for liberating individuals from the distorted identity-formation of male dominated society. Like the collective behavior school mentioned above, with whom they shared many theoretical assumptions, some feminists viewed individual memory as a barrier to collective political action. "Memory work" was one technique developed by feminists after the women's movement moved into the academy, as a way of recalling faded or repressed images of domination.

A more recent development concerns the idea of collective memory itself. The editors of a volume concerning developments in literary theory (Singh *et al.* 1994) define collective memory as "the combined discourses of self: sexual, racial, historical, regional, ethnic, cultural, national, familial, which intersect in an individual." These form a net of language, a meta narrative, which a community shares and within which individual biographies are oriented. Here Foucault and post-structuralism unite with the Durkheimian tradition referred to above. Collective memory is conceived as the outcome of interaction, a conversational process within which individuals locate themselves. This dialogic process is one of negotiation for both individuals and the collective itself. It is never arbitrary.

From this perspective, the past is a collectively shaped, if not collectively experienced, temporal reference point, which forms an individual, more than it is re-shaped to fit generational or individual needs. This is a necessary addendum, especially where political motivation is concerned. In response to what he calls the "interest theory" of memory construction where the past is thought to be entirely malleable to present needs, Michael Schudson (1989) suggests several ways in which the past is resistant to total manipulation, not least of which is that some parts of the past have been recorded and thus obtain at least a degree of objectivity. Supporting this, Barry Schwartz writes, "given the constraints of a recorded history, the past cannot be literally constructed, it can only be selectively exploited" (Schwartz 1982:398). In this context a distinction between collective memory and history is useful. If, as Halbwachs suggests, collective memory is always group memory, always the negotiated and selective recollections of a specific group, then collective memory is similar to myth.[6] This, in fact, is how Neal (1998) conceives of it in his work on national trauma.[7] From Halbwachs' "presentist" perspective, collective memory is essential to a group's notion of itself and thus must continually be made over to fit historical circumstance. While this collective memory makes reference to historical events, that is events that are recorded and known to others, the meaning of such events is interpreted from the perspective of the group's needs and interests, within limits, of course. History, especially as a profession and academic discipline, aims at something wider, more objective and universal than group memory. Of course, history is always written from some point of view and can be more or less ethnocentric, but as an academic discipline, even within the constraints of nationally based institutions, its aims and, especially, its rules of evidence, are of a different sort from the collective memory of a group. At the very least, professional historical accounts can be criticized for their ethnocentrism.[8]

A conversation overheard between an historian and a Holocaust victim can perhaps illustrate what I mean. In this conversation the victim was recalling his memories of an infamous Jewish guard in a Polish ghetto. He vividly recalled his personal experience of this man. The historian pointed out that this could not have occurred, as this guard was in another camp at that particular time, and could document that claim. The victim remained skeptical, but perhaps because he was also a scientist, was willing to consider the claim. Later, the historian, who specializes in atrocities like the Holocaust, recounted that he often faced this problem of the difference between memory and documented history.

While the focus on language and ways of speaking has had many liberating aspects for the study of collective memory and identity, there are limitations as well. According to Alan Radley:

this movement . . . still falls short of addressing questions related to remembering in a world of things – both natural, and products of cultural endeavor – where it concentrates upon memory as a product of discourse. The emphasis upon language tends to hide interesting questions which arise once we acknowledge that the sphere of material objects is ordered in ways upon which we rely for a sense of continuity and as markers of temporal change.   (Radley 1990)

Viewing memory as symbolic discourse in other words tends to downplay or ignore the impact of material culture on memory and identity-formation. From the point of view of discourse analysis, objects gain meaning only when they are talked about. Radley's point is that the way things are organized, whether the objects of routine everyday experience, like the furniture in a room or the more consciously organized objects in a museum, also evokes memory and a "sense of the past," whether this is articulated through language or not. Food and household items can evoke memory, such as the examples found in the African American cookbook *Spoonbread and Strawberry Wine* (Darden and Darden 1994:xi), "Aunt Norma's biscuit cutter, Aunt Maude's crocheted afghan, our father's old medicine bottles (representing a medical practice of over sixty years) all evoke powerful and loving memories."[9] The same can be said of other cultural artifacts, like music and art objects. Listening to a particular piece of music or gazing at a painting can evoke a strong emotional response connected to the past, and be formative of individual and collective memory. Memory can also be embedded in physical geography, as illustrated by Maya

Angelou's vivid description of returning to the small Southern hamlet where she grew up:

> The South I returned to ... was flesh-real and swollen-belly poor. Stamps, Arkansas ... had subsisted for hundreds of years on the returns of cotton plantations, and until World War I, a creaking lumbermill. The town was halved by railroad tracks, the swift Red River and racial prejudice. Whites lived on the town's small rise (it couldn't be called a hill), while blacks lived in what had been known since slavery as "the Quarters." (Angelou 1974:61)

As Angelou recounts in her biography, the memory of slavery colored almost all of her experience, especially in relations to whites. Barton (2001) reveals how race is materialized in spatial organization and thus recollection.

> As a social construct and concept, race has had a profound influence on the spatial development of the American landscape, creating separate, though sometimes parallel, overlapping or even superimposed cultural landscapes for black and white Americans. The spaces forming these landscapes were initially "constructed" by the politics of American slavery, and subsequently "designed" by the customs, traditions and ideology emanating from the Supreme Court's "separate but equal" finding in Plesy v. Ferguson, as well as 20th-century "Jim Crow" statutes. (xv)

There is a point to the post-structuralist argument, however, that the actual significance of a response, what it "really" means, is fashioned through language and dialogue and may change depending on the context. Thus, while the arrangement of material artifacts may evoke a "sense of the past" or of something else, what exactly this "sense" is requires articulation through language.

This points further to the issue of representation. How is the past to be represented in the present, to individuals and, more importantly in this context, to and for a collective? If we take the preceding arguments into account, the past is not only recollected, and thus represented through language, it is also recalled, imagined, through association with artifacts, some of which have been arranged and designated for that purpose. If narrative, the "power of telling," is intimately intertwined with language, with the capacity and more importantly perhaps, with the possibility to speak, representation can be called "the power of looking" (Hale 1998:8) and associated with the capacity to see and the possibility to make visible. The question of who can speak and to whom, as well as the issue of who can make visible, are thus central. This point is made in Ralph Ellison's *Invisible Man*, where according to Barton (2001:1), "the ability to render the world visible and invisible is a concrete form of power, and is part of the social construction of race."

These are matters of great interest to the present study. How was slavery represented, literally and visually, in whose interests and for what purposes? What role if any did former slaves have in this process of collective remembering through public representation? How slavery was represented in literature, music, the plastic arts and, later, film, is crucial to the formation and reworking of collective memory and collective identity by the generations which followed emancipation.[10] What social movements provide is a context in which individual biographies and thus memories can be connected with others, fashioned into a unified collective biography and thereby transformed into a political force. Social movements reconnect individuals by and through collective representations; they present the collective and represent the individual in a double sense, forging individual into collective memory and representing the individual as part of a collective.

The place of generation in collective memory

If collective memory is always group-based and subject to adjustment according to historically rooted needs, what are the spatial and temporal parameters that mark this process of reinterpretation? As social groups are mobile, so are the borders of its memory and collective identity-formation. The spatial parameters marking these borders vary and have attained more fluidity with the exponential development of mass media. While they may be rooted in relatively specified geographic boundaries, with the aid of mediated representation they may span such restricted space to reach exiles and expatriates. Alternatively, they may reflect non-geographical ethnic and religious foundations that can be diffused over great distances. While both Karl Mannheim and Halbwachs root memory in real communities, those which have face-to-face contact, recent approaches expand this notion to include the "imagined" communities described by Anderson (1991). This has to do in part with the rise to significance of the electronic mass media and the migration of populations, both of which fall under the umbrella term "globalization." As Igartua and Paez (1997) put it after studying the symbolic reconstruction of the Spanish Civil War, "collective memory does not only exist in the individuals, but that in fact it is located in cultural artefacts. Analyzing the contents of cultural creations, as for example films, one may see how a social group symbolically reconstructs the past in order to confront traumatic events for which it is responsible" (81). This means that the collective memory which forms the basis for collective identity can transcend many spatial limitations when it is recorded or represented by other means. The Armenian-Canadian film maker Atom Egoyan has, in his films, for example, traces of remembrance of the slaughter of Armenians by Turks in 1915 an event which has shaped the collective identity of Armenians ever since. This group is now spread over the globe, but its identity-forming collective memory remains apparently intact, partly due to such media as film as well as the stories passed within the community itself.[11]

Temporally, the parameters of collective memory appear a bit more fixed. Research on memory has brought forth the generational basis of remembrance and forgetting as key to adjusting interpretations of the past.[12] Survey-based research such as that carried out by Howard Schuman and Jacqueline Scott (1989) has investigated whether or not there are particular events which distinguish generations and which shape the actions of individuals through memory. Their study focused on Americans in the post Second World War era and found that those who came of age during the Vietnam War shared a distinctive collective memory of that period, something that distinguished this cohort from others. Other studies of "traumatic events," such as the Spanish Civil War (Igartua and Paez 1997) have made similar findings. Taking their starting point in Karl Mannheim's theory of generation, what these studies tend to show is that "attributions of importance to national and world events of the past half century tend to be a function of having experienced an event during adolescence or early adulthood" (Schuman, Belli, and Bischoping 1997:47). In Mannheim's original formulation, it was proposed that the events experienced during adolescence are those most likely to "stick" in later life and to influence behavior. Also, those passing through the life cycle at the same point in time are likely to recall the same events, allowing one to speak of a generational memory.

In what would generational memory consist, how would it be produced and maintained? Mannheim had a very optimistic and positive account of generational memory, at least concerning its general "function," before it is filled with the historically determined specifics. The function of generational memory for Mannheim consists in offering "fresh-contact" "with the social and cultural heritage" of a social order, which "facilitates re-evaluation of our inventory and teaches us both to forget that which is no longer useful and to covet that which has yet to be won" (Mannheim 1952:360). Here, collective forgetting is as important as collective remembering for a society's self-reflection; it is in fact the role of youth or the new generation: to provide society with a fresh look at itself. Aside from this general, and generally positive, role, generational memory consists of a record of and a reaction to those "significant" events which an age-cohort directly experiences. As noted, for Mannheim this involves having direct experience. Later investigators have added mediated experiences, both as formative of a generation and also in terms of retention or reproduction of that generation and others. Thus, not all those who lived through the Sixties participated in social movements, but many others saw them on television. Probably those who participated directly would have a stronger sense of belonging to "the sixties generation," but those who experienced it on television and are of the same age might also feel a strong sense of belongingness. The question is, would those of a different age who saw it on TV have any sense of belongingness, and where would the age-related boundaries fall? In any case, the role of the mass media in producing and reinforcing generational identity is a much more central question in the current age than it was in Mannheim's.[13]

The cycle of (generational) memory

The notion of cultural trauma implies that direct experience of an event is not a necessary condition for its inclusion in the trauma process. It is through time-delayed and negotiated recollection that cultural trauma is experienced, a process which places representation in a key role. How an event is remembered is intimately entwined with how it is represented. Here the means and media of representation are crucial, for they bridge the gap between individuals and between occurrence and its recollection. Social psychological studies provide grounds for a theory of generational cycles in the reconstruction of collective memory and the role of the media in that process.

After analyzing various examples, Pennebaker and Banasik (1997) found that approximately every twenty to thirty years individuals look back and reconstruct a "traumatic" past. In applying this account to their study of the remembrance of the Spanish Civil War, Igartua and Paez (1997:83–84) list four factors that underlie and help explain this generational cycle:

1. The existence of the necessary psychological distance that remembering a collective or individual traumatic event requires. Time may soothe and lessen the pain that remembering a traumatic event produces. 2. The necessary accumulation of social resources in order to undergo the commemoration activities. These resources can usually be obtained during one's middle age. The events are commemorated when the generation which suffered them has the money and power to commemorate them. 3. The most important events in one's life take place when one is 12–25 years old. When these people grow older they may remember the events that happened during this period. 4. The sociopolitical repression will cease to act after 20–30 years because those directly responsible for the repression, war, and so on, have either socially or physically disappeared.

If we leave aside their assumption that an event can be traumatic in itself, this framework is useful in the analysis of collective memory. Igartua and Paez emphasize the difference between a generation shaped by the direct experience of an event and those that follow, for whom memory is mediated in a different way. They point to the issue of power and access to the means of representation, which are essential for public commemoration and the framing of collective memory. They also place special emphasis on the role of art and of representation generally in this process.

A discussion of representation seems appropriate here, as this is an issue which will arise throughout this book. Representation can be analyzed along several dimensions, as re-presenting, i.e., as the presentation through words or visual images of something else, where considerations of form are at least as important as content; this can be considered an aesthetic dimension. That the form may itself have a content has been pointed out by White (1987). Representation can refer to a political process concerning how a group of people can and should be represented in a political body, like a parliament, or another public arena or forum, from the mass media to a museum. Representation has a moral dimension, which can involve both aesthetic and political aspects, when questions like "how should a people be represented?" are raised. There is a cognitive dimension, where representation becomes the prerogative of the arts and sciences, and of professionals, such as museum curators, historians who develop procedures and criteria of and for representation, claiming special privileges regarding the materials presented. As in representativeness, representation can refer to types and exemplars, as in Emerson's *Representative Men* (1851) or Du Bois' "talented tenth," where individuals are said to be types which express the "best" of a race or a civilization.

The complex and problematic issues of representation have been of central concern to black Americans from the earliest periods of the slave trade to the present. In what can be properly called "the struggle for representation" (Klotman and Cutler 1999), black Americans have fought for the right to be seen and heard as equals in social conditions which sought to deny this. This struggle for representation occurred in literary, visual, and more traditional political forms. It encompassed a fight to be seen as well as heard and involved the question of who would define what was seen and heard. The first written accounts "from inside the culture" were the slave narratives, from Briton Harmmon's *Narrative* (1760) to Harriet Jacob's *Incidents in the Life of a Slave Girl* (1861) (Klotman and Cutler 1999:xiv). The abolitionist movement and the associated free black press were important mediators and facilitators of this representation, something which affected the mode of presentation, as we will see in the following chapters.

Painting and other forms of visual representation "from the inside" were later to emerge. What have now come to be called the historically black colleges and universities, inaugurated during the Southern "reconstruction" after the civil war, were important in the production, conservation and display of artifacts by black artists. These schools and their collections were central to the education of future artists as well, along with other black scholars and intellectuals. Music, especially as related to work and religion, was one of the few means of cultural expression publicly available to blacks and its importance as a means of representation as well as of expression has been duly acknowledged, not least by black intellectuals like W. E. B. Du Bois, in their attempts to find grounds for the narration of black collective identity in the trauma following the end of reconstruction. What Du Bois would call the "sorrow songs" of the slaves embodied and passed along, across generations and geographical space, the memories of slavery and hopes of liberation. The first film documentary by a black American appeared in 1910, bearing the title *A Day at Tuskegee*; it offered a representation of the "new Negro" and was commissioned by Booker T. Washington. Commercial black film makers and music producers began to play an increasingly important role from the 1920s onwards, as the urban migrations and better living conditions created a sophisticated audience for "race" movies and recorded music.

Even if these representations were made from the inside, by blacks themselves, the issue of whose voice, whose image was not thereby resolved. The black "community" was always diverse, even as it was unified by enforced subordination and oppression. Internal discussions concerning "proper" representation, as well as the means and paths of liberation, were many and divergent. This was especially so in the urban public sphere that emerged with the Great Migration in the first quarter of the twentieth century. After emancipation and the urban migrations, the possibility that a single issue could define and unite the black "community" and focus any and all representation was undercut. Thus, "since there is no single, unchanging black community, the 'burden of representation' involves varying viewpoints, differing degrees of objectivity and subjectivity, and competing facts and fictions" (Klotman and Cutler 1999: xxv). Here different voices and visions clamored to be seen and heard, even as representation was still intimately entwined with subordination and the desire for liberation. This created a situation where representation was a responsibility and "burden"; it could not easily or merely be a form of personal expression, as a black artist was always "black" in the eyes of the dominant culture.

Resolving cultural trauma can involve the articulation of collective identity and collective memory, as individual stories meld through forms and processes of collective representation. Collective identity refers to a process of "we" formation, a process both historically rooted and rooted in history.[14] While this reconstructed common and collective past may have its origins in direct experience, its recollection is mediated through narratives that are modified with the passage of time, filtered through cultural artifacts and other materializations, which represent the past in the present. Whether or not they directly experienced slavery or even had ancestors who did, blacks in the United States were identified with and came to identify themselves through the memory and representation of slavery. This came about not as an isolated or internally controlled process, but in relation and response to the dominant culture. The historical memory of the civil war was reconstructed in the decades that followed and blackness came to be associated with slavery and subordination. A common national history was ascribed and inscribed as memory, as well as indigenously passed on, as groups emerged out of protective necessity and/or collective solidarity In this sense, slavery is traumatic for those who share a common fate, not necessarily a common experience. Cultural trauma articulates a membership group as it identifies an event or an experience, a primal scene, that solidifies individual/collective identity. This event, now identified with the formation of the group, must be recollected by later generations who have had no experience of the "original" event, yet continue to be identified by it and to identify themselves through it. Because of its distance from the event and because its social circumstances have altered with time, each succeeding generation reinterprets and represents the collective memory around that event according to its needs and means. This process of reconstruction is limited, however, by the resources available and the constraints history places on memory.

The generational shifts noted by Pennebaker and others can be said to structure temporally the formation of collective memory, providing a link between collective (group) memory and public (collective) memory. Groups of course, are public, but a particular group's memory may not necessary be publicly, that is officially, acknowledged or commemorated. If a collective memory is rooted in a potentially traumatic event, which by definition is both painful and open to varying sorts of evaluation, it may take a generation to move from group memory to public memory; sometimes it may take even longer, sometimes it may never happen at all. The case of American slavery is an example. As Ira Berlin notes in his introduction to *Remembering Slavery* (1998), slavery is remembered differently in the United States depending upon which time period and which racial group and regional location one starts from. He writes:

Northerners who fought and won the (civil) war at great cost incorporated the abolitionists' perspective into their understanding of American nationality: slavery was evil, a great blot that had to be excised to realize the full promise of the Declaration of Independence. At first, even some white Southerners – former slave-holders among them – accepted this view, conceding that slavery had burdened the South as it had burdened the nation and declaring themselves glad to be rid of it. But during the late nineteenth century, after attempts to reconstruct the nation on the basis of equality collapsed and demands for sectional reconciliation mounted, the portrayal of slavery changed. White Northerners and white Southerners began to depict slavery as a benign and even benevolent institution, echoing themes from the planters' defense of the antebellum order . . . Such views, popularized in the stories of Joel Chandler Harris and the songs of Stephen Foster, became pervasive during the first third of the twentieth century. (Berlin 1998:xiii–xiv)

There was a long history of visual representation to draw upon as well. In his account of the "visual encoding of hierarchy and exclusion," Albert Boime (1990:16), shows how "a sign system had been put into place" (15) which supplemented written and oral justifications for slavery. Especially in the nineteenth century, white artists produced paintings that reinforced beliefs about the "happy slave," contented in his/her servitude. This was filtered through popular culture in minstrelsy, where black-faced white actors parodied black dialect and behavior in staged performances. American culture was permeated with words, sounds, and images which "took-for-granted" that slavery was both justified and necessary, beneficial to all concerned, at the same time as there existed a counter-current which "remembered" the opposite.

Against the attempt to reconstruct slavery to fit particular interests, stood the recollections of former slaves, those passed down orally, in story and song, as well as written slave narratives, being hailed today by many as the origins of a distinctive African American aesthetic. These voices, though significant and strong after emancipation, took second place, at least to begin with, to the optimistic hope for integration. It was the future orientation, not a reflected-upon common past, that unified blacks after the civil war. As the former slaves began to die out the voice of direct experience began to disappear. Already in 1867 a group of interested collectors could write about the songs they were about to publish, "The public has well-nigh forgotten these genuine slave songs, and with them the creative power from which they sprang . . . "[15] By the 1880s, as dreams of full citizenship and cultural integration were quashed, the meaning of slavery emerged as the site of an identity conflict, articulated most clearly by the newly expanded and resourceful ranks of formally educated blacks. Through various media and forms of representation black artists and writers reconstituted slavery as the primal scene of black identity. In this emergent identity, slavery, not as an institution or experience but as a point of origin in a common past, would ground the formation of a black "community." This was not the only source of the revived memories of slavery however. In face of repressive, often violent reaction from Southern whites, many blacks fled the South as reconstruction ended. One of their prime motivations for migrating was the fear that slavery would be reinstated (Painter 1976). In the trauma of rejection, slavery was remembered as its memory re-membered a group. Slavery defined, in other words, group membership and a membership group. It was in this context that the recollection of slavery was articulated as cultural trauma.[16]

As stated previously, the idea of an African American was one result of this identity struggle. It is important to keep in mind that the notion "African American" is not itself a natural category, but an historically formed collective identity which first of all required articulation and then acceptance on the part of those it was meant to incorporate. It was here, in this identity-formation, that the memory of slavery would be central, not so much as individual experience, but as collective memory. It was slavery, whether or not one had experienced it, that defined one's identity as an African American, it was why you, an African, were here, in America. It was within this identity that direct experience, the identification "former slave" or "daughter of slaves" became functionalized and made generally available as a collective and common memory to unite all blacks in the United States. This was a self-imposed categorization, as opposed to, and meant to counter, those of the dominant white society. In this sense, the memory of slavery by African Americans was what Foucault would call a "counter-memory."[17]

This clearly marks a difference between black and white in social and historical understanding. It was in the context of re-narrating the meaning of the civil war that "whites" and "blacks" were articulated as distinctive social groups with a complex, yet common history. Whites, regardless of whether chance had placed them in the North or the South, shared a European cultural heritage, what would soon be identified as part of Western civilization, while blacks belonged to Africa and the "uncivilized." While some whites might have condemned slavery as an evil institution and bemoaned its effects on the body politic of American society, blacks viewed slavery as a social condition, a lived experience, producing a distinctive way of life, a culture, a community, and thus an identity, which affected not only the past and the present, but also future possibilities. A distinct gap emerged between the collective memory of a reconstructed minority group and the equally reconstructed dominant group in post-reconstruction America; the one which controlled the resources and had the power to fashion public memory. Even here, however, differences between regions, North and South, winners and losers of what some have called the first modern war, created conflicting modes of public commemoration and thus public memories. While both sides avoided slavery as a mode of experience, except of course for the North's celebration of its role as liberator and the South's paternalistic romanticism, to focus on the civil war itself as a traumatic event in the nation's history, each side offered a different interpretation and developed different ceremonies and rituals to officially and publicly commemorate that event.

There were some dissenting voices, especially amongst liberals and radicals in the North. Savage (1994) cites one very influential Northern point of view, that of William Dean Howells, America's foremost literary critic writing in the *Atlantic Monthly* in 1866, who believed that commemoration following the war should focus not on soldiers and battles, but on the ideals and ideas over which the war was fought. Howells, in what must have been a minority view, thought "ideas of warfare itself – organized violence and destruction – unfit for representation" (Savage 1994:127). As an alternative he pointed to "The Freedman," a sculpture of a freed black slave done in 1863, as "the full expression of one idea that should be commemorated" (cited in Savage 1984:128). Needless to say, this suggestion went unfulfilled. Instead, each side, North and South, built monuments to its soldiers and their battlefields. In his analysis of these monuments, Savage writes, "issues such as slavery were at best subsidiary in the program of local commemoration, lumped in with stories of Christian bravery and other deed of heroism . . ." (131). This was also the context in which "whiteness" and "blackness" were reconstructed as overarching categories, transcending regional differences. With slavery out of the picture, there could be reconciliation between the opposing sides, each being allowed to mark their own heroes, thus sweeping aside one of the main contentions of the war. Finally, "commemoration and reconciliation, two social processes that were diametrically opposed in the aftermath of the Civil War, eventually converged upon a shared, if disguised, racial politics" (132).

Without the means to influence public memory, blacks were left to form and maintain their own collective memory, with slavery as an ever-shifting, reconstructed reference point. Slavery has meant different things for different generations of black Americans, but it was always there as a referent. It was not until the 1950s, even the 1960s, that slavery moved outside group memory to challenge the borders, the rituals, and sites of public memory. The phenomenon of erecting monuments has become popular for African Americans only recently, because while the 1863 Emancipation Proclamation granted enslaved blacks the imaginary juridical space of constitutional rights, it was not until the civil rights movement a centry later that the physical spaces of the nation – schools, hotels, and public institutions – were made accessible. Today "Black Heritage," as it is termed, has ballooned into a multimillion dollar tourist industry. Cities, historical societies, and citizens groups have identified locales where key events in the struggle for equality occurred and have undertaken preservation measures for the homes of eminent figures and the buildings of important institutions (Barton 2001:13). Again it was a social movement, the civil rights movement, that reopened the sore and helped transform the cultural trauma of a group into a national trauma. Since then and only since then has slavery become part of America's collective memory, not merely that of one of its constituent members. At the beginning of this century the meaning, commemoration and representation of slavery continues to evoke emotionally charged response. Reviewing the most recent American historical literature on North American slavery, George Fredrickson (2000:61) writes "One hundred and thirty-five years after its abolition, slavery is still the skeleton in the American closet. Among the African-American descendents of its victims there is a difference of opinion about whether the memory of it should be suppressed as unpleasant and dispiriting or commemorated in the ways that Jews remember the Holocaust. There is no national museum of slavery and any attempt to establish one would be controversial." While black Americans may be divided in their opinions regarding the commemoration of slavery, most white Americans, Fredrickson continues, see no reason to accept responsibility for slavery or its effects on American blacks.

Along with the narrative frameworks that as "internalized moral force" (Alexander and Smith 2001), give meaning as well as order to collective memory, the notion of emancipation has been a constituent aspect of black American tradition. After the failure of reconstruction to realize the promises implied in the Emancipation Proclamation, American blacks have sought their own paths to liberation. Three distinct models can be identified. The first follows the ideals upon which Lincoln's famous speech was based, Enlightenment notions of individual autonomy and human dignity and the rights to full citizenship as guaranteed by law, the principles which inspired the French and American revolutions. It is this model which was most tightly coupled with the progressive narrative and underpinned the struggle for civil rights which began directly after the end of reconstruction in the efforts to integrate public transport and to pass anti-lynching legislation, as well as for more formal political rights to participation which were removed in the political purges in the late 1870s. This struggle for individual autonomy was, in the context of cultural trauma, necessarily a collective struggle, as "blacks" were ascribed an identity of difference, especially in the South. This model of emancipation was institutionalized in the NAACP and other organizations.

A second model of emancipation was inspired by the anti-colonial and nationalistic movements, like the Irish, Jewish Zionism, and later, national liberation movements in Africa. These movements provided models of cultural and political nationalism, as a means of overcoming marginality and subordination. A third model was emigration, collective leave-taking, a form of political nationalism that coupled emancipation with possession territory, a nation/racial home. This latter was most clearly linked with the tragic, redemptive narrative.

To each of these models of emancipation were attached various strategies for their realization. The full citizenship model called for a long-term struggle of legal confrontation, gathering evidence, accumulating "cases" and changing laws. Tactics varied, from indirect to direct, aggressive confrontation, but they always involved using and challenging the laws of the land, with the aim of acquiring full and equal guarantees for blacks. The national or racial liberation model implied a strategy of racial identification, solidarity and withdrawal, similar to the labor movement. It called upon blacks to recognize themselves as a group in the positive sense and not merely as victims of white discrimination and ascription. Programs of self-help, from producer and consumer cooperatives, to the founding of racial zones based on a varying combinations of economic, political, and religious principles were central to this strategy. Tactics varied from moral persuasion to physical threat and the use of force, both within to enforce solidarity and without, in confronting the dominant "white" society. The model of emigration was the most clear-cut, to unify and remove the "race" from its exile and to return to a homeland, although the location of the latter varied. These strategies were important in the cultural praxis, or the process of collective identity-formation of the social movements which formed their basis.

There are identifiable generational aspects in this process of continuity and change in black American responses to the cultural trauma of the failure of emancipation to emancipate black Americans. Although I use the concept of generation in a social rather than biological sense, I have designated specific time-periods in this study, making use of the convenient principle of decades. My use of the concept "generation" however derives from sociological theory (Mannheim 1952; Eyerman and Turner 1998) and requires a set of conditions beyond biological age and time of birth for its application, and is primarily a collective memory which serves to integrate an age-group.[18] In this sense, the first "generation" is that formed around the turn of the century shaped by the end of reconstruction. This is the generation which articulates the cultural trauma and begins to formulate the responses, including the recollection of collective memory. The second "generation" is that formed by the first waves of the migration, at the end of the First World War. It is here, in the 1920s, that the two dominant narrative frames took shape and the collective memory was significantly reformulated. The third "generation" took form during and just after the Second World War, shaped by new waves of urban migration in the context of Pax Americana and the consumer society, again reforming the collective memory in a significant way. From this time-spread it should be clear that date of birth is not the central aspect in the articulation of a generation. Rather it is the convergence of social forces and the emergence of social movements which are key to the formation of a collective consciousness which forms a generation in my sense of the term. Generation is not merely synonymous with generational awareness growing out of the shared experience of significant events, but requires as well significant collective action which both articulates this consciousness and also puts it into practice and through which collective memory is reformulated. It is in this context that the past is reinterpreted to provide a map for the present/future.

In addition to the theory of cultural trauma, the theoretical framework for the analysis which guides this work derives from social movement theory, especially the cognitive approach developed by Eyerman and Jamison (1991, 1998). Important here is the idea that the articulation of a collective identity is a central task and even a defining characteristic of social movements, an idea contained in the concept of cognitive praxis. This concept will be used in describing the role of social movements in the reconstruction of collective identity and the transformation of collective memory regarding black Americans. Cognitive praxis refers to that process of identity articulation and formation, a process in which intellectuals, both traditional and movement-produced, are central.

The notion of "frames" and the process of "framing" have been central to the contemporary analysis of social movements. Stemming from Goffman (1974) and also European phenomenology, the concept has several connotations. It refers to the process whereby aspects of reality are highlighted and others hidden or forgotten, as when a "frame" is placed around a painting.[19] Frame also refers to the ordering or structuring of story, something which also highlights events and gives them meaning. I use the concept of "narrative frame" in both these senses. In addition to the cognitive emphasis on framing, the role of social movements in the constitution of a collective subject through collective representation will also be discussed. Representation here can be of several sorts, one of which is the more common political kind of representation where individuals represent, stand or speak for others. Here movement intellectuals and leaders are key actors. Another aspect of representation, however, concerns collective memory and the representation of a shared past. Through the context for dialogue they create, social movements facilitate the interweaving of individual stories and biographies into a collective, unified frame, a collective narrative. Part and parcel of the process of collective identity or will formation is the linking of diverse experiences into a unity, past as well as present. Social movements are central to this process, not only at the individual level, but also at the organizational or meso level of social interaction. Institutions like the black church and cultural artifacts like blues music may have embodied and passed on collective memories from generation to generation, but it was through social movements that even these diverse collective memories attained a more unified focus, linking individuals and collectives into a unified subject, with a common future as well as a common past.

The book is divided into six chapters. Chapter 1, "Cultural Trauma and Collective Memory," introduces the themes and concepts used in the study. Chapter 2, "Re-Membering and Forgetting," applies this framework to the period between 1865 and the early twentieth century, when the process of cultural trauma begins and responses are articulated. Here the first black intellectuals play a significant role in constituting a discourse on collective identity. Chapter 3, "Out of Africa," discusses the emergence of the idea of a "New Negro," the significance of W. E. B. Du Bois and the role of popular culture around the turn of the century in articulating a new, racially based, collective identity. Chapter 4, "The Harlem Renaissance and the Heritage of Slavery," covers the urban migrations that followed the First World War, the emergence of an urban black public sphere and the articulation of two narrative frameworks, one progressive and the other tragic/redemptive, which will "frame" the meaning of past/present and future for black American identity. Chapter 5, "Memory and Representation," covers the period between the great depression and the end of the Second World War. Here continued migration and concentration of the black population and rising standards of living alter the two narrative frames developed by the previous generation. Radio offers a new medium for representing as well as communicating to the black "community." Chapter 6, "Civil Rights and black nationalism: the post-war generation," covers the emergence of these two movements and the changes they effected in the narrative frames. This chapter covers the period from the 1950s to the present and includes a discussion on how the image and heritage of slavery continues to affect black America.

2

Re-membering and forgetting

Memories of slavery disgrace the race, and race perpetuates memories of slavery.
Tocqueville

Four million slaves were liberated at the end of the civil war. The exact figure was 3,953,696 (1860) which represents about 12.6 percent of the total American population and 32 percent of the Southern population (these figures also are from 1860, but there was no dramatic change during the civil war). The free black population in the United States in 1860 was 488,070 and in the South 261,918 (Kolchin 1993:241–42). In the first comprehensive historical account written by a black man, George Washington Williams offered this description: "Here were four million human beings without clothing, shelter, homes, and alas! most of them without names. The galling harness of slavery had been cut off of their weary bodies, and like a worn out beast of burden they stood in their tracks scarcely able to go anywhere"(1882:378).[1]

This was written nearly twenty years after the event and is an act of re-membrance as much as historical writing. The author was part of a literary mobilization of a new black middle class emerging after the civil war which aimed at countering the image of blacks being put forward by whites, as the "full and complete" integration promised by radical reconstruction gave way to new forms of racial segregation in the South and elsewhere. In addition to this monumental work, which also appeared in a condensed "popular" version, Williams produced an equally monumental history of black soldiers during the civil war, and Sarah Bradford published *Harriet, the Moses of Her People* (1886), a dramatization of the life of Harriet Tubman, leading black abolitionist.[2] While constantly growing in number, the black reading public was not the prime audience of these and other literary efforts by educated blacks at the time. The prime contemporary audience remained the sympathetic white reader, in need of bolstering in this reactionary period, and later, generations of blacks who would require alternative histories than those offered by mainstream white society. For it was just as plausible to argue, as sympathetic white historians later would and contemporary black novelists (who will be discussed below) were about to, that slavery produced hidden social networks which permitted blacks not only to survive, but also to maintain their dignity and traditions. These networks, which some would identify as a distinct cultural form, were an important resource after emancipation and reconstruction. As McMurry (1998:20–21) writes: "On many plantations and farms, the slave community functioned as an extended family. In freedom those informal support networks became structurally organized as church groups or benevolent organizations and provided aid to families in crisis." Williams painted the former slaves as victims, survivors who would triumph over their condition, proving their worthiness, only to be rejected by a white society busy painting pictures of its own.

Here lie the roots and routes of cultural trauma. For blacks, this rejection after the raised expectations engendered by emancipation and reconstruction forced a rethinking of their relationship to American society. This was traumatic not only because of crushed expectations but also because it necessitated a reevaluation of the past and its meaning regarding individual and collective identity. Many blacks and a few whites had believed that reconstruction would, if not eliminate entirely race as the basis for identity, at least diminish its significance, as former slaves became citizens like other Americans and the caste system associated with servitude disappeared. This was now clearly not the case, making it necessary to reevaluate the meaning of the past and the options available in the future. Once again it would be necessary to attempt to transform tragedy into triumph with the uncovering of new strategies in the struggle for collective recognition, in the face of the threat of marginalization.

After long political debate in which many plans were aired and compromises drawn, reconstruction (1865–77) promised integration and equal rights in the defeated South. The Civil Rights Bill of 1866, passed over the veto of President Andrew Johnson, authorized limited citizenship rights to blacks. The strategy of Federal intervention, which included military occupation, had many motivations, some honorable and some less so. Fredrickson (1971) traces the debate concerning possible scenarios to follow emancipation. Most white thinking assumed a fundamental difference in character between blacks and whites, some of which was considered the result of slavery and some of which had more fundamental causes. An early plan had been to move all blacks either to American colonies abroad or to specified areas within the United States. Finally, after permitting blacks to participate on equal footing in the Union Army, making it "difficult to ask a man to fight for a nation without recognizing his right to live in it" (Fredrickson 1971:167), and rejecting the idea of moving large numbers of blacks to the Midwest or the Georgia Sea Islands, it was accepted that most blacks wanted to remain in the South and that the government must assist in the transition from slave to citizen. Education and limited land redistribution would be the core of this process; one to be energized by paternalistic good will. The emphasis on re-education was supported by many middle-class white Southerners, both during and after reconstruction, as long as it was kept within the bounds of "the civilizing process," that is, under their control. For the most part, it was largely the intervention by the Federal government, more than the policies themselves, which they found most objectionable and degrading.

Along with its military presence, the federal government organized Freedmen's Bureaus designed to assist former slaves, with education and also loans for the purchase of land. Such funding aided individuals but also set school building in motion throughout the South, and many Northern teachers, black and white, moved there to help in the process. According to the report published by the commissioner of the Freedmen's Bureau, Major-General O. O. Howard (after whom Howard University was named), in 1870 (five years after work had begun) "there were 4,239 schools established, 9,307 teachers employed, and 247,333 pupils instructed" (cited in Williams 1882:385).[3] This was only a part of the process however, as "the emancipated people sustained 1,324 schools themselves, and owned 592 school buildings" (385). Thus the federal program was supplemented by the schools and schooling provided by various religious organizations, including those run by blacks themselves, like the African Methodist Episcopal (AME) and Baptist churches.[4]

The church was a central source of community and identity-formation already during slavery and continued to be so until its influence waned during the great migration, at least in the northern cities. In one view, "the Negro church may be regarded as the single institution which has uniquely given a sustained, positive sense of ethnic identity to American Negroes without beating the nationalists' drums" (Essien-Udom 1962:25). In another, the black church was a "nation within a nation," the core of an emergent black social structure and identity (Frazier 1974).[5] The church was also central in organizing and distributing resources during and after reconstruction, as well as in providing leadership in dealings with the larger society and serving as the center of social life. Along with semi-secret associations and fellowships like the Masons and Elks, the church was the central "counter-institution" of black American life. With emancipation, blacks left white churches in great numbers and joined already existing black churches or started new ones. This created a new basis for racial self-determination, as well as liberation, as blacks were no longer forced to listen to sermons dictated by the dominant culture. In the decade directly following emancipation, these black churches organized themselves through a convention, "for the purpose of harnessing traditional feelings of mutuality with new assertions of self-respect and self-determination" (Higginbotham 1993:53).[6]

Even if Essien-Udom is correct in arguing that it sustained a positive sense of ethnic or racial identity without "beating the nationalist drum," as part of a network of separate black institutions it provided the material basis for sustaining separatism. This is nicely put by Drake and Cayton (1945:116ff.) in their discussion of how the meaning of the phrase "social equality" differs in the North and South and between blacks and whites. In answering the question "Do Negroes (in Chicago) Want Social Equality?", they write:

Negroes are generally indifferent to social intermingling with white people, and this indifference is closely related to the existence of a separate, parallel Negro institutional life which makes interracial activities seem unnecessary and almost "unnatural". Since the eighteenth century, a separate Negro institutional structure has existed in America. Through the years it has been developing into an intricate web of families, cliques, churches, and voluntary associations, ordered by a system of social classes. This "Negro World" is, historically, the direct result of social rejection by the white society. For Negroes however, it has long since lost this connotation, and many white people never think of it as such. It is now the familiar milieu in which Negroes live and move from birth till death.

This "world" existed only in embryo in the 1870s and could easily have disappeared had reconstruction functioned as it might have. Because this did not occur, these "counter-institutions" developed into full-scale alternatives and a separate way of life became "natural" and taken for granted by both blacks and whites. It is this development, part of the process of what we have been calling cultural trauma, that clearly marks blacks off from other ethnic groups in the United States, whose integration and assimilation, as measured most clearly by intermarriage, was usually only a matter of a generation or two.[7] This is what transformed ethnicity into race, a more lasting sense of otherness, and laid the foundations for the continuation and further development of black nationalism or nationality. At the same time, however, it must be pointed out that many of the black ministers were trained at colleges where, while segregated, the values of the dominant culture also predominated (Harris 1992:119). It was these values, framed within what I will call the progressive narrative, which were transmitted through sermons to the members.

Some have argued that it was the former slaves themselves, more than the federal government and the various religious organizations, who took the initiative here. Herbert Gutman (1987) writes, "blacks voluntarily paid school tuition, purchased textbooks, hired, fed, boarded, and protected teachers, constructed and maintained school buildings, and engaged in other costly (and sometimes dangerous) activities to provide education for their children" (260). Along with others, he provides sufficient evidence that former slaves were enthusiastic supporters of their own education and that parents sacrificed to see to it that their children went to school, even where they had to bear the full cost themselves (see also Litwak 1979:ch. 9).

Concentrating on basic literacy and moral education, as well as the practical skills associated with good workmanship, it is difficult to imagine that slavery was a topic of study in these makeshift schools.[8] The aim after all was to forget slavery, to move beyond it into the world of paid labor. "Both northern (charitable) societies and the Freedmen's Bureau recognized the values of education in preparing the blacks for practical life, and neither would have understood the need to draw any distinctions between teaching freedmen to read and write and making productive free laborers of them" (Litwack 1979:480) The education of children, on the other hand, was more complicated, as this lesson from a Freedmen's school in Kentucky in 1866 indicates:

Now children, you don't think white people are any better than you because they have straight hair and white faces?
No, sir.
No, they are no better, but they are different, they possess great power, they formed this great government, they control this vast country . . . Now what makes them different from you?
MONEY . . . (Unanimous shout)
Yes, but what enabled them to obtain it? How did they get money?
Got it off us, stole it off we all!   (Quoted in Litwack 1979:387)

This historical account can be compared with the fictional one given by the black writer Frances W. Harper in her novel *Iola Leroy, or Shadows Uplifted*, published in 1892 (Andrews 1992), which portrays it almost to the letter: "One day a gentleman came to the school and wished to address the children. Iola suspended the regular order of the school, and the gentleman essayed the achievements of the white race, such as building steamboats and carrying on business. Finally, he asked how they did it?

"They've got money," chorused the children.
"But how did they get it?"
"They took it from us," chimed the youngsters. Iola smiled, and the gentleman was nonplussed; but he could not deny that one of the powers of knowledge is the power of the strong to oppress the weak.   (Andrews 1992:111)

Litwack's account is based on the diary of a school assessor, perhaps the same one that Harper fictionalizes. Written in the 1890s, Harper's novel, like the historical writings of Williams mentioned above, was part of the attempt by the black middle class to counter the anti-reconstruction revisionism of the time. We will return to her later on.

After basic grammar school education it was possible to attend "normal schools," aimed at teacher training. Fisk University opened its doors the year after the Thirteenth Amendment formally abolished slavery (1866); Howard and Morehouse followed a year later. The Hampton Institute, designed to provide agricultural and industrial education for freed slaves, was established in 1868. Atlanta University, destined to become a cornerstone of higher education, was established in 1867, where "the first classes were held in a church and then a railroad boxcar" (Christian 1995:219). It graduated its first college class in 1876, an important event in the formation of this first generation after slavery.

Morehouse took its name from Henry Morehouse, a white Baptist educator and missionary who served as executive secretary of the American Baptist Home Missionary Society. Morehouse is also the originator of the notion of the "talented tenth" that would become associated with W. E. B. Du Bois. In arguing for the financial support of black education he said: "I repeat that not to make proper provision for the high education of the talented tenth man of the colored colleges is a prodigious mistake . . . Industrial education is good for the nine; that tenth man ought to have the best opportunities for making the most of himself for humanity and God" (quoted in Higginbotham 1993:25). While he used the male pronoun to justify this commitment to black education, the organization Morehouse represented was equally as committed to the education of black women. White northern Baptist patronage based itself on the idea that education would compensate for the deprivations of slavery and prepare blacks for citizenship. "Slavery," it was argued, "had deprived blacks of positive role models" (Higginbotham 1993:30–31) and education was needed to instill self-control and moral discipline. Industrial education was seen as essential for the multitude, as slavery had encouraged the development of bad work habits and an indolent attitude; for women, this implied domestic training, but more sophisticated forms of education were necessary for the "talented tenth," the men and women who would provide the "race" with leadership. The curriculum schools set up under religious patronage and control, like Spelman, were explicitly designed to enhance moral and practical training to ensure that the student might "preside intelligently over her own household, or to do good service in any family," according to the Spelman catalog in 1883 (cited in Higginbotham 1993:33).[9] Motives here were clearly mixed. Education would spread "correct values" and "proper" work habits, i.e., those of the dominant culture. This was a form of cultivation that was also disciplining. From the point of view of the white patrons, "the educated few would become the teachers of many."

However, this commitment to education also created the possibility of creative and critical reflection, something which an emerging women's movement in the Baptist church and small networks of black intellectuals would reveal as the century ended.

These "historically black colleges and universities" would prove central in the reconstruction, preservation, and reproduction of the black past and present. As institutions of higher learning they would produce new generations of educated blacks who would be one of the central forces for social change. They also provided an institutional framework for the housing and display of artifacts of black culture and history, including murals depicting the transition from Africa to America, as well as libraries and collections of works of arts and letters. Black intellectuals, like W. E. B. Du Bois and Alain Locke, both proud of their European education, were both products of and teachers at these colleges. Aaron Douglas, the most important painter of the Harlem Renaissance, would found the art department at Fisk University, where his murals decorated its walls. Edmonia Lewis' "Forever Free" belongs to Howard University's permanent collection, and so on.

The possibility of higher education and the emergence of a relatively large group of educated blacks occurred just as reconstruction was coming to an end. This group articulated the failure of reconstruction to truly integrate blacks into American society as trauma, and formulated the alternative strategies in response. This points to one of the assumptions and limitations of this theory as applied to American slavery. Trauma is articulated in an intellectual discourse, written or visual, factual or fictional, which limits those who can participate, as well as the forms through which one can participate. This discourse "speaks" for the speechless. In other words, it is itself a form of representation. The cultural trauma referred to here, analyzed in this study, is that articulated, and experienced by intellectuals, writers, and artists, as are the responses debated and proposed.

An improved means of communication helped reinforce a sense of community amongst emancipated blacks. Anderson (1991) has argued that it is with the assistance of mass media that "imagined" as well as real communities are constituted and sustained. The first black owned newspaper had appeared in 1827 and "by 1850, black (owned) newspapers were on the streets of most large northern cities" (Banks 1996:15). In his study of four black newspapers between 1827 and 1965, Charles Simmons (1998:5) writes, "the basic editorial philosophy of the black press has not changed much since 1827, when *Freedom's Journal* was founded. The goals of all editors were to deliver messages in unity to their readers, deliver them with passion and emotion, and let white editors and citizens know that black citizens were human beings who were being treated unjustly." The first newspapers were "protest" papers, spurred by outlandish events and thus relatively short lived. *Freedom Journal* was begun in response to an editorial in a white newspaper urging the return to Africa of freed blacks in New York City, in an effort to clean up the streets. Its Prospectus contained the lines, "daily slandered, we think that there ought to be some channel of communication between us and the public, through which a single voice may be heard, in defense of five hundred thousand free people of colour" (Simmons 1998:9). The editor was a Presbyterian minister and his assistant the second black to have graduated college in the United States. The most famous newspaper, *The North Star*, was edited by Frederick Douglass; it began publication from Rochester, New York in 1847. Its purpose was clearly stated in the first issue: "the object of the *North Star* will be to attack slavery in all its forms and aspects, advocate Universal Emancipation; exact the standard of public morality; promote the moral and intellectual improvement of the colored people; and hasten the day of freedom to our three million enslaved countrymen" (quoted in Simmons 1998:13).

With emancipation and expanding literacy black newspapers spread rapidly in the South, their role taking on a new dimension after the end of slavery; 115 black newspapers were started between the civil war and the end of reconstruction, the first in the South in New Orleans in 1862, an event which "signaled the first change in editorial philosophy – one from freeing the slaves to one of reestablishing the racial identity of Afro-Americans and educating them so that they could survive in society" (Simmons 1998:14). Southern black newspapers often met strong resistance, making the publishing of a newspaper and the job of editor a very precarious and courageous choice of profession in the South; newspapers had a shorter life span in the South compared to the North, for these and other reasons, including the size of the readership (Suggs 1983). Newspapers thus became an important medium through which self-definition could be debated and a new, post-slavery collective identity articulated. After all, slavery had been the root circumstance of black identity, previously a condition and an identity under conditions of extreme alienation, as well as white control. Music and other oral forms of communication had been central to the formation of black collective identity during slavery; they articulated an imagined community, as well as the hope of a better life (Davis 1998:7). This was now supplemented in a much more extensive way through literary means and media. Newspapers and the press generally were a central medium of public conversation, as well as reflection, that would help constitute the new "imagined" black community, linking the local and national and moderating the formation of a black public opinion.

Because blacks had been largely dependent upon whites for their self-understanding, the black press, especially after emancipation, was an essential vehicle for the formation of a self-conscious black identity made possible after the war. The press was also an essential weapon in the ongoing struggle over the meaning of freedom being waged, as much of the white press, especially in the South, "highlighted black crime and irresponsibility to justify exploitation, exclusion and segregation" (McMurray 1998:87). One example of this was the interpretation of the Kansas Exodus of 1879, where the memory of slavery played such a central role. While black newspapers tended to explain the mass migration as a rational response to violent reaction and fear, as well as the hope of a better life, white newspapers focused on the irrationality of the movement and its leaders, even organizing trips to Kansas to reveal the "hardships" under which those who left the South now lived (Painter 1976:213ff.).[10]

A prerequisite of a free press was a readership, making literacy and education generally a core issue amongst the first generation after emancipation. Within a few decades a comparatively wide black reading public was established, as illiteracy declined to 79.9 percent in the South from nearly 100 percent during slavery. It had been illegal to teach slaves to read and write in many places. In terms of education, if not work and land ownership, the conditions of the first generation after emancipation differed greatly from those of their parents.

Along with the value placed on education, especially concerning the young, was their elders' interest in the acquisition of land, as former farm laboring slaves and skilled artisans sought to put their experience to use on their own property. In 1866, "freed Blacks popularized a slogan, 'Forty Acres and a Mule', to sum up the help they hoped to receive from the Freedmen's Bureau" (Christian 1995:216). In this, the generation formed by slavery exhibited the yeoman values of their region and their former masters, while their children were acquiring tools that would point in other directions. There were ambiguous feelings involved on all sides. "As the South moved from an agrarian to an industrial economy after the civil war, whites worked diligently to force blacks to remain in a pre-industrial world and to retain the role of agrarian peasants. Yet, in one generation, families . . . equipped themselves to compete with whites in farming, business, and politics. Education buttressed by religion made the difference" (Gilmore 1995:12). The case of Memphis can serve as an illustration, here:

the political roots of black education went back to the first year following the Union occupation of the city in June 1862. White Memphians publicly opposed educating African Americans, and in February 1863 burned down a church that housed a private school for blacks. The extent of opposition was made blindingly clear in the flames of the race riot of 1866, during which whites torched every African American school and church. Before "congressional reconstruction" brought Republicans into office, the city continued to exclude all blacks from public schools. The void was filled by private schools operated by white northern missionaries, the Freedmen's Bureau, and educated African

Americans. In 1866 twelve black schools employed twenty-two teachers: nineteen white northerners and three African Americans, all three of whom had been educated at Oberlin College.   (McMurray 1998:80; see also Gutman 1987)

According to Painter (1976:46) "The Reconstruction legislatures of Tennessee, Mississippi, Louisiana, and Texas had written provisions for public schooling into the new state constitutions in the late 1860s, thereby taking over the primary schools opened and financed by Northern missionary societies and Freedmen's Bureau. But by the early 1870s the public schools were already in jeopardy, especially in Tennessee; there, what little Reconstruction the state underwent ended with Democratic takeover in 1870."

As schools and colleges mushroomed to meet the growing demand, changes in the social structure were occurring. Not only was a working class developing, as blacks freed from the confines of the slave peasant economy could pursue other types of work and move a little more freely to seek employment, but also an educated middle class began to develop in the urban South, and, because most black colleges were coeducational, this included an active involvement on the part of women, especially in the field of education and in religious activity. This had class and regional dimensions, of course, as the working conditions for women in the rural areas changed little between emancipation and end of reconstruction. This does not mean that even here changes were not occurring. As Jones (1985:79) reports: "for black women in the rural South . . . the physical dimensions of their domestic chores and field work had not changed much since slavery, women during this period (1880–1915) toiled with the new hope that their sons and daughters would one day escape from the Cotton South." The high value placed on education and literacy gave high status to the teaching profession and journalism, and it was not surprising that, along with the ministry and law, these professions provided leadership in the struggle to define the meaning of emancipation and the shape of black identity, especially after reconstruction came to an end, just as the struggle against slavery and the abolitionist movement had done earlier.

While the expansion of the black press helped establish and make visible this internal differentiation of the black population, changes included the emergence of a social elite, the white press was not entirely blind or uninterested either.[11] Reporting on the wedding of a prominent black resident, a white-owned Memphis newspaper wrote the following in 1885:

There is as much distinction in the society of colored people of the South as there is among the whites. In every community, town and city the blacks are divided into classes governed by education, intelligence, morality, wealth and respectability. This distinction is scrupulously observed here in Memphis by the colored people. The educated and intelligent who, by honest industry, have accumulated a competency and who live exemplary lives create a fashionable social circle of their own. (Cited in McMurry 1998:32–33)

Different interpretations and ways of recollecting slavery and the past developed along with this social differentiation – amongst blacks as well as whites. As we shall see later on, when it came to models of behavior to guide their lifestyles after slavery, the Southern, urban black elite adopted many of the ways and manners of their former masters, especially regarding gender roles. The same can be said for the yeoman values of the more rural populations. While slavery itself might well have been thought best forgotten, some of its cultural forms lived on in the values and practices of the newly emancipated. This should not be surprising, as with the more or less successful attempts to eliminate all vestiges of their past heritage and the conscious attempts made to ensure illiteracy, where else could former slaves look for models of behavior except in religion? It was partly for this reason that, after the failure of reconstruction, there was a revival of interest in both African and European cultures.

While not directly concerning slavery, the past in the form of a folk culture, a way of life, tastes in food and music, religious practices, sexual practices, and so on was opened up to reflection, moral judgment, and choice. Slavery became a field or a site of memory, an arena of potentiality, which allowed not only different interpretations, but also ambiguity in regard to meaning as well as emotional response. The understanding of trauma depends upon a time sequence like the following: traumatic event – suppression of understanding – reflection. The fact that many, if not most, former slaves wanted to forget the past and look toward a new, more open future, can be interpreted as "latency" if one differentiates active repression, that conscious and forced denial from less engagement, that is, between knowing and denying from knowing, accepting and moving on. Here also, the generational cycle comes into play, where different generations, both within the group and those outside, have different perspectives on the past because of both emotional and temporal distance, altered circumstances and needs. Where one generation, or unit within it, may be actively engaged with a specific aspect of the past, in this instance, slavery, does not exclude terms like latency or psychological theories of trauma, in fact they may be helpful in our understanding of such differences.

At the same time as black life in the South was becoming more differentiated and complex, white views of the civil war and its aftermath were undergoing a transformation. "For most Northerners," writes Merton Dillon (1974:265), "the Civil War and Reconstruction settled the racial question. With the Union armies victorious and the Union restored, a mood of national self-congratulation replaced the guilt that characterized earlier years. After the ratification of three Reconstruction amendments, one could believe that the American system had once more succeeded, that it had achieved a beneficent solution to its most difficult problem." Even the abolitionists, the most actively engaged group in the issue of slavery, could content themselves with the notion that "the historical record also could be interpreted in such as way as to show that the anti-slavery movement had triumphed" (Dillon 1974) and activists could turn their attention to other issues, like woman's suffrage and temperance.

This complacency, coupled with the acquiescence to "states-rights," led to the so-called Compromise of 1877 which marked the formal end to reconstruction.[12] The renewed sense of national unity gained at the expense of blacks allowed Jim Crow laws, including railroad segregation, to be established in the South within a decade. By 1890 Mississippi had incorporated disfranchisement into its state constitution. Lynchings, rare before emancipation probably because of the monetary value of a slave, reached a peak between 1880 and 1890 of 150 per year and their high point, 235, in 1892. A form of racial terrorism, the practice was used, according to Ida B. Wells who devoted her life to its abolition, as an "antidote to black success" (McMurry 1998:xv). In the North, informal segregation was the rule, not the exception. In 1880 blacks finally won the right to education, but not until 1900 was there formal integration of public schools. With the demise of the populist and industrially organized Knights of Labor and the emergence of the skilled-trade oriented American Federation of Labor, the labor movement took on a more exclusionary policy towards blacks. The membership of the radical United Mine Workers was 2:3 black in 1890, however, a glaring exception to the general social drift. The radical agrarian populist movement which first included and encouraged black participation, turned conservative and racist with the end of reconstruction, and the politicization of poor Southern whites led to the exclusion of blacks.

In the face of this onslaught, Booker T. Washington's famous Atlanta Compromise speech of 1895 summed up a major shift in black thinking "from political to economic action, from immediate integration and protest to self-help, from rights to duties; and uniting Northern and Southern whites and Negroes upon a common, even if ambiguous, platform, expressed Negro accommodation on the social conditions implicit in the earlier Compromise of 1877" (Meier 1962:25).

Another form of reaction was to flee the South, in line with an American tradition of geographical mobility when the avenues of social mobility close. Because the Homestead Act of 1862 had offered large quantities of public land for those who worked it, Kansas was a popular destination. Group exodus was not uncommon and black "colonies" were set up in several places. The superintendent of the Freedman's Relief Association wrote the following in

1880: "The great exodus of Colored people from the South began about the 1st of February, 1879. By the 1st of April 1,300 refugees had gathered around Wyandotte, Ks. Many of them were in a suffering condition. It was then that the Kansas Relief Association came into existence for the purpose of helping the most needy among the refugees from the Southern States. Up to date about 60,000 refugees have come to the State of Kansas to live" (Williams 1882:537).[13]

Nell Irvin Painter (1976) recounts not only a history of "Exodusters" who fled the South for Kansas after reconstruction, but also the democratic leadership style and form of black collective identity which was characteristic in the South during the period.[14] In her account, local black communities formed out of necessity in the inflamed racial hatred and anarchy that followed emancipation and the implementation of reconstruction in the defeated South. She reveals how "reconstruction" meant different things in the various states of the region, being more thorough in Louisiana then Tennessee for example, and that the withdrawal of federal troops and the end of reconstruction also occurred at different times and invoked various reactions on the part of whites.[15] More important for our purposes, however, is her discussion of black identity, leadership and reactions to what we have called the cultural trauma which followed the ending of reconstruction.

In the rural areas of the antebellum South, identity was rooted in land and locality, with a particular area and region. This was true for both white and black, of course, as modified by the category "slave" or "freedman" for blacks (including status differences within these categories), and the size of land and slave ownership for whites, along with class differences between owner/holder and worker/laborer (Hale 1998). The civil war helped construct a more general collective identity among whites, as the idea of the Confederacy spanned over geographical and class differences. "Requiring only that an ancestor had fought for the cause, membership criteria of organizations like the Sons, Daughters, and Children of the Confederacy . . . suggested that participation in the war effort superseded class status in determining 'Southerness'" (Hale 1998:69).[16] In the same way, emancipation and reconstruction grouped blacks together as real and potential citizens of the newly reconstituted Republic. However differently the process of reconstruction was realized, the dream of citizenship existed for blacks, along with the attachment to land and region.

Political parties also entered into identity construction. Reconstruction, Painter shows, was an ambiguous Republican Party project, which was strongly, even violently resisted by Southern Democrats, who had their own soon-to-be-realized dreams of redemption and revenge. Against varying levels and types of white resistance, emancipated blacks formed protective alliances and self-help organizations, like cooperatives and mutual aid societies with locally based leadership. These organizations supplemented those programs and protection provided by the federal government and contributed to the locally based racial identity.[17] "Firmly egalitarian and marked by strong racial cohesion, [Southern blacks] commonly spoke of 'our race', 'the colored people', and 'our color' manifesting an enduring communal identity" (Painter 1976:14). The community-oriented, local leadership, which Painter illustrates through the example of two former slaves, Henry Adams and Benjamin Singleton, was counterposed to those "representative" blacks who mediated across the racial and geographical divide, and who were more or less chosen by whites. Local communities tended to be wary of "representative" Negroes and suspicious of "national" racial leadership claims. It was this type of local leader who, in the first place, would be instrumental in dealing with the trauma of rejection. Singleton wrote in 1883 "When we were delivered from slavery we were delivered with nothing and have since been trying to rise up and have some protection and be respected and yet they still try to hold us down but we can't stand to be treated in this manner" (quoted in Painter 1976:124). When reconstruction failed and the Democratic Redemption began, Adams and Singleton were leaders of the Kansas exodus.

Painter and others have described in grim detail the harassment, election fraud and murder that met black claims to the rights of citizenship during reconstruction. The cumulative effect was to set in motion waves of southwestern migration, to Texas, Kansas, and Oklahoma, as well as the attempt to return to Africa. A 'Liberia fever' hit parts of the South in 1877, following the waves of violence which accompanied the election campaign of 1876. It "followed fast on the heels of Reconstruction in the Carolinas, Mississippi, and Louisiana, as Blacks perceived clearly and cheerlessly that they stood alone" (Painter 1976:138). After the bankruptcy of the steamship company which was to carry them abroad, prospective emigrants turned to the American Colonization Society, but demand and costs proved too high and Kansas became a more realistic alternative.

It was in this context of failed reconstruction and rejection that what had previously been a social condition, slavery, became fully transposed into a symbolic one, race, as perceived difference.[18] Slavery after all does not need race. In this historical moment, race was in the air and could serve many purposes and interests. For blacks, some version of the notion could be used as a source of identity, and slavery as a reference point in setting the boundaries of the group-defining collective memory. This of course was double-edged, as race, and indeed, slavery, were also negative ascriptions, although Anglo-Saxons had been using the term in a positive way when referring to themselves. For Southern whites, race was important in both aspects. It was a means for justifying the new subordination of blacks, as a segregated group, but also for asserting their own right to dominate. Race also was an important concept in academic and scientific discourse in this period, especially in the United States, and, as noted, entered into popular discourse through forms of entertainment and education. New academic disciplines would emerge, using race distinctions as their ground and research object, while older ones, like psychology, would find the concept useful for opening up new areas of study. This will be discussed later on.

According to the theories popular at the time and to which even black intellectuals were not immune, human differences were rooted in physical characteristics, the "dark skins, thick lips, spreading nostrils and kinky hair" (Thurman [1929]/1997:12) that Wallace Thurman and Nella Larsen and others would write about so forcefully during the Harlem Renaissance, which then could serve as markers of status, even within the "race" itself – another "memory" of slavery, if one included the reproduction and transmission of values as a form of memory.[19] As previously noted, this symbol system had been in place for a long time, as it served to supplement other justifications for the subjugation of blacks. Nineteenth-century painting was full of images of the "lovable slave" as contrasted to the "monstrous freedman," of "savage brutes who became domesticated under slavery" (Boime 1990:86). Here is an analysis of one such painting taken from the highbrow and "liberal" *Harper's Monthly Magazine* in the 1850s:

> W.S. Mount, the only artist among us who can delineate God's image carved in ebony; or mahogany, has just finished a picture in his happiest style. It represents a genuine sable Long Islander, whom a "lucky throw" of the coppers has made the owner of a fat goose . . . The details of the picture – the rough coat, the gay worsted comforter and cap, disposed with the native tendency to dandyism, which forms so conspicuous an element of the negro character, are admirably painted. The effect, like that of every true work of art, and unlike that of the vulgar and brutal caricatures of the negro which abound, is genial and humanizing.
>
> (Quoted in Boime 1990:90)

These same images, the "happy slave" and the "citified dandy," were staples of the enormously popular minstrel shows which traveled the northern parts of the country during the same period. If there was one area of agreement between class-related cultural tastes, it concerned racial stereotyping.

George Fredrickson (1971) concludes his historical study referred to above of "the black image in the white mind" with the following list upon which there was "widespread, almost universal, agreement," amongst whites, North and South, even after emancipation and reconstruction:

1. Blacks are physically, intellectually, and temperamentally *different* from whites.
2. Blacks are also *inferior* to whites in at least some of the fundamental qualities, wherein races differ, especially in intelligence and in the temperamental basis of enterprise or initiative.

3. Such differences and differentials are either permanent or subject to change only by a very slow process of development or evolution.
4. Because of these permanent or deep-seated differences miscegenation, especially in the form of intermarriage, is to be discouraged . . . because the crossing of such diverse types leads either to a short-lived and unprolific breed or to a type that even if permanent is inferior to the whites in those innate qualities giving Caucasian civilization its progressive and creative characteristics.
5. Racial prejudice or antipathy is a natural and inevitable white response to blacks when the latter are free from legalized subordination and aspiring to equal status. Its power is such that it will not in the foreseeable future permit blacks to attain full equality, unless one believes, like some abolitionists, in the impending triumph of a millenarian Christianity capable of obliterating all sense of divisive human differences.
6. It follows from the above propositions that a biracial equalitarian (or "integrated") society is either completely impossible, now and forever, or can be achieved only in some remote and almost inconceivable future. For all practical purposes the destiny of blacks in America is either continued subordination – slavery or some form of caste discrimination – or their elimination as an element of the population. (Fredrickson 1971:321)

How should those ascribed this new status respond? If, as Judith Stein (1986:14) writes, "new world slavery had destroyed the traditional allegiances and loyalties of the past by severing the power and the ways of life that underlay a man's conception of himself as an Ibo, Ashanti, or Igba . . . creat(ing) a people who considered themselves black, African or Negro – all synonymous for the same person," on what basis could a new collective identity be constructed? The black "community" was no natural phenomenon, but had to be constructed out of the ruins of the Southern economy and on the basis of an ascribed condition, race, that would replace slavery as its defining condition in relation to American society. If they were now formally integrated as citizens of the new post-war America, they were segregated as a race apart. "We want to understand that we are no longer colored people, but Americans," John Mercer Langston told a black gathering in 1866, "we have been called all manner of names. I have always called our people negroes. Perhaps you don't like it – I do. I want it to become synonymous with character. We are no longer colored people simply, but a part of the great whole of the mighty American nation" (quoted in Litwack 1979:539).

The term "colored" was associated by many with slavery. Better to move on from that. But what then?

Even as blacks emphasized their American roots, they could not agree on whether they were Negro, colored, black or African Americans. The ongoing debate in the black press and other fora over how they should be addressed revealed at the same time differences over how they conceptualized themselves as a race and a regard for how whites employed the various terms. The objections to "negro" ... rested partly on its association with slavery and the tendency of whites to use it as a term of reproach. "We call each other colored people, black people, but not negro because we used that word in secesh [secessionist] times", a South Carolina freedman testified in 1863. Both "negro" and "black" also suggested unmixed ancestry and hence excluded large numbers of colored people.   (Litwack 1979:540)

In light of such a broad-based and deeply rooted consensus regarding their inherent inferiority, an almost impossible task faced the first generation of blacks after emancipation. How could one ever hope to overcome such a picture of oneself, created by those with political and economic power, and find dignity in a social order that so firmly denied it. It was not so much the direct experience of slavery that would prove traumatic, but its aftermath as the hope and promise of equality and acceptance were crushed finally and formally in the 1880–90s by a reconfiguration around the views of blacks and whites that Fredrickson lists. In the attempt to deal with this trauma of rejection, the memory of slavery would prove an important resource.[20]

More generally, the question of the effects and affects of slavery on the black psyche had to be addressed in the face of the dominant culture's racism. Blacks were forced to see themselves through the eyes of whites and to test and prove themselves. Frederick Douglass put the issue this way in 1873:

The question, which the future has to answer, is: Whether the negro is what he is to-day because of his mental and moral constitution, or because he has been enslaved and degraded for centuries. If it shall be found, after the lapse of twenty-five years of freedom, that the colored people of this country have made no improvement in their social condition, it will confirm the opinion that the negro is, by his very nature, limited to a servile condition. But if, on the other hand, we supply the world with the proof of our advancement to a plane, even a little above that on which slavery left us, we shall prove that, like all other men, we are capable of civilization ...   (1996:392–93)

This would not be an easy process, for the images of race and the representations of slavery were not simply a matter of intellectual or political discourse, they were reproduced and maintained in popular culture in more seemingly benign ways.

Popular memory and popular culture

Oh, give us a flag, all free without a slave
We'll fight to defend it as our fathers did so brave
The gallant Comp'ny 'A' will make the Rebels dance
And we'll stand by the Union if we only have a chance.
(Massachusetts 54th Regiment)

This was the song of Company A, the all-black regiment of the union army.[21] Slavery was something that was by many, black as well as white, thought best forgotten than remembered or commemorated, even by many who experienced it. Former slaves were more concerned with the future, with education and self-help, than with remembering slavery as something more than a means of orienting collective agency. Alexander Crummell, an early supporter of emigration to Africa, liked to distinguish memory from recollection regarding slavery. He said on one memorable occasion (Memorial Day 1885, Harpers' Ferry, VA) to a young black audience "What I would fain have you guard against is not the memory of slavery, but the constant recollection of it" (cited in Blight 1997:161). For Crummell and many others promise lay in the future not the recollection of the past.

Popular commemoration after emancipation supported this view. Blacks "developed their own political calendar, celebrating four civic holidays: January 1, George Washington's birthday, April 3 (Emancipation Day), and July 4" (Brown 1995). In her study of "African American commemorative culture in the post-emancipation South", Kathleen Clark (1999) recounts how southern blacks celebrated their emancipation. Blacks reinterpreted national holidays, like New Year's Day and the 4th of July, to commemorate their own history and identity as distinct from white Americans. January 1, 1863 was the day the Emancipation Proclamation was read, thus by transforming the New Year's Day celebration into Emancipation Day, blacks appropriated a white holiday into one of their own.

Henry McNeal Turner, a minister and "the first black chaplain" in the US Army at the Emancipation Day Anniversary Celebration in Augusta, Georgia on January 1, 1866, called Emancipation Day "the first New Year's day ever enjoyed" (Clark 1999:12).[22] Traditionally the day when slave owners would reorganize their workforce and thus split apart family members amongst their slaves, "This day which hitherto separated so many families, and tear-wet so many faces; heaved so many hearts, and filled the air with so many groans and sighs; this of all others the most bitter day of the year to our miserable race, shall henceforth and forever be filled with acclamations of the wildest joy, and expressions of ecstasy too numerous for angelic pens to note" (13). After noting that because of slavery the celebration of the nation's birthday, July 4, had previously "no claims upon our sympathies," indicating that with Emancipation this would now change, Turner concluded:

Let me say that I have not referred to the cruelty of slavery to incite your passions against white people . . . To the contrary, let us love the whites, and let by-gones be by-gones, neither taunt nor insult them for past grievances; respect them; work with them; but still let us be men. Let us show them we can be a people, respectable, virtuous, honest and industrious, and soon their prejudice will melt away, and with God our father, we will be brothers.   (Cited in Clark 1999:14–15.)

Slavery in other words was what united blacks in the past and its memory would help forge common purpose in the future.

The abolitionist movement provided a context, a ready audience, a network of media and influential individuals within which to construct and disseminate an image of slavery that was counter to the images and practices of the dominant society. In the visual and plastic arts, they encouraged the representation of the black artisan, as a means of countering the dominant image of the inhuman brute without competence and skill. And they encouraged black artisans and artists, like the daguerreotypist Augustus Washington, who made portraits of John Brown and other leading figures of the movement.[23] They inspired the black artist Edmonia Lewis to create "Forever Free" (1867) a sculpture commemorating emancipation and carved in white marble to break the stereotype (Boime 1990:169).[24] The book that is credited with being one of the first pieces of fiction by a black writer, William Wells Brown's *Clotel or The President's Daughter* (1853) was written by an escaped slave-turned-abolitionist. It was William Wells Brown's reportage of the abolitionist demonstrations in Washington in December 1862, demonstrations which eventually helped force a reluctant Abraham Lincoln to issue his Proclamation on January 1, which gave Lewis the title for her work. "Forever Free" was the chorus of an ode written especially for the occasion which the abolitionists, black and white, chanted that night. Brown wrote, "After singing the final refrain, 'Free Forever! Forever Free!' the demonstrators 'seemed to leap for joy: some were singing, some praying, some weeping, some dancing, husbands embracing wives, friends shaking hands – a sister broke out in the following strain, heartily joined in by the vast assembly'":

> Go down, Abraham, away down in Dixie's land,
> Tell Jeff Davis to let my people go.
> (Quoted in Boime 1990:166)

This mixing of biblical imagery and contemporary politics points to the central most influential literary work, The Bible, in this struggle. Passages and citations from scripture were used by both sides in their attempts to justify and deny slavery and it was more often than not the book that provided the first access to the written word for slaves. The citation also reveals how close spoken poetry and song were at the time, as well as how easily black, and white, could move between the sacred and the secular.

The most famous, if not the most powerful, piece of literature to emerge out of this movement was *Uncle Tom's Cabin* by Harriet Beecher Stowe, which

James Baldwin later called "the first protest novel," and which introduced the tragic image of the gentle slave at the mercy of the evil and brutal taskmaster. The names Uncle Tom and Simon Legree remain etched in popular memory to this day, although the connotation of the first has been entirely altered, from a tragic, heroic figure to its opposite. It was the Abolitionist image of slavery as an evil system totally contrary to Christian beliefs, which degraded whites as much as it brutalized blacks, that offered a powerful challenge to the view of slavery as an economic enterprise with benevolent, civilizing, or at least benign, side effects. Stowe's novel was a bestseller when it was published in 1853. So much so that the author published, *Key to Uncle Tom's Cabin* the following year. Another literary genre to emerge in this abolitionist context was the first-hand accounts written by slaves themselves, the so-called slave narratives. As opposed to fictional accounts like Stowe's, these slave narratives are acts of remembering of the first order. Biographical in form, they offered accounts of the experience of slavery from the point of view of those most affected. The abolitionist context imposed a particular framework on the form and content of these narratives, but still they are the first representations of slavery from the inside, and they form the basis of a counter-memory that is equally important today, as these narratives are seen by some as the founding texts of a distinctive "black aesthetic." From their first appearance, however, they were weapons in an anti-slavery struggle and had essentially two non-literary aims, to recount the dehumanizing effects of slavery and to establish the humanity of the slave. The title of what is perhaps the first such work recounts this: *A Narrative of the Uncommon Sufferings and Surprising Deliverance of Briton Hammond, A Negro Man*, published anonymously in Boston in 1760 (Bontemps 1969:xii).

The slave narratives have been central to the construction of a counter, collective memory and in the constitution and resolution of cultural trauma. Seen as representations, the images presented are framed by the circumstances of their production, and their reception has varied according to time and place. Even as first-hand and first-person accounts, they are structured according to narrative conventions and by the intended effects on, as well as the expectations of, their presumed audience. They tell a story, a moral tale, which identifies heroes and villains, giving voice to pain and faces to perpetrators but, more importantly, however, they turn victims into agents and tragedy into triumph.

In his analysis of exemplary slave narratives, Robert Stepto (1991) uncovers three distinct types that point to a development in literary terms. In addition to the two mentioned above, a distinct characteristic of the slave narrative according to Stepto is that its authenticity must be established. This "authenticating" strategy can be counterposed to the "tale" or story itself. The first type he identifies is that where the authenticating documents, written by well-known whites, append the tale, a practice which was especially common during the abolitionist movement. In the second type, the two are more integrated, where authenticating documents "formally become voices and/or characters in the tale" (Stepto 1991:5), and a third in which the tale itself becomes dominant and the slave narrative slides into autobiography, or the authenticating strategy dominates and the slave narrative authenticates a novel or an historical account. Placed in context, the first is decidedly political, where the narratives were weapons in the anti-slavery movement. Thus they tended to emphasize the brutality of the institution and the humanity of the author. A second type emerged after emancipation and within the context of a budding commercial popular culture, they tend toward the adventure story, where drama is provided by the escape, making this rather than slavery itself the prime focus. A third category was the *Bildungsroman* which focuses on the education and liberation of the subject. This is more like conventional biography, and Stepto sees it as a sign of maturity in black literary development, in that the person rather than the context or the condition becomes central.

If the abolitionist movement provided a context for cultural expression amongst former slaves, as Stepto's analysis reveals, it also shaped them in a particular way. This was also true in the plastic arts and in other forms of popular culture. As Albert Boime (1990:171) writes, "images of emancipation, like the actual emancipation rituals and ceremonies, were designed to emphasize the dependence of the emancipated slaves upon their benefactors as well as their ongoing need for the culture and the guidance of their liberators." Thus works of sculpture showed kneeling slaves under the care of standing whites, even as they broke with other stereotypical images of blacks. As the newspaperman and critic Freeman Henry Morris Murray put it in his analysis of sculpture written in 1916, "So Emancipation – even under the circumstances through which it came about in this country – is conceived and expressed nearly always as a bestowal, seldom or never as a restitution. Hence American art – and foreign art, too, it seems – usually puts it: objectively, 'See what's been done for you', or subjectively, 'Look what's been done for me' " (quoted in Boime 1990:172).[25] In Murray's view, there was another subjectivity here, a black subjectivity, which needed to be represented.[26]

Stepto's final category of slave narrative is exemplified in Booker T. Washington's *Up From Slavery* (1901), which moves the slave narrative into autobiography by focus on subjectivity and agency. At the same time, however, Washington's book also tells a distinct tale and offers a moral lesson. It is a heroic tale of triumph and liberation, of man overcoming circumstances through the power of his own will, discipline and hard work, American virtues that guide the narrative of this former slave. In this sense, *Up From Slavery* is a book for the generation born after emancipation, full of hope for the future, in which slavery is seen as a temporary condition, now overcome, to be recalled primarily as background, thus not to be dwelled upon. I think this can well characterize the one dominant view for the emancipation generation: look forward not backwards, see yourself as agent with a future to construct, not a victim mired in the past. Even those like Alexander Crummell, an outspoken advocate of the return to Africa, and who did just that between 1853 and 1873, shared this view.

In terms of their role in the building of collective memory and identity across generations, Arna Bontemps (1969:xiv), one of the young poets associated with the Harlem Renaissance, had this to say about one representative slave narrative, "It is a book that has had many lives and tends to be revived every time black resurgence occurs. Bibliophiles in Harlem during the Renaissance of the twenties spoke of it with whispered pride as one of the most important books attributed to American Negro authorship. It was they who observed that with the exception of the folk songs, the Negro's worthiest contribution to American literature has been his personal memoirs."

One can uncover in Bontemps' endorsement of the slave narratives the "double consciousness" that Du Bois would point to as characterizing the African American identity, as will later be discussed. On the one hand, the slave narratives are important for blacks in that they reinvigorate collective identity through collective memory. On the other hand, as a literary genre produced by blacks, they prove to a white audience the worthiness of the race as a whole. As Bontemps goes on to write concerning the Harlem Renaissance bibliophiles (including himself, of course), "They realized . . . that pending the emergence of a Pushkin or a Dumas, whose rampant creativity might eclipse his personality, there would continue to be more interest, more significance, in *how* a Negro achieved in the white world than in *what* he achieved" (1969:xiv). Finally, Bontemps likens the slave narratives as a genre of popular culture to the Western: "like the Westerns, they also created a parable of the human condition, but with them the meaning was different. Their theme was the fetters of mankind and the yearning of all living things for freedom. In this context the perils of escape and the long journeys toward the North Star did not grow tiresome with repetition until a new myth, the Western, replaced the earlier one." It seems clear that the slave narratives had different meanings for their different audiences and different rewards and pleasures for their authors as well.

For our specific concerns, the slave narratives accomplished several things, they helped turn victims into agents by giving voice to the voiceless; in recording the experiences of a socially invisible group, they made them not only visible as human beings but also available to others, spanning time and space, thus providing grounds for both contemporary self-reflection and collective memory as they passed through and helped constitute the identity of future generations. They also created a literary genre, one in which culture and politics were intimately interwoven.

The existence of the slave narratives as a literary genre combined with expanding educational and occupational opportunities for blacks to force an opening of the literary field in the years after emancipation.[27] With this the struggle over the memory of slavery took on new form as well as content. Shaped by the promise of emancipation and integration into American society, rather than the experience of slavery, this new generation looked expectantly toward the future, not the past. It included writers and poets like Paul Dunbar, born in Ohio in 1872, James Weldon Johnson, born in Jacksonville, Florida in 1871, and Charles Chesnutt, considered by some to be the first modern black novelist. However, between this new generation and slavery was the work of Frances E. W. Harper, born in 1825 to free parents in Baltimore.

Harper was raised by an abolitionist uncle and began writing in this movement context. Still in her twenties, she worked full time as a traveling lecturer for the Maine Anti-Slavery Society, where the poems she published "went through at least twenty editions" (Andrews 1992:ix). She was be a great inspiration to the next generation of black women, like Ida Wells, who points to Harper as a role model. It was a novel she published in 1892, *Iola Leroy, or Shadows Uplifted*, mentioned previously, which links her to the post-slavery generation, however. A work Harper described as mixing "fact and fiction," *Iola Leroy* traces the history of a black woman and her family from the closing days of the civil war through the beginning of reconstruction. Here slavery is treated not as the ultimate evil it was in abolitionist literature, but as a tragic condition, which brought hardship and misery to black people, but which also provided grounds for racial uplift. A devout Christian, Harper believed that the solution to slavery was to be found in the Bible, as Iola says in the novel, "there is but one remedy by which our nation can recover from the evil entailed upon her by slavery... A fuller comprehension of the claims of the Gospel of Jesus Christ, and their application to our national life" (Andrews 1992:162). While another character, a sympathetic white, replies:

The problem of the nation... is not what men will do with the negro, but what will they do with the reckless, lawless white men who murder, lynch, and burn their fellow-citizens... The negro came here from the heathenism of Africa; but the young colonies could not take into their early civilization a stream of barbaric blood without being affected by its influence, and the negro, poor and despised as he is, has laid his hands on our Southern civilization and helped mold its character.[28]   (Andrews 1992:163)

Although it is not clear whether or not these are views Harper shared, it is clear that slavery is here remembered and dealt with in an entirely different way than in abolitionist literature. Some slaveowners are shown as complex characters, for example, caught up in a system they neither admire nor support. Harper's female heroine, the light-skinned Iola, could pass for white, but chooses to be African American and devotes her life to helping the race through education and literature. Finally, the novel is melodramatic in a way that abolitionist literature could never be.

The ambiguous relationship to slavery which shaped this generation, that slavery was at once degrading and civilizing, as revealed in Harper's novel and in Booker T. Washington's memoirs, was shared by Frederick Douglass ([1873] Andrews 1996:393–94), at least at this late stage of his life: "I have spoken of slavery as our enemy. I have nothing to take back at that point. It has robbed us of education. It has robbed us of the care due us from our mothers. It has written its ugliness in our countenance, deformed our feet, and twisted our limbs out of shape; and yet this same slavery has been, in some sense, our best friend. It has trained us to regular industry, and hardened our muscles to toil, and thus has left in our hands the staff of all accomplishments."

For this generation of black intellectuals and writers, those born after or at the end of slavery, questions of representation were inherently moral concerns of the type, "how should an oppressed minority be represented before and to the dominant society?" Representation was also a political matter, in that considerations of its implications regarding the dominant society were always immanent. Previously, such concerns had been raised and answered to a large extent by sympathetic whites, although not entirely of course, as many free blacks were active abolitionists. These whites had their own moral and political agendas. Later, blacks gained more control of their own representation as the black public grew in size and self-consciousness, they formulated their own specific agenda. The combining of African and European aesthetic influences, consciously or tacitly recognized and applied, occurred in either circumstance as highly politicized, charged with larger meaning and significance than the purely aesthetic. There was no escaping this, and one wrote and sang always under the watchful eyes of the master, even with one's own voice.

This was also a very different picture of slavery from that being presented in white literature. The so-called "plantation tradition" characterized by a nostalgia for the "good old days" populated by genteel whites and contented slaves, emerged in literature and history writing. In other forms of popular culture, minstrel shows and other forms of entertainment contained similar aspects, the nostalgic popular songs of Stephan Foster and others complemented the "Uncle Remus" folk-tales of Joel Chandler Harris and the statues to "Mammy." This cultural offensive – which in "serious" culture was identified with the plantation school and in more popular forms of expression with black face, and in combination identified a "cult of the Confederacy" (Foster 1987:110–19) –

confronted black writers and intellectuals as a powerful opposing ideological force. In addition to this, there was the problem of publishing itself. With the cultural field dominated by whites he or she faced the choice of "conforming to [the dominant vision] of black life . . . and achieve considerable recognition and success; or he could realistically depict the black experience as he perceived it and risk alienating his patrons, his publisher and his market" (Wintz 1988). There was also the question of loyalty to the race and the relation of the black writer to the "community" as it was now forming. In addition to the role of this new group of educated and articulate blacks facing the failure of reconstruction and a reconsolidating white society, popular forms of remembrance also faced a challenge.

Another black author to meet this challenge as part of the middle-class response to the new consensus was Charles Chesnutt.[29] Born in Ohio in 1858, Chesnutt grew up in Fayetteville, North Carolina, where, after having been educated at a school organized by the Freedmen's Bureau, he worked as a teacher, appointed at the age of 16, and eventually as principal of the State Colored Norman School (Andrews 1992:xii; Miers 1969). Frustrated by the disparity between the promise of reconstruction and its reality, Chesnutt returned to Ohio, after having worked in New York, and turned to literature as a means of social change. As blacks were being again excluded from more conventional politics, cultural politics offered an alternative. Having other means of support, Chesnutt turned to literature as a means to counter revisionist attempts to redefine slavery as benign and even beneficial to blacks. He published short stories in the *Atlantic Monthly* and collected folk tales in the late 1880s, "becoming the first African American fiction writer to be published by such an influential arbiter of national taste" (Gleason 1999:33). These led eventually to the *The Conjure Woman* (1899), a collection of eight such stories, considered by many to be one of the first examples of African American literature, and to *The Wife of His Youth and Other Stories of the Color Line* (1899). As opposed to many of his contemporaries who were busy learning to read the white man's texts, Chesnutt aimed to "broaden the cultural record by teaching Whites to read Negro 'texts'" (Molyneaux 1994:164). Chesnutt's conjure woman serves, Molyneaux writes, as a "challenge to forgetfulness" by representing in written form for a wide audience of blacks and whites the folk tales and practices of the oral tradition carried over during slavery. There is more to *The Conjure Woman* and to Chesnutt as novelist than this, however. The novel presents slavery to its white readership in a contrary way to what they had come to expect. Chesnutt describes slavery as a debilitating experience, rather than a paternalistic, civilizing institution, as the new consensus would have it. Cary Wintz (1988) suggests that Chesnutt "skillfully and subtly . . . wove a delicate pattern of racism and the inhumanity of slavery through his stories . . . [that] realistically captured the true injustice of slavery by illustrating the suffering experienced by good slaves at the hands of well-intentioned and humane masters" (56). In a second novel published in 1901, *The Marrow of Tradition*, which he hoped would have the same impact on America's social conscience as *Uncle Tom's Cabin* (Andrews 1992), Chesnutt described the difficulties blacks encountered as they sought to integrate themselves into mainstream society as "the marrow" of inbuilt racism reasserted itself in the "New South." As part of the attempt to enhance racial pride in the face of new waves of racism, Chesnutt also wrote a biography of Frederick Douglass, published in 1899.[30]

"The Wife of his Youth," the short story that gave its title to the second collection of Chesnutt's short stories published in 1899, is a touching tale of the memories and consequences of slavery. A light-skinned, middle-class black man at the center of high society in the black community of a Northern city is about to organize a ball at which he will propose marriage to an equally well-educated, light-skinned woman. Just prior to this, he is visited by a bent and wrinkled quaint looking black woman who asks his help in finding the long-lost husband she married when they were both slaves. Her husband, "a merlatter man named Sam Taylor" (Chesnutt 1968:12), was forced to flee and she "be'n lookin' fer 'im eber sence . . . as though twenty-five years were but a couple of weeks" (13). She shows him an old picture, carried in a locket around her neck and he promises to help. At the ball he recounts this visit to his guests, who listen intently, "for the story awakened a responsive thrill in many hearts . . . there were some present who had seen, and others who had heard their fathers and grandfathers tell, the wrongs and sufferings of this past generation, and all of them still felt, in their darkest moments, the shadow hanging over them" (20). He ends the tale with a hypothetical question concerning the long-lost husband, "suppose that accident should bring to his knowledge the fact that the wife of his youth, the wife he had left behind him – not one who had walked by his side and kept pace with him in his upward struggle, but one upon whom advancing years and laborious life had set their mark – was alive and seeking him . . . my friends, what would the man do?" "He should have acknowledged her," the guests replied in unison (23). "Ladies and gentlemen," he said, "this is the woman, and I am the man . . . permit me to introduce to you the wife of my youth" (24).[31]

Against the emergent revisionist consensus, and the plantation tradition in literature, in which slavery was presented as a civilizing paternalism, Chesnutt and a very few other black authors fought a difficult battle. This sort of revisionism, which successfully replaced the Abolitionist image of slavery with one more congenial to the "New South," was a powerful tendency in popular culture generally. Minstrel shows and other forms of popular entertainment depicted plantation life as anything but traumatic and tragic for blacks for their primarily white audience. Paul Dunbar, Chesnutt's contemporary, wrote lyrics for these shows, as well as poetry and novels.

Dunbar's work is still the subject of debate, as can be gleaned from how he once described his aims and purposes as a writer: to "interpret my own people through song and story, and to prove to the many that after all we are more human than African" (quoted in Wintz 1988:48). This is a telling statement, it reveals a widespread feeling amongst this generation of race conscious blacks, that one had to prove oneself worthy, as much collectively as individually. On the other hand, it exposes a sensitivity regarding the past, even beyond slavery, that was less widespread. Another aspect of controversy regarding Dunbar's work, then as well as now, concerns the use of dialect in his work and, even more controversially, his apparent attribution of subordinate attitudes to slaves, seemingly accepting the plantation tradition's version of slavery, as in one poem where "an old blind slave decides to will his own death so that he can accompany his master, killed during the civil war, to the afterlife" (Mishkin 1998:59).[32]

At a time when many educated blacks regarded dialect as embarrassing and demeaning, because it reinforced stereotypes, Dunbar thought its use presented an authentic picture of black speech and folkways, as, in fact, Irish and Scottish poets had done in Europe. It should also be said that Frances Harper used dialect to mark the different generations of blacks in *Iola Leroy*, where the older generation spoke dialect and the younger did not and Chesnutt, as can be seen in the citations from his short story above, also used dialect to signal the slave past. While Dunbar may have intended to use dialect in the way of his Irish and Scottish counterparts, a major difference between the European examples and the American was the audience. While Robert Burns in Scotland and John Millington Synge in Ireland may have had English readers and audiences, their prime public was their respective national minorities. Dunbar and other black writers confronted a quite different situation. Not only did they have to confront a new consensus in national opinion concerning the recent past, their possibility to survive in the literary field depended entirely upon whites. If they sought to live off their writing alone, they faced a daunting task of walking a treacherous path between loyalty to race and winning a white audience by writing what it wanted to hear and see.

Dunbar's success with white readers was assured when William Dean Howells, the country's leading literary critic, who had also written positively of Chesnutt's work, praised his attempts to "study his race objectively, to analyze it to himself, and then to represent it in art as he felt it and found it to be . . . " (quoted in Wintz 1988:48). Many middle-class blacks felt this degraded the race and preferred moralist melodrama or uplifting romance to such "realism".

In Dunbar's defense, Mishkin points out that while such verse might well have reflected the views and served the interests of its intended white audience, it may also, she suggests, reflect the actual attitudes of many of those older, newly emancipated slaves. An example of this might be the black Mississippi farmer, Gilbert Myers, who owned more than 500 acres of land accumulated during reconstruction, and who, in explaining to a Senate committee in 1879 why he voted for the racially conservative Democratic Party, said "because I sympathize with my own self, knowing that I expected to stay with them [*sic*] to make property if I could, and the South had always been kind to me. My master that I live with I nursed him and slept at his mother's feet and nursed at her breast, so I thought my interest was to stay with the majority of the country who I expected to prosper with" (quoted in Meier 1962:27).

To the extent that this is correct, it would fit well with a generational analysis of how slavery may have been perceived in the postwar period; the younger generation focused on the future and on integration and the older on the past and its ambiguous virtues. Whatever the truth of the matter, Dunbar's intentions in reference to his audience were clearly different from those of Chesnutt and Harper, who used fiction as a means toward social reform and racial uplift. Dunbar, on the other hand, at least in his later work, offered a more realistic approach to black life and a more purely aesthetic approach to writing. His last novel, *The Sport of the Gods* (1902), preempts later attempts by writers of the Harlem Renaissance to reveal the down side of urban life, where not only poverty, but also the lack of real community led to tragedy for newly arrived Southern blacks. In addition to differences in their respective views concerning the role of literature in society, there may have been other factors that explain the differences in the content of their writing. Wintz (1988:55) points out that while Chesnutt maintained a successful career as the owner of a legal stenography business, which afforded him a degree of freedom in his choice of literary topic, Dunbar attempted to live off his income as a writer, something which made him more dependent on the market and on white patronage. By carefully choosing his subject matter and his approach to it, Dunbar was able to support himself on his writing alone during the latter part of his career. He died in 1906, at 38 years of age, the author of nineteen books of poetry and fiction.

Besides literature, journalism and teaching were two other professions through which blacks could do battle in the culture war following reconstruction. Someone whose life well illuminates this is Ida B. Wells, one of the most prominent black activists of the period. According to her biographer (McMurry 1999), "for several years in the 1890s, no African American, except Frederick Douglass, received more press attention" (xiv). When Douglass died in 1895, it was assumed by many that Wells would take over his leadership role.[33] Wells was born in Holly Springs, Mississippi in 1862, during the civil war. Her parents were slaves, but of the more privileged kind. Though a slave, Wells' father was also the son of his master, who had no other children. Because of his high status he was "hired out" as an apprentice carpenter and thus was able to live a semi-independent life as a skilled craftsman. Well's mother was the family cook, also a relatively privileged position. After the war, the Wells family stayed on to work for their former masters, now as paid workers; not an uncommon experience for the more privileged freed slaves, especially those that had held together as family. Had Wells grown up in bondage, she would have begun work at an early age, no matter what her parents' position. Now free, Wells' parents and others like them wanted their children to have childhoods like those they had seen amongst slaveowners. Instead of work, Wells recalled, "our job was to go to school and learn all we could" (quoted in McMurry 1999:9). As a teenager, Ida Wells attended Shaw University which held classes in the Methodist church her religious family attended. Part of the evangelical movement, this school (sometimes called Rust College) was run by white missionaries from the North.[34] The name "college" or "university" did not mean then what it means today; the school, like the ones mentioned earlier, offered basic elementary education up through normal school (high school) for training teachers. At sixteen, after both her parents died in a yellow fever epidemic, leaving her to head the household, Wells began work as a teacher in a country school.

Wells traveled often between Holly Springs and Memphis, where she had friends and family. Segregation on trains was now a hotly debated issue; banned during reconstruction, Jim Crow laws were being slowly reinstated in the 1880s. Black women who could afford it, however, were usually permitted to purchase first-class tickets, which allowed them to sit in a non-smoking "ladies' car." Because of the humiliations suffered by black women during slavery, this newly acquired possibility to be free of harassment on public transportation was an important issue for black women activists and an arena of active protest. Like Rosa Parks would do in 1955, Ida Wells refused to give up her seat in the ladies' car in September 1883, when told to move to the second-class car by a white conductor. As he attempted to force her, Wells bit his hand before other passengers helped the conductor carry her off the train. Angered by the event and viewing it as more than a personal affront, Wells sued the railroad. After many delays and appeals by the railroad, Wells won the case and was awarded $500 in damages. This was only a partial victory, however, as the final ruling charged the railroad with neglect rather than discrimination. However, the event was so important and unusual that even white newspapers carried the story. The headline of the Christmas Day 1884 issue of the *Memphis Daily Appeal* read: "Darky Damsel Obtains a Verdict for Damages against the Chesapeake & Ohio Railroad – What it Cost to Put a Colored School Teacher in a Smoking Car – Verdict for $500" (quoted in McMurry 1999:28).

By this time, Wells had moved to Memphis where she continued her teaching and her political activism. To be a teacher in a black public school was almost by definition to be politically engaged, not only because of the high value and hope placed on education itself, but also, more directly, because of the conflicts over funding with white politicians, especially since education was valued so highly by blacks. Memphis was unusual at this time in that all teachers received the same salary, black and white, male and female. The working conditions of black and white teachers differed dramatically however. "In 1883, when the student – teacher ratio for all schools averaged forty-seven, black teachers were struggling with as many as eighty-four students," and in addition, "almost one-third of black classrooms had split sessions – compared to 4.6 percent for white classrooms" (McMurry 1999:78–99). Black teachers were given a degree of independence to solve these day-to-day issues, but whites controlled the school boards and city councils and thus the budget for education. This power over monies directly linked teaching and politics, an issue that brought many black women, who were an active force in the teaching profession, into politics.[35] Because of the links between education and religion, this was an arena within which many black women defined their contribution to what was now coming to be called their "race." Under these conditions, education was considered to be morally as well as practically uplifting, and a teacher was expected to be exemplary on all accounts, a race leader, in other words.

Because it was a highly valued and esteemed profession, teaching opened doors not only to politics but also to elite black society. As she moved into Memphis, Wells also moved into its black elite, whose circles were organized around an interconnected network of social and cultural gatherings, with the church, in her case now the Episcopalian, as the center. Cultural events included lyceums, book clubs and theater, forming a class-related public sphere whose activities were reported on the society pages of the local newspapers, including the white newspapers on special occasions. This local elite society was interconnected with a larger network which reached into northern cities like New York and Cleveland, whose black newspapers also carried 'reports' on events deemed to be of more than local significance. All of this helped constitute a community as well as to interconnect a society. Wells was also active in professional organizations, such as the national teachers' association, which was integrated by this time, and nationally organized religious organizations. This was a period of great participation by blacks in voluntary, self-help organizations, including secret societies like the Masons, and Wells' activities were not unusual, though they were related to and articulated her social status.[36]

It was through such networks that the possibility of a career in journalism presented itself to Wells. Like education, journalism carried high moral responsibility and visibility; unlike teaching however, there were only a few black women in the field. Through the black press, primarily weekly journals at this point, the "race" re-presented itself, both for each other and to whites. These journals were means of self-reflection, moral education and representation, as well as providing information. This was not something specific to blacks, but these aspects were magnified by the fact of being newly emancipated and marginalized. Because of the latter, the black press was also, in Wells' eyes especially, a vehicle of protest, because it gave voice to the otherwise voiceless. Wells entered journalism on the basis of her contacts in the Memphis elite, but more importantly on the basis of her experience with the railroad. Her first article in the local paper concerned that event, but because of what it entailed it was picked up by other black newspapers, including those in New York. Entering journalism on the basis of her protest activity was significant in that it helped keep Wells from being placed in the role of female journalist, reporting on ladies' issues. She did, however, write on these topics, which also concerned the civilizing or moral role of the black newspaper: she wrote articles on "A Woman's Mission," concerning what a womanly woman was, someone "upholding the banner and striving for the goal of pure, bright womanhood" (McMurry 1999:103), and on a woman's "proper role." With black women especially degraded by slavery, middle-class black women in a position to do so used the church, teaching, and journalism, to "educate" black women generally on their proper role. Though Wells focused on more directly political issues, like criticizing black leadership, especially the clergy, and even the secret societies, she did write such edifying articles as well. This was part of the moral education and re-presentation that black newspapers, through their editors, many of whom were clergy, and journalists, performed.

It was protest, however, and giving voice to the voiceless that primarily motivated Wells in her journalistic writing and editorship. The lynching of two of her closest Memphis friends in 1892 sparked what was to become her life-long concern, one that would carry her, as it had abolitionists like Frederick Douglass, on speaking tours to England and Europe, as well as around the United States. Three black men associated with the People's Grocery Company, a cooperative store in a border neighborhood, were brutally beaten and then shot to death after attempting to protect the store from a white mob. The event had begun, in part, because of economic competition between this store and a privately owned white grocery store which was losing black customers to the co-op. Black economic nationalism was one response to the failure of reconstruction and it greatly angered those whites it most affected. In addition, blacks in Memphis and other areas of the South had formed a militia, which included an armory for the storage of weapons, in order to protect themselves. The men attacked were part of that militia and the fact that they were armed led to their arrest. Later that night they were taken from jail by an angry mob and killed in an outlying field. The following is the first white newspaper account:

The affair was one of the more orderly of its kind ever conducted, judging from the accounts. There was no whooping, not even loud talking, no cursing, in fact nothing boisterous. Everything was done decently and in order. The vengeance was sharp, swift and sure, but administered with due regard to the fact that people were asleep all around the jail, and that it is not good form to arouse people from their slumbers at 3 o'clock in the morning.   (*Memphis Appeal-Avalanche* March 9, 1892, quoted in McMurry 1999:134)

If the event itself were not enough, the reports in the white press incited Wells to devote the rest of her life to a campaign against lynching. One outcome, if not a direct effect of slavery, certainly was connected with it. Lynching symbolized the brutalization and rejection of blacks by white society after reconstruction as nothing else could. It made the fact of that rejection undeniable and crystal clear. While rape and the fear of black sexuality was the usual and prime justification for lynching, its underlying cause, as noted previously, was the fear of black success. There was not even the hint of rape in this case, as these were respected, successful black men, practicing that most common American virtue, defending their economic enterprise; too successfully, it would seem. For this they were symbolically and ritually put to death, "decently and in order." What sort of message could this but communicate to blacks? Writing in her paper, Wells immediately advised blacks to leave, to head West; the underlying message of rejection was clear, however: blacks were not welcome in the United States. And indeed many blacks heeded this advice. Black towns developed in several parts of Oklahoma, including in Boley, a town of over 2,000, which, according to Booker T. Washington who visited there in 1905, had "two banks, two cotton gins, a newspaper, a hotel and a 'college'" (quoted in Christian 1995:294).

This event helped personify cultural trauma and lift it out of the realm of intellectual discourse. It reminded a group of itself and its marginal status, driving home the point as little else could that emancipation had not emancipated them, middle class or not. It also raised fundamental questions concerning their reconfirmed collective identity and their place in American society, questions they thought had previously been resolved, and once again, forcing a reconfiguration of. collective identity and a reworking of collective memory.

Some general issues regarding cultural trauma and representation can be raised here. What are the "appropriate" forms for recollecting potentially traumatic events, such as slavery? Can these be dealt with in all manner and form of representation? Ever since *Clotel or, The President's Daughter* (Wells 1853 in Brown 1995) black writers have used fiction to talk about the truth of their experience. The use of jokes, verbal misrepresentation and the use of double entendre has an even longer history. Oral performance and forms of literary and visual representation can offer a mask from behind which a subordinate individual or group can express true feelings about their social situation or about real events. Are there forms that are not appropriate? Could one think of a musical comedy about slavery, like a minstrel show or a vaudeville act, that was not degrading and which revealed a truth about that condition and institution? Does it depend upon who is doing it and for whom, that is, on actor and audience? Black minstrel shows had some black actors toward the end of the nineteenth century, which not only gave a degree of "authenticity" to those shows, but also work to black performers. As noted earlier, Paul Dunbar and James Weldon Johnson wrote lyrics for minstrel shows. Did this make them more authentic and less degrading? What if the audience was also entirely black, how would that affect the content of the material and its reception? Was *Clotel* more authentic, and thus "true," than *Uncle Tom's Cabin*? I think part of the answer lies in the intent of the authors and the performers and in their connectedness with their public. Another part lies in the sophistication, measured in terms of the distance and closeness they can achieve rather than level of education or snobbishness, from the content or substance of what is being performed or represented. The singing of a song by a slave is one thing, that same song performed in concert is another. The first is the expression of a slave, the second may be about slavery and may recall that experience to a certain audience, those who have experienced it directly or those, like Du Bois, discussed later, who feel themselves intimately connected to those who have had that experience or it may be just a piece of music or noise, appreciated or not. The fact that the former is non-commercial and the latter commercial is not the issue. In other words, a joke may just be a joke, a funny story, or it may have a deeper meaning, but to grasp the difference means to have a special relationship to what is being said and by whom. If a comic story or a musical comedy is as "proper" a means as a poem or a novel to represent such a serious matter as slavery cannot be answered beforehand. Those who attempt to do so may reveal more, about themselves, and their views of culture, than about the forms of representation they wish to judge.

Issues such as these became important for the coming generations of black Americans, when the question "how should blacks be represented?" was posed with increasing intensity and sophistication. This was so because American society had shown black Americans that they were different, a group apart, and would remain so. That this separateness was in part self-willed and the result of unintended historical processes that encouraged group-building, did not detract from the obvious and renewed racism of the dominant white society from the

1880s onwards. This meant that blacks would be forced to identify collectively, whether or not they formed a real, rather than an imagined community and whether they wanted it or not. Their individual actions would always be judged as if they were a community. In this sense, black Americans could never be individuals. An artist or writer who happened to be black would always be judged as a black artist, a reflection on the "race," just as would a black person who committed a crime or an heroic act. Thus, it was argued, each had a responsibility, a duty, to perform well, to present and represent, only the good and the worthy before the critical and judgmental eyes of the observing white public. That such a discussion could occur at all points to some significant developments. First, that articulate blacks had acquired both the status and the means to express themselves in more formalized public arenas. Here the emergence of black media, such as newspapers and journals, were a major development. The clergy were central here and would remain so, but other professions emerged as well, lawyers, journalists, historians, writers, and, most of all, teachers, at first connected to the clergy and religion generally, but soon more autonomous. This created new possibilities, and perspectives, of representation, but also internal social divisions between those who had more access to the means and media of representation, and could claim the right to represent, and those who were represented. This would have consequences for how the past was viewed and collective memory articulated. Again, such developments were not unique to blacks, quite the contrary, but they did take on distinct form because of the new marginalization and reaction to it.

If a distinct "black aesthetic" developed in this period, it had as much to do with the circumstances in which the cultural forms of expression created by black Americans were formed as with a unique blending of African and European influences. While it is certainly true that black music and dance, as well as religious practices and styles of writing, combined African and European aspects, it is also true that this process of cultural creation took shape in a specific social and political context, where forms of representation were intimately interwoven with moral and political concerns. It is certainly possible to argue that this is always the case with any form of representation, but that is neither an issue nor an interesting question. What is more interesting, even if that is the case, is to specify as far as possible how moral and political concerns shape artistic expression. This generation of blacks in the United States faced issues of representation with moral and political concerns forced upon them by the trauma of failed emancipation and in the face of a reactionary cultural and political offensive. As they gained more control over the means of their own representation, they were faced with such opposition that this control was mitigated by the force of circumstance.

In the following generation, blacks would gain more control, and awareness, of their cultural creations and their collective identity, and more opportunities to formulate their own agenda. This was made possible by the distance time allows to select and filter out the past and the power attained through having a larger and more concentrated and self-conscious public. Slavery would look different to this generation, and its collective memory was reconstituted on that basis.

3

Out of Africa: the making of a collective identity

> If we were a people much given to revealing secrets, we might raise monuments and sacrifice memories of our poets, but slavery cured us of that weakness. It may be enough, however, to have said that we survive in exact relationship to the dedication of our poets (including preachers, musicians and blues singers).
>
> Maya Angelou

A new African American Negro

In her discussion of the similarities between the Irish and the Harlem Renaissances, Tracy Mishkin (1998:69ff.) lists three ingredients that were central in the construction of an Irish identity. To counter the degrading racial and ethnic stereotyping perpetrated by the English, Irish intellectuals called upon the past, the peasants, and religion.[1] A similar list could be made for those intellectuals and artists who composed the two interrelated currents of the New Negro movement that emerged out of the cultural trauma spurred by the end of Reconstruction and culminated in the urban Renaissance of the 1920s, on the energy provided by a new generation.[2] Out of this movement emerged the idea of the African American, which reinterpreted the meaning of slavery as it renegotiated the borders of the collective and its memory. In the case of African Americans, the list would include much the same elements, the past, the peasants, and religion but with a slightly different spin. Like their Irish predecessors and contemporaries, most prominently the poet W. B. Yeats and playwright J. M. Synge, black intellectuals at around the turn of the century began to look for some common ground upon which to secure a new collective identity for America's blacks who were once more being degraded by the dominant society.[3]

The Irish rebellion against colonial rule was a source of inspiration which also helped articulate a model of emancipation based on the idea of racial-based community. The concepts and boundaries that would circumscribe and define

58

this collective would change over time, moving between "race," "ethnicity," "community," and "nation," but the underlying force would remain constant: the need and desire for a positive grounding of recognition. One of the first problems facing intellectuals was in fact mediating levels of identity, especially from the local to the national and international levels. Racist reaction in the period of trauma forced blacks into self-defensive, locally based communities; through their representations intellectuals and other leaders sought to broaden this to include other blacks or, for some, Africans and all people of color. The related and coexistent notion of the African American, comprising those in the United States with links to the African continent, past and present, drew upon a different model of emancipation, that of full citizenship rights derived from the Enlightenment and the French and American Revolutions.

Unlike the Irish and most European cultural nationalistic movements, American blacks, writes Mishkin, "lacked an immediately accessible native language in which to center a cause" (Mishkin 1998:48). Black speech patterns were being parodied in popular culture, making their appropriation problematic. If there existed no common African language to draw upon, black dialect and other forms of cultural expression developed during slavery offered a possible starting point. While writers and poets like Charles Chesnutt, Frances Harper, and Paul Dunbar drew upon black dialect, story telling, and jokes in their attempt to locate a distinctive folk culture, the sociologist, W. E. B. Du Bois pointed to another sort of language, the "sorrow songs" that slavery had produced and the humble, good-natured personality this form of music expressed. As he attempted to shift the field of struggle from texts to more direct political confrontation, Du Bois would contrast a "soulless" American culture to the "soulful" slave culture: "Will America be poorer if she replace her brutal dyspeptic blundering with light-hearted but determined Negro humility? Or her coarse and cruel wit with loving jovial good-humor? Or her vulgar music with the soul of the Sorrow Songs?" His answer was a gently put "No!"[4] While Du Bois tended to restrict this positive outcome of slavery to more refined culture, others like James Weldon Johnson would expand this to include the entire way of life produced by slavery (Banks 1996:66).[5] What they had in common was the desire to represent the subjectivity of black American life, though they would have disagreed as to the proper forms of its expression.[6]

The memory of slavery and its representation was a major factor in this struggle to build a new collective foundation. While black intellectuals sought to uncover and mobilize cultural resources to reconstruct collective identity by reshaping collective memory, their counterparts in the dominant white culture were doing the same. By the 1890s the "history of slavery had shifted from recent memory to cultural artifact" (Krasner 1997:23) and its representation was a matter of cultural and political struggle. In the dominant culture a wave of "authenticity" had put an end to the black-faced minstrel show and replaced it with blacks performing as their "real" selves in authentic settings. An example can be found in "Black America," a popular musical which opened in Brooklyn, New York in 1895, where white producers attempted to recreate an "authentic" stage representation of black life on a southern plantation. Here "real" black actors replaced whites in black face in a setting which included live farm animals and where the audience was encouraged to walk through to heighten the experience. This mixture of theater and circus was meant as a sort of living documentary of a way of life and an era just now fading into the historic past. According to the report in the *Boston Herald*, "the people who take part in 'Black America' are not actors. They are the natural production of a section of the United States, and all they are called upon to do in the giving of 'Black America' is to act naturally" (quoted in Krasner 1997:23).

In such "authentic" representations, within what Powell calls "a culture of ridicule and slander" (1997:34) two images of blacks were crystalizing, that of the brute in need of isolation and segregation and that of the "sambo" or "happy darky." Both of these sought to reinforce the recollection of slavery as a benign, pastoral period. For Grace Hale (1998:21), these images were part of the dominant culture's own reaction to a new, assertive black middle class. She writes: "whites created the culture of segregation in large part to counter black success, to make a myth of absolute racial difference, to stop the rising." But, "white efforts . . . to erase the visibility of middle class blacks, to see the world as a minstrel show writ large and all African Americans as a narrow range of characters, proved more difficult." Part of that difficulty stemmed from the growing power of blacks to represent and to speak for themselves. As the educated middle class grew, it also gained access to mass media and to other means of representation, like theater and literature.

It was such representations and the claim to "naturalism" that the New Negro sought to counter.[7] One such counter-image was of themselves, the refined, educated blacks, and in their self-presentation as well as in their aesthetic representations they provided role models and counter-images. As mobilizing ideology, this image was codified in the notion of a "talented tenth," an exemplary elite that would lead the race through projecting its habitus as a form of political practice. While its original formulation encompassed mainly males, a female "talented tenth" was also taking form in the networks and public spaces created within the black church and segregated school system. By the 1920s these essentially Southern based ideas and movements would move northward as part of the Great Migration. Out of this demographic shift, a second wave of the New Negro would crystalize in the cultural upsurge known as the Harlem Renaissance, to offer another, generationally rooted interpretation of the meaning of slavery and the place of Africa in black America. These two developments, the rise of a stratum of more formally educated and cultivated blacks with access to the mass media (thus capable of challenging the reactionary dominant culture) and the urban migration underpinning a cultural renaissance with national impact were both cause and effect of the process of cultural trauma.

A New Negro

Cary Wintz (1988:31) traces the term "New Negro" to a newspaper editorial in 1895 which applied it to a "new class of blacks with education, class, and money" which had emerged since the civil war.[8] What the phrase inferred was that blacks in increasing numbers had achieved social position and influence in at least some aspects of American society and could express publicly feelings of racial pride. This would correspond to the schema of generational memory presented earlier, where it was noted that after a cultural trauma it could take at least a generation before the most affected groups could express their feelings publicly and were also in a social position to do so. The emerging black middle class was a generation removed from slavery, but, as the literature of Chesnutt, Harper, and Dunbar among others revealed, its traces lie just beneath the surface and could easily be recalled, and relived, evoking strong emotional response in the community which shared its memory. The memory of slavery could now be expressed and evoked through the nation-wide public media, such as commercial publishing, which though controlled by whites and with only a small black audience, still permitted a community to imagine itself beyond the borders of face-to-face and defensive reaction. It was against the backdrop of cultural trauma that a new, positive collective identity took form, one that would circumscribe as it characterized an extended community and a new generation. With only a little irony one could say that the newly enforced segregation produced the necessity of a we-identity as it made possible an integrated black community. The same process also fragmented and stratified the black population. The concept and the practices of the New Negro attempted to reconcile these two counter-posed tendencies.

 The predominant responses to the reincorporation of the South and the "civilizing" of the war were the withdrawal from political life into defensive community and an aggressive cultural attack. Central to both was a more "positive" picture of the heritage of slavery, arguing that out of repression and subordination had grown a vibrant culture, a self-help work ethic, and a way to survive, which now in the face of a new wave of separation and marginalization could offer an alternative to the "vulgar materialism" of modern American life. Elements for a dramatic discursive conflict were in place, with a few exceptions. There was categorization, a process of naming self and Other, them and us, each with their own past and present; these categories were seen as unchangeable, two races were opposed and in conflict, but one side refused to play the role of victim or survivor.

Such was the context in which a group of intellectuals around W. E. B. Du Bois sought grounding for a distinctive *African* American identity, one that would expand the boundaries of "community" by reaching out to a racially based, cultural nationalism. Du Bois first tested the notion before sympathetic black audiences before launching it before the white world, first hesitantly in the *Atlantic Monthly* in 1897 and then with greater self-assurance in *The Souls of Black Folk* (1903). The concept of "race" was the key.[9] As Du Bois applied it, race generalized an ascribed commonality in a positive way, connecting the present to the past and a local group to a larger historical one. In the process, several levels of community – local, national and world historical – are articulated and intertwined. The African American was proposed as part of a larger collective, with African origins but now spread across the globe. Du Bois' notion of "race" is distinctly of its time, a European notion with aspects of Darwin as well as Bismark. It grounds race only "superficially" in physical characteristics and "common blood," more important are "common history, common laws and religion, similar habits of thought and conscious striving together for certain ideals of life"[10] (Du Bois 1999:39). Collective memory, embodied and expressed as common history and habits of thought, is here made central to the formation of race. But what is equally important is what this implies, or, as Du Bois puts it the "function of race" today and in the future: "Manifestly some of the great races of today – particularly the Negro race – have not as yet given to civilization the full spiritual message which they are capable of giving." Belonging to a race, in other words, involves mission and duty, giving a message to the world, producing the "greatness" that a great race is capable of.

From the perspective of cultural trauma, race was a conceptual weapon, a trope and an instrument in the struggle to transform negative into positive, lifting a distinctiveness out of a distinction.[11] At the same time, the concept made reference to a real existing collection of individuals, ascribed by others to an inferior category and position, primitive and less developed. The trauma of rejection stemming from what he will later call "the counter-revolution of 1876" (Du Bois [1935], 1973:667) produced the need for positive identification and positive action on the part of a group whose subordination had just been reasserted. From his perspective, reconstruction was as much a cultural project as an economic and political one, as it had to deal with countering the psychological effects of an economic system which "enforced personal feeling of inferiority, the calling of another Master; the standing with hat in hand" (9).[12] As a tool in what today would be called "identity politics," race was an umbrella under which all "black folks" could assemble, an outcome of the slave trade which brought diverse peoples to America. Turning peasants into workers, it gave the victims a common name from which to find common cause. The "race" was no mere victim however, because of a shared African past, it was the bearer of a potential greatness. This greatness was now something that must be both recognized and realized. In the context of the movement, race became exemplary.

The boundaries and borders, in time as well as space, that circumscribed this understanding of race differed significantly from those used by the local black leaders who organized the mass migrations to Kansas and other places discussed in chapter 2. There, race referred to a very visible, local group linked together in the aftermath of emancipation by the fact that they had once been slaves, and who were now in need of collective solidarity. Racial identity here was very concrete, materially based networks of freed men, women, and children who had a real and obvious need for cooperation and protection, an organic rather than imagined community. Du Bois lifted racially based identification to another level – national, but also universal – to the abstract idea of cultural heritage, with links back to an imagined Africa and an abstract America, where the formal identity of citizenship and the romantic identity of cultural heritage were held in a tension filled unity.[13] It was an Hegelian, rather than a pragmatic and practical, idealization.

In *Souls*, Du Bois put forth the idea that blacks in the United States were "American – by citizenship, political ideals, language, and religion – and African, as a member of a 'vast historic race' of separate origin from the rest of America" (Rampersad 1976:61). This African American, Du Bois assured his audience, had something positive to contribute both to American culture and to world civilization. Although shaped by the suffering and trauma of slavery which had produced "two souls, two thoughts, two unreconciled strivings; two warring ideals in one dark body," the African American had but one aim, "to be a co-worker in the kingdom of culture" (1976: 3). To the small, but growing black audience, the notion of the African American offered a middle ground between emigration and accommodation.

Born in Massachusetts in 1868, armed with a Harvard Ph.D. and with influential contacts in the progressive movement, Du Bois became a leading spokesman for the first, post-slavery generation of black Americans. His doctoral thesis, "The Suppression of the African Slave Trade to the United States, 1638–1870" (1896), and his sociological study, *The Philadelphia Negro* (1899), offered objective and dispassionate accounts of slavery and its aftermath. These were path-breaking in a number of ways: for being written by a black man, for their topic, and for their scholarly achievement. But it was *The Souls of Black Folk* that would catapult Du Bois into the center of American cultural politics. Searching for ways to unify this increasingly dispersed, stratified, and discouraged black population, to forge a collective subject as well as to reveal its subjectivity, and to reconcile his own relationship toward it, Du Bois fastened not so much on the memory of slavery as on the forms of cultural expression and personality, or the souls, that it produced. In fact, what characterized the "African American" was not a unified and coherent "soul," but rather two souls and a "double-consciousness": African and American. This divided consciousness was also double-edged. On the one hand, it was positive, in that it potentially combined the best of two worlds, an American who, "has too much to teach the world" and an African whose Negro "blood has a message for the world" (1903:3). On the other hand, it meant "always looking at one's self through the eyes of others, of measuring one's soul by the tape of a world that looks on in amused contempt and pity" (1903:3). The world looks on, Du Bois adds, through a veil, or curtain, which separates two worlds, one black, one white, as the "double consciousness" divides the Negro self. While the world looks in from the outside, the Negro looks out, through the same veil, which not only separates, but also distorts perception. The existence of the veil and the African American double consciousness, Du Bois seems to be saying, requires mediation and mediators, those who can interpret and speak for, and to, both sides. That is the role he clearly means for himself and for those who share his views.

In applying the Hegelian idea of a divided consciousness to American blacks, Du Bois articulated a way of being in the world that was at once particular, class and generation-specific, and more universal. The emergent black middle class, at the turn of the century, could be described as living in two worlds and they were in the process of developing ways and means of mediating them. However, not all, indeed not many, blacks experienced this double consciousness at this time. Except perhaps as a potentiality, it was not the multitudes Du Bois addressed, but those he referred to as the "talented tenth." It was they who could identity with the construct and its meaning.[14] In the "Talented Tenth," an essay published the same year as *Souls* (in a volume edited by Booker T. Washington), Du Bois made a passionate appeal to his socially restricted black and white audiences:

Men of America, the problem is plain before you. Here is a race transplanted through the criminal foolishness of your fathers. Whether you like it or not the millions are here, and here to remain. If you do not lift them up, they will pull you down. Education and work are the levers to uplift a people. Work will not do it unless inspired by the right ideals and guided by intelligence. Education must not simply teach work – it must teach life. The Talented Tenth of the Negro race must be made leaders of thought and missionaries of culture among their people.   (Du Bois 1971:50–51).

Lenin ended his famous call to action with the demand to start a newspaper, as a means toward organizing and directing the masses. In not so dissimilar fashion, Du Bois joined other like-minded black intellectuals and progressive whites to form the NAACP and become editor of a new journal as the first step in his missionary struggle for social acceptance.[15] As a movement intellectual and an educated black American, Du Bois lived the double consciousness he articulated and communicated to others in the hope of recognition.

Du Bois uncovered in the folk culture[16] which emerged in response to slavery a resilience and a moral capacity that would serve well in the future if blacks could shake off the negative aspects of this heritage. At the same time, as a sociologist carrying out empirical studies connected to *The Philadelphia Negro*, he took the perspective of the outsider. Du Bois wrote that he and his wife lived amongst "dirt, drunkenness, poverty and crime" so that he could interview "about 5000 persons" (Rampersad 1976:50–51). Here he experienced first hand a darker side of black life and could reflect upon the negative and positive aspects of what he called folk culture, the living memory of slavery.[17] This of course was measured by his own standards of progress and by his own expectations for the "race." If there were clearly shortcomings in the character of some Negroes, this was no different from any other race, where "talent" was always unevenly distributed and where it was the duty of the "talented tenth" to lead the rest of the race into the future: "The Negro race, like all races, is going to be saved by its exceptional men. The problem of education, then, among Negroes must first of all deal with the Talented Tenth; it is the problem of developing the Best of this race that they may guide the Mass away from the contamination and death of the Worst, in their own and other races" (Du Bois 1971:31). But the American nation must also bear some of the responsibility for the conditions of the poor Negroes of Philadelphia and elsewhere, not merely for centuries of slavery but also for the dashed hopes that followed emancipation. "The Nation has not yet found peace from its sins; the freedman has not yet found in freedom his promised land. Whatever good may have come in these years of change, the shadow of a deep disappointment rests upon the Negro people – a disappointment all the more bitter because the unattained ideal was unbounded save by simple ignorance of a lowly people" (5).

Thus, while the "peasants" embodied the memory of slavery in their residual folk culture and their enforced segregation, the talented tenth drew identity and sustenance from its re-collection, at the same time as they transcended this culture through education, both as educated individuals and as proselytizing teachers. These views laid the grounds for a distinctive aesthetics and theory of representation, as well as politics. The talented tenth should represent the race through exemplification, and the race should be represented with this, its best face, forward. Du Bois (1897) outlined what he meant in an address outlining the aims of the American Negro Academy "it must be representative in character; not in that it represents all interests or all factions, but in that it seeks to comprise something of the *best* thought, the most unselfish striving and the highest ideals"; exemplary, in other words. As we shall see, Du Bois developed criteria for how the race should be represented in aesthetic terms in various forms of cultural expression. In his capacity as spokesman and in his position as editor and board member, Du Bois acted as gatekeeper, determining the types of theater that should be performed and recordings that should be produced. In addition, this trauma-related process marks the emergence of the ambiguous relation to the legacy of slavery which still continues amongst black intellectuals and artists.

In this representative posture, Du Bois speaks of and for the "race," those he would call African American, rather than to them. Although black literacy rates had improved since emancipation, for the first time in history, black illiteracy dropped below 50 percent to 44 percent, down from 57.1 percent in 1890 and 70 percent in 1880 (Christian 1995:288). Du Bois' chosen audience is white, his former teachers and colleagues at Harvard and elsewhere, his fellow progressives and other members of the political and cultural establishment. His role is that of advocate, for a people silent and invisible to this audience, those living behind the "veil," the curtain of ignorance and disinterest that shields white from black and black from white. These blacks have been silenced not by slavery but by its remembrance brought forth again by the disappointment following the failure of reconstruction and the promise of emancipation. If that black audience is deaf to his words, it is because of this disappointment and the bitterness it brought. Through words and, later, organization, Du Bois aimed to create a people, a race, under the banner of the African American, that would react and at some future time form again a moral and a political community. Thus *The Souls of Black Folks* speaks in several voices at once. Du Bois speaks for a new generation of blacks victimized by slavery, as if they could hear and would agree, and he speaks in their name to the dominant culture. Du Bois, the movement intellectual, is advocating, witnessing, and constituting a collectivity, the "race," at one and the same time. The slave songs, well known to blacks, and the lines of poetry, well known to whites, which introduce each chapter of the book, are meant to speak both ways and to perform all these functions.

The concept of race that Du Bois was advocating here has been much discussed (Blight 1995; Rampersad 1976; Stein 1989); it was at once universalizing and particularizing, and a product of the times in which he wrote. Race primarily referred to cultural and physical differences between human beings rooted in their physical environment. The concept was being propagated as an explanation for obvious differences in achievement between the majority of blacks and whites in the United States. Du Bois accepts aspects of what would today be called "essentialism," locating a fundamental and qualitative basis for African American identity in the legacy of slavery rather than in any biological difference. Like the budding Pan Africanism of his time and other forms of cultural nationalism, Du Bois employed the concept of race in a more positive way, one which unified rather than differentiated.[18] As mentioned earlier, while he acknowledged that blacks in the United States were Americans in terms of citizenship, language, religion, and so on, Du Bois declared them also to be "members of a 'vast historic race', which was international" (Stein 1989:82). Like his counterparts in Africa and the Caribbean, Du Bois sought wider grounding for "racial" identity than that imposed by slavery and the United States. This is a culturally, rather than physiologically grounded notion of race, taken from Herder, which makes use of concepts like "folk" and "people," and is designed to unite divergent groups across regional and class differences. Given the emerging class and regional differences between American blacks, it was a fitting choice for Du Bois' political strategies. The same can be said of his notion that each race required leadership from its talented tenth. Here internal differences based on inherent qualities are posited as differences based in class and region are denied. This offered a clear role for the educated, upper stratum of which Du Bois was a part. Armed with this notion of race, "black leaders . . . replaced American institutions as the critical civilizing agents" (85).

The idea of a cultural and political avant-garde was in the air, blowing in fresh ideas not only from Ireland, but also from further east, from Russia. Lenin's *What is to be Done* appeared the year before *The Souls of Black Folk* and made in many ways a similar appeal. In both cases the target audience was not the "masses," nor was the aim revolutionary in any direct sense. The call went out to an educated elite to re-present to and for those without the opportunity to do so themselves. Lenin ends with the idea of starting a newspaper as a means of organization as well as communication, a resource that will link together not disperse the "masses," but also those appointed to lead them. Du Bois' intentions are similar, with a new black-led organization and a magazine being some of the concrete aims of his appeal.

In addition to his white audience, Du Bois had a clear target amongst blacks. One of the chapters of his manifesto attacked the policies of Booker T. Washington, offering a more militantly political program. According to some commentators, this was the most controversial section of the work.[19] The chapter opens "Easily the most striking thing in the history of the American Negro since 1876 [the end of Reconstruction] is the ascendancy of Mr. Booker T. Washington" and closes:

the Black men of America have a duty to perform, a duty stern and delicate – a forward movement to oppose a part of the work of their greatest leader. So far as Mr. Washington preaches Thrift, Patience and Industrial Training for the masses, we must hold up his hands and strive with him . . . But so far as Mr. Washington apologizes for injustice,

North or South, does not rightly value the privilege of voting, belittles the emasculating effects of caste distinctions, and opposes the higher training and ambition of our brighter minds – so far as he, the South, or the Nation, does this – we must unceasingly and firmly oppose them.   (Du Bois 1903: 42).

The audience to whom this is addressed is not only those whites in the Progressive movement and elsewhere who would support Washington's programs for blacks, it is also those educated blacks who are searching for an alternative plan for dealing with the failures of reconstruction and the heritage of slavery. Here the memory of slavery is directed toward whites as part of a moral appeal for their support.

The final chapter of *Souls* is devoted to what Du Bois calls the true black music, the "sorrow songs" of the slaves. The phrase "sorrow song" is perhaps taken from Frederick Douglass, who wrote "The remark is not infrequently made, that slaves are the most contented and happy laborers in the world. They dance and sing, and make all manners of joyful noises – so they do: but it is a great mistake to suppose them happy because they sing. The songs of the slave represent sorrows, rather than joys, of the heart" (Douglass 1969:98). Of the few areas of self-expression open to slaves in the United States, singing was not only permitted but encouraged by many slaveholders. Whatever the reasons for this, perhaps allowing slaves to be heard and thus controlled, work songs were thought to increase productivity, or to entertain slaves and their masters; slaves, as Douglass writes, "were expected to sing as well as to work" (cited in Watkins 1994:58). Because singing was seen (and used) as evidence of the joy and tranquility of plantation life in justification of slavery, a viewpoint reproduced and reinforced in the very popular minstrel shows of the time, both Du Bois and Douglass were forced to offer an alternative viewpoint of the meaning of this activity.[20] Creating such sorrowful songs was evidence, Du Bois seemed to be saying, of deep rooted humanity, as only a people with a great sense of spirituality, human subjectivity, could create such music. Here was the proof of the universal in the African American particular, the human subjectivity once again denied by the dominant culture.

Du Bois found something else besides great sorrow in the slave songs as they were presented in his own time: a basis for identification and empathy, and a model of emancipation. He writes, "Ever since I was a child these songs have stirred me strangely. They came out of a South unknown to me, one by one, and yet at once I knew them as of me and of mine" (Du Bois 1903:177).[21] As he had done throughout the book, Du Bois generalized his own experience to that of the "race." Like the slaves themselves, fragmented and dispersed across the continent, a new generation of black Americans had been traumatized by the dashed hopes of reconstruction and the new national consensus about the meaning of the past. This new generation too, Du Bois reasoned, could find solace and unity in the sorrow songs. In these songs and the cultural heritage represented, the memory of slavery could be carried and passed on. It was here that one could uncover the basis for a community amongst blacks, a community unified through a common memory, one that joins Africa and America. This community could be re-membered through songs "in which the soul of the black slave spoke to men" (177).[22]

The lyrical content of the sorrow songs carried visions of secular emancipation couched in their spiritual form. The Biblical theme of Exodus, of "going to the other side," of being led to the "promised land" carried political as well as religious meaning. Not only was this message transmitted in song, it was also the staple of the religious sermon. While Du Bois may have been emotionally moved upon hearing these songs in their concert performances, for those who heard them in another context, they carried another level of meaning. Not just the lyrical content, however, but also the mood and tone of the music were important in evoking memory and conveying meaning.[23]

The representation of slavery is a sub-text which permeates *Souls*.[24] A central theme of the New Negro movement was the discovery of Africa as a source of imagination and a cultural resource for the African American. It was this that lay behind, in time and as substructure, the resilience and resistance to slavery. As Du Bois recalled the memory of slavery embodied in the sorrow songs, folk tales, and personality of American blacks as the basis of a new collective identity, he again opposed the views of Booker T. Washington, who viewed slavery through an ahistorical evolutionary perspective (Rampersad 1989:107ff.). While both were early exemplars of what the next generation of New Negroes would articulate as the "progressive" narrative frame, Washington represented the slavery he had personally experienced as something which could be both forgotten and left behind, shed like a "dead skin," as Rampersad expresses it (1989:110). Du Bois, who had no such personal experience of slavery, denied this possibility, saying of Washington, "One thing alone you must not . . . forget. Washington stands for Negro submission and slavery" (cited in Lewis 1993:404). And while both believed that blacks gained something from the experience of slavery, they differed as to what this actually meant. Both shared a view of progress, as exemplified in the title of Washington's autobiography (*Up From Slavery*), and in Du Bois' appeal to the racially rooted civilizing process. For Washington, however, progress required forgetting the past and the appeal to "facts," while Du Bois argued for memory and imagination.[25] In a heavily ironic article from 1910, Du Bois linked "progress" to slavery, "We have progressed. The chains are still clinking, the coward and the traitor are still at large, the poor and guilty and unfortunate are still with us. Our enemies smile. So do we. We have progressed" (quoted in Lewis 1993:383).

The memory of slavery is important for Du Bois on at least three counts. It is part of a moral appeal to sympathetic whites. Secondly, it is central to the formation and collective representation of an African American identity. Thirdly, it is important in explaining the behavior, as well as the perception and reception of black Americans in contemporary, post-emancipation America. Like some of his sociological colleagues a century later, Du Bois is interested in naming and studying what he considered the lingering after-effects of slavery amongst black Americans. More importantly, the memory of slavery is central to challenging the revisionist counter-revolution which included, as already discussed, a nostalgic view of life during slavery as well as an attack on reconstruction. Making this memory collective is central to the process of cultural trauma, a process in which collective memory will be formative of collective identity, as recognizable victims and perpetrators are named and acknowledged, marking a membership group off against those outside. This will be done as a defensive strategy, a counter-offensive, in a context of political and cultural conflict, where history is being rewritten and slavery portrayed as either a victimless misfortune or a mutually beneficial social system. From Du Bois' perspective, Washington was partly responsible, part of the problem, rather than the solution. In *Up From Slavery* (1986: 37), Washington had written, "Notwithstanding the cruel wrongs inflicted upon us, the black man got nearly as much out of slavery as the white man did."[26]

From Du Bois' point of view, the collective memory and representation of slavery was essential for the coordinated, collective action necessary to counter similar attempts in the dominant culture. As individuals, black writers and artists could produce significant works which merely by their existence could "prove" the worthiness of the race. But any really significant contribution would come through the directed and conscious efforts of social movements, in which intellectuals would have a leading role. A function of this movement would be to collect and connect individual biographies with others, in the process turning them into a unified political force as a collective actor. The connecting of individuals through collective representation, representing the collective in a double sense, re-presenting by forging individual memory and collective biography and standing for the collective, as a representative individual.

The African American experience was here characterized as unique, an experience which combined in its double consciousness the potential to transcend its own historical conditions and create something distinctive in world history. In the process, this collective consciousness could help others achieve self-understanding through forced self-reflection. Once this consciousness has matured and become a political force, whites would be forced to recognize their own limitations and culpability, their own particularism. It was here that intellectuals would have a leading role to play, in the development of this racial consciousness, and in its transformation into a political force through organized collective action.[27]

In what was "the first collective attempt by African Americans to demand full citizenship rights in the twentieth century" (Lewis 1993:317) Du Bois and William Trotter published the "Declaration of Principles" of the Niagara Movement in 1905. This all-black, all-male, gathering of intellectuals was united primarily by its opposition to Booker T. Washington, whom it ironically referred to as the "Wizard." In a new monthly, *Voice of the Negro* (1904), Du Bois had ventured criticism of Washington, accusing him of bribing newspapers to print favorable stories (Lewis 1993:314). This made visible splits in the ranks of Negro leadership and spurred the formation of an opposition group. It was this group which met on the Canadian side of Niagara Falls in 1905. The result was a statement of purpose which moved from Washington's compromise and negotiation to protest:

> The Negro race in America stolen, ravished and degraded, struggling up through difficulties and oppression, needs sympathy and receives criticism; needs help and is given hindrance, needs protection and is given mob-violence, needs justice and is given charity, needs leadership and is given cowardice and apology; needs bread and is given stone.[28] This nation will never stand justified before God until these things are changed.
>
> (cited in Lewis 1993:322)

The foundation of the Niagara Movement, which was more of a civil rights pressure group than a movement, led to the search for a print medium that was free of the control of Booker T. Washington. This proved difficult because such a venture could not be accomplished without white patronage, something which Washington controlled. The first anti-Washington talented-tenth journal, *The Moon Illustrated Weekly*, which was intended to stimulate "wide self-knowledge within the race," was begun in December, 1905 and lasted less than a year (Lewis 1993:326). This was followed by *The Horizon: A Journal of the Color Line*, which began publishing in 1907. By the second issue, Du Bois announced his acceptance of socialism and his opposition to the Republican Party of Theodore Roosevelt, who had the support of Washington and Thomas Fortune, founder and editor of the *New York Globe*.[29] Besides the yearly meetings, the journals and the network of publishers and intellectuals comprising the talented tenth, the Niagara Movement was coupled to scholarly activity centered on Atlanta University. Du Bois had accepted a professorship there in 1896, carrying out path-breaking research and organizing conferences, which led to a series of books published as the Atlanta University Studies. By 1908, Du Bois had carried out thirteen studies in the same number of years; many of these were published by the US government, including four on the conditions of blacks in the rural South, by the Department of Labor. Du Bois had attended the London Pan African Conference in 1900 and became engaged in a multi-volume project called "Encyclopedia Africana" (1909), which covered "the chief points in the history and condition of the Negro race" (Lewis 1993:379), with the Liberian professor Edward Blyden.[30] His sustained interest in Africa and Pan-Africanism would develop later however, as the current situation demanded his full attention. The need to counter the reactionary drift of the dominant culture by providing an alternative black leadership to Booker T. Washington was now a more pressing concern.[31]

Sustaining the all-black Niagara Movement proved difficult, especially the publication and distribution of the journals which would link the members and their prospective audience together on a more continuous basis. By 1908 the Movement was fading and an inter-racial alternative connected to the progressive movement was in the making. The National Association for the Advancement of Colored People (NAACP) was formed two years later, with Du Bois appointed its director of publicity and research.[32] In November, 1910 the first issue of the organization's monthly journal *The Crisis* appeared and became a resounding success with Du Bois as its editor.[33] This journal would give the avant garde "talented tenth" its medium and be the means for Du Bois' own transformation from progressive academic scholar to movement intellectual.

Du Bois and his male-dominated Niagara Movement was not the only collective force working to create and mobilize American blacks at the turn of the century. A women's movement was emerging within the black church, especially amongst Baptists, the largest denomination. In 1906, the National Baptist Convention, the central organization of black Baptists composing its Northern and Southern regions, had over 2 million members, while its second competitor, the AME, had approximately 1.5 million. The great majority of these members were women (Higginbotham 1993:6–7). As previously noted, the church was the centerpiece of black community life, especially in the South and was much more than a place of worship. Above all, the black church was a meeting and gathering place, a "public sphere in which values and issues were aired, debated, and disseminated" (1993:7), not only through the face-to-face interactions in religious services, theater productions, schools and picnics, but also through various publishing activities. While men were leading figures within the church hierarchy, it was women who were the most active participants in the day-to-day activities and in the so-called "convention movement."

Conventions had been an important part of black public life since slavery. Free blacks had organized yearly gatherings to discuss issues of common concern, such as abolition and emigration, and as pointed out earlier, "conventions" were more than the term usually connotes, functioning more as national

coordinating organizations than annual events. The National Baptist Convention
was formed in 1895 in an effort to coordinate "spiritual, economic, political and
social concerns" (Higginbotham 1993:6). This was a racially based movement,
whose leaders "equated racial self-determination with black denominational
hegemony" (1993:6). Again, while the most visible leaders were men, the large
numbers of women activists were quick to recognize that gender as well as
race was a unifying force. By 1900 the Women's Convention formed within
the larger group, with a membership of 1 million. In 1909 the group had organized the "first school for black women that black women themselves owned"
(1993:6).

With the rise of literacy and the expansion of the black reading public, from
5 percent in 1860 to 70 percent by 1910 (Higginbotham 1993:11), the church's
publishing activities grew in importance alongside the newspapers, some of
which as already pointed out (including the one Ida Wells wrote for) were
church owned. "In 1900 black Baptists at the local and state levels published
forty-three newspapers, the great majority of which were located in the South"
(1993:11). The National convention published the *National Baptist Magazine*
"devoted to the interests of the Negro Race in general" (1993:11), while the
Board reported a "circulation of more than 13 million issues of various tracts
and booklets between 1900 and 1903" (1993:11–12). The links between the
church and the black press also had another side: their common mission in
spreading the idea of racial progress and their role in social integration (Harris
1992:118ff.).

Along with church-based organizations and the conventions, a network of
community-based clubs emerged at the initiative of black woman. When the
National Association of Colored Women was formed in 1896 it united over
200 local women's clubs into a national body (White 1999:22ff.). Their number increased to 1500 by 1916. These clubs formed part of the organizational
network within which Ida Wells drove her anti-lynching campaign, and where
Frances Harper spoke and distributed her novels, as well as political messages
on the duties of womanhood. The resurgence of lynching and women's suffrage were only two of the causes around which black women organized at
the end of the nineteenth century. "The guiding principle behind all the clubs,"
writes White (1999:27), "was racial uplift through self-help." The basis and
orientation of this self-help were the increasingly segregated black neighborhoods, which at times included the black church, but at others transcended it.[34]
Racial uplift was framed through an underlying feminism in that it argued that
"only black women can save the race." As well as being community and family
oriented, this point of view was grounded in a critique of the male-dominated
organizations, the "innumerable conventions, councils and conferences during the last twenty-five years have all begun with talk and ended with talk,"

one club woman wrote at the time, concluding that it was time for black men to stand aside (cited in White 1999:36–37). Club movement intellectuals believed that "it is to the Afro-American women that the world looks for the solution of the race problem" (cited in White 1999:36). This type of language was both a form of mobilizing rhetoric and a reflection of the paralysis and stagnation that may have affected black men in this period. From the perspective of cultural trauma, it could be the case that black men were more affected, traumatized, by the end of reconstruction and the re-establishment of segregation in the South and reaction in the North. It was they, after all, who had been most active in political life due to the exclusion of women generally.

Another argument put forward by both black men and women, was that "a race can rise no higher than its women," as Monroe Majors wrote in 1893. "A race, no less than a nation, is prosperous in proportion to the intelligence of its women . . . The criterion for Negro civilization is the intelligence, purity and high motives of its women . . . The highest mark of our prosperity, and the strongest proofs of Negro capacity to master the sciences and fine arts, are evinced by the advanced positions which Negro women have attained" (quoted in White 1999:43). Part of the process of cultural trauma was the assessment of the state and the progress of the "race," as it was being re-constructed. Du Bois used the last chapter of his 1909 biography of John Brown to access the progress made by American blacks since emancipation. They had, he writes:

already done in a generation the work of many centuries. It [the human force of American blacks] has saved over a half-billion dollars in property, bought and paid for landed estate half the size of all England, and put homes thereon as good and as pure as the homes of any corresponding economic class the world around; it has crowded eager children through a wretched and half-furnished school system until from an illiteracy of seventy per cent, two-thirds of the living adults can read and write. These proscribed millions have 50,000 professional men, 200,000 men in trade and transportation, 275,000 artisans and mechanics, 1,250,000 servants and 2,000,000 farmers working with the nation to earn its daily bread.   (Du Bois 1997:197)

Similarly to Du Bois and his notion of the talented tenth, these club women were looking for criteria of judgment, as well as offering leadership. The situation called for assessment as well as explanation.[35] In this assessment, slavery was both a benchmark of progress and a resource in further development. It was out of slavery that the "race" emerged and the extent of its progress, as well as its mission could be derived from there. As White (1999:39) puts it, "if club leaders considered anything it was the endurance of black women during slavery, their belief in the more humane sensibilities of women, and their acknowledgment of the debilities of black men of white society." Slavery, in other words, created the race and gave strength as well as suffering, preparing black women for their uplifting role. Exactly what this role would be – mother, teacher, political activist – was of course a matter of dispute.

Slavery and popular culture

It was not by chance that Du Bois pointed to music as a foundation of African American culture. Music, including dance, after all, had been one of the few forms of cultural expression relatively open to slaves to participate in and, as noted earlier, was a central means for the constitution of a collective identity and the articulation of hopes and dreams.[36] Paradoxically, it was also in song that the first reference to the notion of the African American appeared, with the opposite reference than that Du Bois intended. In 1863 the "Old Cremona Songster" records these lines: "I'd buy up all de niggers – de niggers – de colored African American citizens" (*Oxford Dictionary*). Here was acknowledged both the new and the old, the citizenship promised after emancipation and the continued desire to own blacks.

As a basis for unification and collective identity in this context of reaction, the slave songs were a curious choice of music, since many middle-class blacks at the time refused to listen to them for the very reason Du Bois was moved by them: they represented a past they wished to forget. However, it was not the slave songs as folk expression that Du Bois referred to, but rather their performance as concert or art music. The songs he experienced were staged performances, not folk expressions. Later, Zora Neale Hurston would write "there are no true spirituals." At the time, however, especially under the onslaught of popular culture parody and "falsification," the search for authenticity and roots was a preview of things to come. De Bois was one of the first and few intellectuals of his generation to argue for a distinctive African basis of slave culture and to call this up to memory. His judgment of this "culture," however, was colored by a distinctive European bias. Du Bois may have found common ground in the slave songs, but it was their "polished" performance that moved him. Du Bois mentions the songs in connection to the Fisk Jubilee Singers and the Hall in Nashville built with the monies earned on the basis of their concert performances in the 1870s, which, he recounts, included those "before the Queen and Kaiser, in Scotland and Ireland, Holland and Switzerland" (Du Bois 1903:179).[37] Du Bois is justly proud of this achievement, but it reflects not only his program of cultural missionary work as a measure of racial progress and pride, but also his model of culture, where racial progress was linked to cultural refinement. He is himself an example of the "double consciousness" he so aptly named: the slave songs speak to blacks and form a potential basis of racial identity, but they also speak to whites, to reveal the "soul of the black man" which "stands to-day not simply as the sole American music, but as the most beautiful expression of human experience born this side of the seas" (1903:178).[38] For this to be recognized and properly judged it was best received in its most polished form as art music in concert performance, not in popular culture or by the untrained voices of the masses. The role of other members of the talented tenth should be mentioned in this context, such as the composer John Wesley Work, who (a few years later) "had succeeded in polishing up the original spiritual for the educated Negro" (Harris 1992:124).

The sorrow songs themselves contained double-edged meanings, moving between the sacred and the secular with an ease that surely confounded slave-holders. Their words were taken from Christian hymns and rooted in Christian mythology, but, as many commentators have shown, the constant reference to "freedom" and the "promised land," among many other ambiguous phrases could be interpreted in many ways, including politically. Like other forms of slave music and culture, the sorrow songs could mask resistance behind a veil of religious metaphor and belief. Du Bois' image of the veil, that which separated black from white and distorted perception, could also be interpreted as a mask, to hide and deceive as well as distort, a common strategy for those in subordinate positions. Thus Angela Davis (1998) writes of these songs: "they retold Old Testament narratives about the Hebrew people's struggle against Pharaoh's oppression, and thereby established a community narrative of African people enslaved in North America that simultaneously transcended the slave system and encouraged its abolition" (1998:7).[39]

The reference to masks and masking becomes all the more plausible when one considers the suggestion made by Watkins (1994:573–4) that "masks were key elements in the religious and celebratory rituals of many West African societies," the area from which most slaves in the Americas were taken. Taking on altered ways of speaking and acting in situations and circumstances that were non-routine and abnormal could be something quite natural for Africans in America. These could also be used to mask true feelings and beliefs and to maintain both continuity and dignity under extreme conditions. The veil in other words could be a mask, and the distortion it produced intentional and functional as well as dysfunctional.

This was certainly the case in the forms of black humor which developed during slavery, where any form of open rebellion, verbal or otherwise, could be severely punished. In his history of the roots of black humor, Watkins (1994:66) writes:

as slaves began to develop rudimentary facility with the language, naive malapropism was slowly but stealthily transformed into double-entendre and self-conscious or willful ambiguity . . . This *deliberate* linguistic misdirection, allowed slaves both to communicate surreptitiously with one another and, without detection, express humorously some pent-up outrage resulting from the treatment of bondsmen.

What could appear as plain dumbness to whites could appear to blacks as "cutting satire," as in the example Watkins provides from a slave narrative written in 1855:

> Pompey, how do I look? the master asked.
> O, massa, mighty. You looks mighty.
> What do you mean "Mighty", Pompey?
> Why, massa, you looks noble.
> What do you mean by noble?
> Why, suh, you looks just like a lion.
> Why, Pompey, where have you ever seen a lion?
> I saw one down in yonder field the other day, massa.
> Pompey, you foolish fellow, that was a jackass.
> Was it, massa? Well, suh, you looks just like him.   (Watkins 1994:67)

Dialogues such as this were the staple of the minstrel shows which achieved tremendous popularity from the 1840s onwards. Here the satire went largely missing, as the white actors in corked-up faces presented at face value a stereo-typed picture of what they and the audience took for ignorance and stupidity. Sambo, the smiling, happy-go-lucky but dumb, black-faced actor was a set piece of minstrel shows into the twentieth century. This was the case even as black actors took on the role and the mask during reconstruction, when, because it was the only entertainment venue open to them "black performers had to fetishize their own race" (Barlow 1999:8). It is certainly possible, even plausible given the roots of this comic dialogue in black humor, that mixed audiences and actors read and heard different things as they performed or observed performances, even as they were embarrassed and undermined by the racial stereotyping. This is precisely what Du Bois meant by "the veil." What he also meant was that there existed behind the veil an authentic black music, which was unavailable to whites, who only observed the distorted versions. The same argument can be made regarding black humor (Watkins 1994) and popular theater (Krasner 1997). In addition to this sort of parody, Krasner (1997:25ff.) identifies another strategy whereby subordinate groups can use their restricted access to forms of representation to their own advantage: reinscription and reversal. Reinscription refers to the process described above where the desire for "authenticity" on the part of white audiences widened the possibility for black actors to find work through "imitating a misrepresentation of blackness constructed by whites," and thereby the possibility to subtly reform that misrepresentation. This is an admittedly precarious project, but nonetheless one that only becomes available under certain circumstances which can be seized and cautiously tested.[40]

One point to be drawn from this is that popular culture played an important role in the struggle over how slavery was remembered, and that different audiences, black or white, could extract different messages and meanings out of it. Minstrel shows helped reproduce an idyllic picture of slavery and plantation life in the South, where naive, happy-go-lucky black-faced "slaves" sang and danced and played the straight man in comic dialogue. It was this image and this type of entertainment, including of course forms of music like the "coon songs" they produced, that Du Bois confronted and attempted to counter with the art music performances of spirituals. His "sorrow songs" were on many counts the direct opposite of the "happy-go-lucky" music of minstrelsy and the vaudeville which replaced it. Another point to be drawn is that this popular culture included aspects of an authentic black expression and, when "read" by an initiated public, formed a type of counter-memory hidden beneath the veil. In this sense, they created a sub-text as well as a means of communication through which an imagined community of blacks could be articulated and maintained. The remembering of slavery provided both form and content for these performances.[41]

Minstrel shows provided something else. They offered a form of entertainment and employment for a new generation of blacks. W. C. Handy (1941), often called the "father of the blues" for his compositions such as the "Memphis Blues" and "St. Louis Blues," records in his autobiography how minstrel shows gave him a career and purpose in life. Handy, born in 1873, "eight years after surrender," took up music behind the back of his minister father, a former slave, who forbad it in his home. Yet it was the traveling minstrel shows which attracted the young Handy and which eventually provided him with both the possibility of leaving his native Florence, Alabama and a professional career as a musical performer and composer. Handy recalls how as a young boy he was impressed by the minstrel shows and other forms of popular entertainment which were performed in his home town and how viewing them provided him with ideas and skills as well as entertainment. At fifteen, he and his companions "had seen the famous Georgia Minstrels in Florence, and we knew how to make the pivot turns. We were all acquainted with Billy Kersands, the man who could 'make a mule laugh', and we remembered his trick of proving on stage that his enormous mouth would accommodate a cup and a saucer. We had seen Sam Lucas and Tom McIntosh walking at the head of the parade in high silk hats and long-tailed coats." What Handy extracted from this experience was not a reinforced sense of inferiority, but its opposite, a sense of skill and accomplishment, and a desire to move out on the road himself. The memory of slavery which Handy's father attempted to pass on to his son was his former white master's cultural values, including musical taste, which his son at once respected and rejected: "my father often pointed out to me the excellence of character and carriage of certain [local white] aristocrats as a sort of object lesson" (Handy 1941:4). And when Handy announced in school his dream of becoming a musician his teacher became furious, waving "his long sinewy arms . . . he gave me his opinion of the musical profession. Musicians were idlers, dissipated characters, whiskey drinkers and rounders . . . Southern white gentlemen, he said, looked upon music as a parlor accomplishment, not as a means of questionable support. Such men should be our examples" (1941:13). Some years later, he became a member of a famous minstrel company and met the same reactions from the family of his prospective bride. About this reaction, Handy writes: "it goes without saying that minstrels were a disreputable lot in the eyes of a large section of upper-crust Negroes, including the family and friends of Elizabeth Price, but it is also true that the best talent of that generation came down the same drain. The composers, the singers, the musicians, the speakers, the stage performers – the minstrel shows got them all." One of those was from the Johnson family of Jacksonville, Florida.

James Weldon Johnson, Du Bois' colleague in the NAACP, shared many of his ideas concerning the role of culture in political struggle and collective identity-formation. Johnson was born in Jacksonville in 1871, two years before Handy and three years after Du Bois. With the latter he shared Caribbean roots, as well as the belief that slavery had produced a unique culture upon which an African American identity could be forged. However, as a musician and composer, Johnson worked with a different model of culture than his movement colleague, one that placed him closer to W. C. Handy. While he shared the idea that the African American needed to prove her/his worth though cultural production, Johnson saw no reason to exclude more popular forms of cultural expression from that process. While Du Bois was a master of the essay, Johnson's form of expression was the popular song and the stage musical, as well as fiction and poetry. Together with his brother Rosamond, a classically trained musician and composer, he wrote "Lift Every Voice and Sing" (1900) for schoolchildren to commemorate Lincoln's birthday. As he recalled in his autobiography, "the schoolchildren of Jacksonville kept singing the song . . . Some of them became school teachers and taught it to their pupils," until it was "sung in schools and churches throughout the South and in other parts of the country" (Johnson 1934). The song was proclaimed the Negro national anthem by the NAACP in 1920.

> We have come over a way that with tears have been watered,
> We have come, treading our path through the blood of the slaughtered,
> Out from the gloomy past,
> Till now we stand at last
> Where the white gleam of our bright star is cast.

This form of counter-memory and racial uplift through popular culture continued when Johnson wrote the poem "Fifty Years" published in the *New York Times* on the fiftieth anniversary of the Emancipation Proclamation, January 1, 1913. The poem recalls Lincoln as the one who "struck off our bonds and made us men" and then continues:

> This land is ours by right of birth,
> This land is ours by right of toil;
> We helped to turn its virgin earth,
> Our sweat is in its fruitful soil.
> (Cited in Bronz 1964:27)

It was for this same celebration that the artist Meta Vaux Warrick Fuller conceived her sculptural work Emancipation Group, the only piece of sculpture on that event "of such great and far-reaching importance" that came anywhere close to expressing its significance, according to Freeman Murray, who found it especially interesting because it was executed by "one of the race of the 'emancipated' " (quoted in Boime 1990:179).[42]

After working as a journalist for a black newspaper in New York city to supplement his earnings as a songwriter on Tin Pan Alley, Johnson joined the staff of the NAACP, becoming its field secretary in 1916 at Du Bois' urging. In an autobiographical novel, *The Autobiography of an Ex-Colored Man*, which was published anonymously in 1912 and later became a great success when republished during the Harlem Renaissance, Johnson wrote that *The Souls of Black Folk* was "a remarkable book (because) it began to give the country something new and unknown, in depicting the life, the ambitions, the struggles, and the passions of those [Negroes] who are striving to break the narrow limits of traditions" (cited by Henry Louis Gates, Jr. in his introduction to Du Bois 1903: xiv). While Johnson may have differed slightly from Du Bois regarding the value of popular culture in the cultural politics of racial uplift and collective identity-formation, they had much else in common. He could easily have co-authored this programmatic statement by Du Bois: "I do not doubt that the ultimate art coming from black folk is going to be just as beautiful, and beautiful in largely the same ways, as the art that comes from white folk . . . but the point today is that until the art of black folk compels recognition they will not be rated as human" (Du Bois 1926 in Wilson 1999). Johnson was not averse to the value of "high" culture in the struggle for racial identity and recognition, after all he is probably best known as a poet, the author of "God's Trombones" (1927), and as the editor of *The Book of American Negro Poetry* (1922), but it was his *The Book of American Negro Spirituals* that became a bestseller in 1925, the year the Harlem Renaissance got its name in the popular press. Like Alain Locke, the movement's chief organizer and promoter, Johnson was sympathetic to the more mundane forms of cultural expression of black Americans.

Johnson's point of view regarding popular culture was shared by others, and as the New Negro exploded into the Harlem Renaissance a distinctive aesthetic position was articulated that would challenge the one put forward by Du Bois. Its main exponent was not Johnson, who was more an artist than an intellectual, but Alain Locke, a Rhodes scholar, critic and professor of literature at Howard University. Nearly twenty years younger than Du Bois, Locke was more removed from the trauma which had shaped the former's views. Du Bois' relation to popular culture was shaped not only by his European education, Locke after all shared some of that, but more by the double consciousness of always viewing oneself through the eyes of the other, in this case the dominant white culture. Locke, on the other hand, while he was as snobbish in many aspects, drew upon other traditions in that culture, a form of modernism that called for artistic independence and an openness to non-European aesthetic forms, including "primitivism" and "realism." While Du Bois developed a theory of representation centered on racial protest, Locke called for the development of a distinctive black Art Theater (Hay 1994). Samuel Hay (1994) developed the idea of the double consciousness into the distinction between inner and outer life as a means of characterizing Du Bois' views. The inner life of black Americans "behind the veil" is for internal consumption only as well as something to be bettered through cultivation, of which the arts are an essential aspect. Artistic representations of black life, on the other hand, were intimately bound with the struggle against racism, part of the "outer life" of blacks, and thus always weapons in a political struggle. Part of that struggle, as discussed earlier, was the fight against the stereotyping of blacks in white popular culture, especially musical theater. Black representations, in other words, could never be "realistic" in the sense of portraying "inner life," no matter how true these portraits might be for a white public. This would only support and reinforce stereotyping, even as they evoked identification and recognition in the black audience. From Du Bois' position popular culture was popular because it was stereotypical, something that was especially true of minstrelsy and the types of musical reviews that Johnson wrote.[43] Locke, on the other hand, could accept the aesthetic as well as entertainment value of recognition and the types that underlay the stereotypes. Their differences can be illustrated through the example of their respective views of musical comedy, the role of drama and of the theater generally in the culture wars. For Du Bois, there existed only one aim for drama, cultural uplift, and only one form of characterization, exemplification. Art was propaganda in the sense that it should uplift; black art should show only the "best" sides of black life, to educate those of both races who needed through this exemplification. Blacks should be heroic and virtuous. What this meant can be seen in Du Bois's own efforts as a playwright.

As part of the NAACP's National Emancipation Exposition presented in New York City in 1913, Du Bois wrote the script for a pageant called "The Star of Ethiopia." The play aimed at representing the story of the African American and contained roles for 350 actors. Its first performances were viewed by over 30,000 people over the space of one week (Hay 1994:79). It was filled with exemplary imagery, such as the production of iron in supposedly primitive society and the extraordinary achievements of Egyptian culture, as well as references to slavery and African participation in the slave trade, all represented as part of the progressive development of the race. The presentations of American slavery focus on rebellion and heroic acts. The play closes triumphantly:

A single voice sings "O Freedom." A soprano chorus takes it up.
The boy scouts march in.
Full brasses take up "O Freedom."
Little children enter, and among them symbolic figures of the Laborer, the Artisan, the Servant of Men, the Merchant, the Inventor, the Musician, the Actor, the Teacher, Law, Medicine and the Ministry, the All-Mother, formerly the Veiled Woman, now unveiled in her chariot with her dancing brood, and the bust of Lincoln at her side. With burst of music and blast of trumpets, the pageant ends.
(Reprinted from Crisis 1916 as cited in Hay 1994:79–80)

Locke, who had actually been recruited by Du Bois to help develop a Negro theater, had a quite different theory of representation.[44] From his point of view drama should reflect "real life," regardless of its effect on a white audience, for such representation encouraged "a positive self-respect and self-reliance" amongst black audiences (from the *New Negro*).

The emerging stratification within the black population following emancipation has been discussed earlier in relation to education, but other bases for differentiation were also forming, including those relating to income and gender. As emancipation made possible a more mobile and flexible black workforce, even in the face of a reinstitutionalized racism and the new plantation economy in the deep South, it created the background upon which the musical traditions from slavery and Africa could be reinterpreted as well as critically evaluated. In addition to the urbanized new middle class finding its voice in Du Bois' notion of the talented tenth and Southern-based skilled workers and the commercially based middle class finding an ideological home in Booker T. Washington's programs of self-help, a new stratum of mobile, unskilled laborers found their form of cultural expression in the blues (Lomax 1993; Meier 1962). For this group the blues served as a means of communication and source of identity as much as a form of entertainment. While some blues traditions originated in the much less mobile agricultural laborers locked into the share-cropping system of the deep South, like the blues of the Mississippi delta, where in the 1890s blacks outnumbered whites by three to one, the roots of the genre grew out of a farm worker's longing for mobility, either geographical or social, which emancipation promised, and a black person's longing for freedom. The blues are basically work songs that became the sorrow songs of the new laborers for whom both of these aims were difficult if not impossible to realize. The fact that they brought memories of slavery other than the uplifting performance of the spirituals, made many of the talented tenth deaf to their calls and moans.[45] This, however, would change in the 1920s, when the discovery of the "aesthetic" qualities of the blues would help constitute a new generation of black artists and intellectuals in their struggle to define themselves against their elders.

At the turn of the century, for unskilled laborers scattered across the mid-Western, Southern and Eastern sections of the United States from Texas to Illinois and across the South from Louisiana to Florida and up to New York, the blues provided a network of shared experience, which migrant workers could immediately plug into as they moved around. It was not by chance that the clubs where the blues were featured or performed lay in the marginal areas of cities and towns. It was to these sections that the newly arrived and the less well off flocked and that the more established and better educated both avoided and disdained. Blues, in other words, helped create a community within a community.

Not surprisingly, many of the songs that can be categorized as blues deal with the problems encountered by this social stratum: work-related problems, traveling, hard times, drinking, social and sexual relationships. One can find also, however, songs which comment on the role of education. As noted earlier, much of this emphasis derived from white middle-class models, and patronage. The mimetic relationship to whites played an important part in internal stratification, as this fragment collected by John Lomax in 1917 reveals:

> Niggers gettin' mo'like white folks,
> Mo'like white fo'ks eve'y day.
> Niggers learnin' Greek an' Latin,
> Niggers wearin' silk an' satin,
> Niggers gettin' mo'like white fo'ks eve'y day.
>   (Quoted in Levine 1978:245)

Music such as the blues functioned to express both the feelings and the social situation of a particular stratum in the Negro population and also as a foil in an internal class conflict. Thomas Dorsey, one of the central figures in the modernization of the blues, wrote this in the midst of this conflict: "Now people look down with derision, discontent, vulgarity on the blues . . . because they use

it in unsavory places – not so up to date . . . But I don't pay any attention to that"
(cited in Harris 1992:98). Dorsey had migrated from rural Georgia to Chicago
where, as a blues pianist and composer/arranger for Ma Rainey, he was a central
figure in mediating between the Southern and the Northern musical tastes and
in the reevaluation of the blues as quintessential black music. He defended the
blues as a "feeling" more than a music form, something which linked blacks to
slavery and to their common religious heritage.

Blues were really born shortly after slaves were free and they were sung the way the
singers felt inside. They were just let out of slavery or put out, or went out, but they hadn't
gotten used to freedom . . . blues is a digging, picking, pricking at the very depth of your
mental environment and the feelings of your heart. It's got to be that old low-down moan
and the low-down feeling; you got to have feeling.   (Harris 1992:98)

For the lower-class, unskilled laborer the blues was a form of communication,
a source of individual identity and collective recognition. It distinguished and
identified members of a group, a range of diverse yet common experiences of a
mobile social stratum, that was both racial and class related. This music, like the
dialect lyrics of the song above, also served as a form of negative distinction for
and from the upwardly striving, acceptance-oriented, middle class, as something
which they did not want to be identified with. This was similar to the use
of dialect by Frances Harper (1892 in Andrews) to mark off the older slave
generation from the younger, emancipated, generation. The term "nigger" used
in the song quoted above carries that positive and negative distinction. For the
singer, the term serves as positive collective identification, "we in this working-
class group recognize ourselves and those who think they are better than us,
but are still 'niggers.'" This "positive" use of the term "nigger," a transposition
of the dominant white culture's racism, is just what the New Negro wanted
to distinguish him and herself from.[46] For the first generation New Negro, the
blues was associated not so much with class as with a peasant way of life, one
intimately connected to the South and thus to slavery. Like the way of life it
reflected and expressed, this was something thought best forgotten or treated
as a remnant of a past which hopefully would disappear. As mentioned earlier
and to be elaborated in the following chapter, another generation would find
qualities in the blues more endearing, as would the dominant white culture in
the decades that followed.[47]

Another form of mediated popular culture emerged around the turn of the
century which would prove of great significance in the representation of the past
and the formation of collective identity. In 1888, Thomas A. Edison invented the
motion picture camera and with it the possibility of producing moving pictures
for large audiences, and, also, the greatly expanded possibility of influencing the
way people interpreted their world and others in it. Regarding blacks and much

else, the new "movies" continued traditions already established and thereby proven successful in minstrel and vaudeville shows. Although he exaggerates slightly, especially when one considers radio and television, Henry T. Sampson has a point when he writes: "there can be no question that motion pictures have had more impact on the public mind than any other entertainment medium during the last ninety years. Although movies did not invent the American Black as a stereotype for stupidity, submissiveness, irresponsibility, laziness, and cowardice, they have contributed mightily to reinforcing and enhancing this stereotype all over the world" (Sampson 1977:1).

Blacks first participated in the new film industry in much the same way as they worked their way into minstrelsy, by adding a degree of "authenticity" to black character-types and, of course, as members of the audience. Outside the theaters blacks sometimes protested against the images represented on the screen. There was no denying either the power or the profitability of the enterprise, however and a black film industry developed alongside the white, just as a black audience was created by racially segregated performances. Movie houses became part of the arena of public life in the expanding black communities occasioned by industrialization in the South and the mobility of blacks out of the region. These factors made it possible for a black film industry to emerge, sparked into existence by the exclusion of black film producers by the white-dominated industry in 1910, so that "by 1921 there were more than 300 theaters in the United States catering primarily to blacks" (Sampson 1977:5). This is the same time as "race records" were being produced for black audiences, some by black owned companies (Black Swan records for example). Racial segregation and growing urbanization combined to produce more concentrated black markets. This market supported the production not only of narrative film, but also of newsreels and documentary, providing the New Negro with not only a mirror to view itself, but also a visual side to the emerging "black perspective" on worldly events.[48]

While black performers were active almost from the beginning, it was not until 1910 that blacks entered into the production and distribution of films, when William Foster produced a series of comedies in Chicago.[49] In the 1910s, a number of black-owned film companies emerged including those with names that recalled the past, Lincoln Motion Picture Company (Los Angeles, 1916), Frederick Douglass Film Company (NJ 1919), but very few of the films they produced concerned slavery, or historical events other than those which recorded the exploits of black soldiers. Most were light-hearted comedies or films which pictured and gloried the cultivated middle class, like the extremely popular *Realization of a Negro's Ambition* (1916) which depicted the rise to success of "a young Negro who has just graduated from Tuskegee, as a civil engineer," who realizes his ambition, "home and family, a nice country to live in and nice people to live by and enjoy it with him," after striking oil (Sampson 1977:90–91). A number of films recorded the efforts of black soldiers in the various wars America was involved in, and were shown in schools and churches as well as theaters. There were exceptions, like *Free and Equal* (1925) which was made as an answer to *Birth of a Nation*, D. W. Griffith's racist chronicle of American history.[50] Although made a with predominately black cast, *Free and Equal* was aimed at white audiences; it opened with "a love scene, with five dancers and six singers, plantation melodies and some fast stepping," that is, it repeated the expected minstrel stereotypes, perhaps in the attempt to open a conversation with its audience.[51]

Perhaps because they were motivated more by political ideals than constrained by commercial considerations, those films which most directly took on challenging the mainstream's representation of the slave past were produced by white-owned independents. These companies often used all black casts in their attempts to reach the black public. One such company, The Democracy Film Corporation, produced *Injustice* (1919), billed as an answer to the racist *The Clansman*, a film adaptation of the novel upon which *Birth of a Nation* was also based. It met with this response from a white Los Angeles newspaper after its first showing: the film "was a frank appeal to the emotions of colored folk to revolt against the social handicaps which has impressed upon them . . . unlike *Uncle Tom's Cabin*, written to be read by white people and to influence them against the continuance of slavery as an American institution, INJUSTICE has been plainly written for colored people" (quoted in Sampson 1977:60).[52]

The most common character in white films concerning the civil war, the devoted slave was a very popular topic with early film makers, just as was the case in plantation literature. Like the later classic in the genre, *Gone With The Wind*, these films usually centered around the hardships of Southern families in the face of invading Northern armies. Here slaves were shown to be both loyal and helpful to their masters and "having no desire for personal freedom and possessing a will to sacrifice everything, including their life for the benefit of their master's family and property" (Sampson 1997:28). Examples of this are *The Confederate Spy* (1910), *The Guerrilla* (1908), *Mammy's Rose* (1916) and *A Slave's Devotion*. For D. W. Griffith this was a favorite theme and in *In His Trust* and *His Trust Fulfilled*, both from 1911, this loyalty is shown to exist even beyond the war itself. The theme "is carried to its extreme in 'For His Master's Sake' (1911), when Uncle Joe, described as an 'old darky', actually sells himself back into slavery to raise the money needed to pay off the gambling debts of his former master's worthless son" (1997:30). The black response was to ignore slavery almost altogether and focus on contemporary events and the New Negro, rather than the "old." Writing about the Chicago-based and black-owned

Micheaux Film and Book Company, founded in 1918, Mark A. Reid (1998) writes

Micheaux's action films, like other cultural productions of the Harlem Renaissance, were imaginative reflections of a proud, aggressive New Negro whose new morality condoned retaliatory action against white racist aggressions. New cultural "objects" such as black action films were created for this group of urbanized, race-conscious blacks who were learning to lessen their need for approval by White America. Blacks were becoming politically and culturally aware consumers, and the black market required products tailored to their new sensibilities.   (1998:11–12)

Like the literary and pictorial works of the core Renaissance writers to be discussed below, Oscar Micheaux's films covered topics not previously ventured upon in cinema. His 1920 film *Within Our Gates* included a racial lynching, other films depicted anti-Semitism as well as racism, while *The Brute* (1920) depicted the urban, black underworld and a black boxer who fought against lynching. Yet, Reid (1998:13) notes, "Despite the moral worthiness of the film's two topics, self-conscious black critics denounced 'scenes of crap games, black dives, wife-beating, and women congregating to gamble' for portraying the New Negro as less than human."

Unlike these critics, the black middle class did not have the luxury of ignoring either the past or those lower-class behaviors they associated with it. In a society where race, as it was now defined by visible characteristics like skin color, was a marker of social status, those to whom these characteristics were ascribed shared the same fate. Linda McMurry (1998:40) succinctly summarizes the dilemma of the New Negro:

Because whites often judged all African Americans by the actions of the most degraded, black elites believed it important to demonstrate the possibilities of the race by setting themselves apart from the struggling masses. At the same time, however, upper class African Americans' own advancement depended on alleviating the poverty and igno- rance of lower class African Americans. Not only would these conditions continue to be used to justify discrimination toward all blacks, but black professionals also depended upon black patronage. They needed people who could afford their services. As victims of oppression themselves, successful African Americans usually felt a moral obligation to those on the bottom of society as well. In addition, after the debasement of slavery, racial pride was seen as essential to advancement, and unity was crucial to success.

For this generation, slavery had become a filter through which the present was interpreted and judged. For those who took on public responsibility for representing the race, the race men and race leaders, the present was filtered through the veil of the past, and present actions could not simply be judged on their own merit, but on how they would be regarded by whites. It was this effect of slavery, a result of the cultural trauma that followed reconstruction and the reinstatement of Jim Crow, that created a distinct generational habitus, not the experience of slavery itself, but rather its memory. It was memory, and habitus, that would set up a conflict between this generation and the following one, which would have another recollection of slavery and the past. This is the generation articulated in the phrase, the Harlem Renaissance, but which formed itself around a cultural or racial nationalism. This cultural nationalism, already present in the previous generation, was a further response to rejection and marginalization by the dominant society. What was unique here, was that for small groups of whites, Harlem and blacks were in vogue. This was based on the view that a distinct black culture had been developed, and this would eventually open a pathway into the society, not through high art, as Du Bois had hoped, but through popular culture and entertainment. Being modern, forgetting slavery and the past, looking to and even returning to Africa, rather than to slavery and the South, these would characterize this generation's search for identity and reworking of collective memory.

4

The Harlem Renaissance and the heritage of slavery

He scans the world with calm and fearless eyes,
    Conscious within of powers long since forgot;
At every step, now man-made barriers rise
    To bar his progress – but he heeds them not.
He stands erect though tempests round him crash,
    Though thunder burst and billows surge and roll;
He laughs and forges on, while lightnings flash
    Along the rocky path to his goal.
Impassive as a Sphinx, he stares ahead –
    Foresees new empires rise and old ones fall;
While caste-mad nations lust for blood to shed,
    He sees God's finger writing on the wall.
With soul awakened, wise and strong he stands,
    Holding his destiny in his hands.
            "The New Negro" by J. E. McCall (*Opportunity Magazine* 1927)

Someone is always at my elbow reminding me that I am a granddaughter of slaves. It fails to register depression with me. Slavery is sixty years in the past. The operation was successful and the patient is doing well, thank you. The terrible struggle that made an American out of a potential slave said "On the line!" The Reconstruction said "Get set!"; and the generation before me said "Go!" I am off to a flying start and I must not halt in the stretch to look behind and weep. Slavery is the price I paid for civilization, and the choice was not with me. It is a bully adventure and worth all that I paid through my ancestors for it.   (Hurston 1928, quoted in Watson 1995)

Both the poem by McCall and the statement by Hurston, a core figure in the Harlem Renaissance, articulate the feelings of a new generation of blacks, those who came of age in the 1920s in the aftermath of the First World War and the Great Migration, two events which reflect and renew cultural trauma. Both offer a modern approach to the past, forward-looking and progressive, though McCall's is very traditional in form. Hurston is more radical, her past is filtered through a narrative that is evolutionary as well as progressive, it is a past that points to the future, rather than to itself. Slavery is not here forgotten, but regarded as a usable past, an experience which can be appropriated. As heritage and tradition the slave past can, and should, be collected, written down and written about, as Hurston and others will go on to do. Conceived as folk culture and compiled as source material, the past can be mined and used, a form of cultural capital to which blacks could be argued to have privileged access, which makes reference to the authenticity discussion raised earlier and which became more and more central as the century progressed. Collecting could also be considered a valuable activity, not only for racial pride, but also from an evolutionary perspective; these expressions of past ways of life may well be threatened with extinction, and recording them is thus socially as well as politically and professionally useful. This brings to the past the attitude and perspective of the outsider, though in Hurston's and in other cases, filtered through the former insider. Raised in the small, all-black town of Eatonville, Florida, Hurston studied anthropology with Franz Boas, Ruth Benedict, and Melville Herskovitz at Columbia University in New York and under their direction returned to her birthplace and other areas of the South to collect this now exotic material.[1] Together with the poet Langston Hughes, born in 1902 in Joplin, Missouri, but raised by his grandmother in a black Oklahoma town, Hurston returned south in search of material for a play under the auspices of a wealthy white New York patron. Hughes was to become one of the most important black writers of the twentieth century, laying the groundwork for a new approach to poetry and literature by fashioning it with rhythms and themes from this folk heritage. In addition to her groundbreaking work as a folklorist, Hurston became a central role model for coming generations of black writers, especially women.

Hurston and Hughes were part of a new generation of American blacks for whom the past was reconceptualized as cultural heritage, useful for understanding as well as orienting present and future behavior. As heritage, the collective past is usable in at least two senses: it is central to the maintenance of group identity, part of a collective memory, and it is source material, a cultural resource for a distinct aesthetic, explored and exploited not only by members of the group itself but by others as well.[2] Opposed to this progressive, evolutionary narrative was another that was tragic and redemptive in nature. This narrative was part of a new form of Pan African black nationalism that was articulated by the Jamaican-born Marcus Garvey and his United Negro Improvement Association (UNIA), what some have called the largest black-based social movement in the history of the United States. Speaking on Emancipation Day in 1922, Garvey began:

Fifty-Nine years ago Abraham Lincoln signed the Emancipation Proclamation declaring four million Negroes in this country free. Several years prior to that Queen Victoria of

England signed the Emancipation Proclamation that set at liberty hundreds of thousands of West Indian Negro slaves. West Indian Negroes celebrate their emancipation on the first day of August of every year. The American Negroes celebrate their emancipation on the first of January of every year . . . We are the descendants of the men and women who suffered in this country for two hundred and fifty years under the barbarous, the brutal institution known as slavery. You who have not lost trace of your history will recall the fact that over three hundred years ago your fore-bearers were taken from the great Continent of Africa and brought here for the purpose of using them as slaves. Without mercy, without any sympathy they worked our fore-bearers. They suffered, they bled, they died. But with their sufferings, with their blood, which they shed in their death, they had a hope that one day their posterity would be free, and we are assembled here tonight as the children of their hope. . . . each and everyone of you have a duty which is incumbent upon you; a duty that you must perform, because our fore-bearers who suffered, who bled, who died had hopes that are not yet completely realized . . . No better gift can I give in honor of the memory of the love of my fore-parents for me, and in gratitude of the sufferings they endured that I might be free; no grander gift can I bear to the sacred memory of the generation past than a free and redeemed Africa – a monument for all eternity – for all times.   (Garvey in Lewis 1994:26–27)

This is a different view of the slave past than the one offered by Zora Neal Hurston. In Hurston's account slavery was a stepping-off point for evolutionary development. This progressive narrative opened the past for scientific excavation, for ethnological and archeological expeditions looking for traces and remnants, which could be collected and perhaps even used by those looking back from a higher plane of social development. Garvey's view is neither progressive nor scientific. The future will look more like the past in his account: the aim of present action is to restore and renew lost glory. Rather than catalogue and trace the steps out of the past, Garvey holds the past up as a model, a vision that will regenerate the present and the future. This is not a progressive narrative but one of tragedy and redemption, of loss and retrieval. While Hurston's ethnological perspective required that the past be treated with respect, as evidence and as resource, Garvey's past demanded retribution. Slavery, which now would also include colonialism, was more than theft and the loss of freedom in forced labor, it deprived a people of their dreams and stripped them of their civilization. This lost generation now had to be redeemed by their progeny. Slavery, in other words, created a duty to the memory of the enslaved.[3]

These two narratives formed opposing and often opposed ways of relating the past to the present and the future. United by the primal scene of slavery and the previous generation's attempts to deal with the trauma of rejection, each in its own way served as the basis for collective identity, by linking the individual to the collective through the concept of racial pride and the role of culture in that process. With their respective interpretations of the past they offered different paths to the future, however. The progressive evolutionary view articulated by Hurston pointed toward eventual integration into American society, on the basis of racial regeneration made possible through sifting the past for present use. The tragic/redemptive narrative pointed to a racial nation in a revitalized Africa.

At the same time, different models of liberation were articulated. The national liberation model was reformulated in cultural terms. James Weldon Johnson wrote:

What the colored poet in the United States needs to do is something like what Synge did for the Irish; he needs to find a form that will express the racial spirit by symbols from within rather than by symbols from without, such as the mere mutilation of English spelling and pronunciation. He needs a form that is freer and larger than dialect, but which will still hold the racial flavor; a form expressing the imagery, the idioms, the peculiar turns of thought; and the distinctive humor and pathos too, of the Negro, but which will also be capable of voicing the deepest and highest emotions and aspirations, and allow of the widest range of subjects and the widest scope of treatment.

(From Huggins 1995:300)[4]

Africa provided an important resource for this generation's search for identity. It had a place in both of these dominant narratives.[5] Again, not as a place, somewhere actually to escape to as Africa had for other generations of blacks and as it would continue to do so for others in this generation, but as a metaphor for a long lost and forgotten past. This can be seen in the following poem by Countee Cullen, another Renaissance poet.[6] The poem appeared in the *Survey Graphic* special Harlem Number (March 1925) and was reprinted in *The New Negro* (1925) edited by Alain Locke, both of which will be discussed in detail.

> What is Africa to me:
> Copper sun and scarlet sea,
> Jungle star or jungle track,
> Strong bronzed men, or regal black
> Women from whose loins I sprang
> When the birds of Eden sang?
> One three centuries removed
> From the scenes his father loved,
> Spicy grove, cinnamon tree,
> What is Africa to me?

The title of Cullen's poem, "Heritage," tells the story. This reconstitution of the collective memory at the base of collective identity adds new dimensions, as well as a reinterpretation of the slave past by looking beyond it to a more glorious past. In other words, it places more emphasis on the African and thus reconfigures the contours of meaning of African American. In his response to the question raised in the title of Cullen's poem, Du Bois wrote:

Africa is of course my fatherland. Yet neither my father nor my father's father ever saw Africa or knew its meaning or cared overmuch for it. My mother's folk were closer and yet their direct connection, in culture and race, became tenuous; still my tie to Africa is strong. On this vast continent were born and lived a large portion of my direct ancestors going back a thousand years or more. The mark of their heritage is upon me in color and hair. These are obvious things, but of little meaning in themselves; only important as they stand for real or more subtle differences from other men.

In this context, Du Bois speaks of race as one long memory.[7] On one hand, the tragic and redemptive narrative that guided black nationalism viewed Africa as the homeland and would drop the "American" altogether.[8]

These perspectives on the slave past were of course fashioned by small groups, "generational units" in Karl Mannheim's terminology, and restricted largely to those in urban environments, who functioned as an avant garde. This was, however, a different sort of avant garde from the talented tenth envisioned by Du Bois and others of the previous generation, where culture would represent only the best and the brightest of the race. This Arnoldian view of culture is rejected in favor of a modernism that is at once "primitive" and realistic, creating an idyllic past as it re-presents the present, warts and all. Through incorporating folk traditions, such as jokes, folk tales ("Hell: Ginny Gall way off in Ginny Gall/where you have to eat cow cunt, skin and all," Hurston, cited in Watson 1995), and blues music into high cultural forms, like poetry and painting, and including sexuality, desire, and everyday life as significant content, this avant garde blurred the borders drawn by their elders, as they reached out to and drew inspiration from, the surrounding mass black public. Its leadership was not exemplary in the same way, manner or form as the moralistic, religious, and Euro-centered, talented tenth. There were exceptions of course, Countee Cullen cited above being one, and overlaps, but there was, as will be discussed below, great tension between these two conceptions of racial representation and their respective views and uses of the past. Africa and the slave past were present as reference points for both, as that from which we came, but were interpreted in a different way by the different generations. And the older generation found such language as Hurston recorded above embarrassing and demeaning, just as they did blues' lyrics and performance. For Du Bois and the generation formed by reconstruction and its failed promise of integration, the cultural trauma generated by the betrayal and the marginalization it engendered, created a standpoint and a filter through which to judge present practice. This constituted the basis of distinct generational habitus. For the new generation, the past and the indigenous culture, as Hurston expressed it, was a jumping-off point, a starting block in the race toward the future which, because it looked back, was an open door. Although offering another way of viewing the past, Garveyism was also optimistic about the future, but with another outcome in mind.

These perspectives were articulated by small groups of activists and spread through a wider community by means of their associated media, which in turn can be said to have discovered itself through this articulation, as individuals took sides for or against these new developments. As such, these perspectives should not be confused or attributed to any wider community, in the imagined or the real sense, but neither should they be said to express only the perspectives of an isolated elite. There were other networks, means of articulation, and perspectives, of course. The commercial black press, the churches, the "secret" organizations, and the black institutions of higher education; in 1917 "there were 2,132 African Americans in colleges and universities, probably no more than fifty of the them attending 'white' institutions" (Lewis 1993: xiii). Each was expanding its influence and articulating points of view on the past and future of the "race." Also of growing importance were the commercial mass media, a force now including radio and records in its arsenal of film and print, as more and more blacks were introduced to the evolving consumer society. These commercial media, largely white owned and controlled, were central to the formation, the reach, and the reception of the Harlem Renaissance.

The changing conditions of community

The war brought unforeseen changes in the material and spiritual conditions of African Americans. For one, even though the American military maintained strictly segregated conditions, black soldiers volunteered for service and went into combat with just as much enthusiasm as whites. African Americans were as patriotic as their white counterparts, which is astonishing given their treatment. Although many of those who volunteered for military service were turned away by the racial ideas and discriminatory practices of admission boards (this was before the national draft) "more than 400,000 African Americans served in the United States armed forces during World War I, and about half of those saw duty in France" (Stovall 1996:5). These veterans would return to the same segregated America and all the frustrations felt by those left behind.

Almost immediately after the war the country suffered some of the worst race riots in its history, something which can at least in part be attributed to the perceived threats of a new, urban Negro. At the same time as the triumphant returning black veterans marched up New York's Fifth Avenue all the way up Harlem to the strains of an all-black orchestra directed by James Reese Europe, other events were equally symbolic. In 1919, twenty-five race riots occurred in Northern cities involving direct clashes between whites and blacks, something which would distinguish them from later occurrences which were largely internal to black neighborhoods. In Chicago alone, 38 persons, black and white, were killed and 500 injured. One of those black veterans returning to Chicago opens his autobiography with these words: "On July 28, 1919, I literally stepped into a battle that was to last the rest of my life. Exactly three months after mustering out of the Army, I found myself in the midst of one of the bloodiest race riots in U.S. history. It was certainly a most dramatic return to the realities of American democracy" (Haywood 1978:1).[9] The same year Edwin A. Harleston painted "The Soldier," a portrait of a black veteran in full uniform "proud, undaunted, admirable, and disquieting – that embodied much of what African Americans felt about their wartime service" (Powell 1997:39).

In the South there was a distinct rise in the number of lynchings, which could be attributed to the threat posed by returning veterans. Eighty-five blacks were lynched in 1919 in what was called the "Red Summer of Hate," as the Ku Klux Klan organized "over 200 meetings throughout the country" (Christian 1995:316). This spurred Claude McKay to write his famous "If I Must Die," sometimes taken as the first public expression of the Harlem Renaissance.[10] Writing in the *Crisis*, Walter White listed the following as causes to the rioting: "racial prejudice, economic competition, political corruption and exploitation of the Negro voter, police inefficiency, newspaper lies about Negro crime, unpunished crimes against Negroes, housing, and reaction of whites and Negroes from war" (Christian 1995:317).[11]

In addition to returning veterans and raised black expectations of integration and acceptance, other changes were occurring in the black population. Stimulated by the war, developments in farm production were in the process of changing the basis of the rural work force, with a significant decrease in the need for unskilled manual labor. The production of cotton, the mainstay of black labor, was particularly affected. Out of these and other factors, such as the need for unskilled industrial labor in Northern cities, there occurred what has come to be called the "great migration," a population shift of such magnitude that it would change the conditions of African Americans forever. In a period of 60 years (1910–70) more than 6.5 million black Americans moved northward, changing from farm labor to industrial labor and from a rural to an urban living environment. During the First World War alone, "the black population of the North increased by almost 80 percent, from 900,000 to 1.6 million. Another 350,000 African Americans joined the armed forces, and many of these soldiers resettled in the North after the war" (Barlow 1999:16). In Chicago the black population increased 148 percent between 1910 and 1920, in Columbus, Ohio 74 percent, Philadelphia, St. Louis, Kansas City and Indianapolis all expanded their black populations by around 50 percent in the same period (Christian 1995:319). This population shift wrought major changes in the social conditions of African Americans. For black authors, artists, and intellectuals it helped produce a new audience and a new self-confidence. In 1920, New York's Harlem "contained approximately 73,000 blacks (66.9 percent of the total number of blacks in the borough of Manhattan); by 1930 black Harlem had expanded . . . and housed approximately 164,000 blacks (73.0 percent of Manhattan's blacks)" (Wintz 1988:20).[12]

What could be called a black public sphere emerged as urban areas expanded to accommodate the waves of migrants arriving from the Southern regions of the country and soldiers home from war. Within the neighborhoods which were created or transformed, small clubs and meeting halls, restaurants, movie houses, theaters, and dance halls sprang up in the teeming black sections of Chicago, Detroit, Cleveland, and Philadelphia. Forms of popular entertainment were created as the newly arrived reorganised their ways of life to fit the urban environment. In a sense, one could say that this new urban public sphere expanded upon and competed with the much smaller circles created and maintained by the educated black middle class of the previous generation. While the book clubs, lyceums, and concerts and theater that helped constitute the previous generation were limited to a small elite with intimate knowledge of each other and were maintained through networks which built on face-to-face contact, this new black public was more anonymous and thus more open. Further, what previously had been carried and motivated by small groups and exemplary individuals, like Du Bois and Ida Wells, was now borne by collective movements of a different type. There existed a tension between these social formations, one exclusionary and personal and the other open and anonymous, that would express itself in part as a generational struggle between an aging New Negro and a younger offspring in the 1920s.

The development of concentrated and literate black populations facilitated the emergence of social and cultural movements which would articulate as well as signal a new social awareness and a revisioning of the collective past. The urban environment made blacks aware of intellectual and political impulses, like the cultural radicalism of Greenwich Village and the political radicalism associated with it – socialism and communism, as well as nationalism. These processes were all interconnected through a range of magazines, journals, and newspapers which served to link together this wide-ranging and socially diverse racial community, and through which "race leaders" sought to influence the formation of its collective identity.

The periodicals included Garvey's *Negro World*, A. Philip Randolph and Charles Owen's socialist *Messenger*, both of which began publication in 1917. Randolph, who would found the all black Brotherhood of Sleeping Car Porters Union in 1925, was the son of slaves. His brand of the New Negro differed, at least at first, from the more culturally oriented version propounded by

Du Bois and the younger generation, like Hurston and Hughes. Besides the *Crisis*, which remained under Du Bois' editorship, another journal central to the development of the Harlem Renaissance was *Opportunity: Journal of Negro Life*, founded in 1923 as the organ of the National Urban League, which published the poem "The New Negro" which opened this chapter.[13] Its editor was Charles S. Johnson, a University of Chicago trained sociologist born in 1893 and co-author of *The Negro in Chicago* (1922), which followed the path opened by Du Bois' *The Philadelphia Negro* in providing a sociological perspective on urban blacks.[14] *Opportunity* was the organizer of literary prizes for promising young blacks. It was at the first awards dinner in 1925 that Hughes and Hurston first met each other, each having been awarded prizes, as was Countee Cullen.[15] At the same time there was a developing interest in black history, literature, and art, especially within the smaller circles of the growing urban African American middle class, and also a market for a race-oriented consumer culture.[16] Arthur Schomburg, famed Harlem bibliophile, wrote:

the American Negro must remake his past in order to make his future. Though it is orthodox to think of America as the one country where it is unnecessary to have a past, what is a luxury for the nation as a whole becomes a prime social necessity for the Negro. For him, a group tradition must supply compensation for persecution, and pride of race the antidote for prejudice. History must restore what slavery took away, for it is the social damage of slavery that the present generation must repair and offset. So among the rising democratic millions we find the Negro thinking more collectively, more retrospectively than the rest, and apt out of the very pressure of the present to become the most enthusiastic antiquarian of them all.   (Schomburg 1994:61)

This statement by a non-professional historian offers a sort of middle ground between the views of the past laid out at the beginning of this section, the progressive and tragic narratives. Here history is reparation, but not redemptive, it should be collected, but more as an end in itself than as a resource for current needs.

Not surprisingly a central issue in this identity-formation concerned the role of culture, past and present, as it was now objectified and held up for reflective judgment. Specifically, this meant the meaning and place of culture in the struggle for acceptance in the dominant, white society, and, particularly those "folk" traditions associated with slavery and the South. Were these traditions a source of vitality or a burden to be rejected and wiped away, or merely curiosities to be codified and preserved in specified arenas? Whatever the answer to this question, what were the criteria to be used in sorting out the living and the dead in these traditions? Further, on what grounds did those who made such judgments themselves stand? These were some of the central questions facing activists in a range of African American movements, from the integrationist and legalistic NAACP to the nationalist Garveyites, as the first quarter of the twentieth century drew to a close.

The older generation had argued that blacks were a creative and talented race, and that would make assimilation all the easier. As James Weldon Johnson expressed it at the time, "through his artistic efforts the Negro is smashing [an] immemorial stereotype faster than he has ever done . . . He is impressing upon the national mind the conviction that he is an active creator as well as a creature . . . that his gifts have been not only obvious and material, but also spiritual and aesthetic" (quoted in Cruse 1984:34). And Paul Robeson said at the time, "it is through our artistic capacity that we will best be recognized . . . it is through art we are going to come into our own" (quoted in Duberman 1989:72). Robeson was on the periphery of the Harlem Renaissance, but the views he expressed were those of its core group as well. This artistic achievement to advance the race, as Martin Duberman, Robeson's biographer, notes, was individual, "not organized, collective action."[17] Yet the memory of slavery permeated Robeson's career; talking about one controversial, yet extremely successful, stage performance he noted:

One does not need a very long racial memory to lose oneself in such a part . . . As I act, civilization falls away from me. My plight becomes real, the horrors terrible facts. I feel the terror of the slave mart, the degradation of man bought and sold into slavery. Well, I am the son of an emancipated slave and the stories of old father are vivid on the tablets of my memory.[18]

The urban environment opened blacks to aesthetic movements like cultural radicalism, the bohemian lifestyle and modernist ideology of Greenwich Village, a new mass consumer culture, and political ideologies like socialism and communism. These, and a new form of African nationalism, would compete for the attention of a black population in a period of great fluctuation. In the 1920s black nationalism would for the first time take the form of a social movement, with the emergence of Garveyism.[19] The figure of Marcus Garvey represents something even more significant than his personal role as leader of this movement, he reflects the centrality of West Indians in the reconstruction of black collective identity in this period. West Indians brought an anti-colonialist perspective into play, as well as an openness to European ideologies like Marxism. They were also central in the development of black nationalism and Pan Africanism in the United States and Europe and the involvement of blacks in the American Communist Party.[20]

Before turning to Garvey and his movement a word about the political left can be said. The 1920s was not a good time for the American left generally and this was even more obvious in Harlem. The economic recession which followed the end of the war had turned into a boom and the expanding American economy reached into Harlem and other cities, a fact which helps explain the black migration. Good economic times are traditionally bad for left-wing politics, which had also been on the defensive after the conflicts created during the war when ethnic and national loyalties split the socialist party. The socialist party got 25 percent of the votes in the race for mayor in 1917, but by 1923, A. Philip Randolph closed the Harlem socialist political club (Naison 1983:9).[21] In addition to this, the twenties was a time of right-wing political reaction, with the "red scare" after the Russian Revolution. Finally, the new immigration laws put an end to the flow of labor from Europe, the traditional home of the left, a fact which made black labor all the more important and attractive to American business. Even the NAACP suffered from these developments, as its membership dropped from 90,000 in 1919 to 20,000 in 1929.[22] Those attracted to the Garvey movement have usually been described as working class in contrast to the middle-class blacks active in the NAACP and other "uplift" organizations. Those on the left found this a matter of timing and of time. By the end of the decade they would be proven right.

Marcus Garvey was born in 1887 in St. Ann's Bay, Jamaica. His father was a stone mason, descended from African slaves who escaped to the island in the seventeenth century. Trained as a printer, he studied in England, where he came in contact with African nationalists and with Booker T. Washington's *Up From Slavery*. On the ship returning to Jamaica in 1914, Garvey had a religious experience which convinced him of his destiny "to build the organization and provide the leadership that would empower the African race" (Lewis 1994:747). In 1916 he arrived at the Tuskegee Institute, just two months after Washington's death. Settling in New York, Garvey set about realizing his mission to readjust the balance between the African and the American. Toward this end he established in 1918, not alone of course, *The Negro World*, a newspaper devoted to black nationalism and the UNIA, the United Negro Improvement Association, shortly after.[23]

This transformation required a wider scope than either the African American or the new Negro, it could not be limited to the Americas, but rather involved the "four hundred million Negroes of the world" (Garvey 1994:23). It would be achieved through organization and leadership provided by the UNIA, a leadership inspired by "a vision of the future . . . a picture of a redeemed Africa, with her dotted cities, with her beautiful civilization, with her millions of happy children, going to and fro" (1994:25).

At its first Annual Convention in 1920, Garvey's UNIA adopted the "Declaration of Rights of the Negro Peoples of the World," a document consisting of a preamble, a list of complaints and fifty-four demands and described as the Magna Carta of the race. It was signed by 122 delegates and observers and reproduced in the *Negro World* (Van Deburg 1997:23). The complaints were directed against racial discrimination and lynching and flogging, drawing parallels between European practices in Africa and those in the United States. Declaring the right to self-determination of all "Negroes" under a banner of the "colors of the Negro race," red, black, and green and that the anthem of that race should be "Ethiopia, Land of our Fathers." The first verse of "The Universal Ethiopian Anthem" is:

> Ethiopia, thou land of our fathers,
> Thou land where the gods loved to be,
> As storm cloud at night suddenly gathers
> Our armies come rushing to thee.
> We must in the fight be victorious
> When swords are thrust outward to gleam;
> For us will the vict'ry be glorious
> When led by the red, black and green.
> > (Declaration of Rights of the Negro Peoples of the World,
> > reprinted in Van Deburg 1997b:29–30)

In line with the policy of establishing ritual celebrations to reinforce collective identity through collective memory, the Declaration of Rights proclaimed "the 31st day of August of each year to be an international holiday to be observed by all Negroes" (Van Deburg 1999:31). The Declaration closed with the words: "These rights we believe to be justly ours and proper for the protection of the Negro race at large, and because of this belief we, on behalf of the four hundred million Negroes of the world, do pledge herein the sacred blood of the race in defense..." (1999:31).[24]

The attempt to establish a new vision also had an aesthetic dimension, as exemplified in the ceremony and costumes of participants. Garvey made conscious use of visual media in his struggle with other black intellectuals to define the new situation and the collective identity of American blacks. He hired the Harlem photographer James VanDerZee to record UNIA meetings and demonstrations. According to Roger Birt (in Willis-Braithwaite and Birt: 1998:48) "Garvey wanted to blanket the black media with images of a vibrant and active UNIA under his own careful stewardship ... the overall intention of the UNIA (photographic) work was to evoke a mood of stability and order." In its aesthetic, the movement exemplified a distinctive gender differentiation. The black man was powerful and heroic, rescuing black women as he redeemed the race. As *The Negro World* proclaimed in 1923, "Let us go back to the days of true manhood when women truly revered us ... let us again place our women upon the pedestal from whence they have been forced into the vortex of the seething world of business" (quoted in White 1999:121).[25] As for the woman on the pedestal, Garvey's poem "The Black Woman" visualizes her:

> Black Queen of beauty, thou hast given colour to the world!
> Among other women thou art royal and fairest!
> Like the brightest of jewels in the regal diadem,
> Shin'st thou, Goddess of Africa, Nature's purest emblem!
> Black men worship the virginal shrine in truest Love,
> Because in thine eyes are virtue's steady and holy mark,
> As we see in no other, clothed in silk or fine linen,
> From ancient Venus, the Goddess to mythical Helen,
> Superior Angels look like you in heaven above,
> For thou art fairest, queen of seasons, queen of love;
> No condition shall make us ever in life desert thee,
> Sweet Goddess of the ever green land and placid blue sea.

In response to cultural trauma, one response already noted is an attempt to turn tragedy into triumph through a reinterpretation, rather than a denial, of the past. The fact that both the New Negro and the UNIA had this in common caused Lawrence Levine (1978) to call both "revitalization" movements.[26] The UNIA and many in the New Negro movement were at opposite poles, however, regarding the use of symbols and commemorative pageantry. The same year the UNIA established "Ethiopia, Land of Our Fathers" as the Negro anthem, the NAACP declared James Weldon Johnson's "Lift Every Voice" to be the Negro National anthem.[27] Both movements might well have sought the revitalization of a people through reconstituting its collective identity, but they did so with different visions of the past, as well as of the future.

Writing of the Garvey movement in *Opportunity* in 1926, E. Franklin Frazier, later to become an eminent sociologist, expressed one position, perhaps the dominant one amongst the educated black middle class, that the "new urban experience for blacks was disruptive, even 'pathological', concluding from this that mass movements, like UNIA, were 'rooted in desperation, not promise' " (Stein 1986:3). From the point of view of cultural trauma this would not be a condemning judgment, but appearing at the time in a journal of a rival organization, although the movement had by this time lost almost all of its force, it was meant as a dismissal not only of the movement but also of the possibility of black mass politics generally. If the situation of blacks in the cities was pathological, all political movements in which they participated could be so judged. Meaning that newly arrived urban blacks could not be trusted to produce grass roots movements, but required "enlightened leadership of the sort offered by Du Bois, the NAACP, and the Urban League, summed up in the notion of the 'talented tenth.' "

Defenders of the movement of course deny such underlying "alienation" or "pathology" in explaining either the popularity or the aims of the movement. Martin (1983) stresses the socializing and educating aims and practices of the UNIA. Like a small public sphere within a larger one, the movement organized clubs, debating societies, reading circles, and the like through which the newly literate could be stimulated and challenged through the arts. Of course, the underlying aim was organizing and mobilizing support for the black nationalism represented by the movement, but the notion of racial pride this ideology built called for and encouraged appreciation of "good" music and literature. That this taste in literature and art was essentially European, the same or similar to talented tenth notions, does not detract from the socializing and educating aspects: people were encouraged to read, write, and discuss, that is, to develop their cognitive abilities, as well as improve their cultural competence.

The weekly *Negro World* also awarded prizes for essays and poetry, in the same manner as *Opportunity* and the *Crisis* did. Younger authors, later associated with these journals and with the Harlem Renaissance, like Hurston, Hughes, and Claude McKay, participated and submitted their works for publication. What may appear today as two opposed movements, a viewpoint encouraged by contemporary activists, was for young blacks excited by the atmosphere, an after-construction. Looking back on those days and on Garvey's significance, McKay wrote:

Garvey assembled an exhibition of Negro accomplishment in all the skilled crafts and art work produced by exhibitors from all the Americas and Africa, which were revelations to Harlem of what the Negro people were capable of achieving. The vivid, albeit crude, paintings of the Black Christ and the Black Virgin of the African Orthodox Church were startling omens of the Negro Renaissance movement of the nineteen twenties, which whipped up the appetite of literary and artistic America for a season. The flowering of Harlem's creative life came in the Garvey era. The anthology, *The New Negro*, which oriented the debut of the Renaissance writers, was printed in 1925. If Marcus Garvey did not originate the phrase, New Negro, he at least made it popular. (quoted in Martin 1983:7)

McKay was looking back not only from the vantage point of time, but also from the point of view of a fellow West Indian. Many on the other side of this struggle concerning how to respond to the trauma of racism and the slave past, tended to dismiss Garvey with names like the "Jamaican Jackass," expressing not only a dislike for his nationalism but also the tensions that existed between West Indians and native born blacks, something which distinguished Harlem from other northern cities.[28] One of the strengths of Garvey's movement, however, was just its capacity to bridge this gap. If there were any distinct sociological characteristics of this movement they were its class character and the appeal of the movement to those newly arrived, either from the South or from the islands. The movement appealed to the less educated, the recently arrived, and the unskilled. It was this basis in lower class and status that made cultural uplift so central to its programs. If the Garvey movement can be considered a response to "alienation," it was no different from many such movements at the time, where the newly migrated or the young sought loosely constructed yet structured settings in which to experiment and reconstitute their identity. This movement had the added dimension of being racially based, that is, open only to those who could meet, or who were ready to meet, certain criteria, skin color being an obvious one, but a slave past being another, unspoken, but not less assumed, criterion. In this, the Garvey movement competed with the NAACP and the Urban League, thus the attempt to define them in a negative way.

The Garvey movement can be understood as part of a new urban black public sphere, in which social learning, socialization, and acculturation as well as experimentation with forms of expression and styles of life, played an important part. This was, in other words, a public sphere where much more than the consumption of mass or consumer culture was important. An argument could be made that this was the case for white workers, especially immigrants, at the time; that is, that participating in the commercially driven public sphere, including the purchase of consumer goods was as much a socialization process as it was anything else. That may well be. The difference here lies in the fact that the black public sphere was defined and permeated by race, and many of the consumer items, records for example, were designed especially for and limited to this public. In other words, they strengthened and reinforced the group in relation to the rest of society, even while creating and or reinforcing internal differentiation.

In this black public sphere different movements as well as different types of entertainment competed for attention. What was considered to be "good activity," uplifting to the race and exemplifying the ideals of the New Negro, was a central matter of concern and controversy. Later we will have the opportunity to discuss the debate on "representation" that was carried out in the pages of the *Crisis* and in other media. In the early 1920s a similar issue was being posed in the *Negro World* and in fora associated with Garvey and Pan Africanism. At issue here was the relationship between art and propaganda, as well as the "racial" component of art. The former concerned the increasingly familiar notion of the "message" an artwork supposedly conveyed, and the latter, the relatively new, but not entirely unique, issue of what was specific to black culture, beyond questions of message and quality. It was here that Africa and the slave past would become central. The issue of the message and purpose of art concerned the present and the future and the relationship

between art and action. The debate about racial art concerned the meaning of
the past.

Propaganda was applied to art "enlisted in the cause of struggle" (Martin
1983:13), a subordination of aesthetic principles to a concern with communicating a distinct message; ideology, in other words, conceived in terms of
ready-made explanations about the nature of the world and one's place in it
and prescriptions for action. The struggle here involved how others perceived
a group as much as how that group perceived itself. The former concerned the
relation to whites, an issue that was more central to Du Bois and the older generation, and the latter, how the race defined itself, and was perceived, by Garvey,
although since both involved racial uplift, there was considerable overlap. There
were fundamental differences between the movements on this issue, however,
in that Garvey and his leadership often referred to the NAACP and the *Crisis* as
"white," because they allowed whites to participate, while the UNIA was more
exclusionary. The debate over the meaning and purpose of Eugene O'Neill's
"Emperor Jones" illustrates these issues and the overlaps where it concerns a
black character in a play written by a white.[29] This became even more complicated regarding art works created and performed by blacks, for example the
black musical shows that were immensely popular with white audiences at the
time. That O'Neill was part of Greenwich Village cultural radicalism, which
was considered sympathetic to the New Negro, further complicated the issue.[30]
The content of the play, however, with its lead character a black ex-convict who
becomes a clownish emperor of a Caribbean island, was cause for concern.[31]
In response to a favorable review of the play by *Negro World* editor, Hubert
Harrison, one reader wrote:

Anything that causes the white man to believe that Negroes are superstitious, immoral
and illiterate . . . can make a hit on Broadway . . . One does not need "an understanding
of drama and its laws," to quote Mr. Harrison, to realize that "Emperor Jones" is of no
racial value to the Negroes of the World. The play does not elevate the Negro, and such
plays never will . . . such men as Mr. Harrison who encourage white playrights (*sic*) by
lauding them to the skies, are of no racial value to the Negroes. Remember always the
man who allows a man to make a fool of him will always be a fool.[32] (*Negro World*
July 30, 1921, quoted in Martin 1983:11–12)

That these issues could be aired in public by and before a generally educated
audience points to the role of social movements and their media in this new
public sphere. They supplemented and complemented the commercial black
press, which continued its role in speaking for the racial community and in
educating as well as informing the public. That the woman who wrote the
letter referred to above lived in Cambridge, Mass., not Harlem, also attests to
the reach of such journals and their ability to link together a more than local

community through discussing issues under the wider notion of race. Here the "race" referred to in the Garvey press stretched farther as it included itself within the pan-African movement, which was of lesser importance for the *Crisis*, and *Opportunity*, and even the *Messenger*, which were more national in scope and integrationist in tone. Writing in the Playbill of another O'Neill play starring Paul Robeson, *All God's Chillun Got Wings* (1924), Du Bois said:

the Negro today fears any attempt of the artist to paint Negroes. He is not satisfied unless everything is perfect and proper and beautiful and joyful and hopeful. He is afraid to be painted as he is, lest his human foibles and shortcomings be seized by his enemies for the purpose of the ancient and hateful propaganda. Happy is the artist who can break through any of these shells, for his is the kingdom of eternal beauty. He will come through scarred, and perhaps a little embittered – certainly astonished at the almost universal misinterpretation of his motives and aims. Eugene O'Neill is bursting through. He has my sympathy, for his soul must be lame with the blows rained upon him. But it is work that must be done.   (Quoted in Stewart 1999:86–87)

Du Bois here reveals his own ambiguity regarding the difference between art and propaganda.

A further issue concerned the possibility of a "Negro" art. This is a question that has roots not only in racial uplift and black nationalism, but in cultural nationalism generally. In the eighteenth and nineteenth centuries, similar questions were raised about the possibility of creating an American art, distinct from European influence. This issue was also posed in connection with political values, that is, European art was characterized as elitist and American art as democratic. In Harlem in 1926 the issue was posed most poignantly by Langston Hughes, a member of the younger generation who moved between movements and camps. Writing in the *Nation*, perhaps to emphasize his independence, Hughes began:

One of the most promising of the young Negro poets said to me once, "I want to be a poet – not a Negro poet", meaning, I believe, "I want to write like a white poet"; meaning subconsciously, "I would like to be a white poet"; meaning behind that, "I would like to be white". And I was sorry the young man said that, for no great poet has ever been afraid of being himself. And I doubted then that, with his desire to run away spiritually from his race, this boy would ever be a great poet. But this is the mountain standing in the way of any true Negro art in America, this urge within the race toward whiteness, the desire to pour racial individuality into the mold of American standardization, and to be as little Negro and as much American as possible.   (Van Deburg 1997b:52)

Hughes' answer, which was also a call to move beyond Du Bois' double consciousness, was that the African American artist should free himself to be himself: "we build our temples for tomorrow, strong as we know how, and we stand on top of the mountain, free within ourselves."

This "splendid article on the difficulties facing the Negro" provoked Amy Jacques Garvey, the wife of Marcus, to respond in the *Negro World* the following week:

Bravo, Mr. Hughes! From now on under your leadership we expect our artists to express their real souls, and give us art, that is colorful, full of ecstasy, dulcet and even tragic, for has it not been admitted by those who would undervalue us that the Negro is a born artist. Then let the canvas come to life with dark faces; let poetry charm the muses with the hopes and aspirations of our race; let the musicians drown our sorrows with merry jazz; while a race is in the making, and steadily moving on to nationhood and to power. Play up, boys, and let the world know "we are Negroes and beautiful." (Reprinted in Van Deburg: 1997b:58)

This made more complicated the relation between art and propaganda. For here the issue was posed as one of self-expression, the desire to be and to express one's true self, i.e., authenticity, rather than communicating a particular message or ensuring a desired effect. For Hughes, a Negro art emerged out of an artist's Negro self or soul, which was collective as much as it was individual. This is what would distinguish his position from the Expressionism that would develop later on in the United States, but perhaps linked it to German Expressionism, if that was considered as much "German" as it was "expressive" of the particular artist. To some critics, this was decadent art, just as certain forms of modernistic realism in the Harlem Renaissance would be. While Amy Jaques Garvey encouraged Hughes to produce a Negro art, one wonders what she might say about particular art works by Negroes, was it enough to say they were authentic expressions or did the content and what it might convey also matter?

On the other side of the art as propaganda issue was the idea of quality, the aesthetic criterion that many believed made it easily possible to distinguish good from bad art, and the idea that politics imposed a constraint on this distinction. Most black intellectuals writing on this issue derived their ideas about aesthetic judgment from European theorists or their perception of them in the practices of whites. They accepted a distinction commonly made at the time between high and low culture and good and bad art. William Ferris, literary editor of the *Negro World*, opted for a middle road on the art versus propaganda issue, while at the same time criticizing what he considered the aping of European values by the black middle class. In addressing the former issue he called upon Harriet Beecher Stowe's authorship as a good example of the middle path: "Uncle Tom's Cabin won more converts to the slave's cause than did the brilliant addresses of Sumner, Phillips and Douglass and the forceful editorials of Garrison." The task of the black writer was thus to create fiction which was both great and influential, "Novels which can powerfully picture the civilization of Africa during the Middle Ages, novels which can powerfully envisage the struggles of the aspiring Negro in a hostile Anglo-Saxon civilization, will undoubted add to the prestige and standing of the Negro Race" (*Negro World* 1920, cited in Martin 1983:13). About the black middle class, Ferris wrote, "One of the stumbling blocks in the pathway to Negro progress is the Negro's false conception of art. Art to him, be it music, poetry, drama, sculpture, painting or literature is a thing that appeals exclusively to the cultural-minded, to the bourgeoisie . . . " Since it was this group that formed the central audience for the black artist, if one wanted to avoid white patronage, this forced black writers into producing romantic, uplifting literature that brought "out the higher aspirations of the Negro . . . that with a brutally sterile puritanism steer clear of the beauty and simplicity of true art" (*Negro World* 1922, Martin 1983:15). Black artists, like black art, were caught between the demands for racial art from all sides, from the white side to produce an art that appealed to white stereotypes or prurient interests, sexuality, primitivism, gambling, and the black middle-class interest in the opposite, romantic and often sentimental stories of the triumph of good over evil and the political interests of movements in mobilization and recruitment; not to mention the problem of making a living. While the market for art works, broadly conceived, by blacks was growing, social movements and their media provided a ready outlet and an audience for young writers; it is unlikely that these young writers viewed the ideological positions of these movements as overwhelming constraints and impositions. They too were learning and experimenting with ideas, as well as forms of expression.

At the same time as these new black communities grew and attracted more and more blacks, they also began to attract the interest of whites other than the reform-oriented, progressives, and those with religious motives who had long been interested in the plight of the African American. Here the newly objectified black "culture," especially music, played a leading role. Jazz clubs were the biggest draw for whites, and it can be argued that through music white interest expanded to include literary works as well, and there appeared more books in print by black authors in the space of a decade than had ever before been the case. It was the jazz clubs that drew cultural radicals like Carl Van Vechten to the "nigger heaven" he imagined he found in Harlem. Vechten's novel of that title about Harlem club life was a bestseller in 1924 and was a major cause of the growth of white "slumming," something which also contributed to labeling the 1920s as the Jazz Age. Van Vechten, helped open doors for Negro writers in the white literary establishment and was in part responsible for the publication of *The New Negro*, the collection of essays which announced the Harlem Renaissance to the art world. The popularity of *Nigger Heaven* amongst whites, like O'Neill's *Emperor Jones*, was cause for concern.

For Du Bois it confirmed the interests of whites, even supposedly sympathetic ones, in downgrading and stereotyping the Negro. This was expressed in the title itself. More than that, white interest in Harlem only reinforced the segregation imposed by society, as it brought it into Harlem itself. Many of the Harlem clubs patronized by whites did not admit blacks, except in service roles, including entertainment. That these were the most popular clubs further reinforced white domination on the value scale, a subject of not a few novels by black writers.

The double consciousness Du Bois characterized was here given another dimension, black artists and writers could not escape the necessity of dealing with the white media, publishers and critics for example, and through that media with the interests of the white public. At the same time, they could never escape being identified as "black" artists and writers, for this audience and for other African Americans. What responsibility did the writer and artist have to the black community in the portraits he objectified for all to see? Was he a "race man" who must be careful in his choice of language and topic, careful in manner and dress so as not to offend whites and to "put the best face forward"? Or, did the black writer enjoy the same artistic freedom of expression and choice of topic that his/her white counterparts were claiming? Was she/he an artist first and a black second or vice versa? Like the role of intellectual, the role of artist was not yet fully defined and available to African Americans, if it ever would be.

This dilemma of always being accountable to multiple audiences with varying interests and claims was discussed in the pages of the NAACP's *Crisis*. In its March 1926 number the journal published a symposium it had sponsored under the title "How shall the Negro be portrayed." While the whites invited to participate, who included Sherwood Anderson, H. L. Mencken and Carl Van Vechten, for the most part agreed that the Negro artist and writer enjoyed the same freedoms whites did in choosing topics and forms of expression, the black participants were more divided and ambiguous on this issue (Tillery 1992:98ff.). While most could agree with the principle that black writers should enjoy the same freedoms as whites, the realities of American race relations made this principle hard to apply in fact. It seemed that history made the claims to universal values, and artistic freedom, luxuries black intellectuals could not afford. For them, Van Vechten's remark that "the squalor of Negro life, the vice of life, offer a wealth of novel, exotic, picturesque material to the artist" could not be taken without reflection. What would be the consequences of drawing on this "wealth" of material for the white perception of blacks, something which was of interest to the intellectual as well as to all other blacks? What was the point of gaining wealth or fame when others of the race, with whom one would always be associated, suffered? On other hand, one could agree that art was not the same as propaganda, although, like Du Bois, some people sometimes seemed to deny any difference, at least in racial matters. These were some of the thoughts that troubled black participants. The very fact that the question could be posed, i.e., "How shall the Negro be portrayed," says much. Race was clearly as much a political issue as a social one. In such a context, Du Bois made the point that all representation was propaganda, that is, it had a political consequence regardless of the intention of the producer. In such a context, artists and writers were intellectuals, producers of representations with political as well as cultural impact and implication.

Alain Locke would soon emerge as the central alternative to Du Bois and the idealist notion of representation. While Du Bois called for the portrayal of blacks as exemplary, with the role of art to be didactic for blacks as well as whites, Locke developed a position within a realist tradition (Hay 1994). For Locke, black art should represent the experience of "real people," whom their audience could identify, if not identify with. This could of course create problems as far as any white audience was concerned, for this sort of realism could easily lend itself to stereotyping. Locke even had a positive attitude toward the musicals that were extremely popular with white audiences, believing, as discussed in chapter 3, that these characterizations not only provided opportunities for black talent, but even offered possible grounds for a new Negro theater, an art theater.[33] By the 1930s, two aesthetic traditions would be codified, one linked to Du Bois and the idea of art as protest, and the other linked to Locke, to realism and modernism.

In *Home to Harlem* (1928), Claude McKay has one of his main characters say "education for Negroes . . . is like our houses. When the whites move out, we move in and take possession of the old dead stuff" (quoted in Tillery 1992:86). The publication of this novel, which was seen by the author as the black answer to Van Vechten's *Nigger Heaven*, caused great controversy in the black media. Du Bois wrote that he became "nauseated" after reading it. As Tillery writes

these controversies revealed sharp divisions within the black community about the nature of the literary movement. Many questions were hotly debated in newspapers, magazines, and private correspondence about the purpose of the Renaissance and who should portray the Negro. But the question that stimulated the most bitter and acrimonious discussion was "How shall the Negro be portrayed?" This issue struck at the heart of one of the fundamental themes of the Renaissance: the relationship between art and society, and most particularly at the problem of defining a writer's obligation – if any – to society.   (Tillery 1992:87)

McKay was accused of pandering to white stereotypes and sensationalism and of having only money in mind. "The most vituperative comment came from fellow West Indian and nationalist Marcus Garvey." In a full-page attack on McKay's novel, he declared:

Our race, within recent years, has developed a new group of writers who have been prostituting their intelligence under the direction of the White man, to bring out and show up the worst traits of our people. Several of these writers are American and West Indian Negroes. They have been writing books, novels and poems, under the advice of White publishers to portray to the world the looseness, laxity and immorality that are peculiar to our group; for the purpose of these publishers circulating the libel against us among the White peoples of the world, is to hold us up to ridicule and contempt and universal prejudice.   (1992:87–88)

Harlem, mecca of the New Negro: from trauma to triumph

Alain Locke's anthology *The New Negro*, published in 1925, is usually cited as the programmatic statement of the Harlem Renaissance, the first attempt to give ideological coherence to the new "state of mind or attitude" and to what were essentially diverse forms of cultural expression.[34] This book actually appeared first in a shorter version as a special issue of *Survey Graphic*, of which Locke was guest editor.[35] The magazine was associated with the progressive movement and the social work profession, with Jane Addams on its board of editors. It was dedicated to producing facts about ethnic populations to counter racist stereotyping in the more popular mass media and to "follow the subtle traces of race growth and interaction through the shifting outline of social organization and by the flickering light of individual achievement" (Editorial Statement "The Gist of it" *Survey Graphic*, 6:6, 1925). After pointing to special issues they had done on the "New Ireland," "New Russia," and "the newly awakened Mexico" the editors wrote, "If the Survey reads the signs aright, such a dramatic flowering of a new race-spirit is taking place close at home – American Negroes, and the stage of that new episode is Harlem." With Locke providing a degree of authenticity, *Survey Graphic* attempted to represent current trends amongst blacks in the United States in an informative and aesthetically pleasing way.

The cover of the Harlem issue featured a drawing of singer Roland Hayes, who along with Paul Robeson – whose drawn portrait appeared inside – helped transpose the spiritual into concert music.[36] The drawing was done by the German-born artist Winhold Reiss, whose portraits filled the issue, and who made many similar portraits of Renaissance figures, including Locke. Reiss was also the teacher of Aaron Douglas, soon to be one of the best-known Renaissance artists.[37] *Survey Graphic* was produced by a mixed group of black and white writers, critics, social scientists, and artists and for a racially varied public. There was no doubt that this was also a commercial and a fund-raising venture. The issue was filled with advertisements, for General Electric, the Metropolitan

Life insurance company, American Telephone and Telegraph, as well as smaller artistic agencies handling black musicians and writers. There were also full page advertisements and statements by the Urban League, the *Crisis*, and the NAACP. The advertisement for the *Crisis* is interesting in that it reveals one target public: under the photo of a young black girl with a white ribbon in her hair, the text asks; "Would you like to know how it feels to be an American Negro? Would you like to know what Negroes are thinking and doing?" After establishing its legitimate right to answer such questions through the credentials of its editor, "W. E. Burghardt Du Bois (Ph.D., Harvard; Berlin; Fellow American Association for the Advancement of Science; Springarn Medalist; Author – "Souls of Black Folk"; "Darkwater"; etc."; "The Crisis A Record of the Darker Races") announces that it is "the most hated, most popular and most widely discussed magazine dealing with questions of race prejudice."

If we were to offer a symbol of what Harlem has come to mean in the short span of twenty years it would be another statue of liberty on the landward side of New York. It stands for a folk-movement which in human significance can be compared only with the pushing back of the western frontier in the first half of the last century, or the waves of immigration which have swept in from overseas in the last half. Numerically far smaller than either of these movements, the volume of migration is such nonetheless that Harlem has become the greatest Negro community the world has known – without counterpart in the South or in Africa. Beyond this, Harlem represents the Negro's latest thrust towards Democracy . . . the special significance that today stamps it as the sign and center of the renaissance of a people, lies however, layers deep under the Harlem that many know but few have begun to understand.   (Locke in *Survey Graphic* 1925:629)

It is Harlem the urban social space that sets forth and represents this New Negro, not a literary movement or a black elite. The latter are merely two expressions of larger social trends like the Great Migration, Locke explains in his editorial. Locke's aim in the selection of articles is to reveal what it is that is lying under the surface of Harlem, what it represents for the race and what this means to white America. Harlem "is – or promises at least to be – a race capital . . . " In clarifying what this means, Locke rejects the view that Harlem is a ghetto or that the Great Migration can be explained by "push factors," like the "boll-weevil" or the Ku Klux Klan, or even "pull" factors like the demand for labor, rather "the wash and rush of this human tide on the beach line of the northern city centers is to be explained primarily in terms of a new vision of opportunity, of social and economic freedom."

What this has to do with cultural trauma and generational effects is revealed in Locke's own contribution "Enter the New Negro": "Each generation," he writes, "will have its creed and that of the present is the belief in the efficacy of collective effort in race cooperation. This deep feeling of race is at present the mainspring of Negro life. It seems to be the outcome of the reaction to proscription and prejudice; an attempt fairly successful on the whole, to convert a defensive into an offensive position, a handicap into an incentive" (*Survey Graphic* 1925: 632–33). Earlier it was proposed that a new generation reconstitutes itself and constructs its identity, what Locke calls its "creed," with the resources provided by past tradition which is modified according to current conditions, which are themselves understood through the framework of tradition. The special circumstance for blacks in the United States is that slavery is the foundation, the primal scene, around which that tradition formed and the failure of emancipation to emancipate created a process of what we have called cultural trauma initiated in the previous generation. This made it necessary to seek alternative responses, race consciousness and the notion of the African American being possible strategies. What Locke identifies as the new race consciousness is a further development in this process. The conditions of the "race" are now, in the urban North, much different than for the previous generation, but there is continuity as well as change. The change relates to the relative strength of the black population, its geographical concentration, education, and access to mass media and other means of communication. The continuity refers to discrimination and prejudice and racial pride as responses. In his study of trauma, Kai Erikson (1978) points to the possibility of turning tragedy into triumph through using the emotional bonds that can result from shared trauma; an ascribed community can become a real community as survivors pull together, using the past to face the future. The racial consciousness Locke speaks of here, which he is also in the business of creating and promoting, can be understood in something of that light. With the traumatic past in common, possibly there can be a more unified charge into the future. This is the hope which both *Survey Graphic* and Locke share and wish to represent. This is something in line with their shared belief in the importance of racial self-consciousness in the contemporary world, which Du Bois had begun to see as early as the turn of the century, but saw more as reaction. At the same time, one can see this as an active attempt to forget, to see the past not as a debilitating burden, but rather as a stepping-off point to a better future. The citation from Zora Neale Hurston which began this chapter is one example of this, framing the past in a progressive, evolutionary narrative of stages of development. One does not need this sort of "theory" in order to do this, simple phrases and constant reminders like, "it's time to move ahead," "let's get past that," may serve just as well. The very phrase "the new Negro" signals an attempt to make a conscious break with the past, not necessarily to forget, for the terms "new" and "Negro" point more towards continuity and renewal, rather than a blank forgetting.

Further along in his introductory essay, Locke represents the poems and literary pieces which make up the volume as comprising a shared vision and collective project whose common roots lie in a transvaluation of the Negro race. In terms that are reminiscent of Marx, which is a strange thing to say regarding a distinguished professor from Howard University, Locke regarded the Harlem Renaissance not as a small literary movement, but rather as the avant garde of a new collective awareness, the leading edge of a positive reformulation of what had previously been a negative demarcation.[38] Harlem, Locke wrote, "is the home of the Negro's 'Zionism' " (Locke 1925:14). The concept of race, like the "New Negro" who bore it, was here endowed with a positive attribution, empowering rather than disempowering, as had been the case up to that point when whites dictated the terms of distinction. As self-attribution, denoting a change from a race in-itself to a race for-itself, if we paraphrase Marx, racial pride would replace self-hate. The Negro was "new" because he could now define himself, taking control over his own self-perception as a step toward control over his own destiny. Again, this view must be seen in light of Locke's view of the importance of racial consciousness in the modern world, first as grounding a collective identity, a racially constituted "people," and secondly as a source and means of self-determination. This is a view which differs from Garvey's nationalism primarily in that it lacks a "nation" in the geopolitical sense. It is cultural nationalism, rather than political nationalism. Locke shares this view with Du Bois, but not with others in his generation loosely connected with the Harlem revival and the new Negro (Hutchinson 1995:62ff.).

Other articles in the Harlem issue of *Survey Graphic* present a more complex picture of the new Negro. Charles Johnson offers a sociological perspective on the black worker in the city, and the effects of the shift from agricultural to industrial labor and to urban living conditions. He reveals how the characteristics of black labor in Chicago and Detroit, where there are large single industries, differ from those of black labor in New York, which has more varied, spread-out, and generally smaller commercial enterprises.[39] As opposed to Detroit, where blacks are concentrated in terms of not only where they live but also where they work, in New York one finds more diffusion of the black population in terms of work and neighborhood. Harlem, Johnson implies, may be a powerful symbol and a magnet in terms of culture and entertainment, but it is not representative of the urban black in the sociological sense. A similar point is made by Elise Johnson McDougald, a Harlem school principal and women's movement activist, in an article entitled "The Double Task, The Struggle of Negro Women for Sex and Racial Emancipation," which has a contemporary ring. Johnson points to the different strata of the urban Negro population and how this has affected both men and women. In terms of work, she distinguishes four types, "a very small leisure group," the "stay-at-home wives and daughters of well-to-do businessmen," "a most active and progressive group" of business and professional women, women in trades and industry and, finally, those in domestic service and causal labor (689). Looking at black women in racial terms, which Johnson appears reluctant to do, she writes,

it is apparent from what has been said, that even in New York City, Negro women are of a race which is free neither economically, socially, nor spiritually. Like women in general, but more particularly like those of other oppressed minorities, the Negro woman has been forced to submit to overpowering conditions. Pressure has been exerted upon her, both from without and within her group. Her emotional and sex life is a reflex of her economic station. The women of the working class will react, emotionally and sexually, similarly to the working-class women of other races. The Negro woman does not maintain any moral standard which may be assigned chiefly to qualities of race, any more than a white woman does. (691)

Such professional, empirically grounded, viewpoints are not inconsistent with Locke's more literary focus or his political strategy of racial promotion and uplift. He would probably gladly endorse the conclusions of both Johnson and McDougald. The latter uses empirically based data to argue against the sexual stereotyping of blacks on the basis of lower-class behaviors, which themselves may or may not be true from an empirical point of view. Such similarity with other groups does not exclude the possibility of distinctive forms of cultural expression or race mission. More troublesome, however, is the article by Melville Herskovits. An anthropologist at Columbia University which borders on Harlem, Herskovits recounts his walk through Harlem looking for racial distinctiveness: "And so I went, and what I found was churches and schools, club-houses and lodge meeting-places, the library and the newspaper offices and the Y.M.C.A. and busy 135th Street and the hospitals and the social service agencies . . . and finally, after a time, it occurred to me that what I was seeing was a community just like any other American community. The same pattern, only a different shade" (Herskovits, *Survey Graphic* 1925:676). There is a short introduction to the article which must have been written by Locke although it is unsigned, which states "looked at in its externals, Negro life, as reflected in Harlem registers a ready – almost a feverishly rapid – assimilation of American patterns, what Mr Herskovits calls 'complete acculturation' . . . social standards may be more or less uniform, but social expressions may be different. Old folkways may not persist, but they may leave a mental trace, subtly recorded in emotional temper and coloring social reactions." Locke then refers the reader to the following article more supportive of his claims, where "Mr. Bercovici tells of finding, by intuition rather than research, something 'unique' in Harlem – back of the external conformity, a race-soul striving for social utterance" (676).

This is a conflict not only between different ways of viewing the New Negro, each of which would imply different strategies of response, but also between different approaches to reality, empirical and intuitive. Locke's position is clear and is tied directly to the idea of continual reflection and the importance of the past for black identity and his belief in the centrality of racial self-determination in modern society. The trauma of slavery may be long past, but its traces are still important for explaining racial uniqueness, even if these are now positive rather than negative. The empirical facts may imply otherwise, but in this instance the facts are wrong.[40]

Representation and memory: high culture and low

The new white interest and the added visibility brought about through con-centrated urban setting combined with the introduction of the mass media to produce new problems of representation. The race man who represented the race to the white world by moving within and outside the veil now competed with images and sounds that represented blacks in a less controllable and less determinate way. Visibility was double-edged, it enhanced racial pride but also stereotyping and misrepresentation of a more intense and anonymous kind. It could also make blacks appear more threatening to whites who had little direct contact or experience with black people. Concern with the nature of respon-sibility had to be adjusted. How did this affect the black writer's and artist's responsibility to "represent" the race in a certain way, or did they enjoy the same freedom of expression that their white counterparts were claiming for them-selves? The notion of race man itself had a number of variants, some of which were turned primarily inward, toward the black community, and others outward toward the white world. Inwardly, the intellectual as race man was a major force in the constitution of this imagined community itself, the intellectual as race man exemplified the community, allowing for its own self-reflection. The in-tellectual, in other words, helped constitute the black community by being a mirror through which it could become aware of itself. In the rural South, the minister had played this role and continued to do so in the urban contexts, both North and South. Now, however, there were secular competitors in the form of journalists, artists and writers, film makers, actors, singers, dancers and so on. Black ministers were rarely known in the white world, outside the circle of their local white counterparts. The same can be said of the journalists who wrote for the black newspapers and magazines. These were rarely read by whites and unknown by the majority of the white population, even those who may have lived in the same neighborhoods. Entertainers and other "personalities" whose performances reached wider audiences through mass media of various sorts were of another type. What was their responsibility, if any, to represent the race? What of these new forms of entertainment and cultural expression them-selves, did they enhance race pride and social standing, quickening acceptance or integration, or were they demeaning in a way that encouraged continued discrimination and racism? Further, what role did these mediated images and performances have regarding the reformation of collective memory and collective identity?

Alain Locke was more open than most of the educated Negro elite to more popular forms of cultural expression. He was sympathetic to the younger generation's openness to all forms of black cultural expression, not only the spirituals, which in the 1920s were being further modified for general consumption by Paul Robeson and Roland Hayes, but also for jazz and the blues, although the latter was a bit harder to accommodate. In a chapter of the *New Negro* entitled "The Negro Spirituals," Locke picked up the argument where Du Bois had left off two decades earlier, "It may not be readily conceded now that the song of the Negro is America's folk-song; but if the Spirituals are what we think them to be, a classic folk expression, then this is their ultimate destiny" (Locke 1925:199). Yet, after acknowledging Du Bois' contribution, Locke went on to criticize the basic categories upon which it was based:

> Interesting and intriguing as was Dr. Du Bois's analysis of their (the spirituals) emotional themes, modern interpretation must break with that mode of analysis, and relate these songs to the folk activities that they motivated ... From this point of view we have essentially four classes, the almost ritualistic prayer songs or pure Spirituals, the freer and more unrestrained evangelical "shouts" or camp-meeting songs ... and the work and labor songs of strictly secular character.   (1925:205)[41]

This characterization widened the understanding of slave songs by including, as it differentiated, more secular forms, or at least those that would develop along secular lines. It was these work and labor songs which would provide a basis for the development of the blues, a form of music that provided entertainment, as well as expressing a changing way of life.

The older generation of Negro leaders continued to discuss "culture" as a strategic medium for recognition and acceptance. Their understanding of the concept was primarily limited to the fine arts, as noted earlier. Most of the older generation, including Du Bois and Garvey, shared the European cultural prejudices of the whites they sought acceptance or distance from: real culture was high culture and serious music was classical music composed and performed by those with formal training or who had at least aspired to it. Those who stood outside this designation were entertainers and untrained players who maintained the oral folk traditions of the rural and slave past. At best, they were tolerated as remnants of a bygone age and at worst as an embarrassment and a constant reminder and reproduction of unfavorable racial stereotypes.

Robert S. Abbott, the editor and founder of *The Chicago Defender*, the black newspaper with the largest circulation in the country, wrote on its pages in the 1930s, "At sometime during our intellectual maturity we are expected to have in our repertoire something more than 'St. James Infirmary', 'Minnie the Moocher', and 'All God's Chillun Have Shoes' . . . We must train ourselves to enjoy formal music, symphony concerts and chamber music. Such music tends to purify the senses and edify the imagination. It helps to refine the feelings by appealing to our higher aesthetic selves" (quoted in Spenser 1993:113). Also writing in the *Defender*, Lucius C. Harper wrote:

While we have failed in these fundamental instances [gleaning political recognition from whites], we have succeeded in winning favor and almost unanimous popularity in our "blues" songs, spirituals, and "jitterbug" accomplishments. Why? . . . Our blues melodies have been made popular because they are different, humorous and silly. The sillier the better. They excite the primitive emotion in man and arouse bestiality. He begins to hum and moan and jump usually when they are put into action. They stir up the emotions and fit in handily with bootleg liquor. They break the serious strain of life and inspire the "on with the dance" philosophy.   (Quoted in 1993:113)

These views reveal an affinity to the evolutionary, progressive narrative identified previously, using it to form a platform upon which to make moral judgments, in a way similar to that which was used to judge literature as a form of representation. The Negro writers preferred by the older generation were those who wrote of protest or, in more popular literature, with a message of moral and economic uplift, similar to those Horatio Alger tales which the ethnic population enjoyed. Like the Southern blues singer of the previous generation, the new generation of artists and writers of the Harlem Renaissance was the first to turn inward, to write about emotions, including the psychological affects of racism, and to write realistically about African American life. These were themes which tended to embarrass the older generation. Cary Wintz writes:

the major problem that confronted blacks [in the 1920s] was no longer how to deal with prejudice but how to achieve racial identity; the major task of black writers was not to expose racial injustice but to uncover, describe, and possibly explain the life of American blacks . . . before the 1920s most black writers avoided detailed and realistic descriptions of the colorful life of lower-class urban blacks because they believed that depicting the squalor and vice of ghetto neighborhoods would only reinforce negative racial stereotypes. They usually described blacks in middle-class settings and emphasized the similarities between white and black society.   (Wintz 1988:67)

For a generation coming to self-awareness in an urban public sphere permeated with mass entertainment this restriction on subject matter appeared oppressive if not ludicrous.

There was thus a gap between the old and the new generation that encompassed the meaning and basis of culture. The new generation was working out its own aesthetic, which included a perspective on slavery and the past, thus reworking collective memory as it forged its identity. In literature and art, this would mean a search for "authenticity" and truth, a turn to realism and modernism and away from the uplifting romanticism of the older generation. It meant the realistic portrayal of Harlem street life in Claude McKay's *Home to Harlem*, a bestseller in 1928, which for Du Bois was an expression of the "debauched" rather than the "talented" tenth, the use of dialect and street slang in the blues-inspired poetry of Langston Hughes, the folk tales and stories collected and transformed by Zora Neale Hurston, and the primitivism and the naive realism in the painting of Palmer Hayden and the bohemian images contained in William H. Johnson's well-known self-portrait (1929). While the best-known artist to emerge out of this generation, Aaron Douglas, combined lyrical images of an idealized past with modernistic forms of expression. For the younger generation, popular entertainers, like the blues singer Bessie Smith, were exemplars of the power of black culture.

In addition to this, the new generation was more open to the "mediated" reproduction of culture than their elders. Participants and supporters were much more open to accepting various forms of cultural expression and reproduction. Radio and recording had begun to play an important role in promoting the fusion of cultural forms and genres, as well as in their dispersion; the new black public sphere embodied and expressed the entry of consumer society into black life. This new generation in the 1920s was more accustomed to listening to music in a mediated form and probably more open to converging styles and transgressions than its elders, even if the basis of experience was still the live music of the clubs and bars of city life. Langston Hughes, one of the central figures of the Harlem Renaissance, had no difficulty fusing jazz and poetry, or writing poems in rural dialect (something which marked the older generation and which the Old Negro elite looked down on), thus mixing the "high-brow" and the "low-brow" genres, as well as musical and literary forms. Nor did he have difficulty taunting those who disagreed:

Let the blare of Negro Jazz bands and the bellowing voice of Bessie Smith singing Blues penetrate the closed ears of the colored near-intellectuals until they listen and perhaps understand . . . We younger Negro artists who create now intend to express our dark-skinned selves without fear or shame.   (Quoted in Floyd 1994:9)

As was said earlier, the slave songs, spirituals, or "sorrow songs," as Du Bois called them, had articulated an imagined community amongst disparate slaves, and in mediated, "cultured" form had done the same for the collective identity of this generation as well as the collective memory of the next. Reconstruction freed black labor and sexuality from white control. The blues expressed one aspect of this freedom. Blues music thus recollected slavery in a different manner from the spirituals, not necessarily because it was more secular then the spirituals or their modern expression in gospel music. Though there is something of a difference here even where both forms mixed the sacred and the secular, the real difference lies in the way each gave voice to the slave past. Blues are also sorrow songs, they express melancholy and are sometimes nostalgic; at the same time, they give expression to the desire for freedom, here of a physical rather than spiritual sort. Central themes in blues music refer to sexual freedom and physical mobility, to traveling, being left behind, and making love, and being made a fool of; all refer to negative as well as positive experiences. There is a fundamental reference point, however, which can be traced back to slavery. It is the memory of slavery, the state of unfreedom with regard to labor and love, which allows the emotional expression of liberation to seep through in the raw tones and words of the blues. As they emerged in the early part of the century, the blues also gave expression to black subjectivity, and they are the first form of black music to be sung primarily in the first person. What is unique about this subjectivity, however, is its being intimately connected to a collectivity, to being black in America ("Why am I so black and blue?") and through this to the shared racial memory of slavery. In this sense, the blues articulated a new imagined community, a community of subjects, of individuals, seen by others, through the veil, as a mass. Cultural trauma was now truly mediated, mediated by the distance of time and mediated through music, mediated through a subject identified as an object. Slavery, a mediated collective memory, was distant but also present.

The blues also represented slavery in gender roles and the sexually linked expectations it articulated. The sexuality it expressed also applied to women. As Angela Y. Davis (1998) reveals, in the 1920s the most popular blues artists were women, like Bessie Smith, referred to by Langston Hughes above, and Ma Rainey, whose "Slave to the Blues" makes one of the very few clear references between the two.

> Blues, please tell me do I have to die a slave?
> Blues, please tell me do I have to die a slave?
> Do you hear me pleadin', you going to take me to my grave.
> (Davis 1998:114)

Sexuality is here identified with slavery as being unfree. The singer is "blue" because her sexuality has become compulsion and unfulfilled. She has become, in other words, a slave to her freedom – a modern twist on these conditions that was only possible with generationally related reflective distance.

Slavery controlled female even more than male sexuality, associating it with breeding. The church continued to impose such control, as did black intellectuals, not so much by associating sexuality with breeding as with morality and social standing. This of course was not limited to blacks or to black women, but since "respectable behavior also represented the race in a more favorable light, it had a racial dimension. While the blues in general expressed the new found freedom of the black working class, blues as written and performed by black women articulated this freedom in a gendered context" (Davis 1998). But the blues expressed both the freedom of sexuality and also the freedom to talk about it. If black women were still oppressed by males, they could see and hear of women who weren't. However reinterpreted and represented, slavery formed a common reference point, a point of departure for a new freedom and a resource for feelings and allusions, a distinctly black experience, slavery from the inside, a cultural resource.

This resource was commercially exploited by some and enjoyed by others as a tool of reflection and catharsis, a memory of the past that made present life more bearable. From W. C. Handy's first composition to Thomas Dorsey's adaptations and arrangements, the blues mediated between Southern and Northern black cultural contexts (Harris 1992), as migrants flooded Northern cities like Chicago and New York. As reflections of the Southern and slave past, the blues were looked upon by concerned church and educational figures in these communities as part of a vernacular culture that needed to be left behind, an embarrassing remnant. At the same time, the blues and other forms of Southern black music transformed the religious services of the very churches where middle-class ministers sought to resocialize the new parishioners into (in their eyes) more sophisticated behavior patterns (Harris 1992). By the second decade of century, a re-evaluation of the blues was in progress, from racial embarrassment to commercial success, and a credit to the race. This would place entertainers like Ma Rainey and Bessie Smith in the role of representatives – exemplars of the race.

In the 1920s, blues became commercially interesting to whites, in conjunction with the cultural radicalism of the Village, under the influence of Freud and "primitivism" from Europe, and its native version, the cult of the Indian and the "authentic" and under its influence, whites flocked to Harlem to slum: it was closer and, as reservation, safer than the West. While it may have been "primitive" to whites, to blacks it meant something else. It cast women and women singers in a new public role. Not only as sexual objects, but, as Angela Davis suggests, as articulators of a new gender as well as racial consciousness. The gender roles rooted in slavery and the Victorian model of women of the black middle class, were hereby challenged in a commercially fed public sphere. It turned black women into stars, but also permitted the public display of new possibilities for black women. This occurred not only in public performance, where a black audience could read sub-texts in the songs and gestures of the singers, but also in mediated form to a much wider, though still largely black audience. Radio was central here.

There were, however, forms of music and types of musicians who made it easier to bridge the gap between these generations. In addition to the jazzy blues of club singers like Bessie Smith, there was a new "jazz" developing which combined larger orchestration with a softer tone and which moved out of the smaller, more marginal clubs and onto the larger, brightly lit and often lily-white, dance floor, and this was an important factor in bridging the generations in interpreting the interface between culture and politics. This was also a reinterpretation that brought to the New Negro a larger and more diverse white audience. While this was not exactly the kind of integration the Old Negroes had in mind, it was at least a step in that direction, or so it might be interpreted. Central to this process of mediating generational (mis)understanding were musicians and "personalities" like "Duke" Ellington.

Raised in Washington, DC's large and education-oriented black middle class, Ellington personified the manners and appearance of "class" which appealed to the Old Negro (Tucker in Floyd 1994). Ellington, as his nickname expressed, was a "duke" in style and bearing, yet he was also "classy" and helped set the tone for the New Negro appropriation of old European as well as urban American modes. The jazz Ellington was instrumental in creating mixed the old and the new, the rural and the urban, in a very creative way which crossed over social as well as musical barriers.

In addition to helping bridge the gap between generations, regions, and races with his sophisticated jazz renditions, Ellington's music was central to the Harlem Renaissance's transvaluation of race consciousness. He was part of the Renaissance generation's interest in black history and was instrumental in transposing this literary interest into musical form. His compositions, *Creole Rhapsody* (1931) and *Symphony in Black* (1934), put the African American heritage to music, and in 1943 his "tone parallel to the history of the American Negro," *Black, Brown and Beige*, opened at New York's prestigious Carnegie Hall (quoted in Floyd 1994:117). For the independent black journalist J.A. Rodgers, writing in Locke's *New Negro* collection, the blues and jazz have common roots in the need for escape from domination and oppression, just as the slave songs, inherent in Afro-American experience:

Jazz isn't music merely, it is a spirit that can express itself in almost anything. The true spirit of jazz is a joyous revolt from convention, custom, authority, boredom, even sorrow – from everything that would confine the soul of man and hinder its riding free on the air. The Negroes who invented it called their songs the "Blues", and they weren't capable of satire or deception. Jazz was the explosive attempt to cast off the blues and be happy, carefree happy, even in the midst of sordidness and sorrow . . . It is the revolt of the emotions against repression.   (In Locke 1925:217)

This would explain both their origin in the Afro-African experience and also the more universal appeal of jazz and blues, and also why, in their less disciplined and sophisticated forms, both were anathema to the respectable and acceptance-seeking talented tenth. Rodgers goes on to write about the great future awaiting jazz in the "sublimated" form offered up by the current jazz orchestras, from Fletcher Henderson to Paul Whiteman, where "there are none of the vulgarities and crudities of the lowly origin or the only too prevalent cheap imitations" (Locke 1925:221). He quotes Serge Koussevitzky, conductor of the Boston Symphony, to the effect that "jazz is an important contribution to modern musical literature. It has epochal significance – it is not superficial, it is fundamental" (1925:221). It should be clear why Rodgers found these comments significant. He makes his position explicit in the closing lines of his essay: "jazz is rejuvenation, a recharging of the batteries of civilization with primitive vigor. It has come to stay, and they are wise, who instead of protesting against it, try to lift and divert it into nobler channels" (1925:224).

Middle-class, educated blacks of this generation tended to view the blues as vulgar and unsophisticated, and thus a cultural detriment. Willie "the Lion" Smith, the greatest of blues piano players, said this was a time when "the average Negro family did not allow the blues, or raggedy music to be played in their homes" (quoted in Lewis 1994:59). David Levering Lewis (1994) questions the sincerity of such appearances, arguing that the same people who forbad such music in their homes in the daytime attended the rent parties and clubs where it was played at night. Such distinctions aimed at keeping up appearances and the duplicity this surely involved were connected, however, with class-related strategies of integration and accommodation. In addition to the ones already mentioned, such strategies had a geographical dimension. Wintz (1988:6) writes, "by the 1920s few black intellectuals still believed that the future of the race lay in the South. As they turned their attention northward and focused their hope on the emerging black communities in the northern cities . . . they also were turning their backs on their southern heritage." The blues was part of that "southern heritage," which was in their eyes rural and thus uneducated in origin, primitive in terms of emotional expression, and unskilled in terms of musical technique. The more blunt stated this straight out, the more subtle, like Du Bois, found aesthetic criteria for dismissing the blues. As mentioned, this was not the view of a younger generation just taking form for whom "blues" and "jazz" meant not "Southern" but black music. The blues they heard were already mediated and modified, an unintended consequence of the Great Migration and the conscious efforts of composers and arrangers like Thomas Dorsey and performers like Ma Rainey and Bessie Smith.

To the extent that blues can be considered secular music, a similar process can be identified in religious music, between spirituals and gospel music.

Black religious music gained respectability amongst a broader segment of the white middle class when the Fisk University Jubilee Singers were formed in 1871. A market was uncovered for concert performances of refined versions of black church music which would have been hard to predict, had not Fisk stumbled upon it. Du Bois was himself moved by their songs and they formed the basis for his own analysis of the sorrow songs. What "refined" meant here was controlled and disciplined performance before an essentially passive public, in the manner of the genteel, white middle class. Taken out of their original collective context and performed in this manner at concerts rather than in church, spirituals became, as Levine notes, more and more like European art music. When Paul Robeson, the Columbia University educated African American singer, performed them in London and on the Broadway stage, the shift in meaning and context of black music became a matter of open controversy among activists and supporters of the Harlem Renaissance.

There were a number of aspects to this controversy. One concerned the solo performance of what was essentially a collective music, another the role of black music in Western civilization and, underlying it all, the more or less hidden class-related strategies we have been discussing. The growing popularity of Negro religious music for a white middle-class concert audience generated debate among black intellectuals not only about its origins, the question of African and rural American roots, but also about their musical elements, which for Locke (1925, 1936) was the source of their distinctiveness. According to Locke, what was unique in the spirituals and essentially all other forms of black music was the way rhythm, harmony, and emotion fused as a form of collective expression. Separate out and emphasize any of these, the harmony, the rhythm, the emotion, or the collective expression, and you are left with a distortion. One such distortion was the solo performance of the spiritual, which, in its focus on the individual performer and the emotional content, removed the music from its collective basis (1925:205ff.). As a remedy, Locke wanted the spiritual and Negro folk music generally to be performed in such a way as to make a "great contribution . . . to the substance and style of contemporary music, both choral and instrumental" (1925:210).

Visualizing the New Negro

Between the publication of the Harlem issue of *Survey Graphic* in March 1925 and in expanded book form later that year a barely visible yet significant change occurred. Aaron Douglas a former Kansas high school teacher was included amongst the contributors. Douglas was in New York studying with W. Reiss and had adopted his mentor's style of realistic illustrative drawing and portraiture.[42]

There were some stylistic differences between the two, as well as differences in age and development, but the main difference was that Douglas was black. The addition of an unknown black artist to this illustrious gathering signaled a new development. It introduced a new player on the field and, more importantly, it signaled a desire on Locke's part to establish a black presence in the visual arts. In the *New Negro*, Locke had posed the following demands regarding the black artist:

the Negro physiognomy must be freshly and objectively conceived on its own patterns if it is ever to be seriously and importantly interpreted . . . we ought and must have a local school of Negro art, a local and racially representative tradition . . . in idiom, technical treatment, and objective social angle, it is a bold iconoclastic break with the current traditions that have grown up about the Negro subject in American art. It is not meant to dictate a style to the young Negro artist, but to point the lesson that contemporary European art has already learned – that any vital artistic expression of the Negro theme and subject in art must break through the stereotypes to a new style, a distinctive fresh technique, and some sort of characteristic idiom.[43]   (Locke 1925)

While the first decades of the twentieth century had witnessed an increasing interest in black literature, including history, and a great increase in literacy and book buying, there were still very few black artists and no tradition of black art to speak of.[44] Locke understood that the visual arts were gaining in significance, that print and music were being complemented and supplemented by visual forms of expression, film and photography were expanding, and there was an increasing demand for visual accompaniment in the print media. Locke also knew there were very few blacks engaged in the arts of this type. He had heard about a young black artist through Reiss and asked to meet him. Later, after being asked to contribute, so that there could be a sample of Negro art as well as literature, Douglas wrote to his fiancée "The book will be some class. It won't cost but five smacks. I'm not making any money, but I'm making a 'rep' and getting up into real class . . . I'll be the only Negro artist with a drawing in it . . . some samplin', eh?" (Cited in Kirsche 1995:92–93).

The closing irony reveals Douglas' self-reflective humor as much as the previous remarks reveal the role of gatekeepers and their significance in the budding Negro art world. With this beginning, Douglas' work spread through the small journals of the black public sphere, his illustrations graced *Opportunity*, the *Crisis*, and the book jackets and inside illustrations of the novels and poems of associated Renaissance writers. His work has come to be identified with the Renaissance, as exemplifying New Negro art, with its African style, its blues and jazz Rhythms, and its historical and narrative focus.

Aaron Douglas was born in Topeka, Kansas in 1899, in a black community with rich roots in the reconstruction and its aftermath. Many of those in Topeka were those "Exodusters" who fled the South to Kansas after the civil war. His path to Harlem was similar to that of his friend Langston Hughes and other, white as well as black, would-be intellectuals. He was middle class, having been raised in a strong and independent black community in the mid-west rather than the South, where the majority of those in the Great Migration came from. In addition, Douglas held a college degree and had served in the Student Army Training Corps, experiences which separated him from the other migrants with whom he shared employment in the various Northern cities he lived in for a short time while working his way to New York. He was 26 years old when he arrived in Harlem in 1925. Harlem were to be only a stopover on the way to Paris, to study art. But friends convinced him New York was the better place for an aspiring young black artist (Kirschke 1995:12). A friend from Kansas working at the National Urban League in New York introduced Douglas to Charles S. Johnson. Given the shortage of black artists and the illustrative needs of the journals he immediately found work designing covers and providing illustrations. His description of Harlem upon first arriving from the mid-west is very much like those provided by Langston Hughes:

My first impression of Harlem was that of an enormous outdoor stage swarming with humanity . . . here life moved across the vast stage without a halt from morning until night and from dusk to dawn. Here one found a kaleidoscope of rapidly changing colors, sounds, movements – rising, falling, swelling, contracting, now hurrying, now dragging along without end, and often without apparent purpose. And yet, beneath the surface of this chaotic incoherent activity one sensed an inner harmony, one felt the presence of a mysterious hand fitting all these disparate elements into a whole to be realized, to be understood only in time and from a great distance.   (Quoted in Kirsche 1995:12)

This is an artist speaking, seeing a flow of color and movement and wanting to give it form and express its meaning. But Douglas was not yet a "black" artist, rather he was an artist who happened to be black. After all, he was on his way to Paris, the mecca of modern art and the center of the European avant garde. He would become a black artist in Harlem, first because of the opportunities afforded him there, but primarily because of the spirit that gripped his generation as exemplified by those he befriended: Langston Hughes, Eric Walrond, Zora Neale Hurston, and Wallace Thurman. It was the older generation that provided the opportunities, they had the resources, the journals, and the contacts. But it was a circle of similarly placed friends that provided the enthusiasm and the emotional support. Interestingly, it was Reiss, the European modernist, who first encouraged him to draw Negro subjects and to draw them without an ideal of beauty in mind.

I have seen Reiss's drawings for the New Negro. They are marvelous. Many colored people don't like Reiss's drawings. We are possessed, you know, with the idea that it is necessary to be white, to be beautiful. Nine out of ten times it is just the reverse. It takes a lot of training or a tremendous effort to down the idea that thin lips and straight nose is the apogee of beauty. But once free you can look back with a sigh of relief and wonder how anyone could be so deluded.   (Quoted in Kirschke 1995:61)

It was to be Douglas' mission to change these internalized ideals of beauty, and the expectations they created amongst blacks, about themselves and about art. Writing to Langston Hughes in 1925, Douglas exalted in the new-found collective mission to represent the new Negro:

Thirty years ago, it was impossible. Twenty years ago we rather felt that the rise of one Negro meant the overshadowing of another. Conflict. Du Bois could not sincerely praise Washington and Washington could not sincerely praise Du Bois. But now, God be blessed, things have changed. We have learned that stars catch fire from stars . . . Langston, we are epoch makers. I laugh, I weep at the same time when I think of the brilliant opportunity, the tremendous responsibility, and magnificent challenge that confronts us. Who chosen people! The Jew lies! It is we, it is we blacks who are chosen . . . We are the echo of a million voices that have travelled over three hundred years, no, three thousand years of laughter, pain, hope. Let's listen to the soul. Let's listen to the soul of black folk, whose hands know toil, whose bodies know pain, whose hearts know passion . . . Let's also make gods, Black gods . . . And then let's laugh at our "Nordic" overlords who sing songs, Negro songs, German songs, Italian songs.   (James Weldon Johnson Collection, Yale University)

Reiss helped in the search for African precedents, especially in Egyptian art and to expand his (Douglas') intellectual horizons, "encouraging him to read books such as Henri Bergson's *Creative Evolution*, which Douglas considered 'the greatest thing I have ever read. It's going to be the bible of my aesthetics from now on" (Kirschke 1995:63).[45] It was this, the linking of African, especially Egyptian, traditions in painting, flat, elongated bodies with faces shown in profile, with an evolutionary modernism, that would crystalize into Douglas' unique style. In this he identified himself as a black artist, rather than an artist who happened to be black. What made the difference was his strong emotional identification with Africa, as the heart of darkness, something that was characteristic of his generation, which drew them to each other and to Harlem, which provided the geographical and cultural context that made it possible. This was an identification, in other words, that linked Douglas as an individual to a group and this group to a wider community. They were links on a chain which now traced its roots beyond slavery to Africa.

Douglas went on to idealize this Africa in his illustrations and drawings, but most especially in the murals he painted on the walls of black colleges, libraries, and other public institutions. Through this he created a black historical space in a modern black context within which a collective identity could be situated in connection with a collective past. Douglas complained about the loss of history amongst black youth: "Present day youth like those of my day is inclined to be impatient of the past. They feel that the past is an obstacle, an impediment, and withal an intolerable burden. The attitude is of course a mistake. The past rather than constituting a burden on our backs or a stone around our necks can become, when properly understood, the hard inner core of life giving bounce and resilience to our efforts which would be otherwise flat and uninteresting" (quoted in Cassidy 1997:123). It was this he sought to change by visualizing history in an easily accessible, yet somber and striking, way which combined aspects of Art Deco, modernism, and American scene painting. Douglas described the Fisk mural in the following way:

the main part of it was designed as a sort of panorama of the development of Black people in this hemisphere, in the new world. I began in Africa. On the one wall I began with African life, the animal life and so on. Then picking it up over the other side, I have the slave situation and then the emancipation and freedom and so on. Then I used Fisk as the model or the pattern of the Fisk University as represented by Jubilee Hall. I put in the sun, the rising sun and across that had a series of graduates from the various faculties of the various sciences and literature and so on as they moved across the walls. But that was the idea from Africa to America to the slave situation, freedom and so on. Now on the other side, on the other walls I used two things: one, the Spiritual as being important or relevant to Negro life and on the other side, the south wall, I used laboring aspects of work. I was thinking labor has been one of the most important aspects of our development.

(Douglas 1994:127)

The underlying narrative theme of these murals, and indeed the space within a space, is the evolutionary, progressive narrative that was exemplified earlier through Zora Neal Hurston. Douglas' vision of black history was progressive and evolutionary; even though the painted African scenes were idyllic, they were also primitive, in the positive sense, where figure and surroundings melded together in a natural, organic totality. These are scenes imagined and observed through the modernist prism: lush, exotic and colorful, although in Douglas' work these colors tended to be muted, more Modigliani than Gauguin. His contemporary images carried traces of this, rhythmical, exotic, colorful primitivism, but he often introduced a political comment, like the threatening hangman's noose that hangs down in the center of a cabaret in "Charleston," an illustration which appeared in Paul Morand's *Black Magic* in 1929. His depictions of slavery, particularly in the murals "An Idyll of the Deep South" and "Slavery Through Reconstruction," both from 1934, are done in the same style, idyllic in their depiction of the slave community, where oppression is amended by collective solidarity, expressed through work, music, and struggle. In all of these, the past is an essential link to the present/future, but nothing to redeem or return to.

Another artist in the visual, plastic arts more influenced by Locke's statement in the *New Negro* was the sculptor/painter Sargent Johnson, whose piece
"Forever Free" (1933) recalls earlier debates concerning how emancipation
should be represented. Born in 1888 in Boston, where he studied at the School
of Fine Arts, Johnson moved to San Francisco in 1915, thus missing the Harlem
aspect of the New Negro Renaissance. His work, however, is clearly influenced
by its ideas.

"Forever Free" depicts a black mother with her two small children engraved
on her skirt, seemingly expressing the close bond between mother and child as
an essential element of freedom. Like Douglas, Johnson cited Egyptian art as
a source of inspiration, something which is apparent in this work. According
to Lizzetta LeFalle-Collins, "the form's self-contained stance approximates
an Egyptian tomb figure, with 'hieroglyphic' toddlers incised at the mother's
sides" (Sargent Johnson 1998:14). The figure was also painted, something which
Johnson also traced to Egyptian art. In explaining this and other works to a
reporter Johnson said:

I aim at producing a strictly Negro Art . . . studying not the culturally mixed Negro of the
cities, but the more primitive slave type as it existed in this country during the period of
slave importation. Very few artists have gone into the history of the Negro in America,
cutting back to the sources and origins of the life of the race in this country. It is the pure
American Negro I am concerned with, aiming to show the natural beauty and dignity
in that characteristic lip, that characteristic hair, bearing and manner . . . And I wish to
show that beauty not so much to the white man as to the Negro himself.

In explaining why he colored his sculpture, Johnson said, "I am concerned with
color not solely as a technical problem, but also as a means of heightening the
racial character of my work. The Negroes are a colorful race. They call for an
art as colorful as it can be made" (cited in LeFalle-Collins, 1998:15).

The Garveyist movement does not seem to have produced artists like Aaron
Douglas and Sargent Johnson to visualize its tragic and redemptive view of the
past. This can be explained partly as a function of the class character of the movement. But in a sense, it did not need artists of this sort. The movement was its own
image. It represented the past through its pageantry and costume, thus denying
the distinction and the need for artistic representation. It was colorful and expressive, and offered redemption through exemplary performance. If one could not
yet return to the glorious African past, one could live it now, as it was imagined to
be, with leaders dressed in military-type uniforms with curved-brim hats, feath-
ers, swords, and gold braids, where everyone had a function and each role a uniform, like the "black cross nurses" in white costumes and headpieces and where
demonstrations took the form of parades. This was an easy target for sarcasm,
and other organizations seldom missed an opportunity to ridicule this aspect of

the UNIA. But it was a powerful device that invited active participation as well as expressing the movement's view of history and the future. The UNIA turned the streets of Harlem into a stage and a canvas, and these ritualized, costumed performances represented the movement for a wide public. Like performance art, however, one had to be there to experience it; thus the public was more limited and more local than that reached by Douglas, but that was perhaps intentional, part of its meaning and purpose. This was a movement of and for newly arrived urban blacks who longed for something else. This something else was quite different from the visions offered by Douglas and his friends and supporters.

In *The Power of Feminist Art*, Norma Broude and Mary Garrard (1994:10) ask "How do we . . . situate the Feminist Art movement on the broader stage, conceptually and historically? Is it merely another phase of avant garde? Or is it not . . . one of those deep-seated shifts of sensibility that alter the whole terrain?" They suggest the latter when they write: "feminism . . . created a new theoretical position and a new aesthetic category – the position of female experience" (1994:11–12). The Harlem Renaissance helped establish "a new aesthetic category" – the position of black experience in the United States. And, like feminist art, in so doing "reduced what had previously been considered universal in art to its actual essence: the position of [white] male experience" (1994). Although this may not have been the intention, and it clearly was not the intention of Du Bois, Locke, and others, who saw the goal more in terms of adding black art to the ranks of world art, this was the achievement of the cultural politics of the Harlem Renaissance and the New Negro movement as a whole. For a new generation of intellectuals, the cultural trauma of rejection solidified a collective resolve to move forward through the past.

5

Memory and representation

> I was theirs and they were mine. I sang the race memory, and we were united in centuries of belonging.   Maya Angelou

The historical context which set the parameters for a reworking of the discursive grounds for black American collective identity was bounded by the Great Depression and the Second World War. These events were significant in that they helped structure the formation of a generational awareness amongst black intellectuals, writers, and artists, and thus condition their attempts to reconfigure the process of identity-formation and collective memory. The new generation re-visioned collective identity through a dialectic of remembering and forgetting within the process of cultural trauma begun earlier, and was structured by the two narrative frameworks set in place by the previous generation. Even as the younger generation struggled to define itself in opposition to the ideas and beliefs of their direct elders, they were bounded by inherited interpretative frames. The mass media, especially film and radio, would play a central role in the contemporary process of collective identity-formation, as would a range of social movements and their organizations.

The two artists mentioned at the end of chapter 4, Aaron Douglas and Sargent Johnson, had something else in common other than their links to the Harlem Renaissance and a vision of the collective past. During the 1930s they benefited from the American government's active intervention to aid in the preservation and representation of American culture. For a time, both artists worked under the auspices of the Federal Arts Project (FAP), part of the Works Progress Association (WPA), and President Roosevelt's New Deal to revive the American economy.[1] The effect was to temporarily lift the cultural production of a few black artists and writers out of the market and patronage and to place it, at least for the moment and partially, in their own hands. The murals Douglas painted at Fisk University and the Harlem branch of the New York Public Library were done with support from that program. Johnson worked in San Francisco first with support from the Harmon Foundation, a privately funded program to encourage African American artists, and then under the FAP. Richard Wright's career as a novelist began with help from the Chicago offices of the WPA, while Chester Himes, who would join Wright in exile in Paris, was employed on the Ohio Writers' Project, a WPA offshoot, and Ralph Ellison, whose novel *Invisible Man* (1953), would be called the "greatest American novel of the second half of the twentieth century," became a writer through the encouragement of Richard Wright and the possibilities provided through the WPA in Chicago, where the painter Archibald Motley Jr. also worked. Zora Neale Hurston continued her ethnographic excursions into the black American South with the help of this program, while Langston Hughes worked in Harlem on WPA projects. Equally significant, a new generation of artists and writers, like the painters Jacob Lawrence and Norman Lewis, would learn the fundamentals of the craft through such federal projects.[2] One of their teachers in the Harlem community art center was the sculptress Augusta Savage, who had returned to the city after years in Europe. It was Savage who created "Lift Every Voice and Sing," a sculpture honoring James Weldon Johnson, for the New York World's Fair in 1939.[3]

The economic depression spurred an interest in reevaluating the "American experience" and in the life of the common man, to which the FAP was one response.[4] Through its auspices Hurston, Sterling Brown (poet, folklorist and professor of English at Howard University), worked with John Lomax and Benjamin Botkin, directors of a special section dealing with American blacks, collected oral histories from former slaves, as well as recording blues music and folk tales.[5] During the 1920s, historians at black colleges throughout the South had collected oral histories and published accounts of the slave experience in the *Journal of Negro History* or privately. These were largely ignored by their white colleagues, who thought them "hopelessly tainted" and "peripheral to what they believed to be slavery's larger meaning in American life – its role in the coming of the Civil War" (Berlin 1998:xiv–xv). Black scholars and scholarship were marginal to mainstream (white) academic discourse, but, as the upgrading of black colleges and universities continued, the power of their voice was increasing, as was their respective professionalization. By the late 1930s, scholars had interviewed and recorded the remembrances of thousands of former slaves, which were later stored at the Library of Congress ready to be rediscovered by future generations.

As part of this reevaluation of slavery and its aftermath, in 1935 W. E. B. Du Bois published a massive study entitled *Black Reconstruction in America 1860–1880*.[6] In addition to providing a new and detailed look at this period from the perspective of an engaged intellectual, the book also revealed how far its author had moved since *The Souls of Black Folk* (1903). Calling the Emancipation Proclamation "easily the most dramatic episode in American history," Du Bois frames his reinterpretation in a Marxian variant of the progressive narrative. It is no longer the sorrow songs of the slaves which ground collective identity, but rather the laboring process, the means of production which through its own dynamic imposes an abstract and functional "class" identity on disparate blacks. Slavery is here analyzed in terms of the need for labor power and is the basis for the making of "the black worker," which is also the title of the book's first chapter. What slavery had done was to transfer a peasant from tribal Africa and transplant him (it is the male worker who is the prime focus of Du Bois' attention) to a similar economic condition in America. What was significant about reconstruction was its role in the modernization of peasants into laborers. Thus the real tragedy of the "counter-revolution of 1876" was devolution, the attempt to return blacks to their previous condition as peasants. "It must be remembered and never forgotten that the civil war in the South which overthrew Reconstruction was a determined effort to reduce black labor as nearly as possible to a condition of unlimited exploitation and build a new class of capitalists on this foundation" (Du Bois [1935] 1973:670). And the significance of consequent events was the return to the path of history, the turning of peasants into workers. As for reconstruction, Du Bois concluded his massive study with this evaluation: "the attempt to make black men American citizens was in a certain sense all a failure, but a splendid failure" (708).[7] Seen from the perspective of the 1930s and the progressive narrative, reconstruction was a mis-step on the road to a new future, as the new social and political context made possible the reevaluation of earlier paths within the process of cultural trauma.

Institutionalizing the progressive narrative

Franklin Roosevelt took office in 1933 largely without the support of black Americans. The overwhelming majority of blacks voted for the Republican candidate in the 1932 presidential election, deferring to the heritage of Abraham Lincoln. Two-thirds of those blacks voting did so against Roosevelt. Up until preparation for war in the early 1940s, the New Deal was interpreted by most American blacks as a "raw deal," just as the NRA (National Recovery Administration), one of its central planks, came to be called everything from "Negro Run Around" to "Negro Removal Act." This can be interpreted as resulting from an inherited skepticism regarding the federal government, a heritage of cultural trauma, and a rational response in the current context. Deborah White (1999:142ff.), for example, provides contemporary voices in both North and

South to reveal how the WPA worked against blacks and most especially black women.

At the same time, the 1932 election reproduced a Congress dominated by Southern Democrats opposed to any alteration of American race relations. All of Roosevelt's initiatives faced close scrutiny, especially concerning race. Programs like the WPA did however provide some benefits to black Americans, especially in the general area of culture.[8] In addition to the support provided for those mentioned above, the WPA provided funding for some of the most popular community arts programs in Northern cities. In Harlem in the 1930s, WPA arts projects

had a dramatic impact on Harlem's cultural scene. They included a Federal Negro theater that employed 350 people, put on sixteen plays, and gave black playwrights, actors, directors, and technicians the best opportunities of their lives; a Federal Writers Project branch that undertook a study of the history of New York blacks and of the cultural, political, and economic life of Harlem's residents; a Harlem Community Art Center which provided studio space for Harlem's best known artists and offered art classes free of charge; a music project that sponsored orchestras, bands and music appreciation classes; a puppet show; and an African dance troupe.   (Naison 1983:204–05)

The Great Depression and these acts of government intervention into economic and social life were thus significant factors shaping a new generation of black intellectuals, just as they influenced the population at large. Aside from the establishment of laws concerning mass public education, the New Deal was the most significant set of government programs to affect the conditions of blacks in America since reconstruction itself. The effects of Roosevelt administration policies, however, were ambiguous, to say the least, calling forth the skepticism noted above. The National Industrial Recovery Act (NIRA) of 1933, for example, aimed at creating national standards for wages and a more standardized national labor market with the possibility of manpower planning, something which in principle was to the benefit of all American workers. Given America's post-reconstruction racial heritage there was no such thing as the all American worker, however, and this notion was just as abstract as Du Bois' black worker. It also established the right of workers to choose their own representatives, which underwrote a wave of union organizing later in the decade and the establishment of the Congress of Industrial Organizations (CIO), as a radical industrial union challenge to more conservative trade-focused unions in the labor movement.[9] This would be beneficial to some of those blacks in or migrating to urban areas and the industrial North, but, again, the benefits were mixed. Because of the need to acquire the approval of Southern states, federal programs were compromised, as well as being under constant threat of reversal. To appease opponents, especially in the South, regional variations were allowed, to the extent of "retaining the legacy of slavery and caste in the Southern labor market by paying blacks lower wages than whites for the same work" (Woodard 1999:35). The NAACP protested to no avail as a dual labor market was created, allowing not only regional variations, but also those based on race. "Virtually everything done by the Agricultural Adjustment Administration (AAA), civil rights spokesmen proclaimed, had made the plight of the black farmer even more desperate" (Sitkoff 1978:53).[10] In another example, the new social security legislation excluded from its jurisdiction farmers and domestics, those agricultural and service occupations where blacks were overly represented. The push–pull of economic depression and the mixed benefits of the New Deal formed the context in which a second wave of black migration swept over America just prior to the Second World War.

New Deal legislation also concerned housing policy, something which had great significance for those blacks migrating North. Cities continued to swell: the percentage of blacks living in cities increased from 22 percent in 1900 to 34 percent in 1920 and reached 40 percent in 1930 (Sitkoff 1978:30). As with the racially structured conditions, dual labor market structured by labor legislation, housing policies helped create what has been called a "second ghetto," where "the federal government facilitated the persistence and extension of high levels of residential segregation" (Woodard 1999:31).[11] From this perspective, the first wave of black migration resulted in a relatively spontaneous ghetto formation in the target urban centers, North as well as South, while the second wave reshaped those ghettoes with the aid of active governmental intervention.[12]

As opposed to the previous decade when the post-war economic boom was accompanied by a wave of political conservatism, high levels of unemployment and ghetto housing conditions proved fertile grounds for renewed political activism. Rates of unemployment in the black ghettoes were often more than double, at times triple, those of whites, with about the same percentage differences for those on public assistance. At the same time, the percentage of black-owned real estate, which in Harlem had been as high as 35 percent in 1929, fell to an estimated 5 percent in 1935 (Naison 1983:31). In the early 1930s, with many blacks out of work and excluded from trade unions, political activity concentrated primarily on local housing and unemployment as fertile areas for organizing workers. An important exception to this general tendency was the long and successful struggle to organize black service workers on the railroads, led by A. Philip Randolph. The Brotherhood of Sleeping Car Porters Union was established in 1925, but did not achieve full bargaining rights until ten years later.[13] A second exception was the campaign mounted in connection with what came to be called the Scottsboro Affair in 1931.[14] Much of this activity formed under the umbrella of the "united front" centered on the American Communist Party, which would expand even more in the mid-1930s into a "popular front."[15]

The Communist Party had undergone a process of "bolshevization" in the mid-1920s, making it more amenable to recruiting American blacks.

In this broad left-wing context, the Harlem Tenants League organized protests which exposed the conditions under which many blacks lived in the city.[16] The organization also pointed the finger at members of the black middle class as being partly responsible. The economic depression had changed the conditions which made the vibrant public sphere that characterized many urban centers in the 1920s, and which had made possible the Harlem Renaissance and other city-centered creative movements. In 1929, the *Daily Worker* declared: "Harlem, in New York, is described as a 'Negro Garden of Eden' by the reactionary parties, the republicans, democrats, and socialists, but the Negro workers know better who are forced by the Jim Crow laws to reside in this overcrowded ghetto, paying 50 percent more rent for dirty, stuffy quarters than white residents, suffering from the regime of brutal police terror, suffering a higher death rate and a tremendous rate of infant mortality" (quoted in Naison 1983:23). The conditions which had underpinned the emergence of the Harlem Renaissance had clearly been altered in the 1930s.[17]

Black urban ghettoes became the centers of community-based organizing not only for the political left, but also for the black church and "middle-class" and "white" organizations, like the NAACP and the Urban League, as well as black nationalist groups.[18] Housing and jobs were the focus here as well. Harlem's ministers, for example, were active in forming groups like the Harlem Citizens' Committee for More and Better Jobs, in 1930, an organization concerned with pressuring local businessmen to hire more blacks. The slogan "Don't Buy Where You Can't Work" was one rallying cry for this community based organizing (Hamilton 1991:90). Central here was the pastor of Harlem's oldest and largest church, the Abyssinian Baptist, Adam Clayton Powell, whose son, Adam Jr., then a college student and aspiring minister, would gain his first taste of public life in such community struggles.[19] The elder Powell was a member of the NAACP's interracial executive board and active in established party politics. His son, who would take over as minister of the Abyssinian in 1937, would be elected to Congress as a Democrat in 1944, a position he held until "unseated" by his fellow Representatives in 1967. According to his biographer, Adam Clayton Powell, Jr. marched with groups of all ideological stripes in the 1930s in support of the community protests for ending job and housing discrimination (Hamilton 1991:92). His father's church was the center of much of this activity.[20]

Conditions were similar in other cities. In Chicago, a city where blacks made up 11 percent of the city's population and 25 percent of its relief cases. the founding convention of the National Unemployed Councils was held in 1930. After a slight upturn in the American economy, in 1932 unemployment for

Chicago blacks remained at 50 percent and 24 percent for whites (Haywood 1978:442ff.).[21] Already in 1929 in Detroit, before the stock market crash and the outbreak of economic depression, newly arrived blacks were on the fringes of industry, and industry itself was on the verge of collapse. To make matters worse in a tense racial climate, blacks were used as strikebreakers, as white workers sought to better their conditions. The emergence of the CIO in the late 1930s proved a turning point for black labor.[22] Led by the United Mine Workers' John L. Lewis, a former vice president of the AFL, and David Dubinsky of the International Ladies Garment Workers Union, the CIO actively sought the support of black workers. This was based as much on pragmatic as ideological grounds. Blacks had been used as strikebreakers in the 1920s, something which not only contributed to racial tension, but also severely undermined union organizing efforts. "To prevent a reoccurrence, the United Mine Workers' campaign in 1933–4 had made an unprecedented effort to gain the backing of Negro leaders, to employ black organizers, to elect Afro-Americans to union offices, and to demand equal pay for equal work for everyone regardless of race" (Sitkoff 1978:179). This "U.M.W. Formula" became one of the guiding principles of the CIO.[23]

Among other things, this program brought a flood of radical white activists into the new movement. Miles Horton, head of the Textile Workers Organizing Committee and founder of the Highlander Folk School, which would be central in civil rights organizing in the 1960s, was one; Walter Ruther, soon to head the United Auto Workers, was another; and Harry Bridges of the Marine Workers Industrial Union was a third. In New York City, even the leadership of the Irish Catholic Transport Workers Union joined in attacking racial discrimination in the labor movement, drawing on the analogy between "the struggle of the oppressed Negro workingmen" and "the Irish workers under the yoke of British imperialism" (Sitkoff 1978:182), recalling the similar connections made by activists in the New Negro movement. This latter example to the contrary, the driving force here was the fact that by the end of the 1930s, when the positive effects of New Deal policies began to become visible, the mass-production industries which these unions were organizing contained large numbers of black workers. Blacks made up 20 percent of steel workers, 25 percent of packinghouse workers. Blacks made up a much lower percentage of auto workers, but these 4 percent were highly concentrated in one factory, making them vital to organizing efforts in the union at large (Sitkoff 1978: 184ff.).

Along with the labor movement, the cooperative movement was an organizing force in the black urban ghettoes. George Schuyler, novelist and publisher of the Harlem-based *Negro National News*, founded the Young Negroes' Cooperative League (YNCL) in 1930.[24] Cooperatives had existed in Harlem earlier, but his was the first to attempt to build a national organization aimed at black youth. In announcing the new organization, Schuyler's leaflet boldly proclaimed:

Twenty-five young men and women from widely separated parts of the United States have now signified their intention of joining with me in putting over this movement which promises to be the most truly revolutionary the Negro race has launched in its entire history. The FIVE YEAR PLAN is destined to emancipate the Negro economically by 1936, or at least better his status as a working man. This is the only movement I know of among Negroes that is actually offering some hope to our bewildered young brothers, sisters, cousins, nephews and nieces who eagerly come out of school with absolutely no hope of employment commensurate with their education. The educational program will revolutionize Negro thinking.   (Quoted in Grant 1998:30)

Echoes of Booker T. Washington's self-help program and the "five-year plans" of the Soviet Union can be heard here. Producer cooperatives had been an active force amongst American farmers since the late nineteenth century, especially in those regions settled by Scandinavian and British immigrants, and had been a part of the self-help strategy adopted by the early labor and populist movements. Consumer cooperatives were a more recent, largely urban-based phenomenon. The YNCL distinguished itself by restricting its membership to the young (18–25) and black. It was affiliated with the Co-Operative League of the USA and local, black-run organizations, like Harlem's Own Cooperative, but sought to steer an independent course. In 1932, the YNCL had a membership of 400 and local organizations in 12 communities (Grant 1998:34).[25] Ella Baker, who would become a major figure in the civil rights movement, was secretary-treasurer of the Harlem council and then national director of the YNCL. During the same period in the 1930s, Baker worked for the NAACP's youth council and later became an assistant to W. E. B. Du Bois. In 1943 she was appointed the NAACP's director of branches by Walter White, revealing the network links that were operative in the black public sphere. Both the labor movement and the NAACP retained links to the cooperative movement throughout the 1930s.[26]

Seen from the perspective of collective identity-formation and social learning, this period of urbanization, combined with the rise of civil protest in which social movements played a central and coordinating role, built upon and expanded already established black protest traditions. A socializing as well as politicizing force, participation in protest campaigns and social movement organizations changed attitudes and taught valuable lessons, especially in the absence of interest from mainstream political parties. For many blacks this was their first experience of interracial activity, working together with whites for a common goal, something not experienced on this scale since abolition. Such activism taught the "importance of mass action, the power of boycotts and disruption, and the organization and discipline necessary for strength" (Sitkoff 1978:188). Also, as in the case of Adam Clayton Powell Jr. and Ella Baker, it prepared a new generation for leadership in the struggles to come. From the perspective of cultural trauma, this period signaled the institutionalization of the progressive narrative.

In connection with this, there was also the professional, academic discourse in which black voices were gaining influence. E. Franklin Frazier, whose study *The Negro Family in Chicago* was published in 1932, continued his influential investigations into the plight of the urban Negro.[27] These studies revealed something other than the renaissance of a New Negro, pointed to an "urban pathology," a "demoralization" and disorganization in black life, a stage, however, which was a necessary part of the "civilization process." Charles Johnson, along with Frazier and other black academics, was involved in sociological investigations in the South and would work with Gunnar Myrdal on *American Dilemma* in the mid-1940s (Myrdal 1944).[28] During the war, blacks would participate as social scientists in studies of the Negro soldier and in radio programs and documentary films aimed at affecting public opinion concerning blacks and their support for the war effort – Sterling Brown and E. Franklin Frazier among them. Diverse as these discourses were, they were bounded by the polarity defined by the progressive narrative on one side and the tragic, redemptive on the other, each of which took the primal scene of slavery as the main point of reference.

This process of social learning and identity-formation amongst a generation in a context of migration and economic depression occurred also in a context where a new intellectual consensus was forming amongst social scientists about the effects of racism. A new concept of race was emerging and the mass media were involved in spreading these ideas throughout the wider society. The rise of fascism in the 1930s provoked a counter-attack by black and white intellectuals and scientists in the United States and elsewhere. Melville Herskovits, an anthropologist and one of the few white contributors to *The New Negro*, attacked the idea that any "pure" race existed. A student of Franz Boas, Herskovits drew on his mentor's idea that all human beings evolved from the same species and that culture "is shaped by experience and historical conditions rather than organic or spiritual 'racial' inheritance" (Hutchinson 1995:70), a tradition which also helped frame Zora Neale Hurston's writings and the progressive narrative itself. At the same time, Herskovits was one of the few social scientists to argue that American blacks "retained African influences in speech patterns, religion, family life, music, food and motor behavior" (Jackson 1990:100). In one study, Herskovits "estimated that at least 80 percent of the Negroes in the United States in 1930 possessed combinations of black, white, and Indian blood."[29] In the scientific mobilization against fascism, Herskovits was joined by a chorus of voices from biologists like Nobel Prize winner Herbert J. Miller who linked the idea of race with "defenders of vested interests . . . Fascists, Hitlerites and reactionaries generally," to popular authors like Ashley Montagu who argued that the concept of race is "meaningless, or rather more accurately such 'meaning as it possesses is false'" (quoted in Sitkoff 1978:191). Science had become a weapon in the struggle against "racism" as well as fascism, which would be waged not only on the battlefields of Europe, but in America itself.

In 1937 the Carnegie Corporation commissioned Swedish social scientist Gunnar Myrdal to lead a study of American race relations.[30] As an outsider, Myrdal made use of "local informants," which included a core of young black social scientists, many of whom came from Howard University in Washington, DC, Ralph Bunche, chair of the political science department and E. Franklin Frazier, chair of the sociology department. By the 1930s, African American social scientists were significant enough in number and reputation to join in what had become a discursive battle around the meaning of race. The nineteenth-century organic notion of race had been bolstered by developments in biology and genetics, which claimed to have uncovered its "natural" basis. This so-called "scientific" notion of race was now being challenged as ideological by more relativistic, historicized notions of cultural differences, and anthropologists, psychologists, and sociologists were central here. Frazier, who published a now-classic study entitled *The Negro Family in the United States* (1939), which expanded on his previous Chicago study, and was elected president of the American Sociological Association in 1948, declared such scientific writings on race "merely rationalizations of the existing racial situation" (Sitkoff 1978:200). This younger generation of black professionals "reacted sharply against the 'race chauvinism' of the older generation of black intellectuals such as Du Bois and (Carter) Woodson and rejected the NAACP's traditional strategy of civil libertarianism and moral appeals to white elites" (Jackson 1990:103). They preferred a professional role to that of partisan intellectual.[31] A new era was emerging in which more positive viewpoints on race relations would dominate the professions in which black professionals and intellectuals would play a major role.[32]

There were other black professionals, of course. Doctors, lawyers, school-teachers, and ministers were the backbone of the traditionally conservative black middle class, or "bourgeoisie" as E. Franklin Frazier (1957) preferred to call them.[33] And there was a growth in black business. According to figures on black-owned businesses gathered by Frazier (1957:54ff.), in 1944 the great majority were retail stores and services with a relatively small cash flow. These were primarily food stores (37 percent) and eating and drinking establishments (40 percent), and the remainder were gas stations, liquor stores, drug stores, and other smaller, family businesses like beauty shops, barber shops, and funeral homes – 80 percent of all black-owned businesses were owner-operated. These establishments were primarily concerned with providing services which white businesses refused to provide. The largest black-owned businesses at this time were those insurance companies which served the growing urban population. In 1945, the National Negro Insurance Association consisted of forty-four companies, with a total income of $42 million (Frazier 1957:59).

The urban migration concentrated the black population as never before, and the market for racially specific professional services also grew. Predominantly black colleges like Howard, Fisk, and Atlanta University provided the education to meet this growing demand. Between 1925, the height of the Harlem Renaissance, and 1939 the number of black Americans holding doctorates increased from 17 to 109 (Banks 1996:93). Already in 1933, Carter Woodson pointed to the need to redirect the education of black professionals. In a collection of speeches published under the provocative title, *The Mis-Education of the Negro*, Woodson pointed out that Negroes had been educated to serve, not to lead. Taking slavery as his point of origin, Woodson articulated Enlightenment ideals concerning intellectual, and collective, maturity: "The Negro finds himself at the close of the third generation from Emancipation. He has been educated in the sense that persons directed in a certain way are more easily controlled . . . The Negro in this state continues as a child" (Woodson 1933:111). To counter this, Woodson called for a new educational program to produce blacks who would be "professionals first, Negroes second" (1933:173). It was this ideal that was now being put into practice. Included in Woodson's book was an Appendix entitled "Much Ado About a Name," where the author addressed the issue of racial naming. He complained about "a participant who recently attended an historical meeting [who] desired to take up the question as to what the race should be called. *Africans*, *Negroes*, *colored people*, or what?" In Enlightenment fashion, Woodson responded that "it does not matter so much what the thing is called as to what the thing is. The Negro would not cease to be what he is by calling him something else; but if he will struggle and make something of himself and contribute to modern culture, the world will learn to look upon him as an American rather than one of the undeveloped element of the population." The progressive narrative clearly framed Woodson's emancipatory ideal.

Mediating race

Throughout the Depression the black press continued to grow and exert its influence. The outbreak of the war stimulated a new wave of migration and a more concentrated as well as prosperous black readership. By 1943, 164 black-oriented newspapers were actively publishing, of these 58 were in cities with 50,000 or more Negro inhabitants. "World War II accelerated the growth and importance of Negro newspapers. During the War four Negro newspapers emerged as the most important organs of opinion among Negroes: the *Pittsburgh Courier* with a weekly circulation of about 270,000, the *Afro-American* (Baltimore, Maryland), with a circulation of about 230,000; the (Chicago) *Defender* with about 160,000; and the *Journal and Guide* (Norfolk, Virginia) with around 78,000" (Frazier 1957:177).

At the same time, popular culture was becoming a more and more important element in articulating and shaping American society, affecting the attitudes and values of its members. On the role of records and their relation to other media, Paul Oliver (1968:2–3) writes

Through the blues record the lower-class Negro was able to hear the voice of his counterpart from a thousand miles away; hear him and feel a bond of sympathy which no other medium could impart at such a personal level. Few radio stations were beaming with Negro audiences in mind when the blues first appeared on record and those that did had small catchment areas . . . Black newspapers were concerned with protest but also improvement and thus did not feature blues, which was seen as part of a past to be rid of, not spread . . . For the Negro in Tuscaloosa, Alabama or Yazoo City, Mississippi, the blues record afforded the first real opportunity of contact through a mass medium with others of his social status . . . Newspapers could only reach the literate, radio stations beamed locally only; records had a greater potential as a communication medium. Their direct impact on the senses made a positive impression and they could be played again and again, repeating their message in every playing.

By the late 1930s and early 1940s, both the US government and black leaders had clearly recognized the centrality of the mass media, and of radio in particular, in negotiating the terms of agreement between the dominant "society" and the "race." In the 1950s television would add another dimension to this process. These developments clearly affected the role and place of the black press in articulating the meaning and bounds of the collective. When the new, more "color-blind" media of radio came into prominence, the black press sought to present the "black" perspective and to represent black "society"; radio appeared more "neutral" and formless. Television would later bring color back into focus. As for "colorless" radio, in the 1930s the controversy over the popular Amos and Andy show transposed black-faced minstrelsy into a new form. By the 1940s and 1950s the black market had grown sufficiently large to attract not only "race" records but also two distinguishable variants, black radio and black-oriented radio (Barlow 1999). While whites had their stereotyped views of blacks reinforced through the antics of two black-faced comedians, blacks could listen to radio broadcasts made in "their" image, at the same time as they sought to influence and re-make those images provided in the dominant media.

The importance of radio increased significantly during the Second World War.[34] Just prior to the outbreak of war, on June 18, 1938, millions of black Americans listened to a live radio broadcast of a boxing match as Joe Louis knocked out the German champion Max Schmeling in the first round. This was seen as a victory for the race and for the United States. It fostered inclusion as it bolstered race pride, drawing on and reinforcing collective memory. Maya Angelou (1969:113) recalls listening to the Joe Louis versus Primo Carnera fight as a child in Arkansas three years earlier, as Carnera had Louis on the ropes "My race groaned. It was our people falling. It was another lynching, yet another Black man hanging on a tree. One more woman ambushed and raped. A Black boy whipped and maimed. It was hounds on the trail of a man running through slimy swamps. It was a white woman slapping her maid for being forgetful . . . If Joe lost we were back in slavery and beyond help."

In the late 1930s, radio broadcasting was dominated by two commercial national networks, NBC and CBS, which had succeeded in convincing the American government that it would uplift American culture with minimum regulation and do it free of charge. The role of radio during the war seemed to indicate the commitment of these networks and of commercial radio to the democratic cause and the "American way of life." After the war, however, a change in political climate followed the outbreak of the cold war with the Soviet Union. This shift also affected the representation of blacks. While prior to and during the war there were attempts to reinterpret the history of the United States to include more blacks, at least in terms of program content if not employment, and to combat the stereotyping that still dominated popular culture, after the war there was a return to normal. No serious discussion of race or race relations could be found on the radio and programming favored and reinforced stereotypes, from Amos and Andy to Aunt Jemima, to Jack Benny's manservant, Rochester, to name some of the most popular. It was only in music programming that blacks appeared in more sympathetic roles, as the voices of Nat King Cole and Billie Holiday, and the music of Duke Ellington, competed for a hearing with the white swing bands and crooners like Frank Sinatra and Bing Crosby and groups like the Andrews Sisters. Holiday's version of "Strange Fruit," recorded in 1939, was an important bearer of the collective memory of racial trauma at a time when popular culture turned more and more to entertainment and escape.[35] As the two national networks effectively seized control of the airwaves in the 1930s and practiced Jim Crow policies regarding the hiring of blacks, local radio provided an alternative.

> Southern trees bear a strange fruit,
> Blood on the leaves and blood at the root,
> Black body swinging in the Southern breeze,
> Strange fruit hanging from the poplar trees.

Pastoral scene of the gallant South,
The bulging eyes and the twisted mouth,
Scent of magnolia sweet and fresh,
And the sudden smell of burning flesh!

Here is a fruit for the crows to pluck,
For the rain to gather, for the wind to suck,
For the sun to rot, for a tree to drop,
Here is a strange and bitter crop.

Although interest in the song and its performance rested primarily in the North, with black intellectuals and sympathetic whites, the mechanically reproduced version spread a counter-image to a wide audience. Even where many radio stations refused to play it, including, one presumes, those local stations aimed at black audiences (Margolick 2000), the very fact of its existence was cause for reflection and recollection.[36]

Local black radio made its first short-lived appearance when the Harlem Broadcasting Company leased air time from a white network in Chicago the same year. Jack Cooper, a theater critic for the Chicago *Defender* and a vaudeville performer, produced a "successful weekly radio show featuring African Americans (The All-Negro Hour, WSBC, Chicago, 1929); pioneering the modern disc jockey format (WSBC, 1931); launching the first successful black radio production company (Jack L. Cooper Presentations, 1932); and creating the first successful black advertising firm specializing in radio (Jack L. Cooper Advertising Company, 1937)" (Barlow 1999:51). Cooper went on to expand his media empire and retire a rich man. In this as a successful black businessman he served as a role model, and also developed a style of black broadcasting that others would emulate. On the air, Cooper spoke in a clear and distinctive way which emulated the popular and successful white network broadcasters. His trained and sophisticated voice gave expression to the successful Negro, one who had assimilated into the white mainstream, just as his business acumen represented and expressed success. Besides serving as an exemplary role model, Cooper's musical programming expressed the promise of the progressive narrative, favoring mainstream jazz and swing.

In 1930, 14.4 percent of black urban households and 0.03 percent of rural households owned a radio; a small but clearly concentrated percentage, which in that sense helped to localize the urban black community. The first radio news program was sponsored by the Pittsburgh *Courier*, which along with the Chicago *Defender* was one of two black newspapers with a national distribution.[37] The depression severely limited opportunities to produce local, independent black radio and it was not until 1944 when the book, *New World a-Coming* by the black journalist Roi Ottley, was adapted for radio on WMCA, a local New York station, that black radio returned to Harlem. With Duke Ellington providing the theme song, and Ottley the scripts, and with Canada Lee, one of the few black radio actors beside Paul Robeson to survive network hiring policies, New World a-Coming broadcast a weekly drama and documentary program for thirteen years, between 1944–57. These drama-documentaries included "Harlem: Anatomy of a Ghetto," "Hot Spot U.S.A.," which looked at housing discrimination, "Apartheid in South Africa," and "The Story of Negro Music," which linked together African music, and the slave songs with modern variants like blues and jazz. This evolutionary, progressive perspective on black music was now generally accepted by black intellectuals, as Alain Locke had articulated in his *The Negro and His Music* (1936), a book written in popular format and published in conjunction with the Associates in Folk Education. In these programs, which took their lead from the docudramas broadcast earlier as part of the war effort, black history was restaged and reconstituted for radio consumption. Slavery and the past were reinterpreted though a voice-over dramatic format within the framework of a progressive narrative, which also pointed toward the future. In 1946, just after the end of the war, New World a-Coming broadcast a program called "The Story of the Vermont Experiment," concerning a church program led by Harlem minister Adam Clayton Powell, which placed black youths from Harlem with Vermont white families. In a voice-over ending the radio program, Canada Lee exclaimed, "The Vermont Experiment is a significant development in the progress of good race relations in this country, a milestone on the road to a New World a-Coming!" (Barlow 1999:79).

Two other programs produced on New World a-Coming deserve mention in this articulation of the progressive narrative through confronting stereotypes born out of slavery. In March, 1947 the theme concerned "The Mammy Legend," a program which uncovered and discussed the stereotyping of black women which had begun during slavery and which was still being effectively reproduced. The program began with Canada Lee saying "If there is one thing that irritates Negroes today it is the Mammy legend, often romanticized in song and story. Yes, of course the Mammy did exist once. For at least two centuries she was an institution of the Old South. But today that Mammy has become largely a fiction, a museum piece of slavery days. Yes, it is true that Mammy doesn't live anymore. Yet you still hear people say . . . " (quoted in Barlow 1999:81). Here the concern was with how the remnants and traces of slavery were determining white readings and expectations of black behavior and how blacks might themselves be affected in their contemporary behavior. This is a theme that has continued to be discussed, often heatedly, and we will be returning to it.

The second program was a "Tribute to Canada Lee," the man whose voice had signified black dignity and determination over the airwaves since the 1930s.

This particular program was part of larger series focusing on achievement, this time that of African Americans, and it was offered to network affiliates, thus reaching beyond the local Harlem radio public. Black music from W. C. Handy and Duke Ellington and the tap dancing of Bill "Bojangles" Robinson was also featured.[38] Richard Wright put in an appearance, after a reading from "Native Son," which was then being performed on the Broadway stage. For our purposes, however, it is the keynote address by Paul Robeson that is the most significant. To complement the reading, Robeson sang a song he had written, which he said was in the spirit of Wright's novel. The song was called "Jim Crow."

> Lincoln set the Negro free
> Why is he still in slavery?
> Why is he still in slavery?
> Jim Crow
>
> This is the land we call our own
> Why does the Negro ride alone?
> Why does the Negro ride alone?
> Jim Crow
>
> When it's time to go to the polls
> Why does the Negro stay at home?
> Why does the Negro stay at home?
> Jim Crow
>
> Freedom for all it is said
> Freedom to suffer until he's dead
> Freedom to suffer until he's dead
> Jim Crow
>
> If we believe in liberty
> Let's put an end to slavery
> Let's put an end to slavery
> From Jim Crow

(Paul Robeson, Feb. 10, 1945, quoted in Barlow 1999:82–83)

We cannot know how many listeners heard this song, but we can speculate that it was more than the radio-owning black community in Harlem. Most likely, however, the audience was primarily black, with a scattering of sympathetic whites. In any case, Robeson's song broadcast over the radio waves probably expressed the feelings of many blacks at the time and reminded them of the links between the past and the present, as well as their collective responsibility.

Local, network-affiliated Chicago radio broadcast a weekly docudrama series entitled "Destination Freedom" between 1948 and 1950. Its creator was also a journalist turned radio writer, Richard Durham, who had previously worked for the Chicago *Defender* and *Ebony* (Barlow 1999:83).[39] This series focused on representations and dramatizations of the black struggle for civil rights in

American history, including slavery, Jim Crow, voting rights, and racial discrimination in employment and housing. Ida B. Wells' campaign against lynching was the subject of one program. One program, "Searcher for History," covered the life and contributions of W. E. B. Du Bois and another, "Recorder of History," focused on Carter G. Woodson, who "worked to uncover the treasures of Negro life so that America's goal of equality and justice may be strengthened by the knowledge of their struggle for freedom in the past" (Barlow 1999:84–85). Here the past was presented as a pathway and an educational stepping stone to a better future; the progressive narrative of inclusion, that is.

With hindsight, one can see how Durham's dramatizations prefigured and prepared the ground for later social movements in their portrayal of American history through the lens of the struggle for inclusion by African Americans, that is, those who adhered to this collective identity. In this, Durham went even further, in that he characterized this struggle not as that of a particular group seeking inclusion, but rather as the struggle of a "universal people," whose own struggles united them with the "downtrodden" of the world. As Durham expressed it:

> It so happens that there have come to be created in America a people whose emotional fabrics and repeated experiences bring them very close to becoming in this Atomic Age the universal people. While some leaders may have difficulty identifying their lives with this mainstream – a Negro personality undergoing the experience of segregation and sharecropping – it is instantly recognizable to the 500,000,000 Chinese people who have undergone the same experience under imperialism for three hundred years. A Negro character confused by the caste system in the land of his birth is instantly identifiable to the 450,000,000 Indians in Asia and the 150,000,000 Africans in Africa, with Burmese Malayans, with the Jewish people whose identical struggle has led to the creation of a new nation, and with millions of Europeans and white Americans who also want to uproot poverty and prejudice.   (quoted in Barlow 1999:87)

These programs were not characteristic of those listened to by the radio public in the United States. They did, however, offer local black communities, primarily in urban areas, a chance to hear another side of American history and their place in it. When the cold war reached its peak in the early 1950s, however, even this voice was quieted as radio turned to the right and to another format, partly, also, in response to television's appropriation of the representation of history and the dramatization of everyday life. What this radio programming most probably did, however, was express the longings of many black Americans in the post-war period and in that sense helped prepare the ground for the civil rights struggles, which began in the South a decade later, a movement which articulated the aspirations that constituted what we have been calling the progressive narrative.

The importance of radio as a commercial medium was discovered in the 1920s, but its use as a mobilizing tool and community-building force was only fully exploited in the late 1930s and early 1940s. In preparation for war, the American government sponsored programs on commercial national radio networks with the aim of representing the United States as a country of immigrants from diverse backgrounds, yet "Americans All," as the title of one such program from the late 1930s proclaimed. In this representation of the nation, each immigrant group was said to have made a unique contribution to the building of a national heritage, called "American culture," which reflected as it absorbed this diversity. Here, blacks were considered to be immigrants, even if involuntary ones, who contributed equally with other groups to this dynamic and diverse heritage. A series called "Freedom's People," dedicated, as its announcer declared, "to – and conceived by the American Negro," was broadcast in the early 1940s. The program opened with the following statement:

From the old world they came – high with hopes and strong. To America they brought this hope and strength and founded a nation of splendid freedoms! But this is not their story. This is the story of those who did not come but were taken! The story of those who lost their freedom when they came upon our shores and for years they tilled our soil, gathered our crops, and made the land good. Some won liberty – others waited. Then freedom came to all – a liberty well deserved, a liberty triumphant. Yes, this is the story of the American Negro – 13 million citizens of the United States.
(Quoted in Barbara Savage 1999:75)

Savage (1999) describes the process through which this program and others like it were produced for radio, and, especially, how and in what way they can be said to be "conceived by the American Negro." Key actors, in both senses of the term, were indeed black Americans, including Ambrose Calvier, an educator with an interest in the mass media, Alain Locke, W. E. B. Du Bois, Charles S. Johnson and Paul Robeson, veterans of the Harlem Renaissance. In the series. "Freedom's People," Calvier gathered political support, including that of Franklin and Eleanor Roosevelt, solicited the participation of black entertainers like Robeson and the editorial and critical skills of Locke and Du Bois. Here the federal government's interest in mobilizing the nation coincided with the interest of these black leaders concerned with affecting the image of black Americans and advancing the cause for integration. The programs met with apparent success, even in the South, where radio network executives had feared a racial backlash (Savage 1999:83).

With this interest from above, the old issue of how blacks should be represented in the media was given new meaning. Blacks were asked to participate and contribute in the "national interest," which meant not only recognition but also a degree of bargaining power. How then was the Negro to be represented, and how was this desired image to be transmitted over the air waves?

The question of what a "Negro" voice was and how it should sound had to be addressed, as much as the literal content of the script. The form of delivery and voice was as much a part of the representation of blacks as the content. In radio, voice performance, if not everything, was at least as central as text. This raised again the issue of dialect and the memory and meaning of the slave heritage. Framed by the progressive narrative, blackness should be represented as cultivated, but still "black," that is, similar to yet different from "white." In "Americans All," the radio network had included a performance by a popular black singer, who some black leaders thought sounded like a black-faced minstrel, and in a trial performance a black actor was thought to sound "too white" over the radio. For Locke, "one of the most important ways to get over to the public that the program is Negro is to have a narrator whose voice is rich . . . I do not mean a cornfield voice. [rather] . . . a characteristically Negro voice" (Savage 1999:74). What exactly this meant was debated by those involved in producing the program, but it was clear to all that a voice that recalled the stereotypes of minstrelsy and other forms of popular entertainment was not acceptable. What was acceptable was a voice which expressed strength of conviction and character, a willingness to serve (the nation), but not to bow.

Reconstructing blacks as immigrants was tactically suitable to those black leaders who favored integration as a political strategy. It also provided a way of reinterpreting the slave past, as an unwanted, but necessary step toward acceptance in a modern, American society. This is something different from the evolutionary perspective which viewed the past as a necessary step toward the future without discussing agency or will. In this reconstructed form of the progressive narrative, blacks were ascribed agency, they had been taken involuntarily from their own civilization – one not judged as better or worse, primitive or civilized – and removed to another. Taking this as a *fait accompli*, rather than a necessary step, did not mean that nothing had been gained or that blacks had not contributed to the development of the country which they had adopted but which had not adopted them. On the contrary, as it was expressed through these radio programs, American culture would have been very different were it not for the contribution of blacks, as slaves and as restricted citizens. The narrative was progressive but no longer evolutionary as it pointed to the changing relations between the group and the surrounding society as a significant factor in development.

Black-oriented radio

After the Second World War a quite different type of radio format, the disk jockey and pop music program, presented an alternative way of interpreting the grounds of inclusion. If Jack Cooper's style of broadcasting in the 1930s can be characterized as black-oriented (as opposed to black-owned) radio, the fast-talking, rhyming disk jockeys who became prominent after the Second World War can be said to characterize black radio. This was a type of radio where the racial make-up of the ownership was less important than the style and content of the performance. The key figure here was also a Chicago broadcaster, Al Benson (Barlow 1999:98ff.). Benson was born in Jackson, Mississippi as Arthur Leaner in 1910 and had moved to Chicago in the 1930s. He broke into radio as a store-front preacher in 1945 only to be transformed into "the Ole Swingmaster" later that year with an hourly program of what would soon be dubbed urban blues or rhythm and blues. Like the disk jockeys who would play it over the air, guitar-based blues music evolved as it accompanied migrants from the South to the North. In order to be heard in the noisy clubs in Chicago and other cities, blues performers like Muddy Waters began using amplification and back-up musicians. The beat of their music also adapted itself to the pace of urban life. It was this louder and upbeat blues that became rhythm and blues and that was broadcast, along with gospel, by black disk jockeys like Al Benson. While Jack Cooper cultivated a soft-sophisticated style of presentation, Benson, who was an educated man, talked in a style he called "native talk," the people's vernacular, as he identified it. In 1948 Benson was voted the most popular disk jockey in Chicago in a poll conducted by the white *Chicago Tribune* and in 1949 he was "elected" as "Mayor of Bronzeville," the local name for the black community, by readers of the Chicago *Defender*. At the time, Benson was on the air 20 hours a week (Barlow 1999:99). Benson gave voice to changes which were occurring in the black community in this early post-war period. During the war another 1 million blacks migrated to Northern cities, Chicago experienced an increase of 100,000 in its black population, Los Angeles 75,000, New York 70,000, and Detroit 50,000. There was also a marked increase in the wages earned by this new urban black working class. This created opportunities for increased consumption and changing styles and tastes in dance, music, clothing, and language. Benson gave voice to these developments and at least to some of the possibilities they entailed. A new urban, hip black style was emerging alongside the professional, assimilationist style of the middle class. It voiced and performed "blackness" in a different way, one that could be "progressive" and "inclusionist," but which maintained a cultural distinctiveness at the same time.

These changes did not go unnoticed by marketing representatives. As early as 1949, *Sponsor*, the radio and television advertisers' trade magazine, featured an article entitled "The Forgotten 15,000,000: Ten Million a Year Negro Market is Largely Ignored by National Advertisers' (Barlow 1999:125). This announced to the largely white trade what many blacks already knew. Some things at least had changed. For one thing, black radio ownership had grown significantly since the 1930s, to the extent that 90 percent of urban black households and 70 percent of rural black households owned a radio. According to the survey, 60 percent of the African American population now lived in urban areas and the "annual income of the nation's black population had reached 10 billion, a significant rise from pre-World War II levels" (Barlow 1999:125). When *Sponsor* made a follow-up study in 1952, they raised that level to 15 billion and found that the median income of the black workforce had increased 192 percent during the 1940s – 50 percent higher than the white workforce in the same period (figures cited in Barlow 1999:127). In response to these changes, black-oriented radio stations, some of them black-owned, some, like the giant WDIA in Memphis, not, developed a style of radio presentation which suited, in both meanings of the term, this new black audience. This was after all commercial radio and *Sponsor*'s editors chided white advertisers for ignoring this explosive consumer market.

It was not only the Northern cities that were undergoing this transformation. As the last example indicates, the South was also experiencing a wave of urban growth and an outburst of black-oriented radio programming. Just as Northern industrial cities had done, Southern commercial centers had prospered and grown during the war. The South was a center of military operations and training and the needs of war created vast demands for cotton, clothing, and other products produced by Southern industry. The economy boomed and the cities expanded and the mix of the racial population altered. By the end of the war, the black population of Memphis was on the way to becoming 40 percent, Atlanta about the same, Charleston, with its large-scale military operations, had a black population of 48 percent. In the latter city a poll by a local radio station conducted in 1949 found that "96 percent of the black households in the city had at least one radio set, whereas only 33 percent owned telephones . . . [blacks] listened to the radio seven and a half hours a day – three more than their white counterparts" (Barlow 1999:126). The difference between radio and telephone ownership was pointed to as an explanation for why the figures for blacks listeners were relatively low in national surveys, since these were conducted by telephone. By 1950, these three cities had successful black-oriented commercial radio stations, with music and public service programming.

At a time when blacks were largely excluded from political participation and representation, especially in the South, radio "personalities" played a major role in the black community, comparable even to ministers. One well-known black female disk jockey in the 1950s, Martha Jean "the Queen" Steinberg explained:

We were the majors back then. At that particular time, you have to understand that you didn't have any black politicians, no black judges, very few black lawyers . . . you didn't have so-called black leaders. So we were the ones who spoke out. We were considered the mayors of the cities . . . We were shaping the minds and hearts of the people, and we did a good job. We encouraged them to go to school, to get degrees, to be educated. Told them about racial pride. We talked to young girls about not having babies. We kept our communities intact.   (Quoted in Barlow 1999:134)

Black-oriented radio in other words fostered inclusion in a multiple sense. It promoted consumer culture and helped integrate blacks into local and national commercial markets; it also, as the citation above reveals, articulated other basic values of American society concerning the importance of education and sexual discipline. At the same time, this new style black radio promoted a sense of distinctiveness, a racial pride which was inclusionary yet not assimilationist.

Barlow's account of the shifts in style and content of black radio, to which we will have occasion to return, can be added to by describing what was occurring on the other side of the racial veil. Even with the hardening attitudes that accompanied the cold war in the early 1950s, or perhaps even because of them, a new form of popular music was being shaped by and for the post-war generation. While black radio was broadcasting rhythm and blues and playing "race" records in a new, fast paced, smooth talking, programming format, young white ears were tuning in. One of the characteristics of radio, as opposed to live music performance, is that no one knows exactly who is listening. Radio waves are oblivious to racial boundaries and neighborhood segregation. Dissatisfied with the music played over mainstream and network radio, young urban whites began tuning in to black radio stations in increasing numbers in the early 1950s. In his study of this slow but dramatic audience-driven shift in race-related musical tastes, Brian Ward (1998) reveals how record companies and radio stations were forced to redirect their programs and products to meet a growing demand for a more integrated form of recorded music and radio programming. It was record producers who had created the notion of "race" records, that idea that consumer-defined musical taste was directly linked to skin color. Contrary to the assumption in the industry, at least since the 1930s, there developed a substantial market for black music amongst whites.[40] As this "cross-over" audience grew, it forced the recording industry to change its assumptions and its products. On this audience-driven wave a new, integrated form of popular music was created, a development with important consequences for both cultural tastes and political attitudes.

In the early 1950s, from about 1953 onwards, the music of cross-over stars such as Sam Cooke, a former gospel singer from Chicago by way of Mississippi, Ray Charles, Jackie Wilson, Fats Domino, as well as "doo wop" groups which covered a wide range from "race" to "pop" (the Paragons and the Jesters, say, to the Flamingos and the Platters), and the most popular of all, Chuck Berry, and of course the white cross-over, Elvis Presley, who was almost as popular with black radio audiences as he was with white, dominated the airwaves and the live concerts. The audience was young and while it did not eliminate them, it bridged racial, class, and urban/rural lines. While it may not be possible to make any strong claims in this regard, it is not unreasonable to suggest that this teen-aged audience, which had in common a taste for a type of music in which racial lines were blurred, was more predisposed than their elders to accept more integrated forms of social interaction. Changes in taste do not in themselves represent social change and cultural trends and fads are not social movements, but when the civil rights movement did emerge as a public force in the late 1950s, this was one segment of the American population which was well prepared and even predisposed to accept its claims, if not entirely embrace them. Popular music, in other words, was an element in the progressive narrative and radio played an unexpected and probably unintended role in its articulation.

In addition to this more preparatory, dispositional role, black disk jockeys, North and South, played an active role in mobilizing support for the civil rights movement, once begun. As Steinberg herself pointed out, in the absence of legitimate political representatives, radio personalities helped connect and articulate an imagined black community. While studies of the civil rights movement have rightly pointed to the role of the church, as a center of local black communities in the South, and of course to the central role of ministers, relatively little attention has been given to local radio. Martha Jean Steinberg takes a different view:

If it hadn't been for black radio, Martin Luther King would not have gotten off the ground in my estimation because we were the first to talk about it . . . It was new, it was exciting. Everybody became curious. We talked like the African drummers used to talk years ago. We talked in code – "Yes Mammy and Daddy, get on down!" We talked about what to do, but some people didn't know what we were talking about . . . We were the cause of the civil rights movement . . . after it started moving about the nation we let everybody know what was going on, because no one would interview Martin Luther King. No one knew Jesse Jackson. Nobody interviewed these preachers, so we did that ourselves, on a low key basis, but we did.   (Quoted in Barlow 1999:210)

Steinberg can be accused possibly of exaggerating her own role and that of her colleagues, but their role seems hard to ignore. While Steinberg worked in Detroit during the movement years, her Southern colleagues supported her point of view and complement it. Atlanta DJ "Jockey" Jack Gibson recalls:

Back then, the SCLC (Southern Christian Leadership Council) had their offices right below our studios. If Dr. King wanted to make an announcement, he'd take a broomstick and hit on the ceiling. That was the signal that somebody downstairs wanted to make an announcement, and we knew by the taps which party it was. So when I'd hear his tap, if I was on the air, I'd say – "We interrupt this program for another message from the president of the SCLC, Martin Luther King Jr. And now here is Dr. King!" But while I was saying it, I'd let the microphone out the window, and it would come down to him, and he'd pull the microphone in from his window, and he'd make his announcement. And then I'd say, as I was pulling the microphone back up – "We've just heard another message from Martin Luther King Jr, and now, on with the programming!

(Quoted in Barlow 1999:208–09)

Radio helped make the civil rights movement and its leaders public, in both the local and national sense. Just as television lifted the movement, its programs, its confrontations, and its leaders, into the national imagination, through visual imagery and voice, radio worked in a more mundane way to give voice to the movement, as it linked and connected organization and public. It gave the movement publicity, not simply in the sense of advertising; radio helped make the movement public by offering it a voice and giving presence. In the 1950s this meant commercial radio, not public or listener-supported radio. Radio presence was financed through selling air time to advertisers. In this sense it was a means of inclusion in that it helped to articulate a community and a movement. The medium was, at least in part, the message. Radio included blacks into the wider American consumer culture as it helped constitute the community and the movement. This would have been the case had the movement in question been a separatist or nationalist movement.

Television helped as well. In 1966, when recounting the impact of the civil rights movement on her life, Alice Walker wrote:

Six years ago, after half-heartedly watching my mother's soap operas and wondering whether there wasn't something more to be asked of life, the Civil Rights Movement came into my life. Like a good omen for the future, the face of Dr. Martin Luther King, Jr, was the first black face I saw on our new television screen. And, as in a fairy tale, my soul was stirred by the meaning for me of his mission . . . and I fell in love with the sober and determined face of the Movement. The singing of "We Shall Overcome" . . . rang for the first time in my ears.

(Walker 1983:124)

Negotiating the meaning of migration

At the same time as the progressive narrative was being reconstructed with government support, sub-narratives concerning the meaning and relation between past and the future were being carried and negotiated through the mass media. The Great Migration was now in its second great wave and the motivation that drove it was being discussed and represented through various media, by blacks and whites, and by professionals and lay persons. In chapter 4 the blues were discussed in relation to the themes of personal freedom and individuality.

In American mythology, mobility is often associated with freedom, with the possibility to begin anew. Additionally, both freedom and mobility are often associated with individual and collective "progress." Together or separately, freedom and mobility can have several sides as well as meanings. They can imply "nothing left to lose," as much as the opportunity to move about and do as one pleases. In a new study of the "migration narrative," Farah Griffin (1995) reveals how blues lyrics also carried messages telling how the fear of lynching and other forms of violent repression motivated people to leave the South.

> Boll Weevil in the Cotton
> Cut worm in the corn.
> Devil in the White man.
> I'm good and gone.

This blues verse, "the closest one gets to the threat of violence as a catalyst to migration," recorded in song (Griffin 1995:22), blends economic and social reasons as explanations for leaving the South. It also mixes the two sides of freedom mentioned above: since there is nothing left to stay for, and it is dangerous as well, one might as well exercise the freedom to leave. Moving North or East, which was for the young writers and artists of the Harlem Renaissance, as for many others of that generation as well, taken as a progressive and voluntary step, may not have seemed so to others. This did not necessarily have anything to do with the "pathology" of urban life, as characterized by E. Franklin Frazier and other social scientists, but it certainly was not the same kind of agency that drew middle-class blacks to the city.[41] Here the South and the past could be perceived as something to get away from, if not forget, and mobility was a less than voluntary step into an uncertain future. The many poor whites leaving the South at this time may also have experienced a similar ambiguity about leaving to take jobs in Northern and Western cities. The urban population of the United States was, in general, rising rapidly. Whites and blacks migrating to urban areas shared economic motivations and faced prejudiced opinions and stereotyping from the more sophisticated and educated "settlers" of previous generations. In this sense they were "migrants all," but still not equal for all that. To judge by their music and their tendency to return, poor Southern whites viewed the South with nostalgia, as a lost home, which still colored their identity and with which they still identified.[42] Among migrating blacks of this generation one can find little trace of nostalgia, rather there are links to the tragic, redemptive narrative which one finds in the forms of black nationalism which emerged during the period. In this migration narrative the South, the land and the way of life left behind, replaces slavery as the focal point of the past, and thus of memory. Here there is no returning, however, and thus no redemption.[43]

Like Billie Holliday's "Strange Fruit" (1939), where black bodies swing from trees in the Southern breeze, the picture of the South as a threatening place replete with memories of the slave past was expressed through literature and documentary photography in the 1930s, perhaps most clearly in the short stories and novels of Richard Wright. Born in 1908 into a sharecropper's family on a plantation in Roxie, Mississippi, Wright knew about what he wrote. All four of his grandparents were slaves and as a child he had been forced to move when local whites murdered his uncle in order to take over his business (a chronology of Wright's life can be found in Wright 1991). Educated in segregated public schools in Mississippi and Tennessee, Wright published his first short story in 1924 in the Jackson, Mississippi *Southern Register*, a black weekly. In 1927 he migrated to Chicago with his aunt whose husband had been murdered. Through a fellow-worker at a Chicago post office, Wright joined a newly organized John Reed Club, a literary organization sponsored by the American Communist Party. Along with the literary magazines and books he was able to coerce out of white librarians in Mississippi, Wright's major literary influences came from the black education institutions in existence since the civil war and the left-wing public sphere.

In the 1930s the latter revolved around a core of political organizations, including the Communist Party, under the umbrella of a popular front. In these circles, Wright found encouragement and great sympathy – as a black man, a worker, and a Southern migrant he exemplified the utopian ideals of the movement. The newspapers and journals of the radical left offered an outlet for his writing, and his emotions as well as his memory. In the mid-1930s, Wright joined the Communist Party (CP) and became a chief organizer of cultural events in Chicago. He was part of a group, the South Side Writers' Group, which included Arna Bontemps, Horace Cayton, who co-authored a classic sociological study of the city's black community to which Wright contributed an introduction, and Margaret Walker, author of *Jubilee*, and also from Mississippi, who later wrote his biography. It was this context – migration, the depression, left-wing intellectual circles, and the post-(Harlem) Renaissance realist literary tradition – which helped frame Wright's portrayal of the South as a site of violence.[44]

Like Sargent Johnson, Aaron Douglas, and Zora Neale Hurston, Richard Wright received support from the WPA, which along with his Party-related network, allowed him to leave Chicago and live in New York. He was appointed head of the CP's *Daily Worker* "Harlem Bureau" in 1937.[45] Harlem in the 1930s, as described above, was no longer what it was during the Renaissance. In *Uncle Tom's Children*, published first as separate stories in the late 1930s and then in book form in 1940, and *Native Son* (1940), both written while he was active in the CP, Wright painted a portrait of the South which differed from that in romantic historical novels like Margaret Mitchell's *Gone With the Wind*, or its filmed version released in 1939, and a different reason for migrating than the progressive narrative of upward mobility or personal freedom. The South portrayed here is little different than during slavery, with the threat of violence hanging in the air like the noose in Aaron Douglas' paintings and book illustrations. In his review of *Uncle Tom's Children* in *Opportunity* (1939), titled "The Negro, New or Newer," Alain Locke wrote: "with this our Negro fiction of social interpretation comes of age" (cited in Introduction to *Uncle Tom's Children*, 1991:ix). The naturalism, irony, and light-hearted social satire which characterized the writing of the Harlem Renaissance was now turning into a more hard-edged social realism. In the Depression, the New Negro got newer. Despite the very different historical contexts, Locke saw a clear linkage between the Harlem Renaissance and the social realism of the 1930s. Speaking at the Second Convention of the National Negro Congress in 1937, Locke claimed that "the class proletarian art creed" of the 1930s was equally as committed to the "expression of Negro folk life" as the writers in the 1920s (Naison 1983:202). What had changed, in other words, was not the aim of depicting "the folk," but rather the conditions which made them what they were.[46]

In this politicized period, the point of writing was to promote the actions of others, not merely to express oneself or to represent the collective.[47] This type of acting/agency is future-oriented, even as it recollects the past. As portrayed by Richard Wright, the future of the American black lay in the industrial North, part of a working class and an American culture in formation, with the South representing a legacy of confinement. At the same time, writing is public self-expression, a form of agency where the emotions attached to experience color its representation. As one who experienced the migration, Wright's literary portrayal of that experience moves between individual and collective memory, anger at the past, and hope for the future. This complexity is the basis of the "we" that comes through in the text Wright wrote to accompany the photographs in *12 Million Black Voices* (1941).[48] There are several aims and sub-texts contained in this collaborative effort with the photographer Edwin Rosskam. The aim of countering the image of the South as it is represented in American popular culture and contributing to the struggle for anti-lynching legislation then being debated is mixed with the desire to preserve, at least in representative form, the memory of a residual way of life.

The critical reception and best-seller status which *Native Son* achieved in 1940 made Richard Wright a celebrity, and the appearance of his name on a book would almost assure a large readership. This and the success of John Steinbeck's *Grapes of Wrath* (1939), which competed with *Native Son* for first place on the best-seller lists and appeared as a film in 1940, had revealed the existence of a market for realist portrayals of the hardships and triumphs of migration – an American tragedy framed within a progressive narrative.[49]

Looking for an author for the text to accompany a collection of photographs from government achives, Viking Press turned to Wright, probably without any real thought about the text itself, or even the photographs. The question of how blacks should be literally and visually represented was left primarily to Wright and "photo director" Edwin Rosskam (David Bradley, Preface in Wright [1941] 1988).[50] But, as a reader of *12 Million Black Voices* will attest, the photographs themselves and the field trips he made in preparation stirred Wright to produce a moving document where his own individual memory melded into the collective. The photographs are organized under four headings, Our Strange Birth, Inheritors of Slavery, Death on the City Pavements, and Men in the Making. The use of the collective and inclusive pronoun "our" in the first section indicates both the collectivity and the author's position, Wright is an intimate of the group he will now represent. The group is "the black folk," the landed peasantry on the way toward becoming an industrial proletariat, whose birth "into Western civilization" is described as "weird and paradoxical" (12), and visually presented as bent but not bowed. As opposed to the "lean, tall blond men of England, Holland, and Denmark" and the "dark, short, nervous men of France, Spain, and Portugal, black people were hurled . . . into another land, strange and hostile, where for a second time we felt the slow, painful process of a new birth amid conditions harsh and raw" (12). The photos depict the worn, yet strong hands of a farm laborer, the weathered, but dignified face of a farmer, the bent back of an urban street collector, the black maid, the black industrial worker, stevedore, waiter, share-cropper, dancer, and cotton picker. The last photo in the section is of a young farm laborer, whom David Bradley, in his Preface, speculates could have reminded Wright of what could have been had he not migrated to Chicago. The inheritors of slavery represent the hard and harsh conditions of economic and political subordination, the cruel reality of Southern justice, from lynching to share-cropping and migrant labor. That little had changed in the more than half-century since the end of reconstruction and that the memory of slavery was much more than that is the clear message. The concluding section represents the future, not only for blacks, but for America, where the story of America's blacks, up to now a people without real history, flows into the river of world history.

We black folk, our history and our present being, are a mirror of all the manifold experiences of America. What we want, what we represent, what we endure is what America *is*. If we black folk perish, America will perish. If America has forgotten her past, then let her look into the mirror of our consciousness and she will see the *living* past in the present, for our memories go back, through our black folk today, through the recollections of our black parents, and through the tales of slavery told by our black grandparents, to the time when none of us, black or white, lived in this fertile land. (146)

The real history of black Americans, in other words, begins with the first steps of migration. It is then that blacks become agents of their own fate, as they leave the inherited subordination that has characterized their collective lives since slavery. In Wright's fiction and his autobiographical works, the South is represented as a place to flee from, a beautiful landscape with an ugly and fearful social structure held together by racism. There is no redemption to be found here, at least not in the real present. If it is to be found in the South at all, redemption may well come symbolically, through memory and with the telling of the tale. As Griffin (1995:32) points out, Wright reveals the agency involved in the act of writing, and, one may add, in the memory it evokes and, in the process of recollection it constitutes. In addition to flight and returning violence in kind, in Wright's early fiction, Southern blacks express the capacity to act in the face of repression through language, in speech-acts, song, and other forms of symbolic representation, recalling the coded dialogue of earlier periods. The difference now is that it is formed as literature, a tool in the reworking of cultural trauma. Language is here conceived as a form of action and an expression of agency, the capacity to exert some control over social and physical determination. As the songs and narratives rooted in slavery and after represented and expressed the humanity and agency of blacks, so Wright's stories of a violent and repressive South in the years between the wars express agency. In Wright's hands, however, the telling is not enough and even literature cannot be an end in itself.[51]

This reconstruction is also evident in the representation of the South and the motivations for migration that are pictured in Jacob Lawrence's series of paintings, first displayed as "The Migration of the Negro" in New York in 1941, with a large segment appearing in *Fortune* magazine the same year.[52] Like Wright, Lawrence proved enormously popular with both black and white audiences. Composed of sixty panels, the series represented as visual narrative the movement of masses of blacks from the South and the formation of a black working class in Northern cities. As opposed to Aaron Douglas, who used the mural format popular in the 1930s, Lawrence painted on small masonite panels. Born in 1917 and twenty-one when he completed the Migration Series, Lawrence was, as he expressed it, "too young for a wall" (quoted in "Introduction" in Turner 1993:14).

Unlike Wright who made the migration himself, Lawrence was raised in the North.[53] The story he painted was that of his parents and neighbors. He presented himself as a voice of these people with whom he closely identified, a role he modeled on the West African *griot*, "a professional . . . praise singer and teller of accounts." In this role, Lawrence sought to represent the move North in a way that its agents could appreciate (Hill 1993:141). The small, colorful panels painted in a modernist naive manner were arranged in chronological form, each accompanied by a caption to narrate it. Like a story board or a comic strip, the series allows the observer to participate in the journey and to understand the multiple motivations that turned it into a flow. The series begins and ends at a train station, with the final caption "And the migrants kept coming," a refrain that is repeated at various points in the narrative. Lawrence is careful to list several motivating factors, including the boll weevil and the hope for a brighter future, as Locke had done earlier. But one of the most striking panels (number 15), like the blues song mentioned above, presents another motivation for migrating North. A headless brown body sits bent forward beneath a tree branch, with an empty noose hanging from it; the caption reads "Another cause was lynching. It was found that where there had been a lynching, the people who were reluctant to leave at first, left immediately after this."

Lawrence depicts the positive and the negative motivations for migrating North and his story is painted with overtones of social realism, yet full of color and pathos at the same time. Those portrayed, while flatly drawn with a minimum of perspective, are not cardboard figures, they are identifiable human agents, even if their plight is largely socially determined. One significant social fact that distinguishes Lawrence's rendering of the black experience circa 1940 from that painted by Aaron Douglas, is the reality of the ghetto as exposed by economic depression. Although his warm optimism concerning the future of the community he so closely identifies with comes through, Lawrence appears well aware of the conditions under which the vast majority are forced to live. His panels depict the overcrowded and segregated housing and the angry whites who feel threatened by the newcomers. Du Bois' middle-class and educated talented tenth is absent from this narration, except for Panel 53 which portrays a well-dressed black couple and the caption "The Negroes who had been North for quite some time met their fellow men with disgust and aloofness." The story told is that of a sympathetic and understanding insider, not a literary or scientific outsider. There is none of professional sociology's "urban pathology" here. Rather, we are presented with a new New Negro, an urban black working class in formation, one whose melding of Southern and Northern cultures is only just beginning. In spite of tensions, internal and external, the overall theme of the Migration Series is that of agency, cooperation, and solidarity that, in the end, result in the formation of a new black community. At one significant level, the migration replaces slavery as the formative experience of the black community in the 1940s.

A different representation of urban black life in the 1930s was offered by the UNIA's "official photographer" James VanDerZee.[54] Although designated to that position by Marcus Garvey in 1924, VanDerZee was in reality the photographer of choice of the "strivers," the urban middle class. Born in 1886 in Lenox, Massachusetts, not far from where W. E. B. Du Bois was born eighteen years earlier, James and the rest of the large VanDerZee family worked serving the wealthy whites who spent their summers in the surrounding Berkshire mountains. Their own tastes reflected those for whom they worked. James was an accomplished musician, playing piano and violin, before discovering his talent for the visual arts. After a short time in Virginia with his first wife's family, VanDerZee opened a photo studio in Harlem in 1912 and became a recorder of the desires of the new middle and upper classes aspiring toward assimilation, if not racial integration.[55] This is the group which Lawrence left out and Wright dismissed as hopelessly bourgeois.

While VanDerZee's photographs can be considered visual documents of Harlem life, they are representations framed within a particular variant of the progressive narrative. His compositions reveal a different image of the 1930s than either Wright's or Lawrence's, in their focus on private family life and the public display of the symbols of success and comfort. In this, VanDerZee's work exemplifies the social ideals of the Harlem Renaissance while modifying its aesthetics. He chose to remove the warts while retaining the exuberance. The blues aesthetic and the documentary impulse is replaced here by classical European forms and the desire to celebrate individual and collective aspiration. Harlem's residents are neither displaced peasants, the victims of disintegrating social forces, nor an industrial working class in the making. Rather, they are black Americans inspired by a particular mix of racial pride, and American identity. Pictured here are families set in comfortable living rooms, dashing young men and women in military uniform and formal gowns in front of expensive automobiles, and children with faces full of hope and promise. In an insightful essay, Deborah Willis-Braithwaite (Willis-Braithwaite and Birt 1998) contrasts VanDerZee's photographs of Harlemites in the 1930s with those made by Aaron Siskind. Siskind was part of the same left-wing tradition as Wright and greatly influenced by the documentary school of social realism which guided the work of the WPA photographers used by Wright in *12 Million Voices*. Defining the situation within this framework, Siskind's photographs reveal a community in crisis, the innocent victims of powerful social forces outside their control. Covering the same territory, VanDerZee represents Harlem as centered around tightly knit family life and guided by materialist values like financial success and conspicuous consumption, and by patriotism. She writes:

comparing VanDerZee's and Siskind's views of Harlem, two separate and distinct notions of the vitality of the African American community emerge. While VanDerZee's best photographs seem to celebrate a sense of self-identity and racial pride, Siskind's most powerful works deal with notions of class distinction and racial segregation. Unlike VanDerZee's photographs, which picture the community as whole and functioning, Siskind was concerned with how racism and poverty defined the character of Harlem. Simply stated, to VanDerZee Harlem was home; to Siskind it was a ghetto. (1998:23–24)

While, on this last point, Wright was closer to VanDerZee, he shared with Siskind the victim to actor progression.

One would have to look hard to find any reference or representation of slavery in VanDerZee's photographs. His images represent the practices and expressions of respectable community, family life, weddings and funerals, sport clubs and the like; primarily, however, they present proud and dignified individuals, full of themselves and their place in the world. These are of course the tasks and projects of a commercial photographer. In this case, the demands of commerce and the desire of racial pride and progress coincided.

Throughout the 1930s, Langston Hughes and Zora Neal Hurston continued their influential careers as writers and intellectuals. Like Aaron Douglas, Paul Robeson, and Richard Wright, Hughes moved to the left during the 1930s and his writing took on a much more obvious political tone. Hurston, now working under the auspices of the WPA continued her ethnological expeditions to the South, collecting stories and writing novels on their basis. Through her eyes and ears the black South remained a storehouse of rich cultural experience, something which distinguished her work from that of Richard Wright. Hurston remained within the progressive narrative, while Wright's work, as mentioned, had had something in common with the tragic, redemptive model of black nationalism. At this point in his life, however, Wright was not a nationalist, but more sympathetic to the universalism that characterized the left, for whom any particular past was best forgotten or seen a useful resource toward a common future. Black nationalism of the Garvey variety was now in the hands of Elijah Muhammad, leader of the Nation of Islam and former sympathizer, if not activist, in the UNIA.[56]

War: the end of Depression

In 1940, the population of the United States was 131,669,275, of which 9.8 percent were black (Christian 1995:360). Three quarters of the 12,865,518 blacks still lived in the South, though the migration Northward continued with greater and greater force as the war created new employment opportunities. The armed forces remained segregated in spite of attempts to redefine blacks as immigrants like any other group. Each branch of the armed forces maintained a quota of 10 percent black participation, set in 1940, although actual participation never reached this. Most blacks served in the Army, where the percentage of blacks reached 8.7 percent in 1944; blacks were not permitted at all in the Navy until 1942, and even after that very few went to sea, until 1943 when all-black crews manned two ships, a destroyer and a submarine. Two black army divisions from the First World War were reactivated; however, in the main part of the Army the great majority of blacks were placed in the Quartermaster

Corps (supply) and in transportation. This was a practice that would continue well after President Harry Truman formally integrated the armed forces in July, 1948. All of this was watched with great interest, especially in the Northern cities: Drake and Cayton wrote in 1945:

> The overcrowded northern Black Belts are highly sensitized areas of discontent whose inhabitants are keenly aware of the treatment of Negroes throughout the country. The advent of the Second World War heightened this race consciousness, for Negroes were not only segregated from whites in the armed forces, but were also Jim-Crowed at post exchanges and theaters in many camps and sometimes humiliated and attacked by civilians in the South... All of this was common knowledge, discussed in the Negro press, on street-corners, and in barbershops. Every rumor of discrimination against soldiers or sailors sent a tremor through Black Metropolis. (1945:94)

The Second World War did not create the same raised expectations amongst black Americans as did the previous world war. Black Americans appeared less eager to serve and the American government was clearly concerned about this.[57] There was even organized resistance to the military draft in the black community, as Elijah Muhammad, the leader of the Nation of Islam, went to jail rather than register, an act of defiance which solidified his leadership and drew headlines in the black press. A race riot in Detroit in 1943 in which six whites and twenty-nine blacks were killed contributed to apprehension more than expectation.[58] At the same time, black leaders, such as A. Philip Randolph and Mary McLeod Bethune, had grown more cognizant of the bargaining power blacks had with reference to their support for government efforts.[59] As the government-supported radio programs and other forms of mobilization propaganda made clear, black support was essential to a united war effort. With this and also the fear of further urban disturbances as background, Randolph and others were able to extract concessions and gain support for civil rights legislation.[60]

Differences between the possibilities available to blacks during the First and Second World Wars related to the labor market as well.

> During the First World War Negroes came into a labor market that needed them. When the Second World War began they were part of a vast labor surplus. It soon became clear that Negroes were not going to get off the relief rolls [where they had been since the Depression, R.E.] until white people had secured jobs in private industry. Black Metropolis seethed with discontent as white men streamed back to work while Negroes generally were being denied employment. Here and there picket lines began to appear around factories on the margins of the Black Belt with signs reading –
> HITLER MUST OWN THIS PLANT,
> NEGROES CAN'T GET WORK HERE
> IF WE MUST FIGHT, WHY CAN'T WE WORK?
> BULLETS KNOW NO COLOR LINE, WHY SHOULD FACTORIES?

It was to such feelings that Randolph and other leaders gave national voice. There was thus not the kind of faith in the good will of the government to accept blacks as Americans after their show of patriotism that characterized Du Bois and others after the First World War. Randolph was able to extract concessions before the war, on the basis of the uncertainly of black participation. In summer, 1941, Randolph and his organization, the March on Washington Movement (MOWM), threatened a massive march on Washington to protest against discrimination in the military and defense industries.[61] In order to prevent this demonstration, Roosevelt banned discrimination in defense work and established the Fair Employment Practices Commission. Although only a small step, this marked a significant victory in political awareness, as Randolph and others "pressed forward with broader demands, creating a pattern of interaction that would characterize the relationship between African Americans and the federal government for the duration of the war years . . . the open threat of mass action, whether organized and peaceful or disorderly and riotous, would remain one of black America's greatest resources of political power" (Savage 1999:71).[62]

Randolph was not alone in this. Similar strategies were being carried out through the black press, by editors and publishers using their power to shape black public opinion. As Charles Simmons (1998:91) puts it, "one of the lessons that the World War II era had taught the black press was how it could fight consistently and effectively with unity for a cause by confronting forces – governmental forces, if necessary – head on without bending and survive." Both locally and nationally through their own mass media, black Americans could act as a pressure group, and perceive themselves as such. Leaders like Randolph could thus serve as representatives, race managers who could stand in for the collective and extract concessions on the threat of withdrawal of support or disruptive behavior. It was this sort of accumulated collective learning that would prove useful later on in the 1950s as the civil rights movement emerged out of long-established, tried and tested, traditions of protest.

Three million blacks registered to serve in the armed forces during the Second World War, almost 1 million saw active duty. By standards established during previous wars, in practices established already in the War of Independence when both sides bartered for the support of slaves, it would be difficult for any government to deny citizenship rights to those who were prepared to die for the national cause. This alone would have raised the expectations of those blacks who served in the armed forces and their families. These expectations were enhanced and extended to others in the "community" by leaders and the black mass media. An addition to these media was the national magazine *Ebony*, modeled after the popular weekly *Life*, which was established in November, 1945 and would go on to become "the most successful and widely circulated Black magazine in the world" (Christian 1995:373).

This did not mean that expectations concerning acceptance and integration, and racial progress, were not raised after the war, especially now that victories had been won from the federal government. Expectations were raised, and attitudes had changed, but now with a more hardened and realistic edge at least at the level of leadership. Already in 1945, President Truman established a national committee on civil rights to recommend action against racial injustice. In 1946, the Supreme Court banned discrimination on interstate bus travel, and in 1947 the Congress of Racial Equality (CORE) organized the first freedom rides to test that ban. Bayard Rustin, who was to be central to the civil rights movement a decade later, was a participant (Christian 1995:375). Also in 1948 the Supreme Court declared all state laws forbidding interracial marriages unconstitutional and also those restrictive housing agreements which denied blacks access to land use and occupancy.[63]

These were hard-won concessions. In a less pragmatic and more exuberant sphere, Jackie Robinson and Roy Campanella began playing baseball for the Brooklyn Dodgers, and Joe Louis, the Brown Bomber, and other boxers had been, were, or would be world champions, winning great pride for the increasingly self-conscious national black community.[64] Black entertainers, especially in the music industry, but elsewhere as well, were also visible representatives of the achievements of the race and their careers were covered with a great sense of pride in the black press.[65] These talents were combined when in 1940 "a group of black artists closely associated with the Popular Front came together to create 'King Joe,' a musical tribute to (Joe) Louis" (Marqusee 1999:26). Richard Wright wrote lyrics to music composed by Count Basie and sung by Paul Robeson, to the effect that Louis not only belonged to the black community, but also to the South:

> Lord, I know a secret, swore I'd never tell,
> Lord, I know what makes old Joe hook and punch and roll like hell,
> Black-eyed peas and cornbread what makes you so strong,
> Cornbread says I come from where Joe Louis was born.
>   (Quoted in Marqusee 1999:27)[66]

Later, with the return home of black soldiers after the war, it almost seemed possible that the idea of the New Negro could spread to the South.

Ralph Ellison's novel *Invisible Man*, which came into print in the form of two short stories published in the late 1940s before appearing in full form in 1953, represented the black male experience through the progressive narrative.[67] Written as a picaresque *Bildundsroman*, *Invisible Man* chronicles the experiences of an unnamed young black man from the mid-1930s to the immediate postwar period. Forced to leave his Southern college, this invisible man travels to Harlem where he is swept along by forces beyond his control and awareness.

From unreflective bearer of the progressive narrative, he is transformed into its self-reflective bearer, who gains both consciousness and also ironic, self-distance in the process. The invisible man is lifted out of the black mass by his talents as a public speaker and his passive and accepting personality. It is these which gain him a college scholarship and which lift him out of the crowd witnessing a Harlem eviction. His spontaneous speech at the latter event transforms the crowd into a protest. This act attracts the attention of the Brotherhood, a left-wing organization. He is offered a job as community organizer and trained in the organization's ideology. He rises quickly, becoming the movement's Harlem chief, engages in a successful struggle with black nationalists, only to be betrayed as the group's shifting strategy calls for the sacrifice of the black community for the greater good of mankind as the Second World War progresses. He is brought to consciousness during the Harlem riot in 1943, when chased by nationalists out for revenge, he lands in an underground coal pile, lost in blackness, he discovers his role as invisible man, capable of playing many parts in the urban environment.

My entire body started to itch, as though I had just been removed from a plaster cast and was unused to the new freedom of movement. In the South everyone knew you, but coming North was a jump into the unknown. How many days could you walk the streets of the big city without encountering anyone who knew you, and how many nights? You could actually make yourself anew. The notion was frightening, for now the world seemed to flow before my eyes. All boundaries down, freedom not only the recognition of necessity, it was the recognition of possibility.   (Ellison 1990:499)

Breaking out of the constraints of the realist "protest" tradition as exemplified by his mentor, Richard Wright, Ellison summarized his own generational experience and opened a new one, where a new balance would be struck between the individual and the (racial) collective. Ellison's novel begins in a South still struggling with the effects of slavery, where white patronage and acceptance is the center around which black identity revolves, and ends in a Harlem sewer, with the realization that blackness is at least to an extent a matter of performance and choice, where whites are important but not determinant.

Black nationalism and the tragic narrative

The UNIA continued to exist in the United States after Garvey's imprisonment for mail fraud in 1925, his deportation a few years later, and eventual death in London in 1940.[68] The movement maintained an active presence in Harlem throughout the 1930s, where among other groups it kept the nationalist presence alive. Encased within a tragic, redemptive narrative frame, nationalism offered an alternative to the progressive internationalism of the increasingly influential

Communist Party, the integration-oriented and progressive nationalism of the NAACP, and the local, self-help perspective of the cooperative movement. Black nationalism's biggest rival was perhaps the Communist Party, which, after the Scottsboro affair in the early 1930s, presented the strongest activist challenge to the NAACP, whose membership didn't really take off until the 1940s.[69] The Communist Party offered a variant on the progressive narrative in that its inclusivity was international in scope: solidarity with the working class and the oppressed of the world. It challenged the implicit capitalism of the NAACP, it did not promise or promote inclusion into the dominant American culture. In the midst of economic depression the viability of these values was certainly open to question, especially in regard to blacks. Here slavery was defined as a form of wage labor, the most extreme example of capitalist exploitation and was compared to the current conditions of the American worker, whose life conditions were also defined as a form of slavery to be overcome. This narrative was progressive in that the formation of a working class was a step forward and beyond the bondage to which blacks had been subjected. The move North and into industrial labor was also described in progressive terms, as a shift from the serfdom of the feudal South to the potential liberation through identification with the industrial working class. Redemption was also a part of this narrative as world revolution would ultimately free all workers from both wage slavery and racial discrimination.

It was especially in cities like New York, Detroit, and Chicago, prime goals of migrating unskilled black laborers from the South, that nationalism and communist internationalism competed for the militant position opposite the NAACP. In Detroit and Chicago, West Indian influence was less than it was in New York as these cities tended to attract more unskilled migrants from the South. As Charles Johnson had pointed out in *Survey Graphic* (1925), each Northern city tended to develop its own particular characteristics regarding its black population. Much depended upon local industry and the labor market, including the strength and openness of its trade unions, especially since at this time there was little city planning or government intervention of any sort.[70] In part because of this, Chicago more than Detroit, for example, with its strong and radical labor unions, became a center of black nationalist organizations.[71] Here, new native-born leaders emerged, with a different religious orientation and a different view of history and interpretation of the slave past than that offered by Garvey and UNIA. The fact that so much is known about Chicago and not other cities may also have to do with the University of Chicago and its sociology department, which encouraged urban studies and attracted and trained black sociologists. The power of the academic discourse to create "reality" should not be discounted. Chicago was also the home of post-Harlem

Renaissance literary circles, with its share of small magazines, like *Anvil* edited by Jack Conroy, who together with Arna Bontemps produced a study of blacks during the migration.[72]

Among the Chicago-based groups attracting and organizing newly arrived migrants was one which traced its roots back to Africa, known as the Abyssinians. Activists in this semi-religious, nationalist sect identified themselves as Ethiopian and not Negro. They were led by Grover Redding, who called himself a prophet and claimed to have been born in Ethiopia. Upon his arrest in 1920, Redding stated the aim of his group: "My mission is marked in the Bible. Even if they have captured me, some other leaders will rise up and lead the Ethiopian back to Africa. The Bible says, 'So shall the King of Assyria lead away the Egyptian prisoners and the Ethiopian captives, young and old . . . to the shame of Egypt'. The Ethiopians do not belong here and should be taken back to their own country" (quoted in Essien-Udom 1962:47). Here Africa is more than a spiritual home, and much more than a cultural resource, it is a site of redemption. Whether or not one actually returned there in a physical sense was probably less important than its symbolic meaning as homeland, beyond slavery and outside history.

While Africa remained the spiritual homeland, and redemption the ultimate aim for "prophets" like Redding and, later, W. D. Fard and Elijah Muhammad, it was a different Africa than the one Garvey had drawn upon. This Africa was "Asian," part of the "East," and redemption was more symbolic than physical. Thus the actual site of redemption, the place of return, was without fixed geographical location. While differing in these aspects, the aim was ultimately the same, to reinterpret history and collective memory in order to create a new, more positive, collective identity.[73]

To recently arrived migrants, with little skill, education, or future promise, this could prove attractive. Especially given the possible negative motivation for fleeing the South and the ties to the community there. As Essien-Udom (1962:47–48) writes:

to differentiate themselves from their "Negro-ness" became a means of escaping the abuse and the insults of the whites. For a dollar, a member could purchase an Abyssinian flag, a small pamphlet containing a prophecy relating to the return of the dark-skinned peoples of Africa, a so-called treaty between the United States and Abyssinia, and a picture of "Prince of Abyssinians". In addition, a member could sign up to return to Ethiopia in order that he might fill any one of forty-four positions, such as chemist, civil engineer, mechanic, chicken farmer, teacher, cartoonist, etc.

Sects like these tended to remain small, attracting the most isolated and desperate of the newly arrived migrants, and could be placed into three categories, emigrationist, Islamic, and nationalist. In the midst of this emerged a sect which can be said to combine all three of these categories and which would grow into the largest and most long lasting, the black Muslims.

The original people

In 1930, W. D. Fard, who claimed to have come from Mecca, founded a temple in Detroit for the purpose of establishing a Nation of Islam, as part of a strategy of constructing a new nationality for America's black population.[74] After effectively organizing this Detroit temple, with members recruited from recently arrived Southern blacks, Fard moved to Chicago in 1934 where he founded the Allah Temple of Islam (Essien-Udom 1962:45). He was thought to have been deported after a "courtroom riot" in 1935. The temples were eventually taken over by an assistant, a migrant from Georgia to whom he had given the "original" name, Elijah Karriem, upon his conversion, which later would be changed to Elijah Muhammad, as the two "invented W. D. Fard (later Fard Muhammad) as the messiah of the Black Nation and then eventually as Allah in the flesh" (Clegg 1997:36).[75]

As part of its strategy of rebirth, revival, and redemption, the Nation of Islam sought to isolate and insulate its converts as much as possible from the surrounding urban environment, which they considered a direct result of white domination. Their interpretation of the black ghetto experience was entirely opposite to that of the Harlem Renaissance, a fact that had to do with the very different economic circumstances of the 1930s, as well as the cultural resources of those the movement attracted and mobilized. The temples were designed to give the feeling of having entered another world, where nothing of the white world was sacred and where the white man was the "devil." As Clegg describes it, "the symbols of the white world were singled out for scorn. On the blackboard in the temple Fard had drawn pictures of the American flag, the Islamic star and the crescent (or 'the National'), and a cross." Something which was meant to "illustrate the life-giving qualities of Islam and the evil and deleterious effects of Americanism and Christianity" (Clegg 1997:28). Such visual symbolism must have had a cathartic effect on migrants escaping from the rural South. To see the images of the dominant culture held up for scorn must have been the source of great emotion. Re-naming was an important ritual here as well. Having mastered the basic lessons which were part of the conversion process, the successful novice was "given an 'original' Arabic name or an X, which represented the surnames of unknown ancestors as well as the fact that the person had given up the vices of the world and was now an ex-alcoholic, ex-prostitute, ex-drug addict, ex-Uncle Tom, and/or ex-slave" (Clegg 1997:27).

Redemption was achieved both through denying the "vices" of the surrounding world and through linkage to a long-lost past.

Converts were few, however, and in many ways the hierarchical structure of the organization, which included "a general secretary, a recorder secretary, a Fruit [Fruit of Islam, the internal police and body guard] secretary, a registrar, a captain, a minister, an assistant minister, and six lieutenants" (Clegg 1997:81), was an end in itself. The "movement" at this time (mid 1930s), "a collection of officers with no general body," reflected the need to create status for those without it, something which Garvey had also done, the difference, however was that Garvey had a mass public for its representative displays. In the midst of economic depression, the urban black public sphere which characterized the 1920s had lost much of its vitality, even as new waves of migrants filled the Northern cities. The black population of Chicago had reached 277,731, 8 percent of the city's population, by 1940 (Clegg 1997:37). By the early 1940s the war-related economic upswing trickled down to the black ghettoes and, in 1942, the Chicago temple reported a membership of 150–300 (Clegg 1997:81), while Elijah Muhammad claimed a total membership of 9,000 the same year.[76] This, in spite of continued police harassment and internal bickering. What had been a sect of leaders without followers was on the verge of becoming a movement, one which would gather and create the original people in America.

Elijah Muhammad was born Robert Poole in 1897 on a tenant farm in Sandersville, Georgia, placing him in the same age-group as the activists of the Harlem Renaissance. His life pattern was both different and similar to key figures in that movement. In common was the urban migration, what differed were the reasons that motivated it. Robert Poole was a 22-year-old laborer, married with two children by the time he and his family migrated to Detroit in 1923. He arrived in the North in other words as full of responsibilities as hope. By the time of the stock market crash in 1929 he and his wife had five young children. Poole worked on the fringes of the auto industry during the Depression, when he and thousands of others were laid off. With the collapse of industrial production, Poole moved between temporary work and unemployment and between alcohol and religion. He was "saved" when a friend introduced him to the teachings of W. D. Fard in 1931. The conversion from the Baptist religion of his forebears to the "heathen religion" of Islam went slowly and it was years before he concluded that he "had little to lose in giving Mr. Fard a hearing" (Clegg 1997:18). After his conversion, however, things moved more swiftly. As Karriem he became Fard's assistant and then Supreme Minister in the Nation of Islam in 1933.[77] After Fard's departure and the ensuing power struggle among the many officers, as Muhammad he moved between groups in Detroit, Chicago, Milwaukee, and Washington, DC, before settling in Chicago as the war broke out in Europe in 1939. Elijah Muhammad began preaching against black participation in the war and refused himself to register for the draft.[78]

His moral convictions and his prison time also clearly separated Muhammad from his Harlem colleagues of the previous decade. Thirty-eight Chicago Muslims were indicted for violating the newly revived draft laws when they announced that since they were not American citizens and had already "registered with Allah, they were not required to register for the draft." "Furthermore, since the Japanese were Asiatics and descendants of the black Original People, to go to war against the emperor would be fratricidal" (Clegg 1997:91). Along with his eldest son, who shouted "I hope the Japs win the war!" as his sentence was announced, Muhammad was sentenced to one to five years in prison in 1942 for violating the Selective Services Act. This refusal was interpreted as sacrifice and martyrdom by many blacks, both inside and outside the movement; by refusing to submit to the laws of the land through appealing to a higher authority, Muhammad had shown it possible "to talk to the white man like he was the white man's daddy" (Clegg 1997:93), as street vernacular expressed it. The prison sentence consolidated Mohammad's leadership and his place as messenger of Allah and prophet of an alternative movement.

If this religious orientation and moral conviction separates Elijah Muhammad from the writers, artists, and intellectuals of the Harlem Renaissance, his rural roots and lack of formal education unites him with thousands of others who made the Great Migration. It is this background, in fact, that allowed him not only to speak to and for the "masses" who became his followers, but also to legitimate this role. Muhammad could speak of himself as "one who has walked the streets with them, suffered in the hell of North America, was humiliated in the South by the devils" (quoted in Essien-Udom 1962:79). While the Harlem Renaissance "negrocracy" may have exemplified the New Negro in terms of cultural outpourings and the desire for self-expression and success, revealing that success to its public and holding out the promise for the race at large, the Muslim leader exemplified another type of success, the transcendence of subservience through adherence to an alternative religious culture, a self-made one at that. At the same time he exemplified or at least appeared to exemplify, another set of values, even as he wore the robes of material success, conspicuously living the American dream. Here the religion of Africa, or a made-up version of it, rather than the place itself was the key and the slave past was a period in hell, a necessary step on the path to salvation, part of a divine plan. At the same time, "Africa" was not the black Africa which Garvey had sought to return to and civilize, but "East Asia."[79]

Slavery played an essential part in the theology of the movement. Formulated by Fard Mohammad in the 1930s and revitalized by Elijah Muhammad, the story of the fate of the original people contained a rich narrative concerning the meaning of slavery. After running out of labor power for their exploitation of the Western Hemisphere, European whites, decendents of Yacub, a fallen god whose "sole destiny would be to destroy his own people" (Clegg 1997:49) by creating a race of people entirely opposite from the original black race, turned to East Asia for slaves. "Through tricknology and coercion, the Europeans brought Original People from Mecca and other parts of the Black Nation to America to serve as bondmen" (Clegg 1997:58). Aboard his ship *Jesus,* John Hawkins carried the first slaves to the shores of America in 1555:[80] "Our slavery at the hands of John Hawkins and his fellow-slavetraders and suffered here in the Western Hemisphere for four hundred years was actually all for a Divine purpose: that Almighty Allah . . . might make himself known through us to our enemies, and let the world know the Truth that He alone is God" (Elijah Muhammad, quoted in Essien-Udom 1962:132–33). This John Hawkins, white slave trader, unknown to himself was an agent in this plan. As slave trader he was actually doing the black race a service.

In the year 1555 when he . . . began bringing our people away from our Native Land and away from our own people, to sell us to his white brothers in the West as merchandise for their slave markets, little did he realize at that time that bringing us as slaves he was actually sentencing his white brothers here to their doom, for the evil that they have since done to us and are still doing cannot be forgiven.   (Essien-Udom 1962:133)

The enslavement of black people was both prophesied and part of a plan, as the Europeans "stripped away from their slaves as much of the original culture as possible . . . and the slave master renamed his chattel *Negro,* which meant 'something dead, lifeless, neutral (not that nor this)'" (Clegg 1997:58). To fill the cultural void and to keep the slave docile, the white man imposed Christianity on the black. Amending the divine plan, the "decreed year for the end of the white man's rule was 1914, but Allah extended the time by fifty to seventy years so that black people in America could regain the knowledge of self and Islam" (1997:58). As the black man had now become a white man in black skin, a savior was necessary to lead them out of the wilderness, "as the white man had been centuries earlier" (1997:59).

This kind of trickery, where white people are shown to be doing the opposite of what they actually intended, must have gone home easily with this audience. It is not unreminiscent of the double and hidden meaning found in the folk tales and jokes told by slaves themselves: where things are not always as they appear and that which is not said is of equal importance to what is said, and even that, what is said, is not what it seems. This was also the case when Darwinian evolutionary theory was played upon and reversed. Speaking about a white race punished by Allah, Elijah Muhammad recounted, they were "deprived of divine guidance, for 2,000 years which brought them almost into the family of wild beasts – going upon all fours; eating raw and unseasoned, uncooked food; living in caves and on tree tops, climbing and jumping from one tree to the other. Even today, they like climbing and jumping. The monkeys are from them. Before their time, there was no such thing as monkeys, apes and swine" (cited in Van Deburg 1997b:101). This playful seriousness reverses not only Darwinian theory, but also racial stereotypes.

Elijah Muhammad's theology offered other perspectives on slavery than the one described above. In continuing the history of the evolution of the white race, he recounted that they were freed from their divine curse of being set by Allah on the "worst and poorest part of the planet" by Columbus and his "finding of this Western Hemisphere. They have been here now over 400 years. Their worst and most unpardonable sins were the bringing of the so-called Negroes here to do their labor" (Van Deburg 1997b:101). One result of the white race's sinful action was that of creating a dependent personality amongst the slaves and their descendents, who are

charmed by the luxury of their slave master, and cannot make up their minds to seek for self something of this good earth . . . the good things of this earth could be theirs if they would only unite and acquire wealth as the masters and the other independent nations have. The Negroes could have all of this if they could get up and go to work for self. They are far too lazy as a Nation – 100 years up from slavery and still looking to the master to care for them and give them a job, bread and a house to live in on the master's land.   (1997b:103–04)[81]

Similar to Garveyism, the current task was "to redeem the Black Nation from centuries of unjust white rule" (Van Deburg 1997b:97). The reinterpretation, or rather reconceptualization of history was thus combined with a very practical program for changing behavior, one that built on strictly enforced self-discipline, and aimed at transforming habits stemming from enslavement which ensured continued subordination. This program provided an "ethos," and new habits, proscribed sets of behaviors, and a framework of interpretation and evaluation, through which the individual with the support of the collective could be, at least partially, redeemed here and now.

We must stop relying upon the white man to care for us. We must become an independent people. So-called Negroes should:

1. Separate yourselves from the "slave-master."
2. Pool your resources, education and qualifications for independence.
3. Stop forcing yourselves into places where you are not wanted.
4. Make your own neighborhood a decent place to live.
5. Rid yourselves of the lust of wine and drink and learn to love self and your own kind before loving others.
6. Unite to create a future for yourself.

7. Build your own homes, schools, hospitals, and factories.
8. Do not seek to mix your blood through racial integration.
9. Stop buying expensive cars, fine clothes and shoes before being able to live in a fine home.
10. Spend your money among yourselves.
11. Build an economic system among yourselves.
12. Protect your women.

This last point reveals the place of women in this type and phase of black nationalism, a legacy that the next generation would be forced to come to grips with, as feminism developed as a movement and an ideology, affecting blacks as well as whites. Elijah Muhammad also sought to reverse white fear of black sexuality: "stop allowing the white men to shake hands or speak to your women anytime or anywhere. This practice has ruined us . . . No black man feels good – by nature – seeing a white man with a Negro woman. We have all colors in our race – red, yellow, brown and jet black – why should we need a white person?" (1997b:104).

Even if it could be interpreted as part of a divine plan, slavery was part and parcel of a cultural trauma, one still lived as such. Trauma was living and vital because contemporary white society was conceived as an oppressing Other, a totality from which one was alienated and against which one must constantly struggle, so as not to be its victim or dupe. The movement and its regimen were thus a means of dealing with trauma, offering a source of strength to resist and a path toward redemption. As opposed to other forms of black nationalism where redemption would come in the form of a place, a state of one's own, whether in Africa or elsewhere, redemption in the Nation of Islam would be attained in the coming of a "New World," where righteous blacks would inherit the earth in its entirety.

6

Civil rights and black nationalism:
the post-war generation

Before I was an African American, I was a black kid living in Los Angeles
who wanted to be a rock'n'roll star. Then I discovered Harlem, and, ever since,
I've wanted to be a Negro.
Shawn Amos

The two narrative frames developed through cultural trauma and transmitted across generations in a discursive process of symbolic representation were
reformed in the 1960s through the cognitive praxis of the black nationalist
and the civil rights movements. As part of the same process of remembering
and forgetting, inherited models of emancipation were transformed and revitalized by a new generation of intellectuals. Through their form and content
these interconnected, yet distinctive, social movements reflected the changes
that American society and black Americans had undergone since the end of the
Second World War. At the same time as these movements were structured by
the inherited narrative frameworks, the frameworks were refigured as movement intellectuals articulated collective identity in an altered historical context.
In one sense, these movements competed with each other in the struggle to
determine how the collective would understand itself and the meaning of its
collective past. In another sense, they complemented each other through the
necessity of coming to terms with slavery as the primal scene upon which the
collective was grounded.

Confrontation occurred at the level of action and cognition, effecting change
in both. At the cognitive level, the progressive and the tragic redemptive narratives were respectively revitalized and altered through the cognitive praxis of
these social movements, as they mobilized actors for political ends through articulating a collective identity which linked past, present, and future. A dialecti-
cal interplay between cognitive frame and social historical context restructured
the narratives, as they, in turn, structured the process of collective identity-
formation within these movements. Perhaps the most affected by the competition

and confrontation between movements and their respective intellectuals was the progressive narrative frame, which had remained more or less stable and increasingly institutionalized since the 1920s (see chapter 5). The renewed migration and the economic growth which followed the war affected the grounds and meaning of progress and inclusion. At the same time, external events like the decolonialization of the African continent would also catalyze cognitive transformation, but it was the confrontation with an expansive, modernized, secular black nationalism that most effected changes in the progressive narrative.

Context

In 1950, blacks constituted 10 percent of the US population as a whole and 12 percent of the urban population. Out of a total black population of over 15 million, 1.5 million or 16 percent had migrated from the South – 34 percent to the Northeast, 42 percent to the North Central part of the country, and the rest largely to the West. A westward shift, especially to California, could be noted amongst migrating blacks, as well as for the population in general, as that state moved from fifth most populated to second, after New York. The average income of urban blacks "rose by 192 per cent between 1940 and 1953, when 90 percent of blacks were in some form of paid employment, and the total value of the black consumer market was $15 million" (Ward 1998:31). However, as family incomes were increasing generally in the United States in the 1950s, black families continued not only to lag behind whites, but to worsen in comparison. Black families earned 54 percent of the median income of their white counterparts in 1950, and this increased to 57 percent in 1952, only to drop back to 52 percent in 1958, returning to the immediate post-war levels. The number of black men and women working in agriculture dropped dramatically in the decade 1940–50, while the percentage of black men in white-collar work increased from 5.1 to 8.3 percent and from 6.3 percent to 12.7 percent for black women. This was the result not only of urban migration, but also of industrialization in the farm industry. Even more significantly, between 1940 and 1950, the number of blacks in higher education, primarily at "historically black colleges," increased dramatically from 23,000 to 113,735 (figures from Christian 1999:379–81). This latter figure is especially important in understanding not only the emergence of the civil rights movement, but also its success. As one commentator put it:

The most convincing evidence that the new civil rights movement functioned to sustain and renew Blacks' faith in education has been the tremendous upsurge in school enrollment and retention on all academic levels, particularly on the college level . . . the number of blacks enrolled in college almost tripled in the 1960s . . . from 192,344 in

1960 . . . to 522,000 in 1970 . . . The rate of increase in the college enrollment of Blacks was considerably higher than that for whites . . . Again, between 1964 and 1968, Black enrollment in all colleges increased from 234,000 to 434,000 or by 85 percent . . . During that same period the increase in enrollment in colleges in the nation as a whole was from 4,643,000 to 6,801,000, or by only 46 percent. (Thompson 1974:18)

Toni Morrison offers a more eloquent rendering of these changes as they belatedly occurred in fictionalized all-black Ruby, Oklahoma.

The women who were in their twenties when Ruby was founded, in 1950, watched for thirteen years an increase in the bounty that had never entered their dreams. They bought soft toilet paper, used wash cloths instead of rags, soap for the face alone or diapers only. In every Ruby household appliances pumped, hummed, sucked, purred, whispered and flowed. And there was time: fifteen minutes when no firewood needed tending in the kitchen stove; one whole hour when no sheets or overalls needed slapping or scrubbing on a washboard; ten minutes gained because no rug needed to be beaten, no curtains pinned on a stretcher; two hours because food lasted and therefore could be picked or purchased in greater quantity. The husbands and sons, tickled to death and no less proud than the women, translated a five-time markup, a price per pound, bale or live weight, into Kelvinators as well as John Deere; into Philco as well as Body by Fisher.
(Morrison 1999:89)

In urban centers like Harlem there were other changes occurring. The April 6, 1952 *New York Herald Tribune*, under the headline "Harlem Losing Ground as a Negro Area," reported a survey carried out by a local radio station which it identified as being aimed at a black audience.

A decrease of 30.3 per cent in the Negro population of Harlem since 1947 . . . recent slum clearance programs and the corresponding growth of public and private housing projects have had an "earthquake effect" on the city's Negro population. Since 1947 a total of 182,000 persons have left Harlem and resettled in other parts of the metropolitan area . . . Other findings were: 1. Income and Wages: The income of the average Negro family has trebled since 1940, with the average middle-class heads of families earning $3,200 a year. 2. Savings: More than $12,000,000 on deposit in postal savings accounts in three Harlem branch post offices. 3. Employment: 95.7 per cent of all employable Negroes were working as of August 1951, and more Negroes were on Civil Service jobs than ever before. 4. New Homes: More than 200,000 New York Negroes in new homes. More than 26 per cent of all New York City housing project apartments occupied by or being readied for occupancy by Negro families. 5. Education: High school attendance highest in history. College enrollment up ten times over 1940. 6. Insurance. Negroes own thirteen banks, seventy-four credit unions, twenty savings-and-loan associations and 204 insurance companies nationally. Fifty-two of these companies have assets of more than $100,000,000. 7. Buying habits: Nationally advertized brand-name products preferred almost exclusively. (Quoted in Schoener 1995:207).

The times were indeed "a' changin'."

At the outbreak of the Korean War in 1950, the American armed forces were formally integrated, but informally segregated. This offered black males, at least, another source of integration and mobility. Blacks constituted 13.5 percent of the total military population in 1950, but the vast majority (80 percent) of those in Korea would serve in all-black units, primarily in support and supply and in the lower ranks, with limited chances for advancement. Contemporary anger over this situation was expressed in the play *A Medal For Willie* (1951) by William Branch, where a mother of a black veteran throws away the medal posthumously awarded to her son with the words "'Yes, Willie's dead and gone now, and I'm proud he was brave and helped save somebody else 'fore he got killed. But I can't help thinkin' Willie died fightin' in the wrong place.' (Quietly intense.) *'Willie shoulda had that machine gun over here!'*" The memory of slavery may have lingered in the mammy role of this character, but if it did it was given a new twist by the playwright. As Hay (1994:88) remarks, "Although [the author] had made her appear typical of [the] Contented Slave stereotype, proud to have given her only son 'for her country', he had the wrong ceremony words issue from this 'tired and wilted' woman."

Racial segregation in the military would undergo further change in the 1960s before and during the Vietnam War when racial and regional mixing was not only formally encouraged, but the norm, at least on military bases.[1] At the same time as expectations of economic betterment were rising in the post-war period, a backlash was also evident, especially in the South. Organizations like the NAACP were under constant attack and even outlawed in some states. While the primarily working-class Ku Klux Klan continued its harassment, new "middle-class" organizations like the White Citizens Councils were formed to challenge integration and assimilation (Grant 1998:121).

In other areas, developments in the electronic mass media, mostly by the emergence of color television, and of a "black culture industry" (Cashmore 1997), added new factors in the representation of the present and remembrance of the past. Television, which seemed to offer an authentic representation of events as they occurred, would play a central role in the representation of the Vietnam War and in the new social movements that emerged in the 1960s, including the choice and role of their leaders.[2] The electronically mediated images transmitted instantly over vast spaces would intensify the power of representation as they magnified events and persons. First impressions could become everlasting, making the choice of representatives with particular expressive qualities, and the tactical selection of issues and confrontations, all the more sensitive and important. With the magnifying power of television, as well as the older more traditional means of communication like the press and the public meeting, movement intellectuals in the new waves of civil rights protest would struggle to articulate and define "blackness" and the African American, the preferred names and collective identities which would constitute the post-war generation. In this struggle the meaning and memory of slavery and the failure of emancipation fully to integrate American blacks would remain the point of departure of collective memory and identity-formation.

Television at first challenged then complemented radio, film, and the print media in reaching and representing the collective above the local level. As discussed in chapter 5, radio had become an important means of reaching, representing, and expanding the parameters of the black "community," complementing the print media. Television would add another dimension. However, a rather unexpected development intervened as this was occurring. In the 1950s an interest in aspects of black life grew enormously amongst whites, especially the young. This growth was sufficiently strong to support the development of what has been called a black culture industry in which "black culture" was produced, packaged, and distributed to a multiracial mass audience, primarily, at first, in the form of recorded music. The concentration of black populations had expanded the value of low-wattage local radio stations. As black purchasing power increased noticeably, white advertisers increased their support of black-oriented radio: "by 1961 [they] were spending $9 million annually on black-oriented radio advertisements" (Ward 1998:31). Between 1954 and 1964 the amount of corporate monies spent on black-oriented WLIB-New York increased from 5 percent to 85 percent.

From the point of view of producers and consumers, this new interest in and for blacks was a quite different phenomenon from the "slumming" of the 1920s and 1930s, where affluent whites ventured into the urban black ghettoes for an evening's entertainment and live performances of dance bands. This kind of controlled face-to-face contact over racial borders was now more or less replaced by a form of mediated contact which was privatized as well as commodified. White teenagers could listen to "black" music in the privacy of their own homes, safe from physical contact and even parental control. At the same time, corporations could produce for and sell to black consumers without direct interaction. However, this form of contact, made possible by both radio and records, may well have contributed to a predisposition to support or even participate in the struggle for black civil rights (Ward 1998). What is more certain is that it helped influence how "blackness" was understood, by both black and white.

Black power

Of great significance in the generational reworking of the past/present in black collective identity-formation was the wave of anti-colonialist movements that swept the African continent following the end of the Second World War, but took off in the 1950s and 1960s. These new African movements helped transform the national liberation model (with echoes of the Irish rebellion, and others such as the Russian Revolution and Zionism), which had existed in the black American protest tradition since the turn of the century. Even more importantly, perhaps, they helped transform the image of Africa as a primitive continent in need of "civilizing," which many American blacks had shared with whites, into a political and cultural avant garde. This was especially important in modernizing American-based black nationalism, but also influenced the civil rights movement, and through both, American blacks generally. Martin Luther King and Malcolm X both visited the "new" Africa and returned inspired.[3]

In 1953, Richard Wright traveled to the Gold Coast as it was being transformed from a British colony into the independent nation of Ghana. A year later, he published his impressions in a book given the provocative and prophetic title *Black Power*. Although presumably written for a white audience concerned not so much with anti-colonialism as with the growing influence of Marxism and the Soviet Union on the African continent, *Black Power* must also have been read with interest by the new generation of American blacks, who perhaps heard for the first time the phrase which would become so important in the near future.[4] Full of self-reflection as well as the acute observations of a gifted writer, Wright's book helped open the door to the new Africa, a dark continent offering a glimmer of hope to black Americans.[5] Thinking about this, Wright reflected:

the fortuity of birth had cast me in the "racial" role of being of African descent, and that fact now resounded in my mind with associations of hatred, violence, and death. Phrases from my childhood rang in my memory: one-half Negro, one-quarter Negro, one-eighth Negro, one-sixteenth Negro, one thirty-second Negro . . . In thirty-eight of the forty-eight states of the American Federal Union, marriage between a white person and a person of African descent was a criminal offense. To be of "black" blood meant being consigned to a lower plane in the social scheme of American life, and if one violated that scheme, one risked danger, even death sometimes. And all this was predicated upon the presence of *African* blood in one's veins. How much of me was *African*?   (Wright 1995:5–6)

The trip eventually answered some of these questions, but most of all it evoked reflections about the meaning and effects of slavery and the linkage to colonialism.

Black Power can now be seen as an important transitional work, not so much in relation to Wright's career (it was his first "travel book") as to the role and place of Africa in black America.[6] Slavery was central. The book opens with a concise history of the slave trade and a Marxist analysis of its function, in the spirit of Du Bois. Slavery is described in economic rather than racial terms, and the slave as filling a position within a social hierarchy. This position, Wright argues, had in fact been filled by whites, the indentured servants who preceded black slaves to America and who they would later replace. A major puzzle Wright seeks to solve is understanding not why whites enslaved blacks, something which can be understood economically, but why Africans sold their fellows into bondage, a question especially interesting in a culture not dominated by economic rationality. He found the answer in pagan religious beliefs: "it was now obvious why Africans had sold many millions of their black brothers into slavery. To be a slave was proof that one had done something bad, that one was being punished, that one was guilty; if one was not guilty, one would not be in a position of a slave . . . To be sold into slavery meant that your ancestors had consigned you to perdition! To treat a slave harshly was a way of obeying the spiritual laws of the universe!" (216). It is religious beliefs such as these that Wright sees as the real hindrance to African liberation and he is dismayed when he observes how movement leaders are able to manipulate tribal beliefs to their own ends. In chronicling the rise of the American-educated Kwame Nakrumah and his political party to political power, Wright records shifts in his own impressions of Africa, as he observes its poverty and superstition, but also its youthful energy and future promise.

The new interest in Africa was confirmed a few years later in 1961 when Patrice Lumumba, premier of the newly independent Republic of the Congo, was murdered as neo-colonialists reasserted their power. Lumumba's career and rise from a small village to world leader was followed with great interest by American blacks (Woodard 1999:54ff.). He had spoken on black campuses in a number of American cities. Protest demonstrations followed the news of his death, including some led by students at Howard University in Washington, DC, in Chicago, and at the United Nations in New York. At the latter, a young black poet named LeRoi Jones was arrested. Jones would soon change his name to Amiri Baraka and become a leader of the Newark, New Jersey community control movement and one of the central forces of the new black nationalism.

The transformation of Africa from site of redemption to ideological inspiration was well suited to the more articulate, better-educated and relatively more affluent urban black population and became a resource in a generational, as well as geographical, conflict. Toni Morrison (1999:104) gives these thoughts to one of her characters, representing an older generation of settlers in Ruby, Oklahoma, as she listened to a speech by a younger member:

All Soane knew about Africa was the seventy-five cents she gave to the missionary society collection. She had the same interests in Africans as they had in her: none . . . Yet there was something more and else in his speech. Not so much what could be agreed or disagreed with, but a kind of winged accusation. Against whites, yes, but also against them – the townspeople listening, their own parents, grandparents, the Ruby grownfolk.

As though there was a new and more manly way to deal with whites. Not the Blackhorse or Morgan way, but some African-type thing full of new words, new color combinations and new haircuts. Suggesting that outsmarting whites was craven. That they had to be told, rejected, confronted. Because the old way was slow, limited to a few, and weak.

Modernized and revitalized, black nationalism divided between religious and secular strands, although the two would slowly move closer to one another, while something of the opposite occurred on the other side. The tradition of civil rights protest, also spurred by post-war changes in race relations, was sparked by a series of legal cases concerning racial discrimination which culminated in the 1954 Supreme Court decision concerning segregated schooling, and was transformed into a broad-based social movement. The long-standing demands for equality and full citizenship which this movement expressed were grounded in a model of emancipation extending back to the Enlightenment and the French and American revolutions, and framed within the progressive narrative. While the new Africa was important here, it was more the heritage of slavery that formed the focal point of identity-formation, as the old and new forms of protest and consciousness mixed with the rituals and traditions of established black institutions in their confrontations with the "Southern way of life." In a 1958 interview, Ralph Ellison neatly summarized these developments in response to questions about the concept of the Negro and Negro culture:

the term describes a people whose origin began with the introduction of African slaves to the American colonies in 1619, and which today represents the fusing of many racial blood lines . . . in light of this, even if culture were transmitted through the blood stream we would encounter quite a problem in explaining just how the genes bearing "Negro" culture could so overpower those bearing French or English culture, which in all other ways are assumed to be superior . . . in the United States, the values of my own people are neither "white" nor "black", they are American.   (Ellison 1972:262–70)

The civil rights and black nationalist movements were thus products of the past/present, as they were reformed in a new social and historical context in which the United States assumed the role of political, economic, and moral world leader and by inherited, institutionalized frameworks of interpretation. The self-image of the United States as a "democratic" nation (previously contrasted with fascism and now communism) where individual freedom and the right to participate in the "pursuit of happiness" were central pillars of legitimation, affected domestic relations, increasing pressures to include blacks both culturally and politically, and adding leverage to the claims by blacks as marginalized second-class citizens. It was such claims, and their remedy, that these two social movements articulated, and in this sense they expressed a continuity with the past, but now with an added weight.

Re-framing the tragic narrative

As nationalism developed in the 1960s, its representations modified the cognitive frame through which the collective situation of American blacks was
interpreted. The tragic narrative was transformed through the new interpretation of Africa, as the situation of American blacks was compared with that
imposed through European colonialism in Africa. Eldridge Cleaver, then a
member of the Black Panthers, spoke these words at the founding convention
of the California Peace and Freedom party in 1968: "We start with the basic
definition: that black people in America are a colonized people in every sense of
the term and that white America is an organized imperialist force holding black
people in colonial bondage." Cleaver went on to say that given this definition
what was needed was a "revolution in the white mother country and national
liberation for the black colony" (quoted in Allen 1970:264). As this quotation
succinctly illustrates, a transformation in the meaning of black nationalism and
of American society had occurred amongst groups of black intellectuals and
"black militants" since the end of the Second World War.[7] African national liberation struggles provided American blacks with new categories within which
to interpret their own situation, as they transformed the view of Africa itself.

Another aspect of this re-framing within the tragic narrative was the shift
from an emphasis on the economic to the psychological effects of slavery.
The writings of the Caribbean-born psychiatrist Frantz Fanon, especially his
The Wretched of the Earth (1963), were extremely influential in this development.[8] Because the effects of colonization were so embedded in consciousness
and embodied in behavior, Fanon argued that cathartic violence was a necessary
part of the process of emancipation, a process which was as much psychological as it was political. While Richard Wright uncovered a predisposition for
violence in African religion and its tribal structure, Fanon pointed to colonialism as a major source.[9] Regarding the psychological effects of colonization
and their remedy, Stokely Carmichael, also Caribbean born and at the time
chairman of SNCC, wrote a "Position Paper on Black Power" published in the
New York Times in 1966 explaining why it was necessary to purge whites from
an organization that had been central to the civil rights movement.

Negroes in this country have never been allowed to organize themselves because of
white interference. As a result of this, the stereotype has been reinforced that blacks
cannot organize themselves. The white psychology that blacks have to be watched, also
reinforces this stereotype. Blacks, in fact, feel intimidated by the presence of whites,
because of their knowledge of the power that whites have over their lives . . . If people
must express themselves freely, there has to be a climate in which they can do this. If
blacks feel intimidated by whites, then they are not liable to vent that rage that they feel
about whites in the presence of whites – especially not the black people whom we are

trying to organize. i.e., the broad masses of black people . . . Ofttimes, the intimidating effect is in direct proportion to the amount of degradation that black people have suffered at the hands of white people.[10]   (Quoted in Van Deberg 1997b:120–21)

In the same position paper, Carmichael refers to racism as "white nationalism" and to the black struggle as one of liberation, thus combining the political and the psychological within the frame of colonialism with a well-drawn linkage to slavery. He writes:

It is very ironic and curious how aware whites in this country can champion anticolonialism in other countries in Africa, Asia and Latin America, but when black people move toward similar goals of self-determination in this country they are viewed as racists and anti white . . . it can be said that this attitude derives from the overall point of view of the white psyche as it concerns the black people. This attitude stems from the slave revolts when every white man was a potential deputy or sheriff or guardian of the state. Because when black people got together among themselves to work out their problems, it became a threat to white people, because such meetings were potential slave revolts . . . It is part of the white fear-guilt complex resulting from the slave revolts. (Van Deburg 1997b:125)

The urbanization and ever-greater concentration of the black population and their increasing relative affluence also stimulated this modernization of black nationalism. A key in this process was Malcolm X, who both expressed and represented changes whose implications only came to fruition after his death in 1965. As it had been earlier, the institutional base of black nationalism centered in the ever-expanding urban ghettos, now including those in California, especially Los Angeles and Oakland. As an ideological framework, nationalism was oriented to articulating the aspirations and organizing the resources of the "black community," which would then be constituted through this frame. Over time, this community would be known through various phrases, as "lost-found fish" to be caught, the "black masses," "the people," "the sacred community." As a social as well as political movement composed of secular and religious wings, black nationalism reformed established institutions and revitalized traditions of resistance and protest, from religious temples and modes of self-defense, to ways of dress, food, talk, marriage and child rearing. These seeped into popular culture and were represented in music (soul being the most obvious), film and fashion (Van Deburg 1997a). Huey P. Newton, founder of the Black Panther Party, called the popular film "Sweet Sweetback's Baadasssss Song" (1971), "the first truly revolutionary Black film made" (Newton 1973:155), on the basis of its representation of the community and of Africa. Prostitutes depicted in the film feeding a small boy "are strong and beautiful Black women, definitely African in ancestry and symbolic of Mother Africa. The size of some of their breasts signifies how Africa is potentially the breadbasket of the world . . . certainly they have the power to raise their liberator, for that is

what the small boy is, the future of the women, of Black people, liberation."
At the same time, works like Elizabeth Catlett's "Negro es Bello II" (1969),
Phillip Lindsay Mason's "Woman as Body Spirit of Cosmic Woman" and Dana
Chandler's "4(00) More Years" (1973) linked cultural politics and the more
traditional visual arts.

Obviously, the new vision of Africa was important here. National liberation movements helped promote a shift from the "Asian"-centered approach
of Fard and Elijah Muhammad which was slowly replaced by an image of
"blackness" more focused on sub-Saharan black Africa and in an anti-colonial,
national liberation, model of emancipation. Continuity was maintained in both
religious and secular forms of nationalism, as "blackness" or being "black" was
associated with freeing oneself from the ways imposed by the "white devil,"
"white society," or Anglo-Saxon ethnic culture. The difference lay in whether
emancipation was to be attained through religious or more secular forms of
re-education, and, later, between reformist or revolutionary means. Common
also was that both religious and secular forms of black nationalism came more
and more to represent themselves through uncompromising images of moral,
mental and physical toughness which many, if not most, whites considered
aggressive and threatening.

The Garveyism which first articulated the tragic, redemptive narrative frame
remained alive. The UNIA continued to exist as an organization and its ideas
were still felt through movement intellectuals like Carlos Cooks, founder of
the Garvey-inspired African Nationalist Pioneer Movement (ANPM), and a
noted Harlem street-corner orator. One of the programs espoused, "Buy Black,"
developed those boycotts and consumer cooperatives of the 1930s but with
more militant aims and means. In his street-corner speeches, Cooks also railed
against "Negroism" which turned black Americans into "zombified Caste crea-
tures whose loyalty is permanently married to the white race; whose God
and idolatry status is white; whose standards of beauty, sense of decency
and opinions on all matters are based on the set of concepts laid down by
white people" (cited in Van Deburg 1997b:85–86). Cooks' "Buy Black" campaign proposed boycotts of all "alien-owned" businesses in the Black community, making buying non-black a crime, and the formation of an African
Legion to guarantee success in enforcing its principles. For Cooks this tac-
tic was no different from those used by other urban-based ethnic groups in
the United States.

Even as the Garvey tradition remained alive, it was the religious wing of black
nationalism which produced the great innovation in the person of Malcolm
X, who helped transform it from small sects into a full-fledged social movement. Malcolm X was a key figure in the transformation of black nationalism,
both as person and as symbol.[11] From his point of view, American blacks had

been "brain-washed" by American culture and "we Muslims regarded ourselves as moral and mental and spiritual examples for other black Americans" (Haley 1965: 396). The solution was a complete change of life, making imagery and representation forms of exemplary action.[12] These images, no matter how they were interpreted, were projected and magnified through television and other mass media, in which the phrase "black power" and the image of the leather-clad, beret man with a rifle complemented the pursed lips and tough words of Malcolm X and Amiri Baracka. This image of blackness contrasted sharply with that promoted by the civil rights movement, whose "good Negro" was represented in either suit or bib-overalls and cotton dress, armed with a Bible and espousing non-violent Christian love. Although at points the images could mix in ambiguous and potentially explosive ways, as in the Reverend Frederick Douglass Kirkpatrick's rendering of a Christian hymn as "Nothing But His Blood" (1970): "Nothing but His blood (3 times)/Gonna free me, / Every time I make a start /White man stab me thru my heart/Nothin' but His blood is gonna free me" (B' side #108. 1970).

The story of Malcolm X is well known, having been reconstructed for and by Alex Haley (1965) in a posthumously published bestselling autobiography, and represented on film by Spike Lee; both of which have been very important in keeping his memory and that of the Black Power movement alive in the contemporary mind. The white world first heard of the Nation of Islam's minister, Malcolm X, through the local New York broadcast of a television news program called "The Hate That Hate Produced" in 1959. Born in Omaha, Nebraska in 1925, with the family name Little, Malcolm X was assassinated in Harlem in 1965. Like others of his generation, his life was shaped not only by skin color and gender which conditioned his participation in the migration to the Northeast, but also by the great Depression and the Second World War.[13] Malcolm X inherited his late-developing nationalism from his parents; his father, a carpenter and part-time Baptist minister, became an fervent Garvey supporter and his mother worked at times as a secretary at *The Negro World*.[14] His father's murder at the hands of white racists represented a personal trauma for the 6-year-old Malcolm.[15] Malcolm X recounts:

I remember seeing the big, shiny photographs of Marcus Garvey that were passed from hand to hand. My father had a big envelope of them that he always took to these meetings. The pictures showed what seemed to me millions of Negroes thronged in parade behind Garvey riding in a fine car, a big black man dressed in a dazzling uniform with gold braid on it, and he was wearing a thrilling hat with tall plumes. I remember hearing that he had followers not only in the United States but all around the world, and I remember how the meetings always closed with my father saying, several times, and the people chanting after him, "Up, you mighty race, you can accomplish what you will!"

(Haley 1965:85)

As a teenager, Malcolm migrated to Boston, going to live with an older half-sister. Here, despite his sister's efforts to push him in the direction of middle-class inclusion, Malcolm discovered the excitement of urban ghetto life. He became a small-time hustler, for whom regular work was called "slavery" and considered something only fools or status-conscious blacks would pursue. He worked as a shoeshine boy, railroad porter and dishwasher only to better allow him to negotiate his hustle and "hip" lifestyle. Eventually this led him to New York and to Harlem, the center not of black art and culture, but of the hustle and the game. Imprisoned along with a friend and two white women for robbery, Malcolm avoided direct participation in the war. In prison, he discovered Islam and the teachings of Elijah Muhammad. According to his own account this occurred through the efforts of his younger brothers and sisters, who, now living in Detroit, had become Muslim activists. He began corresponding with Elijah Muhammad and by the time of his release had himself become a convert. His years of correspondence with Elijah Muhammad created a bond between them and an entry into the inner circle of the religious movement. Putting his street knowledge and hustling skills to work in the service of the movement, Malcolm X was soon rewarded with the title of "minister" and the role of chief organizer. He moved from city to city laying the groundwork for new "temples" through his recruiting talents. In part due to his efforts, the organization grew from a sect to a movement, as temples were established in most major cities with a large black population. The prime sources of recruits were the poorest sections of the ghettoes and the prisons, where blacks greatly outnumbered whites. Favorite targets when "fishing" for recruits, were the recent migrants who peopled the storefront Christian churches. "We went 'fishing' fast and furiously when those little evangelical storefront churches let out their thirty to fifty people on the sidewalk . . . These congregations were usually Southern migrant people, usually older, who would go anywhere to hear what they called 'good preaching'" (Haley 1965:318–19).

What Malcolm X offered potential recruits was "good preaching" about how the "white devil" used Christianity to keep them enslaved and alternative religion was created for and by blacks. At the core of these sermons, at least at this stage of recruitment, was what Malcolm called "the dramatization of slavery" (Haley 1965:312):

I know you don't realize the enormity, the horrors, of the so-called *Christian* white man's crime . . . Not even in the *Bible* is there such a crime! God in His wrath struck down with *fire* the perpetrators of *lesser* crimes! *One hundred million* of us black people! Your grandparents! Mine! *Murdered* by this white man. To get fifteen million of us here to make us his slaves, on the way he murdered one hundred million! I wish it was possible for me to show you the sea bottom in those days – the black bodies, the blood, the bones broken by boots and clubs! The pregnant black women who were thrown overboard if they got too sick! Thrown overboard to the sharks that had learned that following these slave ships was the way to grow fat!   (Haley 1965:311)

Thus represented, the image of slavery acted as a magnet to draw new recruits to a new religion, "a special religion for the black man" (Haley 1965:320). "Well, there *is* such a religion. It's called Islam. Let me spell it for you, I-s-l-a-m! *Islam!*" What the new religion offered was a strict moral code, an ethos, that would circumscribe a new collective identity and an entire way of life. This identity promised to connect the urban black to a global community of black people and to a new understanding of himself and his place in the world. Africa, the black continent, was a source of inspiration as well as a common point of origin. This new identity was necessary, Elijah Muhammad had preached, because "You are the planet Earth's only group of people ignorant of yourself, ignorant of your own kind, ignorant of your true history, ignorant of your enemy! . . . You are members of the Asiatic nation, from the tribe of Shabazz!" (1965:357).

In his *Autobiography*, itself a work of mediated representation, Malcolm X freely acknowledges the centrality of the mass media in the growth and development of what became popularly know as the "Black Muslims."[16] He recounts how it was on his initiative in 1957 that the Nation published its own newspaper. "One day every month, I'd lock up in a room and assemble my material and pictures for a printer that I found. I named the newspaper *Muhammad Speaks* and Muslim brothers sold it on the ghetto sidewalks" (Haley 1965:339). The television program mentioned earlier, "The Hate . . .," was produced with the consent of the movement and greatly anticipated as a form of publicity and an organizing tool. Although they authorized the production of the program, the movement had no control over the actual result, which according to Malcolm X "was edited to increase the shock mood" (1965). Yet, the "shock" was interpreted differently in the black and white communities, at least in the black ghettoes, where it increased curiosity and thus potential membership. The program was followed by similarly "shocking" newspaper and news weekly accounts, which also increased the movement's visibility. No one was more conscious and more skillful than Malcolm X when it came to manipulating the mass media, turning need of powerful imagery and colorful "threatening" characterization to serve other ends.

Malcolm X modified the redemptive narrative inherited from Marcus Garvey through Elijah Muhammad, with special reference to the meaning and recollection of slavery. As well known as the details of his life is the fact of Malcolm X's break with the Nation of Islam and his attempts to redirect black nationalism along more secular lines. Just prior to his assassination in February, 1965,

Malcolm X completed a "Basic Unity Program" that would ground this new nationalism. It was addressed to "Afro-Americans, people who originated in Africa and now reside in America," advising them to "speak out against the slavery and oppression inflicted upon us by this racist power structure." The stated aim of the organization, which sought to unify and represent all black Americans, was to "launch a cultural revolution which will provide the means for restoring our identity that we might rejoin our brothers and sisters on the African continent, culturally, psychologically, economically and share with them the sweet fruits of freedom from oppression and independence of racist governments" (Van Deburg 1997:108).

One of the cornerstones of this new phase of Africanism was the idea of self-determination as a form of redemption, with the locus now moved from the individual and the group to the nation. In the Program, Malcolm X put it this way: "We assert that we Afro-Americans have the right to direct and control our lives, our history and our future rather than have our destinies determined by American racists." Central to self-determination was control over history and its representation: "We are determined to rediscover our true African culture which was crushed and hidden for over four hundred years in order to enslave us and keep us enslaved up to today ... " We, Afro-Americans – enslaved, oppressed and denied by a society that proclaims itself the citadel of democracy, are determined to rediscover our history, promote the talents that are suppressed by our racist enslavers, renew the culture that was crushed by a slave government and thereby – to again become a free people" (Van Deburg 1997b:109).

Here slavery is not something relegated to the past, it is forever present. This slavery is economic, involving the exploitation of black labor, but it is primarily cultural, a form of slavery of the mind which denies to the enslaved the possibility to develop their own "talents." Here it would be impossible to view slavery as a past stage of development, which may have either hindered that development or promoted it. It would also be difficult to see slavery as a resource, itself the basis of a form of culture, no matter how distorted and mis-formed. Rather, as represented here, slavery is something lived and living, an inherited and transmitted habitus which determines current behavior and thus requires a radical spiritual transformation in order to be rooted out. The rediscovery of one's true past is central to this transformation.

As developed in the Program, a central part of this rediscovery was the opening of communication channels between the new Africa and black America. This was meant in a more than symbolic sense and involved developing mass media, "independent national and international newspapers, publishing ventures, personal contacts and other available communications media" (Van Deburg 1997b:110). The new Africa could teach black Americans not only about their past but also about their possible future. Concerning the past, Africa could teach black Americans "the truths about American slavery and the terrible effects it has on our people. We must study the modern system of slavery in order to free ourselves from it. We must search out all the bare and ugly facts without shame for we are all victims, still slaves – still oppressed" (1997b:111). Concerning the future, the new Africa offered a model of society in which tradition and modernity could be combined.

In this narrative, redemption would come through rejecting the legacy of slavery, most importantly the psychological burden it continued to impose on the African American, and then being reborn as blacks, no longer Negroes, hyphenated Americans, or anything other than original and authentic black people. Black self-determination, in a physical and cultural sense, whether in Africa or in separate communities or city-states on the American continent, was the goal.[17] In this narrative, blacks are sojourners, a diasporic condition, an existence which can only be redeemed through rejecting the cultural heritage imposed by the white enemy. Thus the significance of renaming and other cleansing rituals. The taking of a new name, either an African-sounding name, or one with the even more symbolic and provocative "X," was a symbol of beginning again, washing away an imposed identity and a relation to an imposed past. Elijah Muhammad put it this way: "Your slavemaster, he brought you over here, and your past everything was destroyed. Today, you do not know your true language. What tribe are you from? You would not recognize your tribe's name if you heard it. You don't know nothing about your true culture. You don't even know your family's real name. You are wearing a *white man's* name! The white slavemaster, who *hates* you!" (quoted in Haley 1965:357).

A renaming ritual was central to the cultural nationalism represented by Amiri Baraka and discussed below, for adults and also for the newly born: "On this day we commit our child Mali to the Black nation forever becoming. We promise to teach her identity, support her in her purpose and provide her with the direction she needs to build a better place for Black people on earth" (quoted in Woodard 1999:90). Baraka had himself previously changed his name from Leroy to LeRoi Jones, as a means of symbolizing a desired identity change. Renaming had roots in celebrations following emancipation, where freed blacks

commonly celebrated emancipation by taking a new name. A new name was both a symbol of personal liberation and an act of political defiance; it reversed the enslavement process and confirmed the free (black's) newly won liberty just as the loss of an African name had earlier symbolized enslavement. Emancipation also gave blacks the opportunity to strip themselves of the comic classical names that had dogged them in slavery and to adopt common Anglo-American names. Very few Caesars, Pompeys, and Catos remained among the new freemen. In bondage, most blacks had but a single name; freedom also allowed them the opportunity to take another.   (Berlin 1974:51–52)

This might not have always been actively chosen or achieved. In her novel *Song of Solomon*, Toni Morrison recounts with irony and humor how one central character, a successful black businessman named Macon Dead inherited his no less provocative and symbolic name: "His own parents, in some mood of perverseness or resignation, had agreed to abide by a naming done to them by somebody who couldn't have cared less. Agreed to take and pass on to all their issue this heavy name scrawled in perfect thoughtlessness by a drunken Yankee in the Union Army" (Morrison1977:23).

The taking on of a new name was part of a ritual of emersion and rebirth, beginning of a pathway that will lead to redemption, liberation from the past, and the chance to begin again on a new footing. It was an act of self-determination, in which an individual relocated themselves with a chosen as well as reconstructed collective. The name change of the boxer Muhammad Ali, a key figure in the struggle for representation of this generation, illustrates this very well. Born Cassius Clay in Louisville, Kentucky, Ali was given his "original name" by Elijah Muhammad in 1964. Against his own protests, Clay was transformed into Ali without the intermediate "waiting period" as Cassius X Clay (Marqusee 1999:84ff.). At one conscious stroke, Clay "claimed a new heritage, a new nation, a new family" (1999:86). As a representative figure, the impact was immediate and the repercussions severe. This was no mere adoption of a "stage name," it was a *nom de guerre* in the full sense. The heavyweight boxing champion of the world carries much symbolic weight, especially a black champion, and he is expected to be "a credit to his race." In accepting this name change, Ali was also accepting a racial conception that was unacceptable to many blacks and to most whites. He would soon be punished by being stripped of his title, if not of his representative role. This points to another dimension in the notion of representation. Being designated as representative can imply a burden, carrying a symbolic load that one does not expect or want. While Ali appears to have gloried in this role, others have rejected it or found it too heavy to bear for long.

Secular nationalism: cultural and political

The cultural nationalism that developed in the mid-1960s, differed from both Garveyism and the Nation of Islam in that it was neither religiously based nor focused on the African continent as such. Its Africa was modern and revolutionary, forward looking and traditional at the same time. While it had no clear theological basis, its Africa was spiritual and could encompass a variety of religious orientations, including Islam and Christianity. It involved the development of a black nationality, rather than a "nation" in the geographic sense and it was open to various religious orientations. In this sense, it was a nationality that was broad enough, at least in theory, to include nationalists of the former type, i.e., neo-Garveyists, and religious nationalists like the members of the Nation of Islam, as well as black Christians. Several factors contributed to the development of this generationally based collective consciousness which could incorporate what had previous divided segments of the black population. Of course, it was itself only a segment of that population, even if in its own self-presentation it spoke for all of "the people." The basis of black cultural nationalism or black nationality was urban, like the Harlem Renaissance, but it was more populist in its ideology and in its base than the latter. This cultural nationalism called for cultural regeneration, seeking to create a space for what was seen to be African culture within the black communities of urban America. In terms of the two narratives, this cultural nationalism called for inclusion but not assimilation, and in that sense it was neither progressive nor evolutionary.[18] It defined the limits of inclusion in formal terms: American citizenship was a basis, but not acculturation into the core values of the culture. Rather it sought to "create the conditions for the flowering of the African personality" (Woodard 1999:xiii) within the institutional framework provided by modern, urban America.

The 1960s appeared differently to whites and blacks. Whites tend to remember the sixties as filled with political and cultural confrontation, where young college students protested against the war in Vietnam, where a sexual revolution altered the boundaries of what was normal and acceptable, and where feminism changed the way Americans looked at gender, marriage and family life. This view of the decade focuses on college campuses, popular culture, and social movements. It is a view which those on both the political left and right can accept, even where they evaluate the events and results differently. Blacks, especially those influenced by cultural nationalism, remember something different. Here the period tends to be viewed through a perceived defeat of the civil rights movement, the failure to either achieve its goals of inclusion or to speak to the specific needs of urban blacks. The failure, in other words, of the progressive narrative. The 1960s from this perspective is a decade filled with violent urban confrontations, between an increasingly frustrated black community and an unyielding white establishment. While whites may view the war in Vietnam as a still-unresolved national trauma (Neal 1998), for blacks the trauma has deeper roots, resulting from the failure once again of the promise of inclusion, except perhaps for a new black professional elite and a consequent expansion of the middle class. From this perspective, Africa, slavery, and the cultural resurgence of the Harlem Renaissance were focal points of reference. Was the Harlem Renaissance a "success" or not, what does Africa and slavery mean, in terms of positive or negative "heritage," were central issues around which a new generation of intellectuals took form.

The Southern-based civil rights movement faced great barriers in mobilizing urban and middle-class blacks. A song addressed to "all them middle class Negroes" and sung in dialect by the Reverend Frederick Douglass Kirkpatrick and Jim Collier expresses this conflict: "You may laugh at our bushy hair/and the worn out clothes we wear/We got everything when we got freedom/And you're just a laughing fool . . . But when segregation is broken down/you will see every Tom in town/sittin' at lunch counters smokin' big cigars/ (and saying) 'Look what we have done'/Try to take the credit from dead heroes/moldin' in the ground" (B side #89, 1968).

Aside from the problem of class-based freeriders, the problems in the urban ghettoes were more complicated and the resistance even stronger. Urban ghettoes had been cordoned off since the 1930s in cities like Chicago and New York as patterns of segregation were habitually enforced and "natural" in appearance. Black and white worlds rarely met or mixed, except in structured situations, such as at work or in those anonymous public situations where there is no "implication that the persons involved are friends or even acquaintances" (Drake and Cayton 1945:102). Rather, "they are simply isolated, atomized individuals who happen to be sitting, standing, looking, watching, pushing, shoving side-by-side. Each minds his own business and is under no obligation to be friendly or even courteous to others. People are lost in the crowd. This is the equality of anonymity" (1945). In these anonymous urban environments, the things Southern blacks were fighting for had been tacitly achieved. As long as the borders of social segregation, usually invisible, yet commonly known and acknowledged boundaries, were respected, life went on. The famous attempt to march into white Chicago in 1965 and the clashes that resulted are symbolic of this difficulty and difference. As Drake and Cayton had shown more than twenty years earlier, economic expansion had drawn black migrants to a city where jobs were plentiful but housing was not. Forced by habit and white resistance to live in proscribed areas, the "Black Belt," the black population constantly pushed against invisible walls, as when a young black boy swam across an invisible line in Lake Michigan and was drowned in the ensuing protest as whites attempted to protect "their" beach, an incident which sparked a race riot. The civil rights movement made these walls visible, but, with its established tactical repertoire, could not remove them. The causes of the urban "revolts" or "riots," the terminology depends on perspective, were multifaceted and complex, but their ideological outcome was clear, black nationalism as framed through the redemptive narrative became hegemonic in the Northern ghetto for at least a decade. This was a new, modernized narrative, however, one that rooted itself in urban ghettoes, in their street talk and worldview. It articulated a new "Africa" and a new version of black history.

Besides the failure of the civil rights movement to develop tactics to deal with the deeply rooted problems of the urban ghetto, two other factors are significant in explaining this hegemonic shift, the economic and political effects of the escalating Vietnam War and the movements of national liberation in what was now being called the "Third World." The costs of escalating the Vietnam War cut into the "Great Society" programs for fighting poverty and integrating the black population. The program of the Johnson administration, at least in theory, exemplified the progressive narrative; the costs of war made it increasingly difficult to put into practice. These difficulties occurred at the same time as the anti-war movement was growing and as the war itself was coming to be interpreted in racial terms. Stokeley Carmichael of SNCC would later change his name to Kwame Ture, a ritual followed by many urban black activists.

The new black nationalism modernized as it revitalized the nationalism of the 1920s and 1930s. The African national liberation movements provided not only an emotional source of inspiration, but also a Marxist-inspired theory of colonialism and imperialism, which moved blacks from the margins to the center of world history. However, these theories were modified to better fit an American experience. The basic notion of black self-determination was translated into the very American idea of community control, with the principles of direct democracy and grass-roots organization, as well as local leadership, being called for. The approach was also "cultural" in the sense of emphasizing individual-based cognitive transformation as the precursor and prerequisite of social transformation. Ritual and ceremony, as well as other symbolic manifestations, like dress and speech and the display of weapons, were an important part of this activity, but also important were long-established traditions of American ethnic politics. As Baraka and others would point out, immigrant groups to the United States had long used the system of local politics to their advantage, while blacks had not. The Italians of Newark offered Baraka an exemplary model, while the Jews in New York and other cites offered examples of how an ethnic group could pool and exploit its economic and political resources.[19]

The turn to Africa, especially to "African culture," can be seen in this light as well. Symbolic forms of dress, art, and even religion, were seem as "African" but were invented and formed by American needs and conditions, rather than remembered or discovered through personal experience on that continent. Traditions were formed to suit the needs and desires of a new generation of ghettoized black communities, some in desperate need of regeneration and hope for the future. "African" symbols served to solidify an ethnic identity in the United States, one which could be used for political ends. Like the Nation of Islam, secular nationalism made self-transformation central to its program for community control. The nation was to be formed in the neighborhood, and the "community" out of reborn individuals. Name change, like the taking on of "X" to replace the "slave" name, was part of this process, as was the naming of children. This was a tradition begun in the Nation when "once a pupil had mastered the lessons, he or she was given an 'original' Arabic name or an X, which represented the surnames of unknown ancestors as well as the fact that the person had given up the vices of the world and was now an ex-alcoholic, ex-prostitute, ex-drug addict, ex-Uncle Tom, and/or ex-slave" (Clegg 1997:27). In the Nation, this X was meant to be temporary until an Arabic name was bestowed.[20]

West African, non-Islamic religions and kinship systems would also be called upon, sometimes in more or less unconscious ways. The popularization of the terms brother and sister to refer to fellow blacks has been traced to these African traditions. Richard Wright pointed out in *Black Power* that characteristic of the West Africa regions from which the lineage of the majority of American blacks could be traced was ancestor worship and a matriarchal kinship system. Both played a determining role in the practices of everyday life. The return to the ancestral culture, if not place, was a central ingredient in the secular black nationalism of the mid-1960s. These ancestors provided a source of identity that reached behind slavery, to a form of life which could be useful even in urban America, a positive source of identification, a symbolic homeland, and a useable past, like that available to other ethnic groups. A similar process would occur later within the progressive narrative frame when black feminists looked to an imagined matriarchal extended family life in the rural South, to their grandmothers, as a source of inspiration and redemption.

Slavery was important here again. It represented a unifying primal scene, that which all had in common as a point of identification, if not as a resource. Even this localized, positive African culture was represented as a unified and unifying integrated whole – slavery was the shared heritage that re-membered an uprooted (now for the second time after the waves of migration) and fragmented community. This is exemplified in one of Amiri Baraka's most powerful and best-known plays, *Dutchman*, a title which seemingly bears no relation to its content. The play concerns a very contemporary urban experience, the highly symbolic encounter on a New York subway between an aggressive white female and a passive black male. The title, however, apparently refers to the Dutch-owned ships which carried the first black slaves to the American continent. Slavery, in other words, is what first put that black male in the position where he now finds himself attracted to a white woman who will eventually murder him. In addition, tastes in music and food, said to be derived from slavery and the slave experience, will be significant also in grounding this shared identity.

Despite significant gains in supporters among the middle class in the 1960s and 1970s, the Nation of Islam remained rooted in the aspiring lower classes and the middle aged. Cultural and political nationalism appealed more to the young, the better educated, and the aspiring intellectuals who rejected the middle-class path, even if it was rooted in religious separatism. Rather than middle-class standards of behavior, the model and audience was the "street," the tough urban youth culture with an "African" coloring. "African" hats, clothing, hairstyles, and rituals replaced and challenged the suit and tie of the aspiring middle-class "race man," as revitalized by the Nation. Accommodation would be made, however, as the idea of a black united front developed in the mid-sixties.

As Malcolm X was a key figure in both the modernization and the phenomenal expansion of religious-based black nationalism as a political force, Amari Baraka was a key figure in the transformation of secular nationalism. Baraka saw himself as an interpreter of Malcolm X's legacy and the latter's assassination in 1965 as a turning point in his own life. But the two were very different in their role as intellectuals. While Malcolm mediated between the ghetto and the movement, using the street mentality he had acquired through his own experience to "fish" and redeem others, Baraka mediated between the cultural radicalism of Greenwich Village and an emerging generation of black intellectuals formed in the newly instituted black studies programs. Africa and slavery would have a central place here as well, but they would be differently represented and interpreted, as will be discussed below. As previously noted, institutionalized black studies incorporated tensions reflected in the two dominant narrative frames. The redemptive narrative was here enhanced by an Afro-centrism as well as nationalism.[21] As with Malcolm X, the civil rights movement provided a counter-foil against which to define and transform black nationalism. The civil rights movement was deemed a "failure," as well as "white," and participating blacks as "Uncle Toms" and part of the "black bourgeoisie," a term made popular by E. Franklin Frazier, in this generational as well as ideological struggle.

Born Leroy Jones in Newark, New Jersey in 1934, Baraka studied sociology with Frazier and literature with Sterling Brown at Howard University. After three years in the Air Force, Baraka settled in Greenwich Village in 1957, working as clerk for *Record Changer* magazine (*Dictionary of Literary Biography* 1983:3–24). Together with his first wife, Hattie (Cohen) Jones, who worked among other things as advertising and business manager for the *Partisan Review*, one of New York's premier small journals, Jones became a major organizing force in the bohemian avant garde, as critic, editor, and publisher and as a poet and playwright. The couple edited and published *Yugen* "a new consciousness in arts and letters," a journal of contemporary poetry, to which Allen Ginsberg, Jack Kerouac, Gary Snyder, Gregory Corso, William Burroughs, and Frank O'Hara, among many others, contributed. They also founded Totem Press, which published literary pieces and manifestos. Together with the poet Diane DiPrima, Jones put out *Floating Bear*, a newsletter which served to interconnect the various literary circles which composed Greenwich Village at the time and to promote a cross-fertilization (Charters 1992:334). Through these efforts, Baraka became a major force in the literary avant garde of the 1950s. As one contemporary remembered, "LeRoi Jones had a magnetic and powerful personality, and his magazine immediately began to flourish – so much so, in fact, that the poets and writers who contributed to it and were drawn to Jones' apartment . . . became known as the *Yugen* crowd" (cited in *Dictionary of Literary Biography* 1983:7). Their apartment, as Hattie Jones (1990) writes in her own memoirs, functioned as a meeting place and floating seminar, a salon for the bohemian literary culture of New York.

In addition this mediating role, Jones published his own poetry, including the collection "Preface To A Twenty Volume Suicide Note . . . " in 1961. Here, like the Beat poets he socialized with, Jones mediates between popular and high culture, as well as between white and black. As Du Bois had done earlier, Jones came to see music as the central force in black life, one which divided as well as united blacks. An example of the latter can be found in his play *The Eight Ditch*, published in the June 1961 issue of *Floating Bear*. The play centers on a conflict between two boys at a black boy scout camp in the late 1940s, one middle class, who identifies and is identified through the music of Nat King Cole, and the other, lower class, who likes rhythm and blues. Despite these tensions and differences at the level of taste, Jones argues, especially in *Blues People* (1963), but also in earlier articles, that it is music which provides the fundamental basis for a common and distinctive black culture. It is music which provides the basic form of expression, its "primary expressive language." And it is through music that blacks have been able to maintain their identity and alternative to the dominant American culture. Here his views are similar to those proposed by his white Bohemian contemporaries. Jack Kerouac, for example, saw jazz as providing the rhythm for his *On the Road* and Harlem's music clubs as a place from which to escape the pressures imposed by white, middle-class America.

A trip to Cuba in 1960 was a major catalyst in transforming the bohemian poet Jones into the black nationalist Baraka. A member of the Fair Play for Cuba Committee, Jones traveled to Havana together with Harold Cruse, Robert Williams (a NAACP leader who advocated bearing arms), and other black artists and intellectuals.[22] Although he would poke fun at this group, "one embarrassingly dull (white) communist, his professional Negro (i.e., unstraightened hair, 1930s bohemian peasant blouses, etc., militant integrationist, etc.) wife who wrote embarrassingly inept social comment-type poems, usually about one or sometimes a group of Negroes being mistreated in general (usually in Alabama, etc.). Two middle-class young Negro ladies from Philadelphia . . . One 1920s 'New Negro' type African scholar (one of those terrible examples of what the 'Harlem Renaissance' was at its worst) . . . " (cited in *DLB* 1983:10), this trip further politicized Jones, not least through the exchanges with Latin American writers and intellectuals. The contact with Williams would also prove decisive. When the latter was forced to flee the South and then the United States after advocating and organizing armed self-defense for blacks in North Carolina,

Jones worked for the Monroe Defense Committee and organized an interracial group of intellectuals as a way of mediating both personally and more generally between Harlem and the Village.

The assassination of Malcolm X in 1965 sparked the final stages of Baraka's transformation from bohemian to revolutionary black nationalist. In rapid succession, he divorced his white wife, took on an Islamic name and moved to Harlem, into the Black Arts Repertory Theater/School he had helped organize the previous year (*DLB* 1983:17–18). Two essays, "The Legacy of Malcolm X" and "The Coming of the Black Nation," published in a 1966 collection significantly entitled *Home* (Jones 1966), announced this change. In another essay contained in this collection, "Black is a Country" recounted the meaning of national liberation struggles in Latin America and Asia, in addition to Africa, for American blacks. These movements offered a model of emancipation that did not necessarily imply leaving the country, and Jones concluded "America is as much a black country as a white one." Redemption, in other words, could be attained through cultural rejuvenation and control of the local, urban communities in the United States.

The notions of black "community" and the "people" were central to the ideology of secular nationalism, as was the idea of "nation." One of Baraka's most compelling poems carries the title "It's Nation Time," and the phrase was repeated over and over in some of his public addresses. He would ask "What time is it?" and the audience responded "It's Nation Time!" While the civil rights movement in its early phase would speak of a "beloved community," where race was secondary to shared vision, nationalism invoked the idea of a black community, in the real and imagined sense. Since the movement was committed to the idea of community control and of working in "the community," it had a real, geographically based community in mind. The concept also referred to a wider and imagined community which would include all members of the "race" and the "nation." Here the notion of the community can be related to the revived interest in Africa, especially West Africa, where kinship networks form the dominant social system (Wright 1954). The use of the familial "brother" and "sister," which became common in the modern black nationalism of the 1960s, has at least some of its roots in this notion of the family or kinship-based community/nation. The term "the people" carried the same meaning; it was used in a way similar to the notion of the "masses" in Marxist rhetoric and in the American constitution.

As poet and playwright, Baraka was a central figure in what came to be called the Black Arts Movement (BAM), and what Hay (1994) calls the "Era of Black Revolutionary Drama" which evolved in the years between 1964 and 1972. Here, the notion of a black aesthetic grounded the national community as a separate race. As Mitchell (1994:9) explains, "Just as the Civil Rights movement encouraged an aesthetic of integration, the social and political issues of the 1960s generated a new literary politics, a Black Aesthetic, an aesthetic of separatism." Baraka's move from Greenwich Village to Harlem, and the founding of the Black Arts Repertory/School, mentioned above, can be considered as originating events in this cultural politics. The group of artists and intellectuals assembled within the BAM considered themselves as the cultural wing of the Black Power movement. Larry Neal, one of the key figures, put it this way in one of the movement's manifestos:

The Black Arts Movement is radically opposed to any concept of the artist that alienates him from his community. Black art is the aesthetic and spiritual sister of the Black Power concept. As such, it envisions an art that speaks directly to the needs and aspirations of Black America. In order to perform this task, the Black Arts Movement proposes a radical reordering of the western cultural aesthetic. It proposes a separate symbolism, mythology, critique, and iconology. The Black Arts and the Black Power concept both relate broadly to the Afro-American's desire for self-determination and nationhood. Both concepts are nationalistic. One is concerned with the relationship between art and politics; the other with the art of politics. (Quoted in Mitchell 1994)

Where the New Negro movement sought to use art as a means of proving the worthiness and level of development of the "race," accepting European aesthetic ideals as universal criteria, the BAM rejected this idea and the aesthetic and political principles upon which it was based. Instead, criteria would be found in Africa and in the highly charged notion of "blackness," a form of consciousness rather than a color. In "The Myth of a Negro Literature" Baraka had already proclaimed that "Negro literature," because it was produced by the middle class, was "mediocre" and a "myth." Only in music, where a basic rootedness in black culture was maintained, could significant accomplishments be found, "because it drew its strengths and beauties out of the depth of the black man's soul, and because to a large extent its traditions could be carried on by the lowest classes of Negroes, has been able to survive the constant and willful dilutions of the black middle class" (Baraka in Mitchell 1994:165). In other areas of culture, Negroes too readily accepted the European distinction between "high" and "popular" culture, especially in literature and the visual arts. This too was an effect of slavery. "The artifacts of African art and sculpture were consciously eradicated by slavery" (1994:168), he wrote. The "people," not the middle class, were the authentic voice and bearers of blackness, and only music, "blues and jazz have been the only consistent exhibitors of 'Negritude' in formal American culture simply because the bearers of its tradition maintained their essential identities as Negroes' (1994:165–66). Untainted folk culture, in other words, contained roots upon which contemporary blackness could grow and develop. This is not far from the path cut by Du Bois in *Souls* as the process of cultural trauma began, although now in a very different historical context.

It was to and from the "people" and the "community" that the BAM drew its inspiration and addressed its aspirations. These were the real and imagined urban communities, with real and imagined patterns of speech, dress, and needs that would be represented in and through a black aesthetic. Hoyt Fuller (in Mitchell 1994) defined this aesthetic as "a system of isolating and evaluating the artistic works of black people which reflect the special character and imperatives of black experience" (what Bourdieu would call a "habitus"), with writers "deliberately striving to invest their work with the distinctive styles and rhythms and colors of the ghetto." The authentic voice of blackness, the most untainted by "whiteness," was to be found in the ghetto. Where, earlier, Zora Neale Hurston and Langston Hughes has gone into the deepest South to find authentic black culture, black intellectuals and artists were looking to the urban ghettoes for inspiration and redemption. These ideas were unified in the Kawaida theory of black culture formalized by Ron Karenga, another key actor in the development of culturally rooted black nationalism. With this as basis, Baraka developed an ideology and a model of representation to replace the protest tradition identified with Du Bois. In theatrical terms, this meant that "playwrights no longer represented appeals to share power, but depicted seizures of power" (Hay 1994:96). More broadly, artistic representation would be guided by the seven basic principles of Kawaida which Baraka transformed into guiding norms: Umoja (Unity), Kujichagulia (Self-Determination), Ujima (Collective Work and Responsibility), Ujamaa (Cooperative Economics), Nia (Purpose), Kuumba (Creativity), and Imani (Faith) (Hay 1994:97ff.). These ideas and rituals would later gain wider support, primarily amongst the educated black middle class, and become institutionalised in Afro-centric black studies programs, as discussed in a later section. They provide a way of dealing with cultural trauma by offering an alternative history and a set of practices which define a distinct collective, yet which do not necessarily interfere with other forms of social action, or integration, including "success" as defined by the dominant culture.

The civil rights movement and the progressive narrative

Seen through the lens of cultural trauma, the wave of protests which began in the 1950s and became known as the civil rights movement was both an expression and a reformulation of the progressive narrative and its faith in the future. Building upon cognitive and practical traditions originating in the late nineteenth-century reaction to the failure of reconstruction the movement articulated both the gains and disappointments of the post-war period. In terms of audience and activists, the movement was multiracial and assimilationist, as it mediated and negotiated between black and white worlds. The movement exemplified, in other words, Du Bois' "double consciousness" on a mass scale and sought to reconcile the two in a new historical context. In the process it drew upon models of emancipation reaching back to the Enlightenment and Abolitionism, and to the spirituality of the black church, as expressed through movement intellectuals situated in organizations like the NAACP and the Urban League, the labor movement and, most visibly, the church. The movement began with protests concerning public transportation and the boycott of white stores and other services, recalling a long history of confrontation. Its demands concerned social inclusion and its vision of America was decidedly along the lines specified in the Constitution and the Bill of Rights, "one nation, indivisible, with freedom and justice for all."

The black church, as mentioned earlier, originated in response to the seg-regationist policies of white religious denominations and developed parallel to them. The largest denomination and the most central to the movement, the Baptist church, retained a Southern basis, as well as a rural flavor. Du Bois was influential in constituting the sociological discourse on the black church with a study published in 1902, the year before the more famous *Souls*. Since then, black scholars have distinguished between a "class" and a "feeling" church (Lincoln 1974), where the former offers a more staid service for the upwardly mobile and educated and the latter a more evangelical service. It was the latter type of church which was central to the movement, while the former proved more conservative and reluctant. This "feeling" church was more internally oriented and culturally more independent than the former. Its worldview, its form of service, was Old Testament, with ministers giving direct representa-tions of the word of God, rather than offering learned interpretations. Martin Luther King exemplified this in taking on the role of prophet, out to redeem the soul of America – a quite different project than that envisioned in the redemp-tive narrative. Its representation of the good Negro was Southern and rural, in bib overalls, the former slave who now wanted the full citizenship only half promised in the Constitution. This was an image congenial to many whites, especially in the North. Even Northern blacks who traveled south to participate in the movement found this image appealing and took it on, like the Harvard-educated Bob Moses, who had changed his name to fit the Biblical references and model of emancipation which guided the movement.

Although it may have appeared so on the surface, the idea of racial progress did not disappear from the South with the millions who migrated. Even in the rural areas where anthropologists and sociologists did their fieldwork, generational changes in attitude could be seen. As early as the 1930s, Hortense Powdermaker (1968) found generational differences in black attitudes towards whites. She discovered that a older generation, those born before the civil war tended to trust in the good will of "good" whites, "their children . . . born just before the turn of the century, more typically continued to behave as if they accepted the superiority of whites but seldom really believed in it" (Payne 1995:22). This can in part be explained as an unexpected result of the re-establishment of Jim Crow segregation, which had the paradoxical effect of creating spheres where blacks had less contact with whites, allowing a degree of freedom and also the growth of literacy and the spread of radio and other mass media offering other sources of influence in the formation of ideas and attitudes. In this generation one uncovered more resentment, but still no dramatic change in behavior, explainable by the conditions under which they lived. Recalling her childhood in the 1940s, Maya Angelou (1974:62) wrote: "Along with other black children in small Southern villages, I had accepted the total polariza-tion of the races as a psychological comfort. Whites existed, as no one denied, but they were not present in my everyday life." We have earlier described this generation as the one experiencing most directly the cultural trauma, the ef-fects of rejection, and the need to reorient individual and collective identity as segregation was violently re-imposed.

By the 1940s, according to Charles Payne (1995:23), "that attitude . . . had begun to grow into various forms of political mobilization," especially in ur-ban centers. Thus by the mid-1940s the secretary of the Jackson, Mississippi NAACP, had "organized a chapter of the National Progressive Voters League, focusing on voter registration." In 1944 the Supreme Court outlawed the white primary, in which only whites had been permitted to vote, and by 1947 the per-centage of blacks registered to vote in the South as a whole rose from 3 percent in 1940 to 12 percent. By 1952 it was 20 percent. Not only were there rising expectations for inclusion in the train of "national progress" in the South, there were emerging possibilities as well, as more and more black youths attended the segregated colleges and other institutions of higher learning. There was also, of course, massive resistance. A cloud of fear and hatred and the threat of violence, hung above and supported ingrained habits and frames of reference.

The prime sources from which this habitus could be altered, as well as re-inforced, were the black press, the church, the educational institutions, and the carriers of popular culture, radio, records and television. These were sites and carriers of the progressive narrative, the dream of racial progress and inclusion into the American mainstream culture of success and the freedom to move, choose, and be seen and heard.

As it had done since emancipation, the black press in the South contin-ued to provide a vehicle of communication and encouragement for the black community it helped constitute. Run by educated, middle-class professionals, now largely independent of the church, these daily but for the most part weekly newspapers, and monthly magazines, promoted the values of the larger American society. They reported local and national success stories as they also tried to tell the "black" side of the news. And for a racial minority identified through skin color, individual greatness brought respect to the collective. This is why the success of sports heroes was so important, even if, as many were quick to point out, it didn't put more food on the table. In the 1940s and 1950s, these success stories became more frequent and were made more visible through the black mass media, and the media more generally. "The Jackie Robinson Story," to cite an extreme example, was a popular Hollywood film in the 1950s and was shown in public schools in some parts of the nation, like my own in Brooklyn.[23] This was a success "story" for the individual, the race, and the society, now viewed on a larger scale than Joe Louis had been earlier. It was a story of progress through inclusion, and like the radio program "Americans All" promoted the "success" of the nation as well as that of a racial minority. This was made even more important by the cold war which was probably one motivating factor in this struggle for recognition and representation.

Inclusion, like representation, means many things, of course, and involves several levels and dimensions. For the most part, blacks interpreted inclusion to mean being regarded as citizens in the formal sense and human beings in the social sense. Throughout its history, the black press and the other institutions did many other things as well, courageous things, campaigning against lynching and racial violence of all sorts, encouraging voter registration and exposing violations, supporting boycotts and other forms of resistance, and so on, the point here is not to downplay these, but rather to place the press and other black media within a more general narrative framework concerning what "inclusion" meant. At the same time, it is important to realize that the very nature of the society that black Americans were fighting to be included in, was itself changing significantly. By the time blacks had achieved some measure of formal inclusion, not only the right to vote but the possibility of voting and working, and of living where one chose to, the basic rights of citizenship, American society or at least one dominant self-image, was on the way to becoming a consumer society, where success was measured in how much wealth one could accumulate and display. This was no longer a society of yeomen farmers, where land ownership was a measure of success and the basis of citizenship rights, and home life was regulated though religious organizations and small towns and villages, nor was it a society of collectively organized workers, where individual success was linked to collective solidarity at work and leisure time spent in close knit, class and ethnically linked neighborhoods. By the time blacks were actively and collectively struggling to be included, America would be redefining itself as an individualistic, consumer-oriented society, where the mass media were as much organs to promote that consumption and the values that sustained it, as to connect and articulate an imagined community. The black press, as discussed earlier, had contained a measure of this, at least since the Civil War, in reporting the goings on of black "society," which was also a means of displaying the worthiness of the race to the surrounding white public, as well as a means of connecting a black community. Like the press in general, the black press also relied on advertising, as well as a politically diverse black community, to sustain itself.

In his study of the black press during the civil rights movement between 1960 and 1965, Simmons (1998) reveals some of the extent of this diversity. Simmons recounts the coverage of the movement in a sampling of black newspapers, primarily in the South. In the first place, the advent of an active and open civil rights struggle was a stimulus to the expansion of the black media themselves, as "nationally 217 newspapers were begun in response to the civil rights movement; California had at least 32 at one time, while Illinois had 28. Mississippi was third with 18" (Simmons 1998:91). However, the type of activism expressed by the sit-ins and other confrontations revealed not only political but also generational differences in the black community. According to Simmons:

in the previous eras the black press had played the role of leader or "champions of the black people". With the start of the sit-ins, however, the black press responded to the civil rights movement only by reporting the news made by the people, editorializing occasionally about the progress of social or moral events, and taking an occasional jab at governments when legislation was not enacted or properly enforced in a timely manner. With the widespread coverage by commercial television . . . and the attention of the much larger white print press to black affairs, the black press was relegated from being a "fighting press" to being a conveyer of black community news.   (1998:103)

This was not so much the effect of any "structural change in the public sphere" as of the rising power of other forms of mass media.

There were other aspects as well, including the generational and political differences mentioned above. One of the black newspapers covered in Simmons' study was the *Jackson* (Mississippi) *Advocate*, under the editorship of Percy Greene. Greene's editorial policy had supported legalistic civil rights advocacy during the Second World War, but in the 1960s vehemently opposed the sit-ins as an unlawful, backward step for the race, which in addition was part of a "Communist Conspiracy." In the latter Greene included not only the students and their sit-ins but also Martin Luther King, Jr. Two editorial citations are enough to reveal Greene's position:

Despite urgings of the militant and impatient, despite the exuberance of our youths as now being exhibited in the sit-down protests, we say that the future hopes of Negroes for enjoying freedom and citizenship in accordance with the high ideals, without resorting to revolutionary techniques can best await the inevitable actions of the Congress of the United States, and the development of American public opinion.

(March 5, 1960, Simmons 1998:101)

Now comes the Reverend Martin Luther King, magnified far beyond his wisdom, fore-sight, experience, and ability following the Montgomery Bus Boycott, which all things considered, has brought nothing but grief and hardship to an increasing number of Negroes in Montgomery and the rest of Alabama, talking about if Negroes in this coun-try are not soon given full rights as American citizens, they will forsake democracy and turn to some other ideology. Since it is the only other ideology challenging democracy in the world it appears obvious and logical to assume that the other ideology alluded to by Rev. King is communism.   (January 13, 1962, Simmons 1998:108)

The political differences seem clear enough, but there are also generational differences at work here. One of the ways this conflict expressed itself was in the proper name for African Americans. Directly after emancipation, as dis-cussed in chapter 2, this issue of naming was constitutive of what emancipation signified: self-determination. That issue was never settled, but became part of a generationally based struggle over the terms of agreement between a dominant culture and the black minority. The notion of the New Negro was an example of that negotiated settlement, one that was processed both within the "commu-nity" and at the same time between it and the dominant culture. This process of naming was part of a more general struggle to define the situation, that is to say, what things really meant, of which the meaning of the sit-ins was also a part. Greene and other members of his generation used the term "Negroes" when referring to the collective, while the "youths" he referred to called themselves "blacks." There was also the issue of how this should be printed, with a capital "B" which would mean eliminating the need for another noun like "Negro," or with a small "b" equivalent to "white," used to denote color and in need of further clarification, as in black race or black people or simply, blacks.[24]

The meaning of the past and of specific historical events came also into play in determining the significance of current events as part of this internal struggle to define the situation. For Percy Greene, the meaning was clear:

According to the historians and students of the south, the ill manners and the intemperate conduct of Negroes, urged on by the carpetbaggers and other adventurers who had entered the south to exploit the Negro issue, largely for their own benefit without any regard for the Negroes future, was largely responsible for the tragedy of the Post Reconstruction Era. The Era which saw the Hayes – Tilden Deal and the Un-written Compromise, which brought about the withdrawal of the Federal Troops from the south, took away all the gains that had been made by Negroes, made possible the one-party system of politics in the south, and put upon the Negroes all of the handicaps of segregation and discrimination . . . It is important for us, the Negro citizens of the state, in the light of the above brief sketch of southern and Negro history that we make sure that nothing in our conduct and manners, and in our attitude and relations with our white neighbors will contribute to another tragic era . . . to us this is the challenge of history.

(Simmons 1998:127)

While "history" and "experience" were weapons used by the elder generation, those younger had energy and the "present" to draw and focus upon. Like the younger generation of New Negroes in the 1920s, history, if it was important at all, was a resource and a stepping stone to the present; the past was there to be made over, not dwelled upon. This was a conception of history for "blacks," not Negroes. From this perspective, it was the future not the past that would determine the meaning of current events. Both sides had in common, however, the desire for inclusion, for incorporation into American society, although exactly in what that society consisted was a matter of contention, as was the means toward inclusion.

Of course, the *Jackson Advocate* under Percy Greene's editorship was not indicative of the black press generally during the civil rights movement, but this example does reveal a generational tension present amongst Southern blacks concerning the goals of inclusion into American society and the meaning of the past in black identity. As extreme as Greene may have been, his example does indicate that there were strong conservative elements within the Southern black community. These existed not only within the press but also within the black church and educational institutions, those very institutions which were also the grounds for social change. It was not by chance that it was a young, newly arrived minister who assumed leadership during the Montgomery bus boycott – a very reluctant leader as well. Many older black ministers refused to play such a role and would not allow their churches to be used for meetings. Activist accounts of the bus boycotts and sit-ins are full of stories of the reluctance and even the open opposition they faced from their ministers and teachers. They are also full of accounts of support. But this form of activism was essentially that of a younger generation full of hope for the future and with less interest in the "lessons of history" than their elders. Their notion of community was more that of the here and now, a community constituted through activism in a social movement, rather than out of history. This was a community, real and imagined, that sought to challenge the society that had formed around it.

While firmly rooted in the traditions of the black church, Martin Luther King reflected the values and orientations of the new generation. He was greatly affected, for example, by the emergence and success of African national liberation. In a sermon given to his Montgomery congregation in 1957, after he had been in Ghana to witness an independence celebration, King related the situation facing American blacks to the history of colonialism by mediating it through his own experience. He titled his sermon "The Birth of a New Nation" and recounted his feelings upon seeing the new flag being raised in Accra: "Before I knew, knew it, I started weeping. I was crying out for joy . . . and I could hear that old Negro spiritual crying out:

> Free at last, free at last
> Great God almighty, I'm free at last!"
> (Quoted in Lischer 1995:84)

Like the drafters of the American Constitution, King believed "freedom" to be the essence of humanity. While their belief was grounded in the Enlightenment and legitimated with reference to religion, King's grew out of the biblical worldview as developed in the black church and its models of emancipation. Here, as Richard Lischer puts it, "the universal quest for freedom owes its existence to a biblical precedent" (1995:202). In the speech quoted, King links the African freedom struggle with that of American blacks through biblical analogy, at the same time as he makes it clear that freedom will not be achieved by a return to Africa, but rather through inclusion in America. "We find ourselves breakin' a-loose from an evil Egypt, trying to move through the wilderness towards the promised land of cultural integration" (Lischer 1995:203). Both these struggles express the notion of freedom King finds in the Bible.[25]

King rose to national prominence with the Montgomery bus boycott two years earlier, an event which served to catalyze what is now called the civil rights movement. In many ways this movement and Martin Luther King himself exemplified the progressive narrative. As they developed, the aims of the movement were the inclusion of blacks as first-class American citizens. King often expressed this demand in his sermons and speeches. He opened his first public address, a speech given at the Holt Street Baptist Church directly after Rosa Parks' arrest in December, 1955, with, "You are American citizens." He continued later on by saying "This is the glory of our democracy . . . If we are wrong, the Constitution of the United States is wrong. If we are wrong, God almighty is wrong!" In his sympathetic and incisive analysis of King's sermons and preaching techniques, Richard Lischer (1995:148) reveals that King's sermonic material "reflects the same worldview and ethos to which white Baptists, Methodists, and Presbyterians had long been accustomed. The Brotherhood of Man and the Fatherhood of God."[26] This he received from his mentors within the black church and he revitalized and re-voiced it to fit the needs of mobilization in the struggle to include blacks into this brotherhood on the secular plane of American society. One of the tasks King was to perform was to transform the traditions of the black church to fit the framework of the progressive narrative and to convince his fellow blacks to act according to its aims. He mobilized and motivated within the framework set by this narrative. "His goal," according to Lischer, "was the merger of black aspirations into the American dream" (1995:142). To achieve this, King at times criticized the black church and some of his fellow ministers for passivity regarding the struggle for inclusion and civil rights; one must remember that the majority of ministers, especially in the South, were conservative and even opposed to King and *his* movement.[27] Such publicly expressed criticism was made only before black audiences, however. Further, King had to convince those blacks who accepted the goals of inclusion and were willing to participate actively in the movement, that non-violence was the best way to achieve this end. Here it was not so much motivation that was necessary, but more a brake on the choice and use of more aggressive means. The central point however is that this narrative provided a framework for making action meaningful in a different way from the traditional messages of black religion, yet still within bounds set by them. This message mixed the sacred and secular in ways that black religion had always done, with a message that combined sustenance here and now with hope for a better, more just future. This future was usually understood to be on earth as in heaven, that is, there was no sharp gap between the world of man and the world of God. Black preachers can be divided between the "sustainers" and the "reformers." The former was a tradition begun with the slave preachers, slave converts to Christianity and (later) free Black preachers, who "stimulate(d) hope while deferring reward" as they "projected a heavenly vision against the dark, low ceilings of slavery and segregation" (Lischer 1995:29). This preaching strategy does not necessarily have to be classed as "otherworldly," "pie in the sky," or "opium of the people." It can be seen as a strategy for "sustaining" human dignity for a people "not yet able to act and thereby avert(ing) the disaster of premature revolution" (Gayraud Wilmore in Lischer 1995). Coretta Scott King remembered the Alabama preachers of her childhood in that way:

Seldom if ever did the preachers of that period (1930s) deal directly with the plight of their people. Occasionally, when some black person had been beaten or otherwise badly treated by whites, there would be a reference to it from the pulpit. The preacher's role was to keep hope alive in nearly hopeless situations. "God loves us all, and people will reap what they sow", they would tell us . . . They never preached what we would now call "the social gospel", neither did they discuss from their pulpits Negro rights or the issues of segregation. It was too dangerous.   (Quoted in Lischer 1995:30)

Because of this danger and because of the subordinate position of blacks generally, "sustaining" always contained a political dimension, in that the maintenance of hope in such a situation is always subversive. What the civil rights movement did, however, was to take this hope beyond the walls of the church in a more collectively active way. This was a strategy that identified the reformer, a role which King learned from his own minister-father. Martin Luther King, Sr., like many black ministers, combined sustaining with a more active engagement with wider condition of blacks in American society. In the 1920s and 1930s this became known as the "race man," a role, as can be understood from the statement by Coretta Scott King, more easily played in urban areas and in the North than in the South. One of Wright's stories in *Uncle Tom's Children* portrayed the dangers this role entailed in the South, not so much physical as mental danger (being an Uncle Tom).[28]

Here King's preaching within the framework of the progressive narrative provided a frame which offered both sustaining and reforming through collective and not merely individual action. The movement took on the role which the minister had played. Christian doctrine and non-violence provided the sustaining, proving the moral worthiness of the movement activist. Non-violence and the Christian worldview provided a moral high ground from which to reveal the immorality and the evilness of segregation and the goodness of integration. Movement activists thus were doing God's work in bringing justice to the world. This strategy of inclusion thus included whites, not only activists on the side of justice, but also those whites who currently opposed the movement – in the end they would inhabit a better world. This inclusion involved an underlying belief in conversion at the base of King's strategy. As opposed to Malcolm X who viewed whites as "devils," enemies incapable of seeing the potential goodness in a new world which included blacks as equals, King's Christian beliefs were based on the hope not only of inclusion but also of the conversion of enemies into brothers.

In this context, Africa was important, not so much as a root of culture and certainly not as the site of redemption, but as a newly revised symbol for freedom. This was understood through the concept of freedom which liberation movements implied, not through the idea of self-determination. What King brought back from Africa was the notion that "there seems to be a throbbing desire, there seems to be an internal desire for freedom within the soul of every man," a universalist notion that he found expressed in Montgomery and in the civil rights movement as a whole. This is a form of freedom based in the individual and in self-determination at the individual rather than collective level. The collective, the community, was a means to this end, not the end itself.

The idea of community here is one born and borne of necessity, out of segregation, and it is a source of strength and an agent of liberation, if not yet freedom. The basis of this community is the congregation, but its roots are wider, reaching back to slavery and to an ascribed racial identity, that is, to the historically reflective process of collective memory and to cultural trauma. The force of circumstance had created the black community, just as segregation had created the black church. It is this historical memory, accumulated over years of struggle and humiliation, that King recalls and calls upon to gather this community to collective action:

You know my friends there comes a time when people get *tired*
Of being trampled over by the iron feet of oppression.
There comes a time my friends when people get *tired*
Of being flung across the abyss of humiliation
where they experience the bleakness of nagging despair.
There comes a time when people get *tired*
Of being pushed out of the glittering sunlight
of life's July and left standing amidst the piercing chill of an Alpine November.
                                                                    (Lischer 1995:87)

This "tiredness" began with slavery, and intensified with the dashed hopes of emancipation; it is a condition that all recognize as their own and it is one contained in the blues as well as in the spiritual.[29] Just as Du Bois recognized himself in the sorrow songs of slaves, which gave voice to the collective as much as opposition to the present condition, King uncovers the collective in a recalled history of shared humiliation and the desire for freedom contained in the response to Parks' act of resistance. The tiredness he identifies, as Lischer notes, combines "weariness with rage," an impatience and a frustration born of centuries of exclusion and marginalization. At this stage of his life (he was 26 when he made this speech), King could hardly have himself felt this weariness, except in the metaphorical sense. It was later, just before his death in April, 1968, when the dream of inclusion and the emergence of an integrated America had once again been shattered, that he must have personally felt the weariness and rage he inherited through tradition. As Lischer puts it: "In his final sermon to Ebenezer (March 3, 1968), King announces that the dream is dead. Throughout this period of his life, his sermons reflect his growing disillusionment with white America. With the urban riots, the white backlash has set in. The war in Vietnam had undercut his earlier reliance on democratic ideals and served to remind him that the ideals themselves were suspect, that white America had been born in genocide and slavery" (1995:108). The "dream" that was by this time shattered was one King had articulated earlier in his famous "I have a dream" speech. This too was part of a heritage rooted in the black church and colored by the memory and image of slavery as refracted through cultural trauma.

Through his sermons and speeches King linked the individual to the collective, just as he reinvented a black religious tradition through their performance. Through drawing upon set formulas and phrases, common points of reference and association, and couching them in familiar musical speech patterns, King linked the individual and collective, the past and the present, as he "transformed the prosaic discouragement of his audiences into the poetry of a Movement"

(Lischer 1995:104). Whether he quoted from Paul Dunbar or James Weldon Johnson, or lifted phrases from the Bible or Shakespeare, King's "formulaic speech" turned the I into the We and the mundane into the historically significant. "His audiences would cheer when he *began* one of his set pieces the way fans respond to the first bars of their favorite song at a rock concert. The formulas not only verified the identity of the speaker, they also guaranteed a collaborative role for the hearer in an important moment of history" (1995:104).

Slavery was the first point of reference and inclusion into the American dream, the end point around which all revolved. As the dream faded, the references became more "black". "Too many Negroes are ashamed of themselves, ashamed of being black. A Negro gotta rise up and say from the bottom of his soul, 'I am somebody. I have a rich, noble, and proud heritage. However exploited and however pained my history has been, I'm black but *I'm black and beautiful*'" (Lischer 1995: 101). As noted, King spoke differently to black and to white audiences, something which is reflected by the double consciousness stemming from cultural trauma and the role of black preacher/intellectual as mediator between the membership group and the dominant society. Yet his narrative frame and that of the civil rights movement as a whole remained progressive and inclusionary. Towards the end of his life, as the frustrations stemming from the failures of white society and increasingly violent resistance, and the corresponding calls for "black power" by a younger generation of activists, increased King may have more and more played the role of prophet, venting his and others' rage against American society, emphasizing its shortcomings rather than its promise, but this was done within the narrative of universal deliverance and a philosophy of Christian love. As Lischer puts it, "deliverance and love were needed by everyone in America" (1995: 217). Here he was more like Marx who believed that the liberation of the oppressed proletariat would also entail the liberation of their oppressors.

Representing the movement and the memory of slavery

Two related factors are important in understanding developments amongst black intellectuals, writers, and artists since the 1960s. The first is the end of the period of social movement itself. The intensive period of political and cultural mobilization which characterized the period and shaped a generation focused all creative energy on racial matters. Creative individuals, from popular entertainers to academic scholars, were encouraged to take a stand and to become engaged in the movement.[30] Being "merely" a black entertainer or scholar was nearly impossible, more so than perhaps it ever had been, in a country so conscious of difference. With the end of this mobilization and the backlash that was both its cause and effect, it was possible to return to more mundane individual pursuits, careers, and other concerns where race played an important, but not so dominant role. Intellectuals could more easily become or remain professionals, for example. The second, related factor, concerns one of the "successes" of the movement, especially for those engaged in intellectual labor, the establishment of black/ethnic studies programs at nearly all major colleges and universities. The early engagement of black students in the civil rights movement was largely Southern-based. The sit-ins and other forms of direct action which led to the formation of SNCC in 1960 were manned, if not led, by students from segregated high schools and from historically black colleges in the South. Their activity was often framed within religious ideals linked to the progressive narrative, with an Enlightenment model of emancipation as a guiding political principle. This can be gleaned from the religion based freedom songs, as well as the forms of non-violent civil disobedience which aimed at recognition and inclusion and composed the basic repertoire of this activism. As the movement evolved into "black power," partly but not exclusively in response to the increasingly violent resistance from Southern whites, and as concerns and issues broadened to include employment and foreign policy, as the Vietnam War and Third World liberation movements became central, the cognitive framework moved more and more in the direction of the redemptive narrative and the national liberation model of emancipation. "What we're trying to do," wrote the chairman of the Black Allied Students' Association at New York University in 1966, "is to convince the brothers who aren't already nationalists that this is the correct goal" (cited in Allen 1969:258).

As the Southern-based movement shifted its focus northward, so increased the potential influence of nationalism on northern activists from the ghettoes as well as the universities. An unintended consequence would eventually be a convergence of the narratives and, for a period at least, of the hegemony of the tragic/redemptive. The Black Panther Party with its aggressive symbolism was one hybrid outgrowth of this shift and would be an important actor in the transformation of representation, both internal to the civil rights struggle and as viewed from the outside through the mass media. In 1967, SNCC campus coordinator George Ware identified this shift as the "second phase" of the student movement, calling attention to the role of a new generation of activists armed with new frameworks of interpretation (Allen 1969:256). In spring 1966, *The Black Student* was first published by the Students' Afro-American Society at Columbia University. The first number addressed these issues, such that "black Ivy Leaguers" were accused "of seeking to escape their blackness by becoming 'white Negroes' and ignoring the black masses" (Allen 1969:258). According to Allen,

The Ivy League Afro groups were grappling with a problem which worried black students everywhere. The students questioned the relevance of a typical college education to the growing black liberation struggle. Many of the black student activists adopted the position that higher education in the United States simply served to reinforce the status quo by encouraging "selfish individualism" and promoting the "white line" of the assumed superiority of Western cultural and ethical values. The student response has been to espouse a kind of communal black nationalism.

The solidification of diversified black studies programs at colleges and universities resolved many of the tensions within the narratives, if not the movement. Such programs created a cognitive as well as an institutional space for reconciliation, framed within a rhetoric of insurgency.

From the perspective of our themes, the development of black studies programs at many major American colleges and universities can thus be understood not only in terms of the institutionalization of the ideas and values of the civil rights movement, but also a reconciliation of the two narrative frames. As with the population in general, higher education in this context was both an often unnoticed means of social mobility and a site of social conflict. A new cohort entered higher education in a politically charged atmosphere which would shape their experience and understanding of the meaning and aim of education. This would ground a distinctive generational consciousness. In the Black Power phase of the movement, institutions of higher education would be added to other public spaces as cites of conflict, rather than simply being bases of movement recruitment. Here the most immediate aim was the creation of new academic disciplines, including "ethnic studies," African studies as well as black and African American studies. In this process, the core of activists "were frequently young men and women in their twenties and thirties. Many were doctoral students . . . most had been involved in black cultural and political protest activities and organizations" (Marable 2000:8; for an overview see Marable's Introduction). While the exact number of departments established remains uncertain, "in the span of three short years, from 1968 to 1971, hundreds of black studies departments and programs were initiated" (2000:10).

As with the civil rights movement itself, there were both political and demographic aspects to this development. Politically, the new fields of study reflected the conflict (as well as the potential reconciliation) represented in the two narratives, progressive and redemptive; demographically, they reflected the continuing northward migration of blacks (3 million blacks left the South between 1945 and 1965) and the radical shift in the racial composition of institutions of higher education: "In 1950 . . . seventy-five thousand Negroes were enrolled in American colleges and universities. In 1960 three-fourths of all black students attended historically black colleges. By 1970 nearly seven hundred thousand African Americans were enrolled, three-fourths of whom were at white colleges" (Marable 2000:7).

The two developments, the institutionalization of the civil rights movement within higher education and the decline in mass mobilization, widened the intellectual field for college-educated blacks by creating areas in which special competence could be claimed. Not only did opportunities for academic employment and the market for publishing and other forms of representation consequently expand, but the range of possible political positions and roles increased as the demands of activism, if not the need to "take a stand," moderated and at the same time became more complex. With this, the progressive narrative focus on mobility regained some of its earlier hegemony as black nationalism lost its political force in the face of massive repression. Now, however, the means toward integration were more a matter of debate. Black conservatism, always present in both intellectual and religious discourse, became a more acceptable stance even in the less politicized academic discourse. At the same time, in fields such as sociology and political science, the redefinition of blacks as a racially based ethnic group, and a renewed interest in ethnic relations including those with the government, i.e., policy concerns, encouraged more applied research on the extent and causes of racial conflict. Black academics were encouraged to study, as well as to comment on, the ghetto, problems of unemployment, family relations, sexuality and so on and to advise as well as actively become and support local and national political leaders. As the movement was institutionalized and transformed into a pressure group, activist intellectuals became experts, advisors, and scholars.[31]

In addition to the establishment of new academic disciplines, the end of mobilization aroused and expanded public interest in the movement's interpretation. Just as Harold Cruse pointed to the "failure" of the Harlem Renaissance when he sought to identify *The Crisis of the Negro Intellectual* in 1965, a new cohort of black intellectuals emerged around the contested meaning of the civil rights movement. In popular debate and in the flood of books and articles related to the movement by sociologists and historians, the legacy of slavery and the African past remained central. Thirty years later, the fusion of movement and institution has matured into several orientations and curricula from Afro-Centrism to African American studies, reflecting the narrative frames in institutionalized form as academic discourse. Despite the tensions and differences, Manning Marable (2000:1–2) identifies three underlying common "points of departure": descriptive, the aim of "presenting reality from the point of view of black people themselves," with "scholarship . . . grounded in the very subjective truths of a people's collective experience"; corrective, with the aim to "challenge and to critique the racism and stereotypes that have been present in the mainstream discourse of white academic institutions"; prescriptive, with the aim "to use history and culture as tools through which people interpret their collective experience . . . for the purpose of transforming their actual conditions and the totality of the society all around them." The role and place of slavery in this discourse varies from historical analysis to the experience of the slave and its wider meaning. This can perhaps be seen as a "corrective," aimed at explaining and also transforming actual social conditions. In contrast, Molefi Kete Asante, a former SNCC activist and current professor of African American studies and director of the Afrocentric Institute, defends the prescriptive position for its role in empowering marginalized groups. Calling on the nationalist heritage of Crummell, Delaney, Garvey, and Malcolm X among others, as well as looking through them to Africa, Asante seeks to use "African agency as a positive statement against the deagencizing character of hegemonic Eurocentricity" (Asante in Marable 2000:195).[32]

On the opposite pole, one finds Orlando Paterson and William Julius Wilson, two sociologists who base their interpretations on traditional empirical research and who express an underlying skepticism regarding the use of scholarship for prescriptive purposes. They represent one side of the existing tensions within the now institutionalized discourse on the role and use of knowledge (a traditional conflict within the academy), while at the same time offering quite opposite explanations of the current situation of African Americans. Regarding Afrocentrism, Patterson, more explicitly than Wilson, has openly criticized what he calls the "three Ps approach – black history as the discovery of princes, pyramids and pageantry" because it "does violence to the facts . . . is ideologically bankrupt and is methodologically and theoretically deficient" (cited by Gates and Marable (2000:186)). Framing his work within the progressive narrative, Patterson has outlined the "ordeal of integration," as an incomplete project. After a doctoral dissertation on Jamaican slavery, Patterson published a series of books on the "consequences of slavery in two American centuries," as the subtitle of *Rituals of Blood* (Patterson 1998) makes clear. Following what he identifies as Frazier's footsteps, Patterson argues that much of the behavior of contemporary black Americans, which he represents on the basis of statistical compilations, can be explained with direct reference to slavery. On this basis, he writes, "Afro-Americans are the most unpartnered and isolated group of people in America and quite possibly the world" (1998:4). The idea of a "black community" in other words, is a myth, something which we could call the legacy of the 1960s. African American males and females are in constant battle, something which has a devastating impact on family life, especially with regard to children. The root cause of this, according to Patterson, can be traced to the effects of slavery on African American males, who were never permitted to develop in the role of father and husband. Slavery encouraged the production of offspring but not the role of parent, something which affected males more than females. This produced an attitude toward children and toward marriage which continues to this day, apparently passed on from one generation to the next. The consequences of slavery, in others words, are very much alive. If African Americans are to progress, or to integrate, this pattern must be changed. Also within the progressive narrative frame, yet on the other side of this policy debate on the meaning of slavery for contemporary urban blacks, William Julius Wilson (1978, 1987) finds a "declining significance of race" in explaining the social situation and behaviors among the "truly disadvantaged" portion of urban blacks. Rather than appealing to the historical past, Wilson explains the behavior of an "underclass" of African Americans on the basis of a lack of opportunity in their current situation. Slavery remains important here not as a means of explaining contemporary behavior, but rather as a point of origin for the category. Their work can be compared to similar debates amongst previous generations of black scholars and intellectuals and contrasted to the more Afrocentric wing of black studies.

Popular culture

The end of mass mobilization provided an opportunity for the representation and reflection of the meaning of the civil rights movement in literature, music, and film.[33] Just as in the professionalized academic discourse, the movement provided a context of experience as well as the necessity to choose sides. One was forced to take a stand for or against, whether or not one actually participated in any activity. The movement filled the atmosphere, as well as the media, with its political and cultural presence. While everyday life and its concerns continued as the main grounds of experience and identity, the movement made itself felt even there. The question "Which side are you on?" was a dominant one, even for writers and artists. James Baldwin was only one who felt the need to return from self-imposed European exile and take a stand for "the race." His famous essays, *The Fire Next Time*, and interview with Elijah Muhammad, as well as the attack on his person by Eldridge Cleaver (1968) were all testaments to the power of the movement to command aesthetic representation as well as to affect everyday attitude and behavior. The legacy of slavery as well as more contemporary events provided points of orientation. Baldwin's play, *Blues for Mister Charlie* (1964), for example, recounted the lynching of Emmitt Till. Conceived within the Du Bois tradition of protest theater, the play proved to be a precursor of the tension between emerging black power and the integrationist, the redemptive and progressive narratives. Instead of portraying the lynching victim as exemplifying the good and the innocent victim of white racism, Baldwin's character is outspoken in his defiance of Southern codes of behavior, even to the point of inciting his murderers. This breaks with Du Bois' notion of exemplary, idealized characterization as well as with the non-violent tactics of the civil rights movement, and introduces "Malcolm X's early revolutionary philosophy to African American theatre" (Hay 1994:94). It also gave voice to generational as well as class and regional conflicts within the movement.[34]

While mass mobilization provided a context for the framing of experience and a reworking of the collective memory of slavery, its passing provided a context for other forms of representation and reflection. The novels of Morrison, mentioned earlier, and Alice Walker, gave the Southern experience a new, gendered, meaning. Walker's *Meridian* (1976) provides an example where the civil rights movement figures centrally. The story concerns the experiences of a young black woman of that name who comes of age in Georgia in the 1960s. The activities of the local branch of the Student Nonviolent Coordinating Committee (SNCC) are the vehicle of her coming of age. Meridian follows an established pattern for black girls in the rural South, she becomes pregnant in high school and is forced to leave school and to marry the child's father, an equally young schoolmate. She also moves from her own parents' home to his. At seventeen it seemed her life was determined by circumstance. The bombing of a house in her neighborhood used by civil rights workers by white racists is the catalyst which helps her break that pattern:

The next morning as she lay in bed watching the early news, she was again shown pictures of the house – except now the house no longer existed anywhere but on film....She had lived in this town all her life, but could not have foreseen that the house would be bombed. Perhaps nothing like this had ever happened before. Not in this town. Or *had* it?...And so it was that one day in the middle of April in 1960 Meridian Hill became aware of the past and present of the larger world.   (Walker 1976:73)

In this account, television mediates experience and stimulates a form of reflection which leads to fundamental changes in the life pattern of a person. Meridian volunteers to work for SNCC and is immediately asked if she can type by a male activist. She learns about politics, gives up her child, is given a scholarship to a black college in Atlanta and embarks on a new life path. Her sexual encounters with another male activist eventually will lead to the development of a feminist consciousness, as she comes to understand the movement as male dominated.

There are continuous references to slavery in *Meridian*. The campus of Saxon college in Atlanta is dominated by "the largest magnolia tree in the country" which is called "The Sojourner" and was planted by a slave named Louvinie. "Louvinie was tall, thin, strong and not very pleasant to look at... She became something of a local phenomenon in plantation society because it was believed she *could not* smile" (Walker 1976:42). In West Africa, Louvinie had learned the skill of telling stories and she carried this tradition to the plantation of the Saxon family in Georgia, where she was given the task of caring for the children of her white master. One of her tales so frightened a seven-year-old Saxon child that he died of a heart attack. For this she was punished. "Louvinie's tongue was clipped out at the root. Choking on blood, she saw her tongue on the ground under the heel of Master Saxon. Mutely she pleaded for it, because she knew the curse of her native land: Without one's tongue in one's mouth or in a special spot of one's own choosing, the singer in one's soul was lost forever to grunt and snort through eternity like a pig" (1976:44). The spot she chose for her tongue was "under a scrawny magnolia tree." It was this tree which eventually became the center of the Saxon campus. This novel represents the progressive narrative, as the civil rights movement is the vehicle for the transformation of a young black girl whose life appears determined by an established pattern based in class, race, and gender into an upwardly mobile critical thinker and political activist. Africa is a resource in this developmental process. It is the source of tradition and myth, which have been transported and planted in the South by slave women. Slavery helps bring culture to the new world. Irony is part of this culture. The loss of a tongue produces a tree of knowledge, a tree used primarily for sexual encounters by students on the Saxon campus, a site of white patronage and itself the expression of the progressive narrative, a conservative, finishing school for upwardly mobile blacks. There is redemption in Walker's South.

The publication of Alex Haley's *Roots* in 1976 and the television series (1977) based upon it were instrumental in widening the scope of reflection on the meaning and place of slavery in the life of black Americans. The most watched television series to date, *Roots* once again articulated the progressive narrative out of slavery in a powerful visual format and became a model for later programs and films, by blacks as well as whites. In the post-civil-rights era, blacks had moved sufficiently into positions of power and influence, both within the mass media and as a market, to present at least aspects of the black experience to the mainstream, especially when framed within the progressive narrative, however modified. It is here that the negotiation with the dominant culture now began, how should the black experience be represented when blacks themselves have more than a little say in the process: whose voice, which experience, and how would the framer be framed?

Spike Lee's film representation of the life of Malcolm X has already been mentioned in terms of its impact on collective memory. Other media were also important in transferring the ideas and expressions of this exemplar of black power. Lee's co-producer, Monty W. Ross, recounts his engagement with the film in this way, "I have to listen to a Malcolm X tape every once in a while and I'm talking about long before we started doing this film. I've always had to do this, just to remind me . . . My problems now are not what Malcolm's problems were then, or what my father's were in a previous generation. But he laid it out for me, the path" (Lee 1993:18). Tapes have become an important means of transference and of remembering or at least of stimulating recollection and remembrance.[35] Ross offers the following motivations for making "Malcolm X":

I think what Spike and I envisioned a long time ago, back in college in Atlanta, majoring in mass communications, sitting on his/our grandmother's front porch during the summers, was knowing between ourselves that the day would come when Black culture could be represented in its truest forms in cinema, and that we could be the ones to represent that culture ... that's what we envisioned, to be able to put together a project that will represent our culture in the best sense of those words, that would be full of spirit, that would motivate people, that would be educational, yet at the same time be entertaining, so we could stay in business, so we could employ people at the same time, and take advantage of all our opportunities.   (1993:16–17)

This would point to a keen awareness of the social changes brought about through the civil rights movement, at least as far as the middle class is concerned, and a related sense of responsibility for its re-presentation. The movement made possible its representation, not only in its being historically real and present, but also in its effects, in making it possible for blacks to attain the skills and the resources to re-present it. Both Ross and Lee attended Morehouse, part of Atlanta University. This return South, to "their grandmother's porch" (a phrase recalling Alice Walker), Lee had recounted in the previously mentioned film *School Daze*. There followed professional training at New York University's Film School, a career possibility related to the opportunities, both material and cognitive, created by the civil rights movement. Like his "Ivy League" counterparts in the black power days of the 1960s, however, Lee felt a responsibility to "speak to the people," through his art. As opposed to members of that generation, however, he felt it possible to do this through the means provided by the (white) dominant culture. A film about Malcolm X was to be commercial entertainment as well as educational. While a film about Malcolm X had to be produced by blacks, because "the story of Malcolm X belonged to Black film" (11), and had to represent "our inherent system of values, down from the earliest civilizations in Africa" (15), it still had also to be marketable and marketed. As Lee recounts, "While we were shooting *Jungle Fever* in late 1990, I made up an initial design for the 'X' cap. I'd already decided to do *Malcolm X*, and marketing is an integral part of my filmmaking" (21). Accepting the necessity of dealing through the established commercial culture, and being proud of these skills, marks Lee off from the previous generation shaped by the movement, as well as from his own musician father, who, as he himself recounts, was an artist and not a businessman. The same was true of earlier black film makers. "See, I realized that being a Black filmmaker, I'm never going to have the same amount of money spent to market my films as I would have if I was a white filmmaker with the same number of notches on his gun, the same amount of success. And I don't want to duplicate what happened to a lot of the Black filmmakers of the previous generations in front of me . . . They were artists and not businessmen . . ." (22).

Although concerned with the experiences of contemporary, primarily urban blacks, Lee's films recall the heritage of slavery. Although explicit references to slavery are made only infrequently, as in the chain-led teenager forced to attend the Million Man March in *Get On The Bus*, the name of Lee's company, Forty Acres and a Mule, which always is prominently presented in the opening sequences, recalls the false promises of emancipation. Like those of the Armenian film maker, Atom Egoyan (mentioned in Chapter 1), trauma is always present, even in its absence.

Rap music has often been pointed to as the voice of the most silent and at risk black, the young urban male. Rap music, as part of a long tradition of black music, can also be understood as a form of counter-memory, where symbolic expressions of resistance, as well as the ideals of emancipation, are maintained and transmitted. The legacy of slavery and the heroes and values of the black power era are especially present in rap lyrics, performance style, body language, and, in the age of the music video, in recorded image. The popular rap group Public Enemy, a group that came into national prominence through Spike Lee's film *Do The Right Thing*, offers perhaps the most prominent example. Loosely associated with religious black nationalism through the revived Nation of Islam headed by Louis Farrakhan, at least one of the group is a devotee (Cashmore 1997:161ff.). Public Enemy has sought a way to negotiate between the white controlled record industry and the urban ghetto, in a situation where the prime commercial audience for rap music appears to be the white middle class (Cashmore 1997), without entirely losing the political message of cultural nationalism. Their contact with the record industry is mediated through the black producer Russell Simmons, who apparently shares the industry's profit motive. Public Enemy have been consistent and insistent with their high political messages. Trica Rose (1994:115–16) offers a reading of one of their most popular videos, "Night of the Living Baseheads," which sets its anti-drug, anti-establishment message against the visual background of the Audubon Ballroom in Harlem, where Malcolm X was murdered in 1965. The image and the recorded words of Malcolm X are a featured part of their musical repertoire, as is the Nation of Islam and a redemptive, religious nationalism.[36]

Lead singer Chuck D (Carl Ryder) offers an interesting example of a post-sixties urban black youth. Born in 1960 in Flushing, Queens, Ryder grew up in Roosevelt, Long Island, a predominantly black suburb of New York City. He claims to remember the 1963 murder of civil rights activist Medgar

Evers, the March on Washington that same year and Malcolm X's assassination (Chuck D 1997:26). He writes, "My crucial developmental years took place right smack-dab in the middle of the Black Power movement. I witnessed my family, and Black people in general, over a five-year span go from using the term 'Negro' in 1963–64, to using the term 'colored' in 1966–67, to using the term 'Black' and using it with pride by 1968. By the time the TV shows Julia (1968), starring Diahann Carroll, and *The Bill Cosby Show* (1968–71) hit the air *Black* pride was at an all-time high" (Chuck D 1997:27). Clearly television has moved into the center as an indicator, as well as medium, of racial awareness. Ryder also recounts the significant impact post-movement successes in higher education made on his development. Two universities near his Long Island home offered summer programs called the Afro-American Experience for local black youth. Ryder's "future Public Enemy partner" also participated, as did "Professor Griff"(Chuck D 1997:29) . These programs placed "ten-and eleven-year-olds on a college campus. We learned Swahili, African drumming, and facts about African culture, history, and the slave trade" (Chuck D 1997:30).

Ryder met most of his group members when later enrolled at one of those colleges he attended during the summers. He studied graphic design and communications and was active on the school newspaper and local radio station. It was also local radio, reaching out primarily to black youth on suburban Long Island, which offered him the opportunity to develop his rapping style as well as introduce it to others. "We would make original tapes with local artists and play them on the air, because there wasn't enough Rap records at the time (early 1980s) . . . We would have local artists come to our studio and headquarters . . . to make tapes that we would broadcast on the air" (Chuck D 1997:66). An innovative entrepreneur, Ryder helped create as well as spread rap music.

It is the former attitude and practice, black capitalism, which links him to the Nation of Islam, as well as his message. Farrakhan (Gardell 1997) has expressed an ambivalent attitude to this form of expression, deploring its imagery, but seeing it as a real expression of the frustration felt by many black youths. It is also tremendously successful as a commercial product. The fact that the largest audience is white, something which is seen as indicating its lack of authenticity by some (Cashmore 1997), does not appear to worry Ryder, who explains rap's appeal in this way. Young people learn more from "the videos and the Rap songs than they're learning from the schools. That's one of the reasons that Rap and other aspects of Black culture have crossed over so successfully . . . because young whites are able to get a heartfelt perspective through our music . . . Hip Hop culture is an education" (Chuck D 1997:33).

In defining what composes the black community, or what decomposes it, Chuck D turns to slavery: "During my years of crisscrossing throughout major and minor cities in America I've developed a theory with regard to the

Black community. I call my theory the 'Plantation Theory'. The Plantation theory states that Black people don't really have communities; what we have are clusters of plantations. A *community* is an environment that has control over the three E's: education, economics and enforcement" (Chuck D 1997:31). At the same time, he writes about the sense of community he experienced in the real black community of Roosevelt where he grew up. This idealized or normative sense of community, which was destroyed by slavery and replaced by the plantation, is that which black nationalism, for him in the form of the Nation of Islam, represents. There control over education, economics, and enforcement has been achieved. This is also the case regarding the related concept of the "family" or the tribal nation:

Since we've been in America we have never looked at ourselves as being a family to each other. The day our people got off those slave ships bound with shackles by neck, hands, and feet, the first brother was like, "Get this shit off of me", and the enslavers cracked that whip on his back, and the others were like, "I don't know that motherfucker." Three hundred years of brutality, and the breeding of fear was so intense that it broke all ties to the concept of family, and made us hate ourselves and each other. (Chuck D 1997:37)

Similar arguments, made in much different language and to much different purpose, are made by the sociologist Orlando Patterson, discussed previously.

The process of cultural trauma begun after the failure of reconstruction in the late nineteenth century provided the impetus for renegotiating the grounds of collective identity for American blacks. After once again being formally relegated to a "separate but equal" social status and to separate but unequal working and living conditions, the basis of the group itself as well as its relationship to the dominant society needed to be renegotiated. Here intellectuals of the more traditional sort and those emerging in social movements would play a central role in the discursive process of forming a collective identity. The representation of slavery would form a primal scene in the process of collective identity formation, as it was renegotiated in the changing historical conditions of black Americans. The two narrative frames which took form in the context of the social movements of the 1920s as an urban black public sphere was emerging remained in place through the second great wave of social movements in the 1960s; with shifting hegemony between them. Today there is a confluence, allowing the possibility that social mobility, a form of inclusion and a measure of progress and redemption, are not mutually exclusive projects. The meaning and memory of slavery are still unresolved, however, as is the cultural trauma. Perhaps it will never be resolved, there may be no resolution as the collective identity of black Americans, as opposed to individual memory, is filtered through cultural trauma, which means that slavery, the primal scene of the collective, will be recalled every time the collective is questioned. It is through representation within already established discourses that this recalling and reformation takes place, as it appears the notion of the African American has once again become hegemonic but in a form which includes aspects of the progressive and the redemptive narrative. This is one of the central legacies of the civil rights movement and the 1960s.

The contemporary debate amongst black artists and intellectuals concerning the role of knowledge and scholarship recalls similar debates amongst previous generations. In the 1920s in the midst of the Harlem Renaissance, the question of "How Negroes should be represented," along with the wider issue of the relationship between art and propaganda (discussed in chapter 4) presents many similarities, as does the 1940s debate amongst black painters concerning abstract art (discussed in chapter 5). What is continuous is the use of knowledge and the role of representation in combating oppression, as forms of empowerment in the cognitive praxis of social movements and in the formation of collective identity, where history conflates with collective memory. What is specific and contextual in the contemporary reworking of cultural trauma is the rejection of the separatism and Marxism which characterized the 1960s nationalism and thus an implicit convergence through the idea of the African American as black American. This reveals the possibility of accepting the collective identification "African American" without necessarily accepting the linear form of the progressive narrative. Progress can mean something else other than shedding or overcoming the past. It also gives a new meaning to the idea of integration by drawing on the later Du Bois and a modernized nationalism, where a reworking of the past leads through cultural autonomy rather than assimilation.[37] In the context of post-colonialism and the resurgence of ethnic politics generally this permits a reconciliation not only of an internal conflict, but also of cultural trauma. This is accomplished through the coexistence of a distinctive and relatively autonomous collective history and the progressive political and economic integration into an American society which is also altered in the process.

Notes

1   Cultural trauma and collective memory

1. The terms African American and Afro-American, often treated synonymously, appear to have emerged at different historical moments. According to the Oxford etymological dictionary, African American appears for the first time in print in 1863 in conjunction with emancipation in a racist song, to be later appropriated by black Americans around the turn of the century. Afro-American, on the other hand, appears in fairly common usage amongst free blacks in the mid-1800s. In 1880 the Afro-American Press Association was formed. In the 1850s, the abolitionist *Anglo-African Weekly* published literary pieces by blacks, indicating that hyphenated identifications were commonly used. According to Moses (1978:32), "A startling feature in the rhetoric of black institutional leadership on the eve of the Civil War was the popularity of the term 'Anglo-African' ... By 1900, 'Anglo-African' had been replaced by 'Afro-American' and such variants as 'Euro-African', and 'Negro-Saxon'."

2. In Boston as early as 1787, "eighty free blacks petitioned the Massachusetts government for financial aid in getting to Africa" (Redkey 1969:17). In 1815 Paul Cuffee, a well-to-do black ship captain and devout Quaker financed the voyage of thirty-eight Negro colonists to Sierra Leone, Africa. Cuffe died in 1817, but his ideas lived on in the formation of the American Colonization Society, an organization made up of blacks and whites which helped found the nation of Liberia and a movement for black repatriation (Redkey 1969:18ff.). One of the early articles in the *Journal of Negro History* (1923) concerned Cuffee and he is drawn upon by Charles Johnson in the novel *Middle Passage* (1990).

3. The Negro Convention Movement organized by free blacks in Philadelphia in 1817 proposed settling in Canada. In 1830, the Convention recommended buying land in Canada for the purpose of colonization. At the 1832 Convention, where blacks from eight states were represented, "The question exciting the greatest interest was one which proposed the purchase of other lands for settlement in Canada; for 800 acres of land had already been secured, two thousand individuals had left the soil of their birth, crossed the line and laid the foundation for a structure which promised

an asylum for the colored population of the United States" (quoted in Essien-Udom 1962:20). Martin Delaney, a leader of one faction of the Convention movement which favored emigration to Africa as opposed to Canada, wrote in 1861 "The question is not whether our condition can be bettered by emigration, but whether it can be made worse. If not, then there is no part of the widespread universe, where our social and political conditions are not better than here in our native country, and nowhere in the world as here, proscribed on account of color" (quoted in Essien-Udom 1962:19). Woodard (1999) interprets the cultural nationalism represented by Amiri Baraka in the 1960s as a modern revival of the convention movement. According to Higginbotham (1993:2) the word "convention" had a particular meaning in the black church, where the term has almost the same meaning as "denomination." Conventions were also a common organizational form through which a black public sphere was constituted. The open and bazaar-like quality of national denominational conventions is vividly described in Harris (1992). As will be discussed in later chapters, various events, like the Kansas Exodus at the end of reconstruction, occasioned a series of conventions, through which the "race" constituted itself.

4. The work of G. H. Mead, influential in the collective behaviorist perspective, certainly lends itself to this problematic.

5. In her discussion of Hannah Arendt's notion of theory as story-telling narrative, Seyla Benhabib (1996:92) writes "who we are is revealed in the narratives we tell ourselves and of our world shared with others. Narrativity is constitutive of identity."

6. In a review of Peter Novick's *The Holocaust in American Life* (1999), Eva Hoffman (2000:19) writes regarding collective memory: "this kind of memory, Halbwachs observed is, if not exactly false, then tendentiously falsifying. Unlike genuine historical consciousness, which strives to understand multiple aspects of the past, collective memory 'reduces events to mythic archetypes'. It uses the resulting conceptions to support a group's interests, mobilize its loyalties, or express supposedly eternal truths of collective identity."

7. Malinowski described myth thus: "taken as a whole, (myth) cannot be sober, dispassionate history, since it is always made ad hoc to fulfill a certain sociological function, to glorify a certain group, or to justify an anomalous status," quoted in Schudson (1989:105).

8. In an exchange on the difference between "authentic" *vs.* "collective memory," following the previously mentioned review of Novick (1999), Eva Hoffman (2000:78–79) writes: "I differentiate between 'collective memory' and 'genuine historical consciousness' – as does Novik himself when he writes, 'collective memory simplifies; sees events from a single, committed perspective . . . Historical consciousness by its nature, focuses on the *historicity* of events.'"

9. The Darden's cookbook traces the history of their family through "recipes and reminiscences." In recalling the memory of a grandfather they never met they write, "Papa Darden would have been nine when the Emancipation Proclamation was signed, but he did not talk about being a slave. Never did he tell his family about a single day in his life before the day he came to town as his own man" (Darden and Darden 1994:5). Food and cooking, smell and taste, are an underappreciated source and

carrier of collective memory, at least in sociology. Jessica B. Harris (1995) traces food and cooking styles from Africa to the United States. Harris reveals the role of the railroads, where the majority of cooks were black Americans, in spreading African and African American food tastes not only geographically, but also across racial barriers. The same claim can be made about the role of slave cooks on the Southern plantations. Like music and dialect, food linked black Americans across time and space, creating the basis for emergent collective identity. "Looking for a way out of sorrow's kitchen, many thousands of African Americans headed west and took their foodways with them. Texas's cowboy stew ... is a descendent of the long, slow cooking, one-pot meals of the slaves. The addition of innards and other lowly ingredients speak to eating habits acquired during slavery ... While some went west, others (many former house servants among them) found their way to prosperity through the new Pullman and dining cars that were first instituted on trains at about the same time as the end of the Civil War, and remained in use through the first half of the twentieth century ... As had happened in the antebellum South, an Africanization of the railway menues occurred very subtly [31] ... Traditional African American neighborhoods could (and indeed still can) be told by their markets" (32).

10. The role of the mass media in the construction of memory has been the subject of debate recently. What exactly is selected for mediated recollection is only one aspect debated, for mass media are often motivated by commercial as well as political interests. Thus Andreas Huyssen (2000:21–38), writes about a commodified, "imagined memory" created by a memory industry. This raises some crucial points about the politics and policies of representation and will be discussed below.

11. In her article on Egoyan, Lisa Siraganian (1997:130) refers to his "exploration of the limits of an identity formation which follows the cultural 'trauma' model (that is a group of people who define their relation to one another by a primal scene, in this case one of genocide)." In the space of three years, between 1915 and 1918, more than 1.5 million Armenians died. Memory traces of these events can be found also in the work of the Armenian American artist Arshile Gorky (Manoug Vosdanig Adoian), who as a teenager fled with his mother from the Turkish onslaught. What Gorky experienced first hand, Egoyan heard depicted, yet both were moved to representation.

12. Regarding the content of collective memory and of public commemoration, Barry Schwartz makes reference to Thomas Cottle's spatial (as opposed to linear) conception of time where time is "atomic and divisible." "It is spatial because it suggests that instead of conceiving time as an unbreakable chain of events, we can use our imagination to lift a past instant out of its place on the continuum of time and drop it into another place" (Cottle cited in Schwartz 1982:395). In this case, one can use history, i.e., recorded events, in unique ways in constructing a collective memory, where the factual events are placed together in imaginative ways. The line between history and myth would then be thin indeed. Robert Rosenstone's (1995) discussion of the making of the film *Walker*, the "true story" of the adventures of an American diplomat influential in the establishment of democracy in Nicaragua,

is relevant here. Rosenstone argues that even though some of the events depicted in the film had no factual basis, they did not distort the overall truth value of the film's representation of history because, while some of the events depicted did not, in fact, happen, they *could* have happened. In portraying them on film, the director was thus able to give a dramatic and symbolic explanation to the factual events otherwise depicted in the film. Here events are not only placed out of sequence, but also dramatized with "plausible" non-factual additions. This raises interesting questions about the meaning of truth in representations of "real" events. What, in fact, does it mean to say that something "could" have happened. This is a question which the so-called counter-factual approach to history takes as its narrative starting point. Other films which also pretend to recount historical events, like Oliver Stone's *J.F.K.* and, more recently and closer to our topic, *The Hurricane* about the unjust murder conviction of the boxer Ruben "Hurricane" Carter, raise related questions about the relation between history as a discipline dedicated to the unbiased recording of factual events and other forms of representation which make use of "history." In comparing Shakespeare's use of historical events and that of the modern film industry, critic Richard Bernstein (*New York Times* Jan. 18, 2000:E1–2) notes that mixing fact with fiction for the sake of dramatic effect is a common artistic device. While this also applies to Shakespeare, Bernstein argues, there are substantial ethical differences between the liberties taken in Richard III and those taken by "the Oliver Stone of 'J.F.K.' and 'Nixon' or the makers of 'The Hurricane.'" For him, "the basic difference is that Shakespeare's history was complex and ambiguous, while most recent movie history is morally one-dimensional, bite-size and therefore easy to swallow. At least three points can be made in this regard: one, the nature of Shakespeare as a historian; two, propaganda as opposed to art; three, the enormous technical and sophisticated public relations employed by moviemakers that was unavailable to playwrights of Shakespeare's time." All three of these can be applied to or at least asked in reference to Rosenstone's discussion of *Walker*. Rosenstone does not justify the use of fictive events for the sake of drama. Rather, his events, like those of the counter-factual historical, *could* have occurred. In other words, they are made up but were a real possibility, implying historical research of the type Bernstein attributes to Shakespeare. In *Walker* use of such "could have been" events is more for political than dramatic effect, raising Bernstein's second issue. That *Walker* was intended to persuade is undeniable and the fictive events are there for just that reason. While the producers of *Walker* are not Hollywood moguls, they still employ the power of modern film technique to reach an essentially passive audience, most of whom probably have no historical knowledge of the events being portrayed. In this situation, the filmed version replaces rather than manipulates history.

The relation between fact and fiction in black film and other forms of representation is addressed by Klotman and Cutler (1999:xx), including the "truth about nonfiction." Among others, they cite *Blurred Boundaries: Questions of Meaning in Contemporary Culture* (Nichols 1994): "the definition of nonfiction, documentary, or even historiography remains elusive, and strongly debated. Claims of authenticity butt up against evidence of story telling; claims of objectivity confront signs of dramatic intensification; claims that what we see belongs to the historical world of actual occurrences come up against indications that the act of representation shaped and determined the event in fundamental ways." Huyssen (2000:29) argues that "public memory" is necessarily permeated by mediated representation in contemporary society, thus making the distinction between mediated and unmediated memory and "serious" and "trivial" memory problematic, if not impossible. "For once we acknowledge the constitutive gap between reality and its representation in language or image, we must in principle be open to many different possibilities of representing the real and its memories . . . The question of quality remains one to be decided case by case. But the semiotic gap cannot be closed by the one and only correct representation . . . phenomena such as Schindler's List and Spielberg's visual archive of Holocaust survivor testimonies compel us to think of traumatic memory and entertainment memory together as occupying the same public space, rather than seeing them as mutually exclusive phenomena."

13. Jorge Semprum (1997:200) recounts his first viewing of a newsreel after his own release from the same concentration camp shown in the film, "Yet although the newsreel footage confirmed the truth of the actual experience (which was sometimes difficult for me to grasp and situate among my memories), at the same time these images underlined the exasperating difficulty of transmitting this truth, of making it, if not absolutely clear, at least communicable."

14. Alberto Melucci (1995:44) defines collective identity as "an interactive and shared definition produced by several individuals (or groups) and concerned with the orientations of action and the field of opportunities and constraints in which the action takes place."

15. From Introduction (in Allen, Ware, and Garrison 1867). Regarding remembering and forgetting, a black film maker has remarked "I looked at *Schindler's List* . . . and the film reminded me of how much we'd lost in black culture. There were few people who put our pictures under the floorboards to hide them; there were few recorders going up to the slave and saying 'How do you feel on this cotton picking day?' . . . so you don't really have the visual information that would allow you to organize and to have the world be sympathetic to your cause because the things that the world is used to seeing, the evidence, does not exist" (cited in Klotman and Cutler, Introduction: xxiii).

16. As Neil Smelser (in Alexander *et al.* 2001) recounts, Kai Erikson (1994) reveals how "trauma" may be both identity-disrupting and identity-solidifying.

17. Besides "counter-memory" there existed the more or less mimetic practices of some former slaves as they searched for ways to express their freedom. This can be seen for example in the post-Reconstruction practices of the small black elite, which apparently mimed many of the mannerisms and values of their former masters. The reproduction of an upper-class habitus amongst former slaves is a fascinating phenomenon, whether or not to consider it a "memory" of slavery or just an effect is also an interesting question. In the North, freedmen had early on formed fraternal organizations, like the Freemasons and other exclusive societies which can be said to have prepared the way for later, post-emancipation, distinctions and status hierarchies. In the South, especially but not exclusively, skin hue was an important factor, in part because it stemmed from mixed relationships between masters and

slaves, sometimes also leading to higher material standards and working conditions even during slavery itself. In any case, there could be no direct miming of behavior as the circumstances between white and black elites were entirely different. In the case of gender roles, for example, it has been argued that former slaves, now part of an educated elite, accepted the "Victorian" ideals of womanhood, that were central to the genteel image of the Southern Lady during slavery, but black women were still subject to the prejudices and practices of segregation and this affected their ability to mime white elite society, no matter how hard one worked at insulating oneself from it. This had the effect of making a social practice reflexive, not mimetic, and thus a form of memory.

The complex relationship between individual and collective memory and identity can be appreciated in this context. While individual identities are formed through daily practices, collective identities are mediated through collective representations. Such representations involve the articulating practices of "representative voices" like artists, writers, teachers and intellectuals. These practices re-present the individual as part of a wider collective, with a distinctive past as well as present. They offer or present the individual with a wider framework and horizon in which to interpret their identity. This is not to say that intellectuals, to use the general term, construct an individual's identity, or that the identity of former slaves was a product of intellectual reconstruction and then handed down to passive individuals. In contemporary discussions, this would be similar to arguing that the "subject" is determined through "discourse." My point is rather that individual identity is filtered through representations of the collective. This collective emerges both out of everyday practices, through social practices, like work and interaction, and also, with varying degrees of intensity and success, out of mediated collective representations, visual and verbal. In the latter, the work of "intellectuals" becomes important. It was with the emergence of an educated middle class with access to mass media, that this latter aspect became important to black identity in the United States. It was here that the African American became a form of collective identification.

18. Eyerman and Turner (1998: 93) offer the following working definition of generation: "a cohort of persons passing through time who share a common habitus, hexis and culture, a function of which is to provide them with a collective memory that serves to integrate the cohort over a finite period of time. Such a definition draws special attention to the idea of a shared or collective cultural field (of emotions, attitudes, preferences and dispositions) and a set of embodied practices (of sport and leisure and activities); that is it identifies the importance of collective memory in creating a generational culture or tradition . . ."

19. According to one popular usage, frame refers to "schemata of interpretation that enable individuals to locate, perceive, identify and label occurrence within their life space and the world at large" (Snow *et al.* 1986:464).

2   Re-membering and forgetting

1. Even after compensating for the literary style of the time, this reads very much like descriptions of survivors from prison camps after World War 2. These descriptions

after release from the concentration camps make for useful comparison. "During the first years after the war, the energies of the survivors were absorbed in finding their way back to some semblance of conventional life. Most had to learn a new language, search for other occupations, and meet some of the challenges of a society in a foreign land. Many families clung together in their new neighborhoods, creating new ghettos, hoping to create their original communities, surrounded by an alien culture, which, though not usually physically threatening, nevertheless regarded them at best with an ambivalent mixture of awe and mistrust, the very embodiment of a past the survivors wanted to forget. It was rare for an entire family to have survived intact. New partners, more often than not, fellow survivors, had to be found, new families started. While life was safer and certainly more bearable, adaptation was by now means easy" (Bergmann and Jucovy 1982:5). While one can question whether or not the emancipated slaves considered themselves "survivors" in the same way as those liberated from the camps at the end of the Second World War, descriptions of their social if not their spiritual conditions have much in common. The theory of cultural trauma may well provide a bridge in understanding.

2. On black abolitionism, see Ripley (1993). G. W. Williams was a controversial figure within the black middle class. On his death in 1891, Ida Wells, editor of the black newspaper *Free Speech*, wrote an article describing his failings as a husband, as well as praising his achievement as a writer, which also created a debate within the black press on the ethics of public discussion of private failings (McMurry 1999:126). A new biography, by John Hope Franklin, appeared in 1998.

3. In their cookbook/family history, Darden and Darden (1979:92–93) recount this story of a relative, R. R. Wright: "as a ten-year-old, Wright had electrified General O. O. Howard of the Union Army . . . and his party during their inspection of the Atlanta schools after the signing of the Emancipation Proclamation. At the end of his address, the general asked the little black children who had assembled around the abandoned freight car that served as their school, 'What message shall I take to the people in the North?' Wright's stirring reply from one so young – 'Tell them, sir, that we are rising!' – was immortalized in a poem by John Greenleaf Whittier."

4. Regarding education and religion, the historian Carter Woodson wrote: "the first real educators to take up the work of enlightening American Negroes were clergymen interested in the propagation of the gospel among the heathen in the new world," Woodson (1915:18). To which Frazier (1974:44) adds, "the purpose of education [prior to emancipation] was primarily to transmit to the Negro the religious ideas and practices of an alien culture. In the North the strictly religious content of education was supplemented by other elements, whereas in the South limitations were even placed upon enabling the Negro to read the Bible. By 1850 there were large numbers of Negroes attending schools in northern cities . . . individual Negroes managed to acquire a higher education and most of these were men who were preparing to become ministers." The AME Church was founded in Philadelphia, in 1786. The use of African in its title indicates the ties felt to that continent and, according to Essien-Udom (1962:24), reveals early roots of black nationalism in the United States.

5. Frazier (1974:13) disagrees with Du Bois over the significance of African heritage regarding the black church and its role under slavery. He writes "Du Bois evidently thought that social cohesion among slaves was not totally destroyed . . . he makes the assertion that the Negro church was 'the only social institution among the Negroes which started in the African forest and survived slavery' and that 'under the leadership of the priest and the medicine man' the church preserved the remnants of African life." Frazier replies "From the available evidence . . . it is impossible to establish any continuity between African religious practices and the Negro church in the United States."

6. As mentioned earlier, "conventions" were a common means of opening a black public sphere, creating a space for discussion and representation. The Kansas Exodus, for example, created the occasion for a series of "conventions" to discuss its meaning and consequences for the "race." It was here that the conditions of blacks as a group could be discussed and alternative strategies weighed. Painter (1976:221) calls them a "shadow government," where those who under normal conditions in a democracy would have been elected representatives gave voice to public opinion.

7. Regarding intermarriage, Drake and Cayton (1945:122) write, "Despite the almost complete adjustment to social segregation, there are situations in which resentment against the pattern is openly expressed. A Negro may have no desire to marry a white person or to make sexual excursions across the color-line; but he usually gets boiling mad at any attempts to break up mixed couples in a public place or to legislate against intermarriage." It is the right to things, rather than the thing itself that is seen as essential, in other words. This, too, can be said to follow from the necessity to accept the status of otherness and of living in separate worlds.

8. Literacy was valued not only as a source of knowledge, but also because it was a requisite of voting and jury duty. Writing about the white reaction, Painter (1979:50–51) notes; "Progressive strangulation of the public schools also aggrieved Southern Blacks because literacy carried juridical value. Once Reconstruction amendments made freedmen United States citizens, many Southern states, such as Texas, required literacy of prospective jurymen . . . thus, literacy and the state of the public schools were inextricably tied to Southern politics and to the perpetuation of the old social system based on Black dependency."

9. Spelman College was made part of the Atlanta University complex. It took its name from a benefactor, Laura Spelman Rockefeller, wife of John D. Rockefeller. The Spelman family had been active abolitionists. In 1885 Spelman College had an enrollment of 645 students, functioning as an "elementary and secondary school rather than a college" (Higginbotham 1993:33). It began training nurses in 1886 and awarded its first B.A. degree in 1901. Most of the graduates became teachers, however. A survey of graduates in 1906 found that 87 percent had been or were engaged in teaching (Higginbotham 1999:39).

10. In 1879, the black-owned New Orleans weekly *Louisianian* carried this explanation of the Exodus, "The constantly recurring, nay ever present fear, which haunts the

minds of these our people in the turbulent parishes of the State, that slavery in the horrid form of peonage is approaching; that the avowed disposition of the men now in power is to reduce the laborer and his interests to the minimum as freemen, and to absolutely none as citizens, has produced so absolute a fear that in many cases it has become a panic. It is a flight from present sufferings, and the wrongs to come. Kansas with her freedom and broad prairies, with the memories of John Brown and his heroic struggle, seems naturally the State to seek . . . the same longing and all-pervading desire to leave here and to go there as the magic name Canada gave in that time to the slave. The feeling is identical, occasioned, too, by nearly like conditions" (cited in Painter 1976:215).

11. Some would argue for continuity between the post-emancipation black elite and the infamous distinction between house and field slaves during slavery. McMurry (1999) supports this view in her study of the Memphis elite that spawned Ida Wells. Ira Berlin (1998) contests the continuity thesis in his claim that the cotton boom in the deep South all but forced all slave labor out into the fields, while the plantation system, upon which most idealized pictures of the antebellum South were built, was all but passed over by this development. Garwood (1990) argues for a continuity between slavery and post-slavery social hierarchies when he writes "the emphasis colored aristocrats placed on ancestry and family heritage . . . was in large measure bound up with blacks' experience with slavery – their place in the slave system, their role in opposing it, and to the extent which their families had been free from it" (9). He also argues for calling these hierarchies caste rather than class hierarchies, to distinguish them from those of white society, which were ordered, he suggests, around different criteria.

12. Congress and the Supreme Court worked hand in hand to undercut the civil rights legislation passed during reconstruction, preparing the way for the reinstitution of Jim Crow in the South and informal segregation in the North. This was aided by trends in academic and cultural discourse, where "the rediscovery of the Mendelian laws of heredity . . . sparked new interest in the genetic transmission of racial characteristics" (Sitkoff 1978:6). A eugenics movement was blossoming by the turn-of-the century among the educated elite, championing racial hygiene in the name of improvement of the species. Blacks were given a lower place on the scale of civilization, as their "genetic" makeup was considered inferior to that of whites. See Sitkoff (1978, esp. ch. 1) for a valuable summary of this history.

13. Later on, the Harlem Renaissance novelist Wallace Thurman (1929:7–8) has one of his characters recount how her grandparents, "both mulatto products of slave-day promiscuity," moved from Kansas because "Kansas was too near the former slave belt, too accessible to disgruntled southerners who, deprived of their slaves, were stricken with an easily communicable virus – nigger hatred."

14. Painter is clearly influenced by recent discussions about the role of "ordinary people" in making history and by discussions about the democratic process. She offers an historical account shaped by that desire, for example, stressing the antagonism between local black leaders and so-called "representative" blacks, those educated and more sophisticated blacks chosen more or less by whites to represent the race.

The idea of the "talented tenth" which developed a little later in history and which has spurred much current controversy is anathema here. Painter also appears to be influenced by the idea of a working-class public sphere and the emergence of local leadership, which later would be associated with Ella Baker.

15. Darden and Darden (1994:4–5) recount this about the town of Wilson, North Carolina where their grandfather, a former slave, lived after emancipation: "Wilson was a small, slow-paced, rather quiet tobacco town with about 4,000 citizens, 40 percent of whom were black, so the climate looked encouraging for black progress. But by 1875, Reconstruction had given way to terrorism. In Wilson as well as throughout the South, the Ku Klux Klan had spread its sheets. Voting was over [three black senators and nineteen black members of the House had been elected to the North Carolina legislature during reconstruction]. First by intimidation and finally by law, blacks were banned from the ballot box. Political power as a tool of black advancement had failed, so Charles Henry Darden focused his energies on his business, the education of his family, and the leadership of his community. He was convinced that economic self-reliance now held the key to the survival of the black community."

16. Hale (1998:69) continues "White war stories erased the bread riots and desertion of poorer recruits, denying class tensions between whites in both the past and present. The 'civil' war became not just the paradoxical space of national reconciliation but also the moment that counted, when the distant plantation past and the postbellum South met, the touchstone of modern 'classless' southern whiteness."

17. Painter (1979:14) writes "Black America had never been culturally monolithic, for Western-educated or at least culturally assimilated Negroes played a prominent part in the abolitionist crusade. In the South, however, where most Blacks were slaves, they shared a rural, nonliterate folk culture, which of course endured well past the Civil War."

18. As Powell (1997:10), points out, blackness is a "state of being that was rooted in perception. Notwithstanding the spurious biological basis of the definition of race, 'black' has almost always initially meant racial identity, and only thereafter a social and/or political condition: an ingrained way of thinking that has been difficult to overcome."

19. Whether or not mimesis is a form of memory can be debated. Later on we will see how the black elite that emerged in the South during and after reconstruction mimed the values and manners of their former masters, including the Victorian "cult of womanhood." This pattern of behavior and value system was molded out of the slave past and reproduced under different conditions by former slaves and their offspring. As long as it is not seen as direct copying, but involving reflection and choice, this can be considered memory. Bourdieu's notion of "habitus" is helpful here, especially as it implies the transmission and acquisition of cognitive, evaluative frames as well as practices.

20. It would also prove a detriment. This was especially so in reference to material culture and habitus. Traces of slavery remained in the separate living conditions of whites and blacks, in the obvious differences in the quality and quantity of possessions. It was also embodied in the "arts of survival and accommodation,

the posture of demeanor and deference" which black parents taught their children (Litwack 1998:39).

21. There were 178,975 black soldiers in the Grand Army of the Republic, of which the Massachusetts 54th was a part. They accounted for 10 percent of the Union Army by the war's end. Not much of the history of their participation was generally known until the post-Civil Rights era encouraged a reinterpretation of American history, and especially the role of blacks and other minorities in its making. In 1989, a narrative film entitled *Glory*, depicted their exploits. Starring prominent actors such as Danzel Washington and Morgan Freeman as footsoldiers and Matthew Broderick as Robert Shaw, the film offered a Hollywood version of black participation in the Civil War. Three years later, Jacqueline Shearer, a black director, produced a documentary "The Massachusetts 54th," with Morgan Freeman and other prominent black actors providing the narration (Klotman 1999).

22. In his autobiography, Turner (1917) recounts that he was born to free parents in 1834 in South Carolina. He was elected to the Georgia legislature during reconstruction, while serving as postmaster in Macon, Georgia. In the late 1870s, as reconstruction began to collapse and what we have called the process of cultural trauma began, Turner, who was thrown out of the legislature and forced to resign his post as postmaster, would become a spokesman for black separatism, as "Liberia Fever" swept the South (Frazier 1974:47; Clegg 1997:166). For C. Eric Lincoln, writing in the heat of the black power revolution and seeking roots for a "Black theology," Turner "was probably the first Black clergyman of note to define God as black" (Lincoln 1974:148).

23. Washington (*c.* 1820–75) was freeborn in New Jersey and attended Dartmouth College. With the establishment of the Fugitive Slave Act in 1850, which made all blacks potentially slaves, Washington and his family fled to Liberia (Michaels 2000:162).

24. Mary Edmonia Lewis was born in upstate New York in 1843, the daughter of a Chippewa Indian mother and a freeborn black father. One of the first persons of color to attend Obelin College, she was expelled in 1862 after being accused of poisoning two of her classmates. With the help of another black Obelin graduate, the attorney and abolitionist leader John Mercer Langston, she was cleared of suspicion due to lack of evidence. With money earned through portraits she created of John Brown and Robert Shaw, the white officer in charge of the all-black Massachusetts 54th, which fought in the Civil War, Lewis worked in Rome. It was there, under the influence of Greco-Roman neo-classicism, that she produced "Forever Free" (Lewis 1990). While Lewis' rendering of the hopes of emancipation broke stereotypical expectations in using white marble and classical facial features, it reproduced and conformed to many as well. The male figure towers over the kneeling female, conforming to nineteenth-century gender idealizations, and the whole rendering, including the use of broken shackles and other forms of obvious symbolism would later be criticized for kitsch-like simplemindedness. The very fact of a black artist producing such a statue just four years after the Emancipation Proclamation can itself be seem as a powerful expression of liberation. As Richard Powell (1999:106) put

it "Representations of emancipation were capable of being more than just images of broken shackles or genuflecting slaves. For some, the very idea of an African American operating outside of the sphere of slavery was enough to signify bodily freedom. Similarly, for many painters and sculptors of color the avoidance of the black subject altogether and the conscious demonstration of artistic skills and a command of the academic ideals of art denoted another kind of emancipation: freedom from the vexing, worrisome subject of a democracy gone awry; sovereignty from a *de facto* American caste system; and independence from assumptions of black inferiority."

25. The only piece of sculpture that came close to expressing the true significance of this event according to Murray was that done by the African American artist Meta Vaux Warrick Fuller for the 50th Anniversary Celebration in 1913. Murray wrote of this work: "The portrayal is emptied of the usual accessories as well as of the frequent claptrap – no broken shackles, no obvious parchments, no discarded whips, no crouching slave with uncertain face; no, not even a kindly . . . Liberator appears; in short, she essays to set forth and to represent, not a person, not a recipient – not the Emancipator nor one of the Emancipated – not even the Emancipation itself, as a mere formal act, but far higher, the Emancipation as an embracing theme" (in Boime 1990:181).

26. Powell (1997:16–18) writes "for Murray, black subjectivity . . . presupposed that there was a world in which black peoples and their cultures, rather than always being filtered through white supremacist eyes and mindsets, could be seen and represented differently: either through the non-racist (or at least, multidimensional) lens of whites, or through the knowing and racially self-conscious eyes of blacks themselves."

27. As far as supply and demand is concerned, the slave narratives were probably more popular before emancipation than immediately after. This can probably be explained with respect to their association with abolition. As the example of Bontemps indicates, however, their significance goes far beyond sales figures. They are still central to current debates about slavery in the United States, as the previously mentioned review of the literature by George Fredrickson (2000) reveals.

28. Black authors writing about whites is a new phenomenon with this generation. The same can be said of Edmonia Lewis sculpting in white marble, mentioned earlier. This can be viewed and analyzed from a number of perspectives. One is the attempt to write a "raceless" novel, to appeal to a white audience – this was "a commercial venture, usually a love story" (Pinckney 2000:86). Another possibility that the inclusion of whites added was of saying things that would be more difficult or sensitive without the white mask. One could, in other words, say and do things with white characters that would be impossible or more difficult with black. Later generations of black writers would find this a useful tool.

29. August Meier (1962:258–66) locates Chesnutt in the radical "cultured" middle class, distinguishing this group from other, more commercially oriented middle-class blacks. The focal point for these sub-groups of the black middle class, according to Meier, was Booker T. Washington's program of racial self-help. Those

dependent on a white market, like Chesnutt, were "radical" in the sense of their opposition to Washington, while those who were more dependent on the new black market were more supportive of Washington and his notion of what Du Bois would call the "group economy."

30. William Gleason (1999) analyzes Chesnutt's work with reference to architecture and spatial references, arguing that these spurred recollections and reflections concerning the slave past amongst contemporary black readers. This view of memory aligns itself with the views outlined by Alan Radley (1990) cited previously.

31. This collection also contains a story parodying the "loyal slave" character of the minstrel show and the plantation school of Southern fiction. "The Passing of Grandison" recounts the attempts of the son of a slaveowner to please his would-be fiancée by freeing one of his father's slaves. The "loyal" slave undermines all such attempts, until in the end he is able to free both himself and his future wife. The moral tale is told with humor and irony.

32. In his autobiography, James Weldon Johnson (1934) wrote: "I could see that [Dunbar] writing in the conventionalized dialect, no matter how sincere he might be, was dominated by his audience; that his audience was a section of the white American reading public; that when he wrote he was expressing what often bore little relation, sometimes no relation at all, to actual Negro life; that he was really expressing only certain conceptions about Negro life that his audience was willing to accept and ready to enjoy; that, in fact, he wrote mainly for the delectation of an audience that was an outside group." Beginning his essay with this quotation, Lawrence Rodgers (1991) goes on to defend Dunbar, even while conceding much of what Johnson maintains. Rodgers compares Dunbar and Chesnutt regarding their respective "characterization of blackness" (46) and finds Dunbar more original in breaking out of the stock set of available black characters, especially in allowing them to move North and thus open an "uncharted territory in African-American literature" (47). According to Rodgers, Dunbar's *The Sport of the Gods* is the first migration novel, which "explores the consequences of migration and the urban setting in a two-stage process. First appearing to offer his readers a plantation story at its most conventional, he 'undercuts the southern code of chivalry and the legendary paternalism of master to servant' so that his characters *must* go North, a strategy that has personal as well as literary consequences for Dunbar. Having cleared a geographic space, he sends them to a setting that is relatively free of white racial stereotyping and is instead informed by urban naturalism" (48). For further discussion of the reception of Dunbar's work see Rauch (1993).

33. The struggle over who would succeed Douglass was fought primarily between Du Bois and Washington, with Wells supporting the former. Wells and her husband were active in the Niagara Movement and, after it failed, in the founding of the NAACP. Du Bois may have attempted to keep Wells off the Executive Council of that organization, but others forced her in (Lewis 1993:394ff.). Since she was more the accomplished journalist of the two, it could have been she who was offered the editorship of *Crisis*. According to Lewis (1993:397), "Wells-Barnett was a woman of unrestrained outspokenness who seldom acknowledged the gender etiquette of

her day when fighting for a cause. She may have presumed a good deal on Du Bois's large ego." Although Du Bois was a great supporter of women's rights, he wanted the job of editor badly and was an accomplished journalist. He also was much better placed amongst the powerful white patrons who supported the NAACP. It was not only Wells' gender and personality that excluded her from the role. She was considered too radical.

34. Shaw University was originally run by the American Baptist Home Mission Society, and became coeducational in 1872. According to Higginbotham (1993:21), by 1880 this white-led organization "owned and supported eight schools for blacks – only two of which were exclusively male."

35. This is an interesting point to contemplate, as one of the explanations given for why black ministers, rather than teachers, were the most prominent leaders of the civil rights struggles in the 1950s was just the fact that they were more financially independent of whites, while teachers, then as previously, were more dependent and therefore more fearful of political activism.

36. "The first Negro lodge, the Masons, received its charter from England in 1787, and African Lodge No. 459 was formally organized with its founder, Prince Hall, as the Master. Other fraternal societies were organized later in the nineteenth century, such as the Elks in 1898. Like the Negro church, the fraternal societies were organized because the free Negroes had been denied membership in the white lodges. The lodges appear to have been more race-conscious than the Negro church. The secrecy, rituals, and the spirit of brotherliness and equality fostered by the lodge members are similar to some of the practices of the nationalist and separatist religious movements of the present (20th) century" (Essien-Udom 1962:26–27). E. Franklin Frazier (1974:42ff.) places great emphasis on the role of the black church in the formation of self-help organizations, including fraternal societies. One example was the Grand United Order of True Reformers founded by Reverend Washington Browne, a former slave from Georgia. "In 1876 he succeeded in bringing together in a single organization, known as the Grand Fountain of True Reformers, twenty-seven Fountains with 2000 members" (1974:43). This organization produced "a weekly newspaper, a real estate firm, a bank, a hotel, a building and loan association, and a grocery and general merchandising store" (1974:43). They also organized an insurance program. The roots of what later would be called "black capitalism" and the cooperative movement can be found in such activities.

3 Out of Africa: the making of a collective identity

1. The Irish rebellion provided both a source of inspiration and a model of liberation for American blacks. Another source was the historical plight of the Jews. Davis (1999:57–63) identifies three models of liberation which American blacks have shared with Jews. The first is the biblical theme of Exodus, which can be found in many spirituals and sermons, the second is the Zionist ideal of a national center "that would radiate pride," the third is the struggle against discrimination based on Enlightenment ideals of full citizenship and acceptance, which also inspired the

French and American revolutions. Writing about the 1919 Pan African Conference in *Crisis*, Du Bois said "The African movement means to us what the Zionist movement means to Jews . . . the centralization of the race effort and the recognition of a racial front" (cited in Powell 1997:40).

2. I use the term movement in the sense outlined earlier to indicate a confluence of social forces containing within it individuals, groups, and organizations struggling to give meaning and direction. In that sense, the term is broad enough to encompass all the meanings of the concept of New Negro which Powell (1997:41–42) discusses.

3. According to Powell (1997:24) "The belief that black people, apart from physiognomic and genealogical ties with the inhabitants of Africa, had comparable experiences, identical struggles for full acceptance in society, and shared destinies, was widely held by social commentators and thinkers in the second half of the nineteenth century." This could be taken either as evidence of the "primitive" culture they supposedly shared or as grounds for a common struggle. It was obviously the latter that inspired American black intellectuals. In any case, it was here that the idea of a common black culture began to take form. The bounds and borders of this culture, whether it was universal or particular, would become a central matter of conflict.

4. In his analysis of the reception of slave songs Cruz (1999:107ff.) lists three modes of hearing that applied to contemporary whites: incidental, a sort of proto-ethnographic interested but chance hearing; instrumental, that of slaveowners, buyers, and overseers, who linked music and social control; and pathos-oriented, a form which opened understanding, which developed within the abolitionist movement. Du Bois offers another sort, from the inside, yet distanced, and also a little instrumental/strategic.

5. This idea of "slave culture" is different from one that later came into use, for example in Stuckey (1987). As part of a much later debate concerning the interpretation of black nationalism, Sterling Stuckey traces the origins of "slave culture" through the living memory of African tribal roots. Stuckey's book also contains interesting interpretations of Du Bois and Paul Robeson with reference to nationalist theory and practice.

6. This subjectivity was visually expressed in the paintings of Henry Ossawa Tanner and Leigh Richmond Miner (whose work was reproduced on the cover of a book of verse by Dunbar, published in 1901).

7. They also had to counter the locally based identity that formed in the process of trauma. Frazier (1974) and others have argued the significance of the church and the local community which formed around it, as the first grounding of black collective identity after the failure of emancipation to fully integrate blacks as citizens. National leaders like Du Bois and Washington sought means to transcend this identity in their struggle for civil rights. They did so in different ways, however.

8. According to one biographer, however, Du Bois had used the term already in 1887, as the title of a magazine article which was never published and is now lost (Lewis 1993:73).

9. On the presuppositions and shifts in Du Bois' notion of race, see Appiah (1985).

10. In the same speech, Du Bois also asked the rhetorical question "Here then is the dilemma . . . What, after all, am I? Am I an American or a Negro? Can I be both? Or is it my duty to cease to be a Negro as soon as possible and be an American?" (Du Bois [1897]1999). Also cited in Redkey (1969:10).

11. Gates (1985) raises some very interesting and relevant issues around what he calls the trope of race. As he reveals, there are imminent dangers in appropriating this concept: "we must understand how certain forms of difference and the languages we employ to define those supposed differences not only reinforce each other but tend to create and maintain each other" (1985:15). Du Bois was surely aware of this danger, but willingly and consciously took the risk.

12. *Black Reconstruction* was published in book form in the mid thirties, but the ideas had been presented by its author as early as 1909. That year Du Bois presented a paper at the meeting of the American Historical Association called "Reconstruction and its Benefits," which even in its title challenged prevailing views. The view that reconstruction was both a mistake and a joke was the dominant one, thus to claim that any "benefits" could be found was radical revisionism (Lewis 1993:383ff.) Du Bois' paper was published in the *American Historical Review*, July 1910, "after which virtually nothing more was ever said among white professional historians . . . (Lewis 1993:384).

13. According to Howe (1998:51) "Du Bois offered probably the least romance-bound, most factually grounded view of Africa yet published by a black American writer" in his *The Negro*, published in 1915.

14. Du Bois developed his particular notion of race out of the Hegelian philosophy he studied in Germany and through its American reception in his Harvard teachers, like William James, whose psychological theories propounded the notion of a divided self and multiple role playing in social situations. David Krasner (1997:52) points this out in his discussion of African American theater. Sociologists will immediately think of Erving Goffman. William James was the forerunner of this tradition of American thought, a tradition which universalized a distinctly modern experience. The class and time specific character of Du Bois' notion of double consciousness has also been pointed out by Zamir (1995).

15. Du Bois had made use of the concept of the "advance guard" already in 1897, in referring to the mission of the American Negro. In a speech before the American Negro Academy he said "the advance guard of the Negro people – the 8,000,000 people of Negro blood in the United States of America – must soon come to realize that if they are to take their just place in the van of Pan-Negroism, then their destiny is *not* absorption by the white Americans." This statement has been used to link Du Bois early on in his career with Pan-Africanism and black nationalism (see Essien-Udom 1962:27). The NAACP emerged out of the shortcomings of the Niagara Movement, a group of black intellectuals united around opposition to B.T. Washington, and the revived interest of the progressive movement in racial issues. After a wave of lynchings and riots in Northern cities (as well as one in Atlanta in 1909), most prominently in 1908 in Springfield, Illinois, Abraham Lincoln's birthplace, "two white settlement house workers, Mary White Ovington and Dr. Henry

Moskowitz . . . prevailed upon Oswald Garrison Villard, editor of the New York *Evening Post* and grandson of the abolitionist leader, to issue a call 'for the discussion of present evils, the voicing of protests and the renewal of the struggle for civil and political liberty'" (Sitkoff 1978:16). The confluence of this white protest movement, with roots in Abolition, and the black intellectuals of the Niagara Movement, led to the emergence of the NAACP in 1910. For a full account of this process, see Lewis (1993).

16. Similarly to Charles Chesnutt, whose short stories he would later print when he became editor of *The Crisis* in 1910, the official journal of the NAACP, an organization he had helped to found a year earlier.

17. Earlier in his life, Du Bois worked for a time in a country school in Tennessee, living a simple life amongst rural blacks. This sort of pilgrimage was not uncommon for educated blacks of this generation, especially those from the North. It was often experienced as a return to one's roots, lest one forget. These were roots connected with slavery and its memory. James Baldwin recorded a similar experience upon his first journey South during the civil rights movement.

18. In *Darkwater* ([1920]1999), Du Bois broadens the "race" to more explicitly include Africans.

19. Sitkoff (1978:13) is one of those. He describes the rise and fall of the Niagara Movement as a direct response to Washington's policies of "accommodation." However, Sitkoff and others, including Du Bois' most recent biographer (Lewis) emphasize the double-edged tactics employed by Washington, where his public utterances (to white audiences) differed from his behind the scenes and private (to black audiences) maneuvering, something of which Du Bois must have been aware. Moses (1998:143–49) discusses the basic similarities in outlook between Washington and Du Bois, especially in regard to the work ethic grounded in Calvinism and in Puritan morality. According to this analysis their religious views were in general very similar. Moses also notes "the burden of his (Du Bois') religious writings identified him as in irreconcilable opposition to both the modernism and primitivism of the so-called Harlem Renaissance . . . It put him in unacknowledged ideological harmony with such working-class cults as the Black Jews of Harlem and the Black Muslims, groups that still appeal to black puritanical traditions and that stand in opposition to the latitudinarianism of intellectual and artistic elites" (1998:48).

20. The popularity of minstrelsry amongst blacks, as well as whites, was a cause for concern and reflection amongst black intellectuals then and now. Why did black and white audiences laugh at the comic characters in black face and flock to such performances? For whites, the answer seemed clear, these characters reflected and reinforced stereotypical, racist preconceptions. But why would black audiences laugh, as appears to be the case judging from contemporary accounts? Although he writes about a slightly later historical period, Hay (1994:18ff.) provides several possible explanations. In addition to seeking escape, relief from everyday life, through viewing such performances, and therefore ready to laugh at almost anything, "actors and spectators alike understood that minstrel and musical comedy characters were but collections of the same peculiarities that often provoked laughter in real life."

Some stereotypes work in strange ways, because they evoke recognition, even on the part of those they consciously misrepresent. The affects and effects of this recognition were and are one of the critical areas of debate. Should characters represent only ideal-types, be exemplary rather than realistic, even if it means a lack of popularity? Or, should recognition and identification between character and audience be central? Then there is the issue of the double audience and the double consciousness. What if recognition means two very different things, is the price of self-recognition on the part of blacks worth the cost of reinforcing racial stereotypes? This issue of how black artists and writers should depict black Americans would be a matter of continuous debate. In the era of the civil rights movement the issue raged again and in the 1970s and 1980s the painter Robert Colescott would jibe both blacks and whites with his historical parodies and flouting of sexual taboos and racial stereotypes (on this, see Sandler (1996:204–7)).

21. Fifty years later, Maya Angelou (1976:170) would uncover similar feelings during a visit to Yugoslavia. Upon hearing the name Paul Robeson she writes, "I made no attempt to wipe away the tears. I could not claim a forefather who came to America on the *Mayflower* . . . My great-grandparents were illiterate when their fellow men were signing the Declaration of Independence, and the first families of my people were bought separately and sold apart, nameless and without traces – yet there was this:

> Deep River
> My home is over Jordan.

I had a heritage, rich and nearer than the tongue which gives it voice. My mind resounded with the words and my blood raced to the rhythms."

22. E. Franklin Frazier (1974:77) would make a similar argument sixty years later in writing about the changing nature of the black church in relation to an evolving class stratification amongst American blacks. He writes "They [the lower black strata] continue to be influenced in their thinking and especially in their feelings and sentiments by the social heritage of the Negro which is represented by the Spirituals and religious orientation toward the world contained in the Spirituals." Frazier also turns to music in explaining the effects of social change upon blacks and their accommodation to American society: "This accommodation is symbolized by the Gospel Singers . . . Since the Negro has become urbanized, there has been an amazing rise and spread of 'gospel singing'" (1974:77). And, in explaining the ground for collective identity amongst a rising strata of "new middle class," Frazier writes, "This new class is largely without social roots except the traditions of the Negro folk represented in the Spirituals" (1974:81).

23. Michael Walzer (1985:3) recalls listening to "the most extraordinary sermon that I heard – on the Book of Exodus and the political struggle of southern blacks" in a small Montgomery, Alabama Baptist church in 1960. "There on his pulpit, the preacher, whose name I have long forgotten, acted out the 'going out' from Egypt and expounded its contemporary analogues: he cringed under the lash, challenged the pharaoh, hesitated fearfully at the sea, accepted the covenant and the law at

the foot of the mountain." Such performances, especially when underscored with music, carried and conveyed enormous emotional as well as cognitive content. The Exodus theme was also prominent in the mass migrations to Kansas in 1879.

24. Rampersad (1989) interprets *Souls* in this light. For him, Du Bois challenges the benign view of slavery presented in Booker T. Washington's *Up From Slavery*, published two years previously. While I am indebted to this analysis, my interpretation of the differences between their views of slavery differs from Rampersad in that I see more similarity than he does.

25. Hale (1998:24ff.) portrays Washington's actions as performance, calling him "a master of minstrel performance" (24). "Booker T. Washington wrote the slaves' old means of survival, the weaving of the mask of acquiescence and dissembling in front of whites, into the new era . . . If whites wanted the world to be a minstrel show, Booker T. Washington, like the black entertainers before and after him, would point out the masquerade . . . If a black man must play the white man's black man, then the 'king' of the race could go one further and play the white man's black man's white man as well" (1998:25). Her point is that in a world where whites controlled the images, black leaders were forced to perform expected roles, but that they could play and turn the game around at the same time. Krasner (1997) makes a similar point regarding black theatrical performance. Du Bois' tactics were otherwise, he worked out of a different tradition of the role of intellectual, as well as leadership. This too involved performance, but of a different character, and a different mask.

26. While Washington and Du Bois disagreed fundamentally on the meaning and place of slavery for the black present, they agreed that racial solidarity and pride were essential to progress. How best to achieve this progress was also a matter of dispute, however, with Du Bois emphasizing confrontation in politics and culture and Washington more group-oriented practical, economic activity.

27. These ideas would re-emerge in new form in another wave of social movements in the 1960s, where the uniqueness of the black experience in America would be called on as the grounding of black theology and black sociology, as well as of movements for institutional change. C. Eric Lincoln (1974) describes the new black theology as a unique development rooted in the experience of "Blackamericans." This experience, the result of slavery and the formation of a black Christian church in a dominant white society, created at one and the same time a particularistic "Black" perspective and the possibility of a new universalism. Black theology emerged out of negation, yet created a new, positive perspective, a black perspective, which made it possible for white Christianity to renew itself. Similarly, black sociology developed in the same period and made similar claims about a scientific discipline, which was shrouded not only in racism, but also in European domination. Like theology, which Lincoln found distorted by European thought and therefore neither truly American nor universal, proponents of black sociology described the discipline as dominated by European theory as well as distorted by white racism. In freeing blacks, the new perspectives would also liberate these ideological systems.

28. Washington would later dismiss these "principles" as "idle talk" (Lewis 1993:323).

29. Black support for Roosevelt, the most popular president amongst black Americans since Lincoln, began to erode with his dismissal of black soldiers after the so-called "Brownsville incident." In 1906 as group of men from the all-black 25th Infantry allegedly "shot up the town," Roosevelt ordered the discharge, without trial, of "167 of the First Battalion's 170 soldiers without honor and with forfeiture of pension, among them men with twenty-five years' service, six of them Medal of Honor winners" (Lewis 1993:332); 1906 was also the year of the Atlanta race riot, where "ten thousand white people (most of them under twenty) had beaten every black person they found on the streets" (1993:333). This and other events undermined Washington's leadership position; Du Bois and others were quick to link them to the "failed" strategy outlined in the Atlanta Compromise speech of 1895.

   Rayford Logan (1965:11), a Howard University historian, reveals the uncertainty regarding the turning point toward progress after the end of reconstruction (Preface to the New Edition); is it 1901 or is it as late as 1923, as John Hope Franklin, another Howard historian, claimed in 1961? From his perspective, "progress" is measured in terms of both formal inclusion, i.e. legal measures and the treatment given in the public culture, especially the mass media.

30. Blyden had visited the United States earlier at the invitation of the American Colonization Society. A native of the Danish West Indies, Blyden was sent to Liberia as a missionary in the 1850s. He visited the United States often, propagating for Negro nationalism and repatriation to Africa. Because of his call for racial purity, which involved an outspoken criticism of "mixed descent," he was controversial not only in the United States, but also in Liberia (Redkey 1969:50ff.). He contacted Du Bois from Sierra Leone about the Encyclopedia project (Lewis 1993:379).

31. Washington was more passive in his support for Pan Africanism, according to Powell (1997:23) "although generally unsympathetic to political agitation and assertiveness by blacks, [Washington] gave his tacit approval for such a conference and urged those 'colored Americans' who were able to attend to do so." Du Bois' biographer (Lewis 1993:249) writes "Washington felt about as much need for solidarity with Africans as did the explorer Stanley (who once explained to the like-minded Wizard that African-American emigration to Africa was impracticable), but Washington was sure that the more black people in America learned about European treatment of Africans, the more tolerable the conditions in the South would seem to them." This was the reason he urged them to attend the London congress.

32. "'Colored' was chosen instead of Afro-American or Negro in order to proclaim the association's intention to promote the interests of dark-skinned people everywhere" (Lewis 1993:405). In the prospectus announcing the coming publication of *The Crisis*, Du Bois used the term "Negro-American" (1993:409). The usage of the term "colored" instead of "Negro" or Afro-American was also discussed when the National Association of Colored Women formed in 1896 (White 1999:51). According to White (79), "The term 'colored' . . . was preferred by some mulattos because it allowed for recognition of white or Indian ancestry." However, in discussing the 1920s she also writes "inasmuch as many light-skinned and more

affluent blacks preferred the term 'colored' to Negro, the popularity of 'Negro' [in the 1920s], also reflected a rejection of the color/class hierarchy that existed at the beginning of the century" (White 1999:154).

33. The title was inspired by James Russell Lowell's poem "The Present Crisis," marking New England roots. The editorial board included the NAACP's chair Oswald Garrison Villard, Max Barber, "formerly editor of the *Voice of the Negro*," William Stanley Braithwaite, a poet and writer of "international reputation" (an African American, was poetry editor of the Boston *Transcript*), and Mary Dunlop Maclean, "a staff writer on the New York *Times*" – an editorial board made up of two white men and one white woman, and three black men" (Lewis 1993:410).

34. Mary Church Terrell, the first president of the National Association of Colored Women, exemplified this opposition. As a decidedly "modern" woman, Terrell dressed and acted the part as she called upon black women to organize and lead the race. Wearing a "pink evening dress and long white gloves, with her hair beautifully done" (White 1999:21) as she delivered her speech on "The Modern Woman," she must surely have irked the conservative, male-dominated church leadership. The organization organized child care, mothering and homemaking education, crisis centers, religious instruction, art and book clubs, professional and business associations.

35. Racial identity was the ground of collective identity not by choice, but the result of white racism. Other identities, like gender in this case, but others as well, would complement, but the overpowering racism of white society forced the issue. Like Du Bois, women activists sought to transform this tragedy into triumph. Anna Cooper "thought that it might be God's way of preparing the race for something nobler than what white Americans had wrought" (White 1999:38). In what would become one of the key phrases of the progressive narrative, Cooper wrote, "the race is young and full of elasticity and hopefulness of youth, all its achievements are before it" (quoted in White 1999:38).

36. According to Barlow (1989:29), "The Saturday night social gatherings were communal rituals of resistance that originated during slavery. Since the slaves worked six days a week from sunup to sundown, Saturday evening was the only time they had for recreational activities. Most plantation owners allowed their slaves to hold a dance or attend one on a nearby plantation, and these get-togethers were the highlight of the week."

37. Du Bois studied at Fisk University between 1885 and 1888. He also managed the glee club after having failed to impress them with his singing voice (Du Bois 1986). His train travel from New York to the Nashville campus was his first experience of the newly imposed Jim Crow South. About the 17-year-old Du Bois making this trip his biographer writes, "Willie says nothing about accommodations aboard his train, but segregation in interstate travel was already imposed. Tennessee, in fact, had been the first state to enact race separation laws in travel and public accommodation" (Lewis 1993:60). In her discussion of the origins of the blues, Southern (1983:333) writes, "In 1903 a black scholar published a rare example (of the three line stanza common the blues) that had been passed down through several generations of his

family from an African great-great-grandmother." The "black scholar" turns out to be "William E.B. DuBois" [*sic*] and the book *The Souls of Black Folk*.

38. Moses (1998:149) asks, "one sometimes wonders if Du Bois ever regretted writing the passage . . . that has been quoted with such stupefying frequency in which he confesses to struggling with 'double consciousness' . . . This was almost certainly an instance of rhetorical oversimplification because, like all persons of intellectual depth, 'the Doctor' experienced numerous conflicts within his complex identity . . . There was a warfare between his loyalties as social democrat and racial romantic, another battle between his impulses as traditionalist and iconoclast. There was a tension between his austerity and his enthusiasm, another between his elitism and his folkishness, and yet another between his blatant Prussianism and his latent bohemianism."

39. Her claim that they were an important means of preserving the memory of Africa is harder to substantiate. More plausible is the claim that the biblical references in the spirituals provided a model of liberation, the theme of Exodus being one example: "Way down in Egypt's land . . . Let my people go." Comparing black spirituals to their contemporary white counterparts, David Brion Davis (1999:59) writes, "Whereas white Christian hymns tended to spiritualize 'Egyptian bondage' and 'the Promised Land', American slaves, more attracted to the Old Testament, concentrated on the fact that God had punished oppressors in *this* world. 'And the God dat lived in Moses' time is jus' de same today.'"

40. The notion of reinscription derives from Edward Said and through him from Franz Fanon and Hegel. According to Said, in the Hegelian struggle for recognition subordinate groups must "rechart and then occupy the place in imperial culture forms reserved for subordination, to occupy it self-consciously, fighting for it on the very same territory once ruled by a consciousness that assumed the subordination of a designated inferior Other" (cited in Krasner 1997:26). The blossoming of the black urban public sphere in the 1920s would create a different context, one in which black artists and performers were more in control of their role-performances because of the larger black audience. This was the case even if blacks did not own or control the means of representation, as Harold Cruse (1984) and other later critics of the Harlem Renaissance pointed out in explaining its "failure." In this context some of the previously taboo topics and stereotypical representations, gambling and prostitution, large lips and broad noses, could now be painted with vitality and pride. This, of course, was not to everyone's taste, as will be discussed in Chapter 4.

41. Sorrow songs or spirituals and "coon" songs were at the time popular both as performance and as sheet music. One of the most popular and prolific producers of the latter was a black vaudeville performer named Ernest Hogan. It was his song, "All Coons Look Alike to Me" published in 1896 which gave the name to this genre (see Powell 1997:25 for a reproduction of the cover sheet).

42. Powell (1997:36) called "The Awakening of Ethiopia" (1914) Fuller's most important work. Rather than slavery, this work looks back to Africa, perhaps inspired by the "utopian, Pan-Africanist novel *Ethopia Unbound* (1911) by the Gold Coast activist and newspaper publisher J. E. Casely Hayford." Fuller had an interest in

this movement and her work "served the representational needs not only of a disillusioned but hopeful black elite in the years 1914–17, but also of successive generations of 'race' men and women" (Powell 1997).

43. Musicals were popular with black as well as white audiences. This popularity bothered Du Bois and Locke. According to Hay (1994:15), "the quintessential question concerning this period [1898–1923] is Why did Locke – and even Du Bois – have a difficult time persuading African Americans to repudiate the clown images in the musicals?"

44. Locke had been recruited by Du Bois in 1916 to help develop the form of protest of "The Star of Ethiopia" type, but resigned after a conflict with the steering committee (Hay 1994:81).

45. The well-known example of W.C. Handy's encounter with the blues is illustrative. Handy, often called the father of the blues, was a musician, composer, band leader, and college band director who offered the first written account of what is now called Delta blues. As Handy waited for a train at a Mississippi railroad depot in 1903, "A lean, loose-jointed Negro had commenced plucking a guitar beside me while I slept. His clothes were rags, his feet peeped out of his shoes. His face had on it some of the sadness of the ages. As he played, he pressed a knife on the strings of the guitar in a manner popularized by Hawaiian guitarists who used steel bars. The effect was unforgettable. His song too, struck me instantly. 'Goin' to where the Southern cross the Dog'. The singer repeated the line three times, accompanying himself on the guitar with the weirdest music I ever heard" (Handy [1941]1970:78). "The weirdest music I ever heard," not at all like the recognition that Du Bois felt with the art-performance of the sorrow songs, but still striking. In fact, Handy will later go on to say that the blues recalled the songs he heard as a child growing up in the South, and to write them down for sale as commercial sheet music. As opposed to Du Bois who identified with the history embedded in these songs, Handy saw immediately their commercial potential. After observing the money thrown at the feet of a small group of musicians playing "our native music," Handy writes, "There before the boys lay more money than my nine musicians were being paid for the entire engagement. Then I saw the beauty of primitive music . . . That night a composer was born . . . My idea of what constitutes music was changed by the sight of that silver money cascading around the splay feet of a Mississippi string band" (Handy 1970:81).

46. The debate and controversy over the term "nigger," who can use it, and what it means still continues. Randall Kennedy, a black law professor at Harvard, gave a series of talks at Stanford in May 1999 on the topic, concluding, not uncontroversially to judge from the audience reaction, that since the term was so grounded in the culture there were times when its use in public discourse, even by whites, was acceptable, if not desirable. In the 1920s, as we shall discuss below, the book by Carl Van Vechten, *Nigger Heaven* evoked controversy as did use of the term in plays by Eugene O'Neill.

47. Like W.C. Handy before him, Dorsey would be a central figure in the transformation of the reception of the blues. Like his predecessor, Dorsey composed and stylized,

making it more acceptable and accessible both to Northern blacks and to interested whites. He also arranged blues numbers and performances, such as those of Ma Rainey mentioned earlier. A deeply religious man, Dorsey stressed the universal aspects of the music and went on to became the "father" of gospel blues and the author of one of the most famous hymns, "Take My Hand, Precious Lord."

48. As noted, the first black documentary was commissioned by Booker T. Washington to promote the Tuskegee vision. Black film companies and photographers also recorded "newsworthy" events covering conventions and meetings, like the 1913 Philadelphia meeting of the National Negro Business League, and events in the all-black town of Boley, Oklahoma (Bowser 1999:16).

49. Concerning Foster's work as a whole, activists in the 1960s Black Arts Movement, such as Larry Neal, "argued that the first wave of black independent film makers, such as Foster and other creative artists of the Negro Renaissance, did not address . . . [themselves] to the mythology and the life styles of the Black Community" (Neal's remarks can be found in Reid in Gayle (1972:75).

50. The NAACP led a protest against the film, with Du Bois writing articles and editorials in *The Crisis*, Both the representation of blacks and the effect on whites were prime targets. Du Bois wrote, the "Negro [is] represented either as an ignorant fool, a vicious rapist, a venal or unscrupulous politician or a faithful but doddering idiot." When the film was released in 1915 lynching was rampant (according to Du Bois the "number of mob murders so increased that nearly one hundred Negroes were lynched during 1915," "after seeing *The Birth of a Nation* in Lafayette, Indiana, a white patron would shoot a teenage African American boy to death. In Houston, audiences shrieked 'lynch him!' during a scene in which a white actor in blackface pursued Lillian Gish. In St. Louis, real-estate interests would distribute leaflets in front of the cinema calling for residential segregation ordinances" (Lewis 1993:507)). In this inflamed context, Du Bois and others in the NAACP leadership called for governmental censorship.

51. There were other attempts to "answer" Griffith's film, such as *Birth of a Race*, which began as the project of a white-owned independent film company using an all-black cast and based on Booker T. Washington's *Up From Slavery*. In its promotional brochure to raise production funding, the company described the film as telling "the true story of the Negro, his life in Africa, his transportation to America, his enslavement, his freedom, his achievements, together with his past, present, and future relations to his white neighbor" (quoted in Sampson 1977:59). Production of the film dramatically changed with the outbreak of the First World War and its entire content was changed to deal with anti-Semitism. "In its final version, Birth Of A Race was not about blacks and did not feature a black cast" (1977:59).

52. The still remembered *Uncle Tom's Cabin* appeared on film in 1903, with white actors playing the roles in black face and again in 1916, featuring black actors.

4 The Harlem Renaissance and the heritage of slavery

1. Eatonville was incorporated in 1888 and may well have been the first black run-town in the United States. It remains so to this day (Christian 1995:270). The town was

named after one of the white benefactors who donated the land. The controversy surrounding Hurston's birth place and date may finally be resolved. In her auto-biography, Hurston (1942) claims to have been born in Eatonville in 1901. This date, although not the place, has been contested since then. In a recent biographi-cal essay accompanying a collection of Hurston's writings from the 1930s, Pamela Bordelon (1999:3) presents strong evidence to suggest that Hurston was born in 1891 in "the tiny hamlet of Nostasulga, Alabama, a farming community situated in the shadow of the famous Tuskeegee Institute." Bordelon reveals that Hurston moved to Eatonville with her parents when she was two years old. Her father was a Baptist minister, who later became the town's mayor. Hurston apparently con-structed her biography to suit her needs, especially in relation to white patrons. The circumstances around her death seem to have been controversial (on this see Walker 1983). Langston Hughes (1990) wrote a short story satirizing his relationship with a particular white patron, while Hurston often referred to herself as a "pet darkey," caught up in "The Pet Negro System," as she described it (Bordelon 1999:18).

2. Similar evolutionary views were expressed ten years later in a retrospective anal-ysis of black creativity by Alain Locke, the most influential critic of the period: "Anti-slavery controversy and the hope of freedom brought poetry and fire to the Negro tongue and pen; whereas the setbacks and strained ambitions of Re-construction brought forth . . . leaden rhetoric and alloyed pedantry. Thus the 70s and the 80s were the awkward age in our artistic development. They were the period of prosaic self-justification and painful apprenticeship to formal culture. Yet these years saw the creditable beginnings of Negro historical and sociologi-cal scholarship . . . and saw also an adolescent attack on the more formal arts of the novel, the drama, formal music, painting and sculpture. Before this almost all of our artistic expression had flowed in the narrow channels of the sermon, the oration, the slave narrative and didactic poetry . . . [then, in the 1890s] there was a sudden change of trend as (a) blaze of talent ushered in a new era of racial ex-pression. It was more than a mere accession of new talent; it was the discovery of a new racial attitude . . . the leading motive of the new era (1895–1910) seems to have been radicalism and its new dynamic self-help and self-assertion . . . the formula of special gifts and particular paths had been discovered, and became the dominant rationalization of the period . . . the leading conception of the free-dom was the right to be oneself and different" (Locke quoted in Spencer 1997: 114–15).

3. In describing the Garvey parade of August 2, 1920, White (1999:110–11) writes, "it stretched for miles. First came the mounted African Legionnaires, dressed in spanking dark-blue uniforms with narrow red trouser stripes, its members proudly conscious of the effect their colorful garb and marching precision had on the mar-veling crowds. Although the African Legion was unarmed except for its officers' dress swords, its very existence hinted that the redemption of black people might come through force, and the two hundred Black Cross Nurses that followed them spoke of the readiness of UNIA women to come to their aid should they fall in battle. The Nurses were followed by squads of children singing songs in praise of the African homeland."

4. Rogers, a free-lance journalist who published a weekly column concerning "little known facts about black history," qualifies as an organic intellectual in Gramsci's meaning (Marable 2000:4). In the Preface to the first edition of his anthology, *The Book of American Negro Poetry* (1921), Johnson wrote, "The Negro in the United States has achieved or been placed in a certain artistic niche. When he is thought of artistically, it is as a happy-go-lucky, singing, shuffling, banjo-picking being or as a more or less pathetic figure. The picture of him is in a log cabin amid fields of cotton or along the levees. Negro dialect is naturally and by long association the exact instrument for voicing this phase of Negro life; and by that very exactness it is an instrument with two full stops, humor and pathos. So even when he confines himself to purely racial themes, the Aframerican poet realizes that there are phases of Negro life in the United States which cannot be treated in the dialect either adequately or artistically. Take, for example, the phases rising out of life in Harlem, that most wonderful Negro city in the world. I do not deny that a Negro in a log cabin is more picturesque than a Negro in a Harlem flat, but the Negro in the Harlem flat is here, and he is but part of a group growing everywhere in the country, a group whose ideals are becoming increasingly more vital than those of the traditionally artistic group, even if its members are less picturesque." Johnson was an important actor in the re-evaluation of the spirituals "which many Negroes had rejected as a part of the heritage of slavery" (Frazier 1957:122).
5. Du Bois' references to Africa, at least early on, are close to the progressive narrative I've here exemplified through Hurston. "we are Negroes, members of a vast historical race that from the very dawn of creation has slept, but half-awakening in the dark forests of its African fatherland" (Speech before the American Negro Academy 1897, cited in Essien-Udom 1962:29).
6. Cullen was born in 1903 in Lexington, Kentucky, but attended De Witt Clinton high school and New York University in New York City, where his step-father was a Harlem minister, before receiving an MA from Harvard. Cullen later taught at De Witt Clinton, where he had James Baldwin as a student.
7. This quotation from *Dusk of Dawn* (Du Bois 1940) is cited by Appiah (1985:33) in conjunction with a discussion of the changing grounds upon which Du Bois bases his notion of race. The paragraph opens with a direct response to Cullen's question: "Once I would have answered the question simply: I would have said 'fatherland' or perhaps better 'motherland' because I was born in the century when the walls of race were clear and straight; when the world consisted of mutually exclusive races; and even though the edges might be blurred, there was no question of exact definition and understanding of the meaning of the word . . ."
8. The notion of "heritage" is interesting in itself. Here it is used as part of the search for and discovery of identity, the notion of "the heritage of slavery" or its "legacy" can be and was drawn upon in this period, and also more recently, in a academic/professional discourse bent upon explaining certain contemporary patterns of behavior, e.g., single-parent families and so on. Writing about the aims as well as the "heritage" of the Harlem Renaissance in 1937, Sterling Brown wrote that it was concerned with "(1) a discovery of Africa as a source of racial pride, (2) a

use of Negro heroes and heroic episodes from American history (3) propaganda of protest (4) a treatment of the Negro masses (frequently of the folk, less often of the workers) with more understanding and less apology and (5) franker and deeper self-revelation. Some of this subject matter called for a romantic approach, some for a realistic" (quoted in Frazier 1957:123). In the debate concerning how blacks should be represented which took place in the pages of the *Crisis* in the late 1920s, Cullen's poem came up for criticism. Allison Davis (1902–83), a young psychologist and graduate of Howard University, criticized the poems' "primitivism." In an article entitled "Our Negro 'Intellectuals'" she wrote, "even Mr. Cullen makes especial use of the jungle urge in his early poems, HERITAGE and SHROUD OF COLOR. This whole primitivistic interpretation of the Negro is the white man's facile point of view, and our Negro 'intellectuals' wanted to appear as the white man would have them" (*The Crisis Reader* 1999:329). Along with Cullen, Davis included Langston Hughes, Claude McKay, and Rudolph Fisher amongst these "intellectuals." In the visual arts, Aaron Douglas was also mentioned, as was his white teacher W. Reiss whose illustrations in the *New Negro* were the source of debate.

9. Haywood continues "It came to me then that I had been fighting the wrong war. The Germans weren't the enemy – the enemy was right here at home. These ideas had been developing ever since I landed home in April, and a lot of other Black veterans were having the same thoughts."

10. McKay's anti-lynching poem "If I Must Die" was first published in the *Liberator* in 1919. The poem was at one point publicly quoted by Winston Churchill without acknowledging its author.

11. Walter White (born in 1893) succeeded James Weldon Johnson as secretary of the NAACP the same year (1931). He also wrote a book on lynching.

12. The two sides of this process are not often discussed together. The activists in the Renaissance tended to glorify the cultural possibilities and downplay or even ignore, except as it became a basis for their literature or art, the poverty and the overcrowding that also characterized Harlem in the late 1920s. *Black Metropolis* is also the title of the classic study of Chicago by St. Clair Drake and Horace Cayton from 1945. Spenser (1993:109ff.) discusses this book in relation to the blues.

Garvey's *Negro World* took its name from *The Irish World* and the movement's meeting place was named after Liberty Hall in Dublin (Lewis 2000:61). This clearly reveals the source of the model of emancipation the movement articulated. The *Messenger* went through several dramatic shifts in ideology and aim. It was founded in 1917 by Randolph and Chandler Owen, calling itself "The only radical Negro magazine in America." Randolph ran for local NYC political offices in the 1920s and changed the masthead of the magazine to read "A Journal of Scientific Radicalism" (Sitkoff 1978:173–74). Langston Hughes records the following in his autobiography *The Big Sea*, "The summer of 1926, I lived in a rooming house on 137th Street, where Wallace Thurman and Harcourt Tynes also lived. Thurman was then managing editor of the *Messenger*, a Negro magazine that had a curious career. It began by being very radical, racial, and socialistic, just after the war. . . . then it later became a kind of Negro society magazine and a plugger for Negro business, with photographs of prominent colored ladies and their nice homes in it . . . I asked Thurman what kind of magazine the *Messenger* was, and he said it reflected the policy of whoever paid off best at the time . . . Anyway, the *Messenger* bought my first short stories. They paid me ten dollars a story. Wallace Thurman wrote me that they were very bad stories, but better than the others they could find, so he published them" (Lewis:1994:81).

13. The National League on Urban Conditions was founded in 1911 "by an interracial group ideologically close to Booker T. Washington, it sought to find jobs and housing for black migrants to the city" (Sitkoff 1978:24). It was established in other words in direct response to migration and its basis was in the progressive movement and the social work profession.

14. Johnson was the student of Robert Park, one of the key figures in the Chicago School of sociology. Before coming to both sociology and Chicago, Park had worked for ten years as "chief assistant, ghost writer, and publicity agent" to Booker T. Washington at Tuskegee (Hutchinson 1995:53). Under his direction *Opportunity* focused on cultural issues and "not until 1928, when Elmer Carter succeeded Charles S. Johnson as editor, did *Opportunity* change its focus and begin to highlight the economic and political plight of Afro-Americans" (Sitkoff 1978:24).

15. The *New York Herald Tribune* wrote of the event, "A novel sight that dinner – white critics, whom everybody knows, Negro writers whom nobody knew – meeting on common ground" (cited in Watson 1995:66).

16. *The Journal of Negro History* produced its first issue in January 1916. It was conceived by "The Association for the Study of Negro Life and History," a group formed in Chicago in 1915. The first number contained an article on "The Passing of Tradition and the African Civilization" by Monroe Work which, after discussing African civilization, concluded "Negroes should not despise the rock from which they are hewn. As a race they have a past which is full of interest" (1: 1:41 (34–41)), and "The Mind of the African Negro as Reflected in his Proverbs," by A. O. Stafford. The second issue (April, 1916) contained a series of letters from thankful readers, W. E. B. Du Bois being one and the historian Frederick Jackson Turner another, and positive reviews from newspapers, including *The New York Evening Post*, which wrote "This is a new and stirring note in the advance of the black man . . . he will gradually learn that he, too, has a heritage of something beside shame and wrong" (1:2, April 1916:230).

17. Individual strategies of social mobility were mixed into this as well. Paul Robeson's wife Essie was apparently instrumental in the process of transforming the spiritual into an art song while assisting her husband with his career. As Robeson was in the process of establishing himself as a stage actor in the 1920s, his wife "began to cast about for a way to establish a separate career as a concert artist, so that he could alternate between the two professions . . . The way, she decided, was through the spirituals – those very songs she herself had earlier dismissed as 'monotonous and uninteresting'" (Duberman 1989:78–79).

18. From an article entitled "Paul Robeson, Son of Slave Parents, Reaches Pinnacle," in the *Pittsburgh Courier*, May 17, 1924 and cited by Musser in Stewart (1999:94). The article was reprinted from an interview with a London paper, where Robeson

was on tour. Robeson was born in Princeton, New Jersey in 1898. His father, as a teenager, "had escaped from slavery in Martin County, North Carolina, become an honor graduate from Lincoln University in Pennsylvania, entered the Presbyterian ministry, and married Maria Louisa Bustill, a schoolteacher and member of a noted Philadelphia family of free black abolitionists" (Lyoyd Brown "Happy Black Boy" in Stewart 1999:21).

19. Woodard (1999:26) characterizes Garveyism as composing a "united front" that "embraced both the Moorish Science Temple Movement and the African Blood Brotherhood." The Moorish Science Temple Movement will be returned to later on when the Nation of Islam and its founder Elijah Muhammad are discussed. That both the ABB and the Moorish Science Temple Movement could be considered part of the same "movement" would indeed make it broad based, as the former was socialist and communist inspired and the latter religious-oriented. What allows Woodard to place them in the same sphere is not so much what I've been calling the black public sphere, an ideologically more neutral term, but rather their common "nationalistic" basis. He says, "looking to Islam for inspiration, Noble Drew Ali [leader of the Moorish movement] argued that black people in the United States were a distinct nationality. Similarly, the ABB, founded by Cyril Briggs, insisted that black people in the United States were a nation within a nation and demanded self-determination."

20. Other central figures who were West Indian included Hubert Harrison who had invited Garvey to make this address at Liberty Hall and Cyril V. Briggs mentioned above. Close to Garvey before turning "leftward," Briggs became active in the Communist Party around 1921, at which time Garvey accused him of being a "white man passing as a Negro," whereupon Briggs sued him for libel (Naison 1983:32). Briggs recruited several other fellow West Indians to the CP after the ABB fell apart. Early on, in the 1920s, this group sought to be both nationalist and internationalist; they thus maintained an ambiguous relation to Garveyism, liking the movement, out of which they sought recruits for the CP and disliking the leader and what they perceived as his political conservatism. Out of the first five blacks to join the CP, four were West Indian (1983). According to Woodard (1999:24), "142,868 West Indian immigrants . . . entered the United States between 1899 and 1932; 46 percent of those black immigrants lived in New York State."

21. Randolph, born in Florida, founded the club while a student at New York's City College in 1917.

22. Sitkoff (1978:25) blames this decline on the leadership of James Weldon Johnson, "an artist more suited for the theater and poetry than the arena of politics and agitation."

23. An early editor of this paper was William H. Ferris, a black nationalist influenced by social Darwinism, as was Garvey. Ferris, who graduated from Yale in 1899 and then from Harvard Divinity School in 1900, was editor of the *Negro World* from 1919 to 1923 (Gaines 1996:100ff.). In 1913, Ferris published *The African Abroad, or His Evolution in Western Civilization, Tracing His Development under Caucasian Milieu*. According to Gaines (1996:103), Ferris belonged to a "nationalist

circle of intellectuals that included John E. Bruce, former slave, journalist, and founder in 1913 of the Negro Society for Historical Research, Pauline Hopkins, Anna Julia Cooper, and American Negro Academy members John Wesley Cromwell, Alain Locke, and W.E.B. Du Bois." This would place both Locke and Du Bois together with a future Garveyite, who was one of their prime ideological foils in the 1920s. To Darwinians like Garvey and Ferris, racial uplift was part of a struggle for racial survival, implying that it was more than a test of character or culture. "To Ferris, the race's manhood was on trial against the military, economic, and cultural achievements of European nations . . ." (Gaines 1996:102).

24. Ethiopia and Egypt were the traditional places referred to by black Americans in their attempts to reconstruct their past. As early as 1829, David Walker's *Appeal to the Coloured Citizens of the World* made reference to the ancient civilization of Egypt as the place of origin. For Walker, Egyptians "were Africans or coloured people, such as we are – some of them yellow and some dark – a mixture of Ethiopians and the natives of Egypt" (quoted in Howe 1998:86). The cover of Howe's book reproduces Lois Maolou Jones' painting from 1932, "The Ascent of Ethiopia," which depicts the climb from Africa to modern America in a style similar to Aaron Douglas.

25. Yet, according to White (1999:138) it is the Garvey movement which would later carry forward a feminist tradition within black women's organizations.

26. "Revitalization movements" is a term which developed out of Weber's typification of authority relations, the notion of the charismatic leader and the "routinization of charisma" through the formation of bureaucratic organization. Talcott Parsons pointed the way for social movement theorists like Neil Smelser (1962). Wallace (1956) discusses revitalization as a movement developing through several stages, with a focus on traditional society. Smelser's range is broader, but he is concerned primarily with developing industrial societies. Like Parsons, Wallace sees the normal social condition as one of equilibrium, a "steady-state," where an all-encompassing cultural design orders the lives of members. When this is disrupted, for whatever reason, Wallace speaks of internal and external causes, like colonization or the intrusion of capitalism, Smelser speaks of "strains." A disrupted steady state is followed by "cultural distortion" and "individual stress," what Durkheim called "anomie" and Marx "alienation," which can lead individuals into despair, criminality, alcoholism and even to suicide. In such periods, a revitalization movement led by a charismatic figure can come to the rescue. They offer individual salvation through collective redemption, a new system of values and mores "which inspire, validate and make meaningful a new way of life." Smelser cites recent migrants to cities as a group prone to "value-oriented" movements of which revitalization movements are a subcategory (1984:326), and the "colonially dominated" are another sub-category.

27. According to Harold Cruse (1984), Garveyism was colored by West Indian perspectives and prejudices regarding culture. Garveyism was constructed, according to Cruse, around a deep structure of Euro-centered ideas about the meaning of culture despite a surface ideology which was Afro-centered. Cruse goes on to cite a description of a Garvey meeting in New York in the 1920s: "Garvey held a mass meeting at Carnegie Hall, in downtown New York City. It was packed to overflowing; white

people attended too, as it was well advertised in white newspapers.... Items on the musical part of the programme were: Ethel Clarke, Soprano, singing Eckert's Swiss song, and Cavello's Chanson Mimi; The Black Star Line Band, in smart uniforms, rendering Overtures from 'Rigoletto' and 'Mirello'; New York Local Choir, fully robed, singing The Bridal Chorus from 'The Rose Harmony Four' in Sextette from 'Lucia'; Basso Packer Ramsay sang Handel's 'Hear me ye Winds and Waves.' The second half of the programme was speeches by the Officers and [Garvey]. Subjects were: 'The future of the black and white races, and the building of the Negro nation'" (1984:539).

Cruse goes on to note how it was "likely that all of these singers were West Indians, which accounts for their Anglicized or Europeanized tastes. Not a note of the American Negro musical heritage was sounded on this occasion (and this was typical), not even a spiritual, not to mention jazz or a classical melody by an Africanized composer such as J. Rosamond Johnson or Samuel Coleridge Taylor. This nationalist blindspot on cultural affairs is characteristic, and the general lack of rapport between nationalistic trends and the creative intellectuals is no one-sided affair" (1984:539–40).

28. This tension is recounted by W. A. Domingo's "Gift of the Black Tropics" collected in the *Harlem Renaissance Reader*, which also notes the following: "From 1920 to 1923, the foreign-born Negro population of the United States was increased by nearly 40 per cent through the entry of 30,849 Africans (black)... the foreign born Negro population is about 35,000... the largest number come from the British West Indies" (10). In the Harlem number of *Survey Graphic*, Charles Johnson confirms this, "there were in New York City in 1920, by the census count, 152,467 Negroes. Of these 39,233 are reported as born in New York State, 30,436 in foreign countries, principally the West Indies, and 78,242 in other states, principally the South" (*Survey Graphic* 1925: 641). For Du Bois' views and relations with Garvey, see Lewis (2000: esp. ch. 2).

Domingo was an ally of Garvey's, a former editor of the *Negro World*, who eventually revealed the hint of fraud in the movement. He was also radical socialist, founder of the African Blood Brotherhood (ABB) with Cyril Briggs, who wrote for the *Messenger* as well as the *Crusader*, the ABB's journal. Domingo's article attempts to document the differences between West Indians and native-born blacks and the contributions of the former. He concludes "the outstanding contribution of West Indians to American Negro life is the insistent assertion of their manhood in an environment that demands too much servility and unprotesting acquiescence from men of African blood" (16).

29. Paul Robeson made the story famous when he played the lead role in the filmed version released in 1933. In the early 1920s, Emperor Jones was a theater piece performed by O'Neill's Provincetown players, with Charles Gilpin, one of the foremost black actors, in the lead role. Gilpin offered a different interpretation of Brutus Jones than Robeson, who took over the stage role in 1924 (Musser 1999:81–102). Robeson's size and charisma fit more easily into the brutal and foolhardy stereotype, than Gilpin's "sense of inner struggle and torment," a "complexity that

O'Neill undoubtedly found compelling . . . and why he preferred Gilpin to Robeson" (1999:85). According to Musser, Gilpin refused to comply with O'Neill's frequent use of "nigger" in the play's text, changing the term to "Negro" and "colored man" in his performance whenever possible. This foreshadowed a debate that still continues.

Musser (1999) contrasts not only Gilpin and Robeson, but also the latter's performance in Oscar Micheaux's film *Body and Soul* (1926), as well as how the different genres, film and theater, offer different possibilities of control and performance to actors and directors. According to Musser, the two should be seen as counter-posed, with Micheaux intending an engaged black perspective to the art-for-art's-sake aim of O'Neill. Micheaux's own views regarding art and propaganda were stated in the *Philadelphia Afro-American* in 1925, "I have always tried to make my photoplays present the truth, to lay before the race a cross section of its own life, to view the colored heart from close range . . . it is only by presenting those portions of the race portrayed in my pictures, in the light and background of their true state, that we can raise our people to greater heights" (quoted in hooks 1992:133).

30. O'Neill had himself used and played blackfaced in his own works, for example in the 1916 production of *Thirst* by the Provincetown Players.

31. When *Emperor Jones* was released as a film in the 1930s, Paul Robeson played the leading role. From exile in England, Garvey renewed the debate, calling Robeson "a good actor but a poor representative of the race" (quoted in Martin 1983:11).

32. Paul Robeson took over the lead role in 1924, when the play was revived. In his "Reflections on O'Neill's Plays" which appeared in *Opportunity* in December 1924, Robeson defended both the role and the playwright. "Any number of people have said to me: 'I trust that now you will get a truly heroic and noble role, one portraying the finest type of Negro'. I honestly believe that perhaps never will I portray . . . a more heroically tragic figure than 'Brutus Jones, Emperor', not excepting 'Othello' . . . I have met and talked with Mr. O'Neill. If ever there was a broad, liberal-minded man, he is one. He has had Negro friends and appreciated them for their true worth. He would be the last to cast any slur on the colored people" (in Lewis 1994:59–60).

33. These arguments are elaborated in Hay (1994), where he traces their historical evolution. He writes that by 1936, "Locke had finally accepted the early musicals – stereotypes and all – as the foundation of his Art-Theatre" (1994:21).

34. One article, commissioned by Locke for the magazine version, which displeased him but still appeared in the book, was written by the white anthropologist Melville Herskovits. Locke had asked Herskovits (who later would be a prime candidate, along with Gunner Myrdal who eventually got the job, to carry out a major study of the American Negro for the Carnegie Commission), to contribute an article answering the question "Has the Negro A Unique Social Pattern?" As a major promoter of the Harlem Renaissance and the view that the New Negro was producing a unique culture which blended African and American patterns, Locke was hoping for a positive answer (Jackson 1986:101). What he got was the opposite. Herskovits argued that Harlem was a typical American community and that the New Negro was well on his way to cultural assimilation in a wider American culture. "Not a

trace" of African culture was to be found in Harlem, Herskovits wrote, concluding, "that [Negroes] have absorbed the culture of America is too obvious, almost to be mentioned. They have absorbed it as all great racial and social groups in this country have absorbed it" (quoted in Jackson 1986:102).

35. Hutchinson (1995:391ff.) provides an account of the circumstances surrounding the making of the magazine and Locke's participation in this special Harlem issue.

36. Robeson and Hayes were two of the most influential interpreters of the spiritual for white audiences. In an article written in 1925, Carl Van Vechten complained about the "dangerous tendency toward sophisticated over-elaboration" in the concert use of spirituals. Given the situation, however, he still preferred the "evangelical renderings" of Paul Robeson to the refined representation of Roland Hayes (Locke 1925:207–08). Hayes attended Fisk University and toured with the Fisk Jubilee Singers.

37. According to Hutchinson "many members of the Harlem elite ... objected to Reiss's artwork – and to the fact that a white artist's work was featured at all ... Jesse Fauset [a Renaissance author, R.E.] objected especially to Reiss's portrait of two dark-skinned schoolteachers, one of them depicted naturalistically with 'nappy' hair, just a bit tired after a hard day, but ... with Phi Beta Kappa keys clearly revealed, and a magazine the size of *The Crisis* or *Opportunity* open before them" (Hutchinson 1995:294). Langston Hughes would poke fun at this type of thinking by "a Philadelphia clubwoman" in "The Negro Artist and the Racial Mountain" (1926). "She doesn't care for the Winhold Reiss portraits of Negroes because they are 'too Negro'" (reprinted in Van Deburg 1997b:55). The reception of Reiss's portraits is also discussed in Stewart (1989:50ff.). Locke was quick to respond to these criticisms. In the May 1925 issue of *Opportunity*, "To Certain of Our Philistines," Locke recounted that it was he who had selected the drawings and that the criticism reflected internal black sensitivity to dark-skinned figures, that is to prejudice within the black community (Stewart 1989:50). Powell (1997:43) explains that Locke's choice "made sense given Reiss's cultural distance from the assorted forms of American racism. He had artistic affinities with both pictorial realism and modern industrial design, qualities that Locke and the other creators of the 'New Negro' considered essential for constructing an African American identity in art."

38. Even when it used traditional means – the rhymed and metered verse of poetry, for example, the standard novel form, and the bounded space provided by a canvas – the HR was political by the fact that it was produced by African American artists at a time when the dominant culture denied or ignored their very existence, and also because, as a movement, its activists were intent upon representing forms of black in "political" ways. The Harlem Renaissance was also an innovative, elite avant garde in the European tradition, in that it broke with the norms of the established aesthetic discourse, introducing dialect and blues rhythms, of Langston Hughes' poems, for example, and in so doing infuriated elements in the educated, black bourgeoisie in ways similar to its European counterparts.

Similarly, the artists and writers of the Harlem Renaissance infused the content of their work with themes taken from the everyday life of more marginal African

American groups, thus opening a line of communication with other than the usual middle-class art-appreciating public. Here the form and content of their works were in tension with one another, just as was the case with the European avant garde in the 1920s. The avant garde literary and artistic forms used by the Harlem Renaissance restricted access to their work, just as did the means through which they were distributed or displayed, while at the same time the content made them more accessible to a wider audience. The HR was not an avant garde in the sense meant by P. Berger, since it accepted and did not challenge the culture industry for artistic products. In fact, it may have been an important factor in reviving that industry (Wintz 1988).

39. In their study of Chicago published in 1945, Drake and Cayton point out that the 1920s needs to be seen in phases rather than as a whole, as far as black employment is concerned. They distinguish the lean years of economic downturn, 1922 and 1924, from the "fat years" of 1924–29, which "were no doubt the most prosperous ones the Negro community in Chicago had ever experienced" (78). During those years, "a professional and business class arose upon the base of over seventy-five thousand colored wage-earners."

40. What is understated in Alain Locke's programmatic statement *The New Negro* for the Harlem Renaissance, but which was probably obvious to many contemporary blacks, as it is to black intellectuals and historians today, is the linkage between the project of the New Negro and the strategy of the Old Negro for racial integration (Huggins 1994). It is a matter of controversy as to whether W. E. B. Du Bois is an Old or a New Negro. The same could be said of Locke himself. In the opening lines of the aforementioned introductory essay Locke writes "In the last decade something beyond the watch and guard of statistics has happened in the life of the American Negro and the three norms who have traditionally presided over the Negro problem have a changeling in their laps. The Sociologist, the Philanthropist, the Race-leader are not unaware of the New Negro, but they are at a loss to account for him. He simply cannot be swathed in their formulae. For the younger generation is vibrant with a new psychology; the new spirit is awake in the masses, and under the very eyes of the professional observers is transforming what has been a perennial problem into the progressive phases of contemporary Negro life" (Locke 1925:3). The reference to Du Bois, one of the most radical of the old guard, is obvious, as is Locke's attempt to distinguish himself from others of his own, older generation.

   For the black editors of the socialist magazine *Messenger*, there was no doubt about this in 1919. Du Bois, then 51 years old, was an "old" Negro: "Du Bois's conception of politics is strictly opportunist. Within the last six months he has been Democrat, Socialist, and Republican . . . he opposes unionism instead of opposing a prejudiced union. He must make way for the new radicalism of the New Negroes" (quoted in Cruse 1984:41). The same magazine also disputed whether or not Du Bois deserved the title "sociologist," because, they said (in Cruse's account), "none of his sociological studies were strictly scientific, but more historical and descriptive" (1984).

41. The personal relationship between Locke and Du Bois was ambiguous. According to Hay (1994:32), "Locke belittled Du Bois in *The New Negro*: Although honoring

Du Bois by letting his essay "The Negro Mind Reaches Out" anchor the book, Locke selected other pieces that attacked Du Bois. Du Bois had good cause not to consider Locke "a particularly good friend."

42. Douglas was not alone. According to Stewart (1989:60), "Reiss's influence extended to the entire design aesthetic of the Harlem Renaissance, with adaptations of his style appearing on the covers of the small literary magazines, civic club meetings brochures, and literary contest announcements." This influence is explained by "the shared romantic idea articulated by Alain Locke in *The New Negro*: that the Harlem Renaissance was an aesthetic revival of African forms."

43. In the paintings of the Renaissance one can detect the influence of European movements, like the "new objectivity" in Germany, as well as French post-impressionists, like Cézanne and Gauguin. Especially the glorified "primitivism" of the latter. The wave of interest in tribal art that struck Paris in the early part of the twentieth century and which influenced modernists like Picasso and Modigliani, was an important ideological support for the artistic efforts of the New Negro. It was used as support by writers like McKay and, especially, painters like Aaron Douglas. Many black American artists moved to Paris in the 1920s, including Albert Alexander Smith whose "A Tap Dancer" (1928) was much admired by younger New Negroes. Paris was also the subject of American-based black artists, like Archibald Motley Jr.'s "Jockey Club" (1929). And of course, there was Josephine Baker. The German influence is interesting because of the intrusion of self-irony into the realism that grounded the desire to paint "things as they really appear," not in an ideal state. It was this aspect of Harlem painting and literature that moralists and political activist like Du Bois disliked. For Du Bois, influenced both by his political motives and his Arnoldian notion of culture, the seedy side of everyday life, whether it be card games or dance halls or whore houses, was not an object of true art. Modernists, from Picasso onwards, had followed Baudelaire's advice that the painter of modern life should focus on the whorehouse and the umbrellas of Cherbourg. German realists from Dix to Groz took this to the extreme, when they included warts and all. These notions came to Harlem with the end of the war, with the Germans and the irony included. Thus along with the allegories painted in modernistic fashion by Douglas, whose illustrations graced the pages of the Locke's volume, there were the ironic portraits of daily life by Palmer Hayden.

44. Gwendolyn Bennett was one of the few woman artists associated with the Harlem Renaissance. She produced one cover drawing for *Opportunity* (July 1926), which "featured a young black woman in a pose that had sexual seduction etched all over it...while neither the flapper nor Bennett's seductress looked like most female Americans, black or white, both signaled the advent of new attitudes about female sexuality and individualism" (White 1999:124).

45. Reiss began his career within a German romantic tradition which gloried in the peasantry. His father, who was also a painter and his first teacher, traveled around the southern German countryside painting idyllic landscapes and representations of a "spiritual" peasant life (Stewart 1989). With the First World War threatening, the pacifist Reiss carried this tradition to the United States, hoping to portray the

American Indian, a subject popular with many European artists at the time. Landing in New York, he immediately found a place in the German community there and was influential in the budding Art Deco movement. One of the basic tenets of this movement was the blending of art and design, something which Weiss would eventually pass along to Douglas. It was thus in the United States that Weiss moved more to modernist styling, but still retained his romantic urge to portray ethnic groups in a positive way. In his representations for the New Negro, Weiss blended modernism and romanticism, as well as African and urban American themes. His stylized portrayals of Harlem women, which were the cause of the controversy mentioned earlier, mixed sympathetic realism with Egyptian and tribal hair styles. In addition to this blending of styles and traditions of representation, or perhaps because of it, the distinction and often thin line between type and stereotype can be discussed. The romantic tradition within which Reiss worked sought to portray the peasant as a distinctive type. As this was a typification based on a positive valuation, it represented the peasantry, and in Reiss's case, ethnic groups, as proud and dignified in their more primitive appearance and way of life. To this Weiss added modernistic stylizations, flatness of figure and color contrast, to reveal both type and individuality in his representations. He thus avoided stereotyping. This at one and the same time continued and countered an American "nineteenth century tradition of realist depictions of Blacks, most notably Winslow Homer's historical and genre studies" and "such early twentieth-century modernists as Robert Henri and Stuart Davis (who) had occasionally produced sensitive genre treatments of Blacks." However, "Robert Henri could create dialect jokes and racist cartoons, while Stuart Davis produced stereotyped caricatures for *The Masses*" (Stewart 1989:50). Weiss' romantic realism never ended in stereotyping, because it synthesized the two in a progressive, movement context. Thus while Weiss maintained the romantic belief in fixed racial types, something which he shared with black intellectuals like Du Bois and Locke as well as whites like the now Chicago sociologist Robert Park (Stewart 1989:83), this was modified by a modernism which allowed for and even gloried in individuality.

5   Memory and representation

1. Franklin Roosevelt initiated the Public Works of Art Project in December 1933 and 3,749 artists produced 15,633 works during the first five months of its existence (Sandler n.d.:5). This success led to the Federal Art Project set up in 1935 under the WPA; it lasted until 1943. The FAP did not require as strict proof of qualification and during its first year over 5,500 artists and related cultural workers were employed. "They received an average of $95 monthy, in return for which they were required to work 96 hours or – if in the easel division – to submit periodically pictures painted in any style in their own studios" (Sandler n.d.). While the governement offered no explicit guidelines for artistist production, it did have an "implicit 'style' prototype: the human figure conceptually placed within a 'social' narrative" (Powell 1997:68). This was a style that sought, in other words, to visualize the progressive narrative.

2. In assessing the political effects of the 1930s and the WPA, Powell (1997:72) writes "the socially explosive realities of U.S. race relations in the 1930s ... created a whole school of artists informed by African American culture who, even under the sponsorship of the WPA/FAP, found their own, independent voices." The work of Lawrence and Lewis will be discussed later in the chapter. As children, both attended the Harlem Art Center, a WPA sponsored project. In the 1960s, Lewis was a member of the "Spiral Group, an organization of artists committed to documenting the essence of the Civil Rights movement" (S. Lewis 1990:119). In this period, Lewis painted only in black and white, colors he felt expressed the essence of the time. In the 1940s, Norman Lewis was one of a small group of black painters who produced abstract works, others were Ronald Joseph and Romare Bearden. All three were outspoken modernists and reacted strongly against the "primitivism" that was part of the call to return to an African heritage (Gibson 1997:65ff.). For them, abstraction offered the chance to produce art with a universal appeal and a way out of the ghetto of the "black" artist. According to Gibson (1997:67), Lewis had the idea that his work must both be socially relevant and that it "must have something African about it." As part of his Guggenheim application of 1946, he wrote, "For about eight years I have been concerned not only with my own creative and technical development but with the limitations which every American Negro who is desirous of a broad kind of development must face – namely the limitations which come under the names, 'African Idiom,' 'Negro Idiom,' or 'Social Painting.'" While in the 1930s Romare Bearden attempted to paint just those social realities that social realism called upon the black artist to represent, by the early 1940s he rejected this view and sought more abstract forms. In 1946 he published a refutation of Alain Locke's ideas about the role of Negro art, in which he wrote "It would be highly artificial for the Negro artist to attempt a resurrection of African culture in America. The period between generations is too great, and whatever creations the Negro has fashioned in this country have been in relation to his American environment" (cited in Gibson 1997:69). In rejecting realism and the racial motifs of "Africanism," Joseph, Lewis, and Bearden, and others, like Hale Woodruff, did not reject politics. They argued rather that realism was ineffective and that the "abstraction was a vehicle of integration – or at least that it held the potential to diffuse the burden of difference that white culture imposed on African Americans" (Gibson 1997:71). In this they represented the progressive narrative and the dream of integration.

3. On this, Powell (1997:74) writes "the community spirit in this piece ... clearly resonated with Claude McKay's expressed notion of an African American 'group-soul' and prophetically looked ahead to the flowering of black culture in the early 1940s."

4. The "man" is consciously chosen. Barbara Melosh (1991) demonstrates this male-orientation in her study of New Deal public culture. The "response" of the FAP, at least on the part of its government sponsors, was run through with political considerations. Sitkoff (1978) reveals how this concern with black history had much to do with the role of the black vote in Roosevelt's reelection. Once that was secured, interest cooled and Southern politicians regained some of their power over New Deal

programs. In 1939, control over the FWP shifted from the federal government to the states, something which greatly affected the form and content of its projects, especially in the South. This directly affected Zora Neale Hurston, working in Florida. The infamous House Committee on Un-American Activities emerged in 1938 as part of a Southern backlash against the New Deal and its chairman, Representative Martin Dies of Texas, went directly to work attacking the WPA arts projects (Bordelon 1999:36).

5. Born in Washington, DC, Brown taught English at Howard University from 1929 and was a folklorist and historian as well as poet. Some of his poems appeared in a collection compiled by Countee Cullen in 1927. Brown began publishing collections of folklore, music, and poetry in the 1930s, *Southern Road* (1932) being the first. The issue of whether or not Brown should be included in the Harlem Renaissance is discussed in Tracy (1998:28ff.). The relation of Brown and Hurston to the WPA, and to each other, is discussed in Bordelon (1999). Bordelon reveals the political expediency and the institutionalized racism in the WPA, as well as the stigmatization involved in accepting its support. It was, after all, a welfare program. Sterling Brown worked in the Washington, DC office, where he was "Negro Affairs Editor" and assistant to Henry Alsberg, the national director of the Federal Writers' Project. Hurston worked for the Florida office, which meant a world of difference. Although the most accomplished and best-known writer, as a black woman she was placed at the bottom of the office hierarchy, a place she rarely visited as blacks were not permitted to work in the same office as their white colleagues. Her relationship with her white, female supervisor resembled the one she had developed with her earlier New York patrons (see above).

6. The essential argument had been formulated and presented in essay form already in 1909. Also, Du Bois was not alone in the attempt to revise the representation of American history from a black perspective. The *Journal of Negro History* had begun this process in the 1920s (see also White 1999:118).

7. The book concludes with a chapter entitled "The Propaganda of History." Du Bois here analyzes how Reconstruction is presented in school texts. He asks "What was slavery in the United States? Just what did it mean to the owner and the owned? Shall we accept the conventional story of the slave plantation and its owner's fine, aristocratic life of cultured leisure? Or shall we note the slave biographies . . .?" (715). In discussing the use and validity of sources he writes: "Nearly all recent books on Reconstruction agree with each other in discarding the government reports and substituting selected diaries, letters, and gossip" (723). The writing of history is clearly linked to partisanship, especially "in a field devastated by passion and belief" (725). "Negroes have done some excellent work on their own history and defense. It suffers of course from natural partisanship and a desire to prove a case in the face of a chorus of unfair attacks . . ." (724). After recalling the "older" historians, George W. Williams and Joseph T. Wilson and "the new school of historians led by Carter G. Woodson" and his students, he comes to his own position. "Naturally, as a Negro, I cannot do this writing without believing in the essential humanity of Negroes . . . I cannot for a moment subscribe to that bizarre doctrine of race that

makes most men inferior to the few. But, too, as a student of science, I want to be fair, objective and judicial; to let no searing of the memory by intolerable insult and cruelty make me fail to sympathize with human frailties and contradiction, in the eternal paradox of good and evil" (725).

8. According to Sitkoff (1978:49), the WPA often worked as a patronage system for local politicians, a system from which blacks were excluded: "Of the more than ten thousand WPA supervisors operating in the South, eleven were Negro." This certainly fits the description of the conditions under which Zora Neal Hurston worked in Florida.

9. The American Federation of Labor (AFL) had "reaffirmed its refusal to admit blacks in 1927" and continued to make good on that promise (Sitkoff 1978:24).

10. Sitkoff thinks this protest "overestimated the damage done by the AAA" (1978:53). He writes: "according to the 1940 census figures, the number of Negro farmers declined in the 1930s by 67,000 or 4.5 percent, considerably less than the 15 percent drop between 1910 and 1920 or the 8.6 percent decline in the 1920" (1978:53). While it may be true that "no clear correlation existed between AAA policies and the black exodus from the cotton counties," Southern blacks saw no reason to believe that federal programs of any sort were designed to help them. Especially when "not a single Negro served on an AAA county committee . . . Yet every Negro farm operator had to abide by their decisions" (1978:53).

11. The Federal Housing Administration (FHA) and the National Housing Act (NHA) of 1934 were openly discriminatory. The FHA's *Underwriting Manual* warned "that property values deteriorate when Negroes move into predominately white neighborhoods" (Sitkoff 1978:50). At the same time the agency refused to approve loans to blacks seeking to move into such neighborhoods. Discrimination was also visible in the rates of public assistance, especially in the South. "Atlanta distributed average monthly relief checks of $32.66 to whites and $19.29 to blacks. Some Southern politicians defended the discrepancy with the argument that Afro-Americans had always had less than whites, that they required less to live" (1978:49).

12. This was something which would have unforeseen effects. "Combined with the slum clearance, urban renewal, public housing, and highway construction programs of the 1950s and 1960s, these government initiatives encouraged and subsidized white flight to the suburbs, helped strip older towns of their middle classes, and practically ensured that blacks would remain locked in economically weakened central cities" (Arnold Hirsch, cited in Woodard 1999:31). See also Lehmann (1991).

13. The Ladies Auxiliary of the Brotherhood of Sleeping Car Porters, formed as a national organization in 1938, was one of the most influencial woman's organizations of the 1930s through the 1950s (White 1999:160ff.). Although originally organized as locally based support groups for working men, it attained great autonomy, especially as a national organization. According to White (1999:161): "the Brotherhood and its Auxiliary set a stellar example for black people. Slavery had fixed the race in a servile role, and the kinds of jobs black people were forced into after slavery only reinforced that role in the minds of white Americans. No matter that racism had made porter work the only option available to some of the best educated and

most capable black men; servility was part of the porter's job definition ... In winning these victories the Brotherhood and its Auxilliary demonstrated that perseverance and organization were the keys to the race's economic security" (White 1999: 163–64).

14. Randolph and his union struggled against entrenched resistence. In 1929 blacks made up only 2 per cent of all union members, of which at least half belonged to the Sleeping Car Porters. According to Sitkoff, that union was itself nearly extinct in 1929 and "ignored by the federal government, the Pullman Company, and the AFL alike" (Sitkoff 1978:25). The union gained new life after the passage of the Wagner Act, the NIRA, and the 1933 Emergency Railroad Transportation Act, all of which guaranteed collective bargaining rights. Even the AFL was forced to change its discriminatory polices, largely due to Randolph's activism and the emergence of the rival CIO (1978:175ff.).

In late March 1931, nine black young men, aged 13 to 21, were charged with gang-raping two white girls in a freight train box car traveling near Scottsboro, Alabama. The case was immediately taken up in the black and left-wing press and the case quickly became a symbol of Southern racism. The NAACP and the American Communist Party competed with each other to represent the case, both in the legal and the wider cultural meaning of the term. The case dragged on over two years and ended in freeing of the defendants, one of whom had during the course of those years been sentenced to death. Protest marches were arranged in Harlem and other Northern cities and culminated in a march on Washington in May, 1933. Support also included many of the artists, writers, and musicians previously associated with the Harlem Renaissance, such as Langston Hughes, who wrote a poem entitled "Scottsboro," and Duke Ellington, who performed at benefits; a film was also made.

15. The popular front was also a "cultural front" (Denning 1997). Many white activists were engaged in organizing the unemployed: "Since ... young artists and writers were themselves often unemployed, they were active in the unemployed councils and relief demonstrations: in New York, an Unemployed Artists' Group and an Unemployed Writers' Group emerged ..." (Denning 1997:66).

16. "Bolshevization" was the name given to a program designed to model the American Communist Party after the centralized Soviet party. It "stripped the foreign-language federations of their power and required their members to join street units where they lived, or shop units where they worked. An Americanization program accompanied this reorganization: Party members had to learn the English language and work cooperatively with other nationalities" (Naison 1983:12). For communists in Harlem these changes meant much improved conditions under which to organize in their local communities. Also, however, it meant more centralized control and closer ties to the Soviet leadership, which while it helped black organizing, had dire consequences for the future of the party.

17. Figures gathered from the US Census reveal another side, "the death rate per thousand Negroes dropped from 25 in 1900 to 16.3 in 1930. Between 1915 and 1930 the infant mortality rate per 1000 live Negro births was almost halved – 181.2 to 99.9.

Black expectation of life span at birth increased from 33 in 1900 to 48 in 1930. Similarly, Afro-American illiteracy decreased from some 45 percent of the adult population in 1900 to 16.4 percent in 1930. By then New York blacks had a lower illiteracy rate than whites in Alabama, Georgia, Louisiana, Mississippi, South Carolina, Virginia, or Kentucky. Over 98 percent of Afro-Americans aged seven to thirteen in New York, Ohio, and Illinois attended school in the twenties, compared to less than 65 percent of their counterparts in Louisiana, Georgia, and Alabama. Overall, the percentage of Negro youth enrolled in school doubled in the years from 1900 to 1930; the number of public high schools for blacks increased from 91 in 1915 to nearly 1000 in 1930; and total Negro college enrollment rose from less than 2000 in 1915 to about 14,000 at the start of the Great Depression" (Sitkoff 1978:31).

18. As reported by Harlem Renaissance veteran Claude McKay (1940), a colorful black nationalist calling himself Sufi Abdul Hamid was a key figure in Harlem protests. McKay, along with Langston Hughes, had by this time become affiliated to the Communist Party.

19. The Abyssinian Baptist Church was "founded in 1808 by a handful of merchants from Ethiopia . . . who had attempted to worship in a local white Baptist church and were insulted by being herded to the back upstairs. They immediately left and formed their own church" (Hamilton 1991:73).

20. In 1942, Powell, along with a Harlem businessman, began a weekly newspaper called *The People's Voice*, to which he contributed an editorial column in addition to being editor-in-chief. The paper characterized itself as "100 percent owned and operated by Negroes" and as a "working class paper," since "we are a working class race" (Hamilton 1991:119).

21. Harry Haywood, born in Omaha, Nebraska in 1898 to former slaves, moved along a similar geographical path as Aaron Douglas and Langston Hughes, first to the northern mid-west then to Harlem. After serving in France in the First World War, something which in addition to his working-class background distinguished him from the Renaissance intellectuals, he became active in the American Communist Party as one of its central organizers. Haywood worked first in Harlem and then in 1934 just as the new wave of strikes and union organizing swept industrial America, he moved to Chicago to lead Communist Party organizing activities in the city's black ghetto (Haywood 1978).

22. As a field secretary for the NAACP in the 1930s, Ella Baker negotiated between blacks and the labor movement. From her experience, the CIO was generally more favorable to black workers, however, "in some situations an AFL local, even one that was all-black, was a step forward" (Grant 1998:71).

23. NAACP president, Walter White, told Lewis in 1935: "Negro workers feel confident that the new movement will be guided by the same policy of freedom from racial discrimination which has characterized the United Mine Workers under your leadership" (quoted in Sitkoff 1978:181).

24. Schuyler had been on the periphery of the Harlem Renaissance and wrote an early satirical piece on it called "The Negro Art Hockum," to which Langston Hughes had responded with "The Negro Artist and Racial Mountain," one of the best-known

position papers of the movement. Both were published in *The Nation* in 1926. Schuyler would become more conservative with age.

25. The Ladies Auxiliary of the Brotherhood of Sleeping Car Porters was another organization interested in consumer cooperatives, tracing the roots of this idea to Booker T. Washington (see White 1999:164–65).

26. Ella Baker was born in Norfolk, Virginia in 1903. In the words of her biographer: "Ella Baker's family came out of slavery, and that fact lived with her. She grew up with grandparents and other family members who had been slaves" (Grant 1998:3). She moved to Harlem in 1927, migrating after having graduated from Shaw University, the Baptist College founded in 1875 in Raleigh, North Carolina. Baker attended Brookwood Labor College on a scholarship from the Cooperative League of America and worked for the WPA in the 1930s. Bob Moses, a central activist in the civil rights movement and Baker protégé, worked for a Harlem consumer cooperative in the 1940s.

27. As Frazier explains in his Preface, this study was carried out in 1927 while he worked as a research assistant at the University of Chicago. Robert Park and Ernest Burgess were the responsible parties, as was the Chicago Urban League. In the editor's Preface, Burgess explained its aim and uniqueness: "This study . . . for the first time in anything like an adequate fashion presents a description and an analysis of the Negro family in the process of social change. Nowhere in the history of the world is there so striking an example of the transplanting of a group of people from their native habitat to an alien environment with so complete a loss of their own culture" (Frazier 1932:x). Frazier was then professor of sociology at Fisk University, before moving to Howard. He aimed in the study to explain the "continued low standards of sex morals among the masses of Negroes in spite of the general progress of the race in the accumulation of wealth and in overcoming illiteracy." Progress in other words in some areas but not in others. After dismissing theories that would explain this by reference to African cultural patterns and as the result of the complete absence of family form during slavery, Frazier concluded that migration to the city had destroyed the fragile family forms evolved in the South after emancipation. It was this that led to "demoralization" and disorganization of the Negro. However, all this should be interpreted as part of a necessary "civilizational" process, that is, a temporary set-back in a larger modernization process, as well as the "development of a race consciousness" (1932:244). "As the Negro is brought into contact with a complex world through increasing communication and mobility, disorganization is a natural result. The extent of the disorganization will depend upon the fund of social tradition which will become the basis for the reorganization of life on a more intelligent and efficient basis . . . This seems to be the inevitable price which the Negro must pay for civilization" (1932:252). This is the same social evolutionary theory which Hurston gave voice to, here presented in the professional language of the sociologist. Other sociological studies of the migration included that by Guy B. Johnson (1924:404–08).

28. Myrdal's study was not only path-breaking in its magnitude, but also provided the basis for policy debates between black leaders and the American government. It

was central to the decision by the Supreme Court to integrate the southern school system.

29. Boas was the leading figure here. He sat on research councils which funded the research of Herskovits and others like Margaret Mead. His organized the Institute of Race Relations at Columbia University in 1933 and "with the assistance of Ruth Benedict . . . turned the Department of Anthropology at Columbia University and Popular Front organizations like the American Committee for Democracy and Intellectual Freedom toward a preoccupation with racial issues" (Sitkoff 1978:196). The role of the anthropological profession in the changing conception of race is traced in Baker (1999).

30. W. E. B. Du Bois had been a strong candidate to carry out the study, but internal antagonism led to the search for an outsider, a "Tocqueville" (Jackson 1990:25). The Carnegie Corporation had previously contributed to the completion of W. E. B. Du Bois' *Black Reconstruction in America*.

31. Frazier worked early in his career at Atlanta University's sociology department which Du Bois had founded. He was influenced greatly by Du Bois' sociological studies but distanced himself from his role as partisan intellectual. Frazier, like other educated blacks of this generation, preferred the role of professional sociologist. He wrote "I have studiously avoided what has appeared to me to be a pitfall which lies in the path of most educated Negroes, namely: being forced into the role of Negro leader" (quoted in Jackson 1990:391). Ironically, Du Bois had faced the same dilemma nearly three decades earlier and moved in the opposite direction.

32. The development of new statistical techniques was important to this rise of professionalism in the social sciences. It was in this period that the case study, once the core of social science, was being replaced by the social survey. The study and measurement of racial "attitudes," which began in the late 1920s, was one outcome, as was the notion of racial stereotyping. Robert Park was a major force in this development.

33. *Black Bourgeoisie* first appeared in a 1955 French edition, two years before it was published in the United States. Frazier worked in Paris between 1951 and 1953 as a researcher for UNESCO, writing his book in cafés in the style of a Parisian intellectual (Stovall 1996:214). This may explain its more partisan and polemical tone, something which separates it from his earlier more "professional" writings. In her study of black women's organizations, Deborah White (1999:188ff.) discusses what she calls Frazier's "vicious attacks" on these organizations: "Describing them as frustrated people who led ineffectual lives, Frazier dismissed their service as minimal." She goes on to explain the popularity of the book as partly due to its resonance with an emerging generation of young blacks who were tired of the ways of their elders, especially those in leadership positions. The young people "repudiated traditional styles of black leadership and middle class consumption. All signified a rejection of the time-honored methods of people who thought of themselves as the talented tenth . . ." (White 1999:189).

34. Charles Johnson's (1941) field studies in the 1930s and 1940s of rural black life in the South revealed the importance of records and musical instruments.

35. As Deveaux (1997:27) points out, for black musicians, a new professional group that was optimistic even in the 1930s Depression, swing was extremely popular and black talent played a leading role, "Advances were dramatic and tangible: for the next several years the entertainment industry expanded rapidly, providing steady and lucrative employment for a small but influential elite of black musicians . . . as a class of skilled professionals who had proved their worth in open competition with their white counterparts, musicians were uniquely positioned to further their cause of black social and economic progress" (1997:27).

36. Margolick (2000) offers a history of the origins and reception of "Strange Fruit." He recounts first-hand accounts of black and whites who either loved or hated the song's performance, but all who heard were moved in one way or the other.

37. In the late 1920s the *Courier*'s circulation was over 50,000 and the *Defender*'s over 100,000, which was down from its peak of 280,000 in 1920. The two papers competed with one another, and, among other things, they took opposing sides in the Amos and Andy controversy, with Robert Abbott's *Defender* being supportive and Robert Vann's *Courier* against (Barlow, 1999:41).

38. Bill "Bojangles" Robinson was one of the first black stars of popular film, as well as an accomplished dancer and stage performer. His first Hollywood films were musicals with all-black casts, including "Harlem is Heaven" (1933). Such films were aimed at black audiences in segregated movie houses. But the success of these films, like the Broadway musicals which preceded them, led to wider distribution and to integrated film performances. Robinson made a series of films with the white child star Shirley Temple, including *Littlest Rebel* (1935) and *Little Colonel*, both civil war films which repeated steroryped roles, but which extended them by presenting a warm picture of the relationship between Robinson and Temple. For the most part, Robinson played the acceptable and expected roles in the many Hollywood films in which he appeared, the loyal slave, the butler, and the janitor.

39. The black press was rapidly expanding as the Northern migration continued. As reported by E. Franklin Frazier (1957:244), "*Pittsburgh Courier* (all editions) 277,900; *Afro-American* (all editions) 235,600; *Chicago Defender* (both editions) 193,000; *Amsterdam News* (weekly total) 105,300. In 1947, the first three newspapers and the *Journal and Guide*, which are nationally circulating weeklies, had a total circulation of 750,000."

40. In the South, where radios were scarcer, especially amongst blacks, and audiences more spread out, it was urban white tastes that dominated the air waves. In the 1940s these tastes did not differ greatly from more rural populations and religious-based music, including forms of country music, were most common. Those black families who owned radios listened to the same music as whites. One of the most popular programs was the Grand Ol' Opry, which had broadcast from Nashville since the 1930s. Here the opposite of what I have been describing occurred, blacks listened to "white" music. Even though it is rare to find a professional black country singer, the boundaries between "white" country and "black" blues, for example, are easier to locate in record stores than they are in reality. There was more music intermarriage than most Southerners would have liked to admit. When a more integrated popular

music emerged in the mid-1950s and the number and popularity of cross-over singers and groups reached into the South, this created a situation similar to that in the urban North. There was one additional complication, however, which had to do with live performance. After being restricted to the occasional enthusiast or collector, one of the first public audiences for black music among Southern whites was college fraternities, which as private clubs were permitted a degree of autonomy from the reigning norms and customs. As the popularity of this music spread, performances by blacks, and black and white acts before segregated audiences created controversy amongst the performers as well as the local authorities. Some black performers refused to perform if the audience was segregated, and this not only made a public issue out of long-standing taken-for-granted customs, it sometimes actually changed them. The role of music, both in recorded form and as live performance, has long been underestimated in social change of this sort.

41. In some sense one might speak not of "pathology" (as Frazier did) but of alienation (as Du Bois might have) and of a difficulty or an unwillingness to give up "the South" in the urban environment. Farah Griffin (1995:70ff.) points to the potential difficulties faced by the newly arrived migrant in the foreign environment of a Northern city. It was definitely not "home" and questions concerning "what am I doing here" and "what does one do here," rather than "who am I" find expression in Wright's novels and in the urban blues lyrics sung by migrants. In her analysis of a section of Jean Toomer's "Seventh Street," a fictional account of Southern migrants living in Washington, DC, Griffin (1995:66) uncovers four alternative strategies of accommodation: total transformation into "materialistic automatons," becoming a class-conscious social climber, steadfastly retaining "Southern" sensibilities or, finally, seeking to balance "Southern spirituality and Northern ingenuity."

42. In addition to New York where the larger music companies had their recording studios, Los Angeles was becoming one of the centers of "country music" in the 1930s. While the great influx of migrants to southern California really took off as preparations for war began to gain momentum, the industrial development of the LA basin was a magnet for whites and blacks from the South and Southwest. Groups like the Sons of the Pioneers and Stuart Hamblen and His Covered Wagon Jubilee recorded classic cowboy songs there on the British owned Decca Records, which opened its American branch in 1934. White country blues, much of it recorded between the late 1920s and late 1930s, contains some of the same themes as black blues: leaving home, loneliness, the problems of city life, and so on. A major difference however concerns what could be called nostalgia for the place left behind. Although the so-called country music in this period was largely a production of the commercial "culture industry," as Richard Peterson (1997) reveals, the themes which drew its audience were based in real feelings. The Beverly Hill Billies, a creation of a Los Angeles radio station manager, broadcast nightly performances over KMPC in LA between 1930 and 1932, were native Californians, but apparently protrayed as producing "authentic" music from the Arkansas Ozarks (Peterson 1997:79). The "cowboys" and "hillbillys" were made up to fit the images of the production staff, but many of those who purchased the recordings and listened to their radio performances

were white migrants who continued to identify with their rural past. The music reflected these needs and desires as well. Radio played a major role in representing these desires, as the Grand Ol'Opry' broadcast out of Nashville, was complimented by the "National Barn Dance" broadcast from Chicago over the NBC network chain. However, as with the blues there was more than just the cynical production of culture involved here. As Klein (1980:78) recounts regarding Woody Guthrie, "The whiny old ballads his mother had taught him were a bond that all country people shared; and now, for the migrants, the songs were all that was left of the land. Singing for these people was a totally different experience from playing a barn dance . . . It wasn't just entertainment; he was performing their past."

43. This also relates to the question of how to view the "folk culture" associated with the South. Many educated and middle-class blacks viewed with disdain what they considered remnants of the slave past in music, religion, food habits, etc., that they associated with Southern migrants. What the avant garde of the Harlem Renaissance and white political radicals viewed as positive, they saw as something to shed and be ashamed of. From this perspective, "progress" would involve forgetting the South and with it the "culture" it had produced, glorifying instead "the people" who survived it. This conflict also entered into the churches, as the "citadels of progressive American black Protestantism" sought new membership through offering housing and other forms of assistance to recently arrived migrants. While the latter at first "seemed ready to lay aside the hand-clapping, foot-tapping, and shouting that had characterized their worship for the security and status of an old-line church affiliation," it would not be long before "the growing presence of migrants slowly eroded the norms of mainline assimilationist worship" (Harris 1992:xvii).

44. Wright, who left the Communist Party in 1942, wrote in the *Daily Worker* in 1938, "I owe my literary development to the Communist Party and its influence, which has shaped my thoughts and creative growth. It gave me my first full bodied vision of Negro life in America" (quoted in Naison 1983:210–11). Yet, Harry Haywood (1978), key black organizer for the party in Chicago and New York, makes no mention of Wright in his autobiography.

45. In 1938 Langston Hughes and Louise Thompson ran a repertory theater company called the "Harlem Suitcase Theatre" for the International Workers Order, part of the American Communist Party's program for black arts. The company had planned to adapt Wright's "Bright and Morning Star," a short story which appeared in the *New Masses* in May, 1938 and was later collected with others in *Uncle Tom's Children*, for the stage, but the Hitler–Stalin Pact put an end to that (Naison 1983:209).

46. This is not to say that Locke had become a Marxist in his approach to literature, but he had clearly moved a little to the political left. Others associated with the Harlem Renaissance were more explicit in their politicization.

47. This "political" aspect moved James Baldwin to label Wright's work "protest" literature and place it together with Stowe's *Uncle Tom's Cabin*. To the young Baldwin, such literature built around "cardboard" characters who merely acted out political ideologies, which left no room for real human emotion and complex character or story development. Despite this criticism, Baldwin learned much from

Richard Wright. He along with Wright and Chester Himes (1909–84) made up the central trio of the black American writers-in-exile in Paris in the early 1950s. According to one account, the "three achieved a level of success and recognition in the French capital unmatched by any other African American writers, and by few Americans generally, before or since" (Stovall 1996:206). Both Baldwin and Himes will be discussed in more detail later on.

48. The American public, at least in the North and West, showed a great interest in reading about and looking at itself. In the eyes of many, the 1930s was the documentary era. During the Depression, government sponsored collective representation reached a peak. Claude McKay's *Harlem: Negro Metropolis* (1940), and Wright's book (1941) were the two major documentaries to deal with blacks.

49. For a thorough account of the social, cultural, and historical background of the *Grapes of Wrath* see Denning (1997), especially chapter 7 on "The Art and Science of Migration."' Denning also places Wright's work in the larger context of the "cultural front" and the migration genre. He writes, "many of the most powerful works of art of the cultural front are migration stories: the portrayals of the Alabama terror become the first act in the grand narratives of African American migration in Jacob Lawrence's *Migration of the Negro*, Langston Hughes's *One Way Ticket*, Duke Ellington's *Black, Brown and Beige*, the Chicago novels of Richard Wright, the Chicago blues of Muddy Waters, and Ralph Ellison's *Invisible Man* . . ." (Denning 1997:264).

50. Rooskam offered this explanation about the photgraphs: "The photographs in this book – with the exception of a few otherwise credited – were selected from the files of the Farm Security Administration, U.S. Department of Agriculture. They form part of a document on contemporary America which at this writing has reached a total of some 65,000 pictures. None of the photographs here reproduced was made for this book; they were taken by Farm Security photographers as they roamed the country during a five-year period on their regular assignments" (Rooskam in Wright [1941] 1998:149). Rooskam himself was one of those who "roamed the country" on such an assignment, as well as Dorothea Lange, Walker Evans, Arthur Rothstein, Russell Lee, Jack Delano, and other well-known photographers. Rooskam also thanks "Mr. Horace R. Cayton, director of the Good Shepard Community Center, Chicago, Illinois, for his invaluable advice on the pictorial interpretation of the urban Negro" (149). Cayton would later co-author the classic study of black migration to Chicago cited earlier, to which Wright contributed a preface.

51. Like Hurston and Sterling Brown, the author of *Blues as Folk Poetry*, Wright draws on the folk traditions of the South.

52. The "Migration Series" as it has come to be called was painted in its entirety by Lawrence in Harlem on a foundation grant. Lawrence received the grant after being highly recommended by Alain Locke and other well-known intellectuals. Along with Locke, who saw Lawrence's work as fulfilling his own vision of a Negro, Lawrence received much needed help in mediating the white art world from Edith Halpert, a Russian *émigré* artist and art dealer. Halpert was shown photographs of Lawrence's work by Locke after she had written to him concerning her desire to

exhibit Negro art that would "demonstrate to the public the valuable contribution made by American Negro artists" (Tepfer 1993:130). It was Halpert's gallery on 51st in New York that first exhibited the Migration Series. It was then shown at the Phillips Memorial Gallery in 1942 and at New York's Museum of Modern Art. The Phillips Gallery and MoMA each purchased half of the series. Between 1942 and 1944 the *Series* circulated to smaller museums around the US.

53. Lawrence, who died in 2000, was born in Atlantic City, New Jersey. At seven he was placed in a foster home after his father abandoned the family. He was eventually reunited with his mother, then living in Philadelphia. In 1930, they moved to Harlem. It was Charles Alston who led Lawrence to painting, during classes at the Harlem Community Art Center. Here he met Aaron Douglas, Langston Hughes, Alain Locke, and Ralph Ellison. After producing a series of paintings of Harlem street life in 1936, Lawrence turned to slavery, painting a series based on the life of Toussaint L'Ouverture, leader of the Haitian slave revolt and independence movement. In 1937, he made a series of paintings depicting the life of Frederick Douglass and a year later over thirty paintings on the life of Harriet Tubman (Cash 2000:166).

54. According to Rodger Birt (in Willis-Braithwaite and Birt 1998), "VanDerZee photographed the activities of the UNIA in the spring and summer of 1924, particularly the fourth International Convention . . . an assignment which produced several thousand prints and even a 1925 calendar" (1998:47). This was part of Garvey's media strategy in his struggle against other black intellectuals to define black collective identity. "Garvey wanted to blanket the black media with images of a vibrant and active UNIA under his own careful stewardship" (1998:48).

55. Kate VanDerZee's family lived near the Hampton Institute and the Whittier Preparatory Academy which served it. James VanDerZee offered music instruction at Whittier at the same time as he took photographs of the school classes. In addition to blacks, Hampton also admitted Native Americans, who comprised approximately 10 percent of the student population (Roger Birt 1998:34). VanDerZee also photographed life in Slabtown, a local black neighborhood which began as temporary living quarters for runaway slaves. The buildings offered material for the remembrance of slavery. The novel *1959* by Thulani Davis (1992) is set in Hampton, called Turner in the book, and concerns the developing political consciousness of the local black community, many of whom have lived there since slavery. The novel is filled with references to slavery, its memory, and its representation and will be discussed in chapter 6.

56. The extent of Elijah Muhammad's relationship to Garveyism and the UNIA is contested. Tony Martin (1986) calls him an active member. Muhammad himself denies being a member, but acknowledged both the UNIA and its rival Moorish Science Temple as forerunners (Essien-Udom 1962:63).

57. Archibald MacLeish, liberal writer and poet, was appointed as head of the government Office of Facts and Figures (OFF), an agency commissioned by President Roosevelt in 1941 to help inform the public about the war and the government about the public. MacLeish was convinced American blacks supported the war because, like Vice President Henry Wallace he was convinced they saw it as a "fight between

the slave world and the world" and that they who had been slaves would clearly make the connection (Savage 1999:109). Others had their doubts and in 1942, MacLeish ordered a survey which would track "The Negro Looks at the War." "The survey results showed that African American support for the war was tempered by the reality of discrimination in defense industries at home and the denial of equal opportunity to blacks in the military" (Savage 1999:113). "The survey also addressed ongoing concerns about African Americans' perceptions of the German and Japanese governments. Asked whether they thought they would be treated better or worse under Japanese rule, nearly a third of black respondents said 'about the same', another third 'worse', and nearly 20 percent answered 'better'. Regarding German rule the figures were a little better from the government's point of view, however, there was still '20 percent of blacks thought their life would be about the same' " (1999:114). It was this 20 percent that worried the American government.

58. A nationally broadcast radio program arranged with the help of NAACP leader Walter White followed in response. The opening statement by the CBS announcer: "Dear Fellow Americans: What you are about to hear may anger you. What you are about to hear may sound incredible to you. You may doubt that such things can happen today in this supposedly united nation. But we assure you, everything you are about to hear is true. And so we ask you to spend thirty minutes with us, facing quietly and without passion or prejudice, a danger that threatens all of us. A danger so great that if it is not met and conquered now, even though we win this war, we shall be defeated in victory; and the peace which follows will be for us a horror of chaos, lawlessness, and bloodshed. This danger is race hatred" (quoted in Barlow 1999:71).

59. Mary McLeod Bethume (1875–1955) served as director of the Division of Negro Affairs at the National Youth Administration, acting as advisor to Roosevelt. A former president of the National Association of Colored Women, Bethume was a founding member of the National Council of Negro Women established in 1935. According to White (1999:146), this new organization exemplified a shift in black women's organizations, from self-help and local community development to lobbying at the national level.

60. Under the direction of Ella Baker, who championed a mass party rather than an elite oriented one, NAACP national membership rose significantly during the war. By 1943, membership had reached the quarter million mark, and in 1944, with a membership of 429,000, the annual report noted: "This marked increase in membership was, in large measure, the direct result of the First NAACP Annual Nationwide Membership Campaign . . . Charters were granted to 136 newly organized units of the Association during 1944, setting a record in the history of the NAACP" (quoted in Grant 1998:74). It was also the result of the expanding economy and job opportunities that accompanied the war effort. This growth in membership added force to the NAACP's role as pressure-group in gaining concessions from federal and local governments.

61. The MOWM held conventions and mass protest meetings in various cities throughout the war, the last one being in Chicago in 1946. In an article in *Survey Graphic* in 1942

entitled "Why Should We March?" Randolph explained "The March on Washington Movement is essentially a movement of the people. It is all Negro and pro-Negro, but not for that reason anti-white or anti-Semitic, or anti-Catholic, or anti-foreign, or anti-labor. Its major weapon is the non-violent demonstration of Negro mass power." The reason for marching was the lack of full citizenship rights and the "challenge both to win democracy for ourselves at home and to help win the war for democracy the world over." The article ended with a series of eight demands on the federal government (Van Deburg 1997b:73–77).

62. Joanne Grant (1998:55) recounts that this was in a context where the federal government "was concentrating on the war effort and powerful forces were attempting to dampen the fight for Negro and labor rights; struggles which were felt to be a distraction from all-out pursuit of the war." This conflict was also felt within the NAACP, where some leaders and rank-and-file felt that blacks should moderate their demands in the national interest. The conflict lead eventually to the firing in June, 1942, of NAACP director of branches William Pickens, who favored the moderate approach. The conflict expressed itself also in relation to support for Randolph's efforts.

63. The series of executive orders that black leaders like A. Philip Randolph were able to extract out of American Presidents Roosevelt and Truman should be seen in the light of a foreign policy and ideological struggle against totalitarian regimes, first in Germany, Italy, and Japan, and then in the Soviet Union. The United States could hardly claim the high ground of moral superiority if its largest minority group was making public issue of its discrimination. This in part, as Doug McAdam (Preface to new edition of *Political Process*, 1970) and Skrentny (1998) point out, explains the rapidity with which Truman, who was no less dependent upon Southern support for his presidency than Roosevelt, issued his executive orders. He appears to have been as concerned with winning the cold war as Roosevelt was the hot one.

64. Ernest J. Gaines' (1997) portrait of life on a Louisiana planation in the 1940s presents the following scenes "From where I stood, about halfway down the bar, all I could hear was Jackie this and Jackie that. Nothing about any of the other players, nothing about the Brooklyn Dodgers as a team. Only Jackie . . . They could recall everything Jackie had done in the past two years. They remembered when he got his first hit, and who it was against. They remembered the first time he stole two bases in one game and the first time he stole home" (1997:87). The men go on to act this out in all its detail, how it looked and how it was done. "Listening to them, I could remember back to the time before Jackie came to the major leagues, when it was Joe Louis everyone talked about . . . I could still remember how depressed everyone was after Joe lost the first fight with Schmeling. For weeks after that. To be caught laughing for any reason seemed like a sin. This was a period of mourning. What else in the world was there to be proud of, if Joe lost? . . . And we waited and waited, and finally the big [second] fight did come. There were two radios in the quarter . . . Praying and hoping for the only hero we knew. . . . For days after that fight, for weeks, we held our heads higher than any people on earth had ever done for

any reason. I was only seventeen then, but I could remember it, every bit of it – the warm evening, the people, the noise, the pride I saw in those faces" (1997:88–89). What is significant here, besides the role of common heroes in the construction of the collective, is the place of imagination in collective representation. Although Gaines does not tell us how these men learned of Robinson's feats, we can assume that the mass media, especially radio and film newsreels, were important carriers. But imagination, as well as remembering, was a feature of the constitution of the collective, as the mediated images were interpreted and articulated as collective memory.

65. Mike Marqusee (1999) makes a point about the burdens of representation with reference to black boxers like Joe Louis and Muhammad Ali. He writes, "Louis was groomed as a role model for black America, inoffensive but dignified, respectful and respected. The symbolic burdens that this would involve became apparent in his first fight in New York City, against Primo Carnera in 1935. At the time, Mussolini was engaged in highly public preparations for his invasion of Ethiopia. Although neither Louis nor Carnera had said anything about the issue, they were seen by many as representatives of Africa and Italy respectively" (1999:24). Regarding Schmeling, "Louis was made aware by the press, the churches, the president of the United States and the Communist party that knocking Schmeling's block off was his duty to America, the cause of anti-fascism and 'the Negro'" (1999:25). The runner Jesse Owens had carried a similar burden in the Olympic Games in Berlin in 1936. It was not only amongst blacks that these athletes were endowed with great symbolic weight and expectation. Paul Oliver (1968) compares Joe Louis to Jesse Owens and asks why the latter did not carry the burden of racial representation to the same extent; there is no song about Owens for example. He explains this by the fact that Owens was part of a team, which included whites while "Joe Louis fought as an individual, as an individual Negro and, in winning his way through a succession of bouts in which contender after contender fell . . . he enacted in real life the struggle that the Negro felt in his heart was his own" (1968:150) and "it was this essential loneliness that made some meaning for the blues singer, himself an individual and speaking more for himself than in abstractions for his society. Identification was simpler and could be for the blues singer almost complete." The fact that both were males might also have helped. Louis, born in Alabama in 1914, the grandson of slaves, moved to Detroit with his mother in 1926. Louis lost his first fight with Schmeling, a fact which no blues song recorded. As Oliver explains, "though the blues frequently express anger, frustration and often passive acceptance of adversity, disappointment as an emotional stimulus to the blues is extremely rare . . . There seems little doubt that as a commercial proposition a blues on Joe Louis' defeat would hardly have offered the incentive for purchase that one of his successes would have done, but it is likely that his defeat . . . destroyed for the singer the quality of an invincible folk hero which he had assumed" (1968:155–56).

66. The burden of representation, of embodying the progressive narrative, would later be passed on to other boxers, like Floyd Patterson. Others, like Muhammad Ali, would reject it and bear another. Marqusee (1999:140ff.) offers a powerful description of

their title match as one between two visions, not two individuals. Before their bout, Patterson wrote in a popular sports magazine "Cassius Clay is disgracing himself and the Negro race . . . The image of a Black Muslim as the world heavyweight champion disgraces the sport and the nation. Cassius Clay must be beaten and the Black Muslim scourge removed from boxing" (cited in Marqusee 1999:140). To which Ali (who had been given an "original name" by Elijah Muhammad) responded

> "I'm gonna put him flat on his back,
> So that he will start acting black,
> Because when he was champ he didn't do as he should,
> He tried to force himself into an all-white neighborhood."

And during the fight itself, when he had easily beaten Patterson, "Ali dragged the fight out to the twelfth round, punishing Patterson with his fists, then stepping back and allowing him time to recover while taunting him, "Come on America! Come on white America!" (Marqusee 1999:141). Floyd Patterson, who openly and seemingly gladly carried the burden of representation, fell victim several times to its weight. After losing twice to Sonny Liston, Leroi Jones remembered, "Each time Patterson fell a vision came to me of the whole colonial West crumbling in some sinister silence" (quoted in Marqusee 1999:44).

67. As Ellison explains in his 1981 Preface, significant parts of the novel had appeared as short stories already in 1947 and 1948 (Ellison 1990:vii–xxiii). Ellison's portrait of black college life and its upwardly striving students can be contrasted with those portrayed by Alice Walker and Spike Lee. Walker's portrait is colored by the 1960s civil rights movement and a politicized progressive narrative, while Lee's film *School Daze* represents the post-sixties institutionalization and stylization of both the civil rights movement and black power/nationalism. In Lee's version, the two movements are replaced by competing fraternaties and sororities.

68. As late as 1961, C. Eric Lincoln (1994:61) could write "Garveyism is not dead . . . Various nationalistic cults in America, Africa, and Jamaica still celebrate 'Garvey Day' each August 1 with appropriate speeches and ceremony. And Garvey's own stature continues to grow as more and more observers concede that, for all his faults, he had a profound effect on the black communities of the world."

69. The Communist Party also offered a direct challenge to Garvey-inspired black nationalism on another ground as well. Four of the first five black American communists in Harlem, as mentioned earlier, were West Indians. These men sought to navigate a path between Garvey's movement and Marxist communist. Like later Third World Marxists, they saw no necessary contradiction between nationalism, in the form of national liberation, and communism. And since they interpreted support for black nationalism as deriving from those they considered "working class," they saw the Garvey movement as a potential basis for recruitment.

70. Nicolas Lehmann (1991) in his study of the black migrants to Chicago could later point to the role of government programs in either helping or hindering their plight; similar to the programs of the 1930s in this respect, but now with a much more conscious design.

71. The Ford Motor Company played an ice-breaking role in employing blacks. At the same time, one of the New Deal programs, the National Recovery Act (NRA) encouraged union organizing and the CIO organized blacks at the same time as it secured contracts with Chrysler (1936) and General Motors (1937). Arna Bontemps and Jack Conroy (1945:222) report that there were "about 14,000 Negroes among the 85,000 workers," when the CIO organized its famous sit-down strikes against Ford in 1941. Black workers were torn between their loyalty to Ford, the conservative black ministers who advised them to support the company which offered them work when others wouldn't, and their fellow workers and the union. The NAACP, through Walter White, encouraged them to support the labor movement.

72. Wright wrote an introduction to *Black Metropolis*, Drake and Cayton's classical sociological study of black Chicago, and claimed to have been influenced in his fiction by the Chicago School's notion of the "marginal man."

73. Writing in *Ebony* in the 1960s, Amy Jacques-Garvey claimed that her former husband had viewed, or at least would have viewed, the homeland more or less in this symbolic sense as well. "After Marcus Garvey had returned millions to Africa spiritually, he had done his work. It was finished in the real sense. I believe if Garvey had lived, he would have studied the conditions in Africa even more than in the New World and he would have realized that the return to Africa had taken place . . ." (quoted in Essien-Udom (1962:61).

    There were other groups as well including the Garveyist. "The Peace Movement of Ethiopia" founded in Chicago in 1932, which later supported a Southern senator's bill to "repatriate" Negroes; the Moors, and two black groups which supported the Axis powers, the Iron Defense Legion, black fascists, and The Pacific Movement of the Eastern World, sympathetic to the Japanese. There was also the Forty-Ninth State Movement which sought to establish a new state for blacks. Writing in the early 1960s, Essien-Udom listed the following nationalist groups and organizations active in Chicago: "the Joint Council of Repatriation; World Wide Friends of Africa; American Economic League; the Garvey Club; Royal Ethiopian Jews; Washington Park Forum; and the United African Federation" (Essien-Udom 1962:50).

74. According to Clegg (1997:18ff.), the roots of Islam in North America can be traced as far back as the Spanish settlements in Florida which predated English colonization; And, he writes: "before 1808, when the transatlantic trade was still legal in what was by then the United States, possibly tens of thousands of Muslims from Senegambia and other Islamic parts of West Africa were transported to North America as slaves. Numerous notices in Georgian and South Carolinian newspapers for runaway slaves with Arabic names confirmed the presence of a significant Muslim minority among African-American slaves. Even after emancipation, some blacks could still trace their ancestry to a Muslim past." Ethnologists on the Sea Islands in the 1940s "found some descendants of a small Muslim congregation" (Gardell 1996:34).

    Fard "was born in New Zealand or Portland, Oregon, on February 25, 1891, to either Hawaiian or British and Polynesian parents" (Clegg 1997:20). After serving time in prison in California for selling narcotics, and abandoning a family in Los Angeles, he established himself in Detroit through selling cheap items of clothing to the newly arrived Southern migrants. He added a symbolic value to this clothing by claiming that it was "the same kind that the Negro people use in their home country in the East" (Clegg 1997:21).

75. Renaming was central to Fard's redemptive strategy. As a means of gaining financial support for himself and the sect, Fard had sold "original names" to converts. After recognizing the potential in his disciple, Fard is thought to have said "I will give you a better name than Karriem . . . You take my name" (Clegg 1997:33). Thus Elijah Karriem became Elijah Muhammad in 1933. This name and identity change was not without complications. Elijah Muhammad was one of the more successful, in that he was able to convince "most of his relatives in Detroit to adopt the new surname, including his father and mother, who became Wali and Marie Muhammad" (Clegg 1997:33–34).

76. The apparent paradox, that "redemptive" movements are most attractive to those most desperate, does not necessarily correlate with economic desperation. Rising expectations rather than complete desperation are more likely coupled with the willingness to join such movements.

77. In contemporary newspaper and police accounts and in the sociological literature of the time, the Nation was described as a "voodoo cult." A ritualist murder in 1932 led to Fard's imprisonment and eventual departure. The outbreak of war and Elijah Muhammad's militant stand against participation changed this view, and led to the eventual transformation from sect to social movement.

78. The Nation of Islam was not the only group in the Chicago black ghetto to oppose the war, others included the Brotherhood for Liberty for Black People of America and the Peace Movement of Ethiopia (Clegg 1997:90). This anti-war stance was also something which clearly separated the Nation from the NAACP, although as noted there were tensions within that organization as well concerning black participation in the war effort, at least as soldiers in a segregated armed forces.

79. According to Clegg (1997:48), this made sense as a mobilizing strategy, as it "made the continent more palatable to those converts who harbored a sense of shame in having roots in Africa." However, it had the effect of reinforcing stereotypes about the continent, as "sub-Saharan Africa was depicted as a savage place populated with uncivilized people." These were views which even Garvey to some extent had shared. At the same time, "Europe was described as a wasteland and whites as waste" (1997:54). This turned the tables on white "civilization," making it equally savage and uncultivated, and blacks into the superior race, without the burden of any "civilizing" mission. The conspicuous display of wealth can also be considered as a mobilizing strategy. Muhammad himself justified it in this way, stating that it was necessary in order to convince poor blacks that the movement was worthy of their support. Changes in tactics and in recruitment occurred as the war ended. One of the lessons Muhammad took with him from prison was the necessity of economic self-sufficiency for black people, the heritage of Booker T. Washington was reinforced through the experience of prison as a model institution for organizing economic life. The Muslims purchased a farm and set up bakeries, grocery stores, and other small businesses to produce goods and services necessary to the community. In the same way the Fruit of Islam acted as an internal police force. These changes

had some appeal to the middle class, especially those with entrepreneurial interests. Shifts such as these made possible the changes in the recruitment base of the
movement which began post-war. Along with the American population at large, the
economic conditions of urban blacks began to improve in the economic upswing.
To ensure that the movement would appeal to more affluent blacks, Muhammad
focused more and more on black capitalism, on the grounds that it aided local
control and provided employment for blacks. The Muslims, in other words, began to exhibit some very fundamental American values, leading Clegg to argue
that the movement was essentially conservative in its economic as well as moral
outlook.

80. John Hawkins is an historical figure, however "conventional histories of John
Hawkins's first voyage describe him as arriving in Hispaniola in 1563, not North
America in 1555, as part of the English effort to break the Spanish monopoly on the
slave trade. The slave ship *Jesus of Lubeck* perhaps did not make the trip across the
Atlantic until Hawkins' third voyage in 1567" (Clegg 1997:59).

81. There existed a long tradition from which Muhammad could draw. The previously
mentioned Alexander Crummell and Henry Turner had in the post-reconstruction
era described slavery as a necessary evil which had provided America's blacks with
necessary skills. For the missionary Crummell, this was grounds for a "black man's
burden," where enlightened ex-slaves had the responsibility to return to Africa to redeem their uncivilized brethren. In similar fashion, Turner, for whom the black man's
future lay in Africa after the American Supreme Court declared the Civil Rights Act
of 1875 unconstitutional in 1883, argued that "returning ex-slaves would evangelize
Africa and defend the continent from Europeans" (Gardell 1996:21). It was the civilizing effects of Christianity in this case, imposed during slavery, which underwrote
the African mission of the American Negro. Booker T. Washington also found some
beneficial aspects to slavery, "We must acknowledge that, not withstanding the cruelty and moral wrong of slavery, the ten million Negroes inhabiting this country,
who themselves or whose ancestors went through the school of American slavery,
are in a stronger and more hopeful condition, materially, intellectually, morally, and
religiously, than is true of any equal number of black people in any other portion of
the globe" (cited in Gardell 1996:16).

6 Civil rights and black nationalism: the post-war generation

1. This was of course especially true on military bases in the South. It was also true
overseas, however. Once off-base, soldiers usually frequented strictly segregated
"recreation" facilities. Bars and other sorts of leisure activities were racially divided, often in separate districts of the surrounding towns and villages, where the
local population learned and exhibited the same kinds of racial prejudices as the
Americans they entertained. Military police patrolled and enforced the codes of
these segregated areas, as a means of "keeping the peace." On the practice of informal segregation, Toni Morrison (1999:112) offers these grisly reflections of a black
father whose two sons were killed in Vietnam and whose bodies had been returned
home. "He knew that bodies did not lie down; that most of them flew apart and that

what had been shipped to them in those boxes, what they pulled off the train . . . was a collection of parts that weighed half of what a nineteen-year-old would. Easter and Scout were in integrated units and if Soane [their mother] thought about it, she might consider herself lucky to know that whatever was missing, the parts were all of black men – which was a courtesy and a rule the medics tried hard to apply for fear of adding white thighs and feet to a black head."

2. The well-known leadership conflicts within the SCLC can at least in part be understood as a consequence of television. Ella Baker, the only non-minister and female in that organization's leadership group, was also strongly opposed to being a media performer, a role enjoyed by her chief rival, Martin Luther King, Jr. This was part of a more general conflict over leadership styles and the role of the organization itself. Baker understood the organization's role as one of promoting local leadership, as a means toward the formation of a mass-based movement. Others in the SCLC, including King, favored the role of national leadership and the projection of a leading figure. According to her biographer, Baker was "exasperated by the failure of SCLC to function as a 'group-centered leadership, rather than a leadership-centered group', and appalled by its unwillingness (or inability) to organize a mass movement" (Grant 1998:123). Similarly, the struggle surrounding the excommunication of Malcolm X from the Black Muslims involved the latter's powerful media representation. Malcolm X was a skilled media performer, something which was at first encouraged by Elijah Muhammad, who was less skillful in this regard. This created some jealousy amongst others in the leadership and may have been a factor in his eventual exclusion and murder.

3. According to David Du Bois, the son of W. E. B. who had lived in Ghana for extended periods and had met Malcolm X there, "It was this mood of liberation that Malcolm attached himself to when he came to Africa, this euphoria of African liberation. I'm sure it impacted him tremendously" (interviewed by Spike Lee (1993:39)). Du Bois also reported: "Cairo and Accra were two independent African capitals in sixty-three and sixty-four, near the high point of African liberation . . . Both cities hosted and welcomed and supported the liberation organization representatives from all over the continent. Maya Angelou and I sort of worked as the liaisons between the African-American members of this mission, the U.S. mission in Cairo, and the liberation organizations. Maya was a great hostess. She would give these fabulous functions to welcome the visiting African-Americans" (1993). One of those visiting was Muhammad Ali, and Angelou was witness to a chance meeting between him and Malcolm X after the latter had broken with the Nation of Islam of which Ali had become a member (Marqusee 1999:129).

4. While the title *Black Power* may not have been of Wright's own choosing, it certainly was prophetic. Its meaning at the time, however, was different than what it would come to mean in the 1960s. For Wright and his publishers, it referred to the assuming of political power by black Africans, something which had no necessary connection to a racial consciousness, which was the core of its later meaning. Especially when associated with the cultural nationalism which developed in the US in the late 1960s–1970s, the term would refer to a racial consciousness, which existed as a

potential but was not necessarily realized by those with a particular hue of skin. As it was expressed at the time, "all Negroes are potentially Black" (Amari Baraka).This was clearly not Wright's meaning.

5. Wright was forced by his editor and publisher to describe his relationship to communism (see the Introduction by Amiritjit Singh). The book was published in the midst of the cold war and anti-communist hysteria. As explanation for the party membership he admits to, Wright says "my belonging to a minority group whose gross deprivations pitched my existence on a plane of all but sheer criminality made [radical] changes welcome to me. From 1932 to 1944 I was a member of the Communist Party of the United States of America and, as such, I held consciously in my hands Marxist Communism as an instrumentality to effect such political and social changes . . . Yet, as an American Negro whose life is governed by racial codes written into law, I state clearly that my abandonment of Communism does not automatically place me in a position of endorsing and supporting all the policies, political and economic of the non-Communist world. Indeed, it was the inhuman nature of those policies, racial and otherwise, that led me to take up the instrumentality of Communism in the first place" (Wright: 1995:xxxvi).

6. The Mau Mau movement in Kenya (1952–57) was one of the first African national liberation movements to catch the popular imagination, especially amongst whites. Their violent acts made in an attempt to recapture ancestral lands were seen in newsreels and in Hollywood films, as well as widely reported in the press. Jomo Kenyatta, who had studied anthropology in London and later became president of the country, was jailed for his alleged role in this movement, something which he denied. In this context, other movements appeared moderate, even where their leaders were jailed, like Kenneth Kaunda in what later became Zambia and Nkrumah in Ghana.

7. The term black "militants" came into common usage in the 1960s, although Richard Wright used the term in Black Power (1953). It was created and made popular through the mass media and connoted a range of representative practices, from forms of speech to dress and behavior.

8. Fanon was born on Martinique in 1925 and died of cancer in Washington, DC in 1961 at the age of 36. He studied medicine in France and was assigned to a hospital in Algeria during the national liberation struggles, where he discovered his sympathies with the rebels. The Wretched of the Earth appeared in French in 1961, just before he died. His first book, Black Skin, White Masks, based on his psychiatric practice in the Antilles, appeared in 1950. A third, A Dying Colonialism also based on his Algerian experiences, was published posthumously. The 1963 Grove Press edition carried the subtitle The Handbook for the Black Revolution that Is Changing the Shape of the World and contained a preface by Jean-Paul Sartre who urged readers to "Have the courage to read this book." Fanon's Black Skin, White Masks has proved equally long-lived. The metaphor of the mask, which has many similarities with Du Bois' veil, has proven attractive to those black intellectuals influenced by poststructuralist theory. A revival of interest in Fanon occurred in the late 1980s and 1990s, spurred primarily through black studies programs.

9. Describing the Ashanti of the Gold Coast, Wright notes "Their homicidal attitude toward the stranger is evidence of their present but deflected lust to kill the not-yet-quite-dead but prospective ancestor whose edicts they hate deep in their hearts. The tight vice of taboo-ridden tribal life, holding the hearts of simple, nonreflective men in a strait-jacket, finds its apogee of protest, its psychological balance in venting its hate and lustful rebellion upon the stranger, but that stranger is symbolically the living dead which that heart hates and fears. So crime and forgiveness for crime are magically combined in a single act of ritualized violence" (Wright 1995 [1954]:328).

10. "Black rage" became the title of a book as well as a concept to refer to the sub-conscious frustration felt by American blacks, especially men. It was this "rage" that needed to be vented in order for emancipation to occur, a point of view stemming from Fanon. *Black Rage* was written by William Grier and Price Cobbs, two black psychiatrists, who suggest, according to Jeff Donaldson, a founding member of AFRI-COBRA (African Commune of Bad Relevant Artists), "that black men defensively equipped with paranoiac personalities survive the experience of America much better than those who are not so fortunately equipped" (cited in Van Deburg 1997:217). The notion that "paranoia" can be "healthy" connects to the "anti-psychiatry" of the then popular British psychiatrist R.D. Laing and the American-based radical therapy movement of the 1960s. Regarding movement developments, earlier in the 1960s, Ella Baker, then a member of the governing board of SCLC had encouraged the organizers of what would become SNCC not to affiliate themselves with her own organization. Rather, she encouraged them to form their own independent organization in a more democratic and less hierarchical way, in order to encourage the development of local leaders. Carmichael's thoughts can be seen to be related to this idea, but now with a new twist – racial psychology. Carmichael and Charles Hamilton, a political scientist and (later) biographer of Adam Clayton Powell, Jr., published a program of political action which they titled *Black Power* (1967). The 1992 edition contains a retrospective Afterword by the two authors which reveals different personal trajectories and interpretations of the meaning of the concept black power. Carmichael (who died in 1998) was then writing from Ghana under the name Kwame Ture (which also appears on the cover of the new edition, 1992). In his interpretation, black power implied the necessity of social revolution leading to racial redemption. For Hamilton, on the other hand, black power implied a strategy of racial or ethnic politics within the American democratic framework. The different paths the two co-authors took aptly illustrate the effects of the confluence of the two narratives frameworks. By maintaining his revolutionary interpretation of Black Power, Ture was excluded and could either leave the country for a more hospitable one or try to maintain his ideology in marginal opposition in the United States. Hamilton, on the other hand, was recruited by Columbia University in New York City to help establish a black studies program (Marable 2000:10).

11. This is not to say that Malcolm X was equally important as a political figure. Thurgood Marshall and others, who accepted the Enlightenment model of emancipation and the legalistic methods of the NAACP, viewed Malcolm X as a failure, if not

worse. "What has he ever achieved?" Marshall asked. Martin Luther King's civil disobedience was also questionable from his perspective (Goldfarb 1998). According to Ishmael Reed, "Malcolm made wolfing and jive into an art form, and though his battles were fought on television (Marshall McLuhan referred to him as the 'electronic man') and his weapons were words, he was a symbol of black manhood . . . manhood being very much on the minds of black men during the sixties," Preface to a new edition of *Soul On Ice* (Cleaver 1992:xiii).

12. For the developing feminist consciousness these movements were considered to represent and be dominated by "male" values and by educated, middle-class blacks as "ghetto" or "street" culture, one that was at the same time attractive and repelling, a continued sign of social maladjustment as well as an outcome of marginalization and racist exclusion perpetrated by the dominant society.

13. Although Malcolm X can be included with the millions of other migrants of his generation, by his own description there remains an important distinction. He regarded himself as product of the Northern ghettoes, "a creation of the Northern white man," who knew "nothing about the South" (Haley 1965:377). Regarding his education, he had this to say: "I finished the eighth grade in Mason, Michigan. My high school was the black ghetto of Roxbury, Massachusetts. My college was in the streets of Harlem. My masters' was taken in prison" (1965:389).

14. In an interview with Spike Lee, as he prepared to film *Malcolm X*, Malcolm's brother revealed, "I can remember Marcus Garvey dictating to [our mother] some letters he wanted her to write. And my mother used to write articles for *The Negro World*" (Lee 1993:47). Malcolm's mother was born in Grenada.

15. In his *Autobiography*, Malcolm X attributes his father's death to members of the "Black Legion," a local white supremacist organization, and as politically and racially motivated.

16. This term itself was media produced, and was not the favored term of the movement, which did its best both to change it and to use the media, rather than be used by it. According to Malcolm X, the term was popularized after the publication of a book based on his doctoral thesis by Eric Lincoln, a sociologist at Boston University. "Just as the television 'Hate That Hate Produced' title had projected that 'hate-teaching' image of us, now Dr Lincoln's book was titled *The Black Muslims* in America. The press snatched at that name" (Haley 1965: 350). Malcolm X attributed his own popularity as a speaker on college campuses to the curiosity created by Lincoln's book (1965:388). Both the knowledge and the interpretation of the Black Muslims, including that very term itself, was significantly affected by a doctoral dissertation in sociology. Eric Lincoln's *The Black Muslims* (1961) was described by Malcolm X (Haley 1965:337) as the first treatment of the movement to provide a fair and adequate account of its meaning and development. This he counterposed to the sensationalist and biased representation offered by television. He wrote "On the wire of our relatively small Nation, these two developments – a television show, and a book about us – naturally were big news. Every Muslim happily anticipated that now, through the white man's powerful communications media, our brainwashed black brothers and sisters across the United States, and devils, too, were going to

see, hear, and read Mr Muhammad's teachings which cut back and forth like a two-edged sword" (Haley 1965:338). This citation reveals the at times close linkage between the academic and the popular discourse. Not only does Malcolm X view an academic study as an opportunity, he also accepts and makes use of its concepts, in this case the very name of his own group. From his perspective, an academic study gave legitimacy as well as publicity. It indicated that the movement was taken seriously, even by opponents, and was no longer considered a mere "voodoo cult."

17. Black nationalists in the United States have also used the Bible as a reference point, often turning around that of apologists for slavery who referred to the "curse of Ham." "Creative black interpreters, however, showed how the negative aspect of Genesis 9 had been superseded in the Christian gospel. Black nationalists such as Martin Delany, Edward W. Blyden, David Walker, Henry Highland Garnet, and J. W. Hood, among many others, combined the reinterpretation of the 'curse' with the prophecy of Psalms 68:21, Princes will come out of Egypt; Ethiopia shall soon stretch out her hands unto God. They produced a powerful affirmation of the historic black peoples of Africa. Far from being the object of a curse, Ethiopia was the source of nobility for the church and world" (Haley 1965:216).

18. Komozi Woodard (1999:6) prefers to oppose "acculturation" to assimilation. He argues that it was the acculturation of black intellectuals in the 1960s–1970s, i.e. the inclusion of blacks into white universities in greater numbers that, paradoxically, produced black nationalism rather than assimilation. Blacks in other words did not become "white" ("assimilate"), but discovered their "blackness." Similarly, one could argue that the inclusion of women in great numbers in this same institution produced feminism in response, i.e., women discovered their difference and each other rather than becoming "male" or accepting "male" values. This is certainly an important insight, however, there was much more going on during this period and had this inclusion happened decades earlier, it is possible to imagine different results.

19. This in part explains some of the expressed love–hate relation that existed between black leaders and intellectuals and other ethnic groups, most especially Jews. The latter were often painted as exploiting poor urban blacks, as "aliens" in the community who owned the buildings and the local stores in which blacks were forced to live and shop, at the same time as this form of ethnic capitalism was pointed to as a positive example for blacks to follow. Italians were vilified for their use of local office for ethnic gain, especially in the political and judiciary systems; while the Irish were pointed to for their use of civil service occupations, especially the police force, for the same ends. Blacks were decried for never having successfully taken advantage of this form of local, urban politics, something which was explained both by racism but also by the late arrival of blacks to the urban areas. The modernization of black nationalism, even where it used the rhetoric of national liberation and neo-colonialism, can be seen as contributing to an "ethnicification" strategy in politics if not identity.

20. Toni Morrison's novel *Paradise* (1997:84) contains the following response to the phrase "ex-slave" spoken by a younger black to his elder: "That's my grandfather you're talking about. Quit calling him an ex-slave like that's all he was. He was also

an ex-lieutenant governor, an ex-banker, an ex-deacon and a whole lot of other exes, and he wasn't making his own way; he was part of a whole group making their own way."

21. A key figure here is Molefi Asante of Temple University in Philadelphia. Born in Georgia in 1942 as Arthur Lee Smith, Asante is called the "godfather of Afro-centrism" by Howe (1998:230), who also summarizes the central principles of the doctrine. Asante authored *Afro-Centricity: The Theory of Social Change* (1980) and edited the *Journal of Black Studies*. "The Afrocentrist seeks to uncover and use codes, paradigms, symbols, motifs, myths, and circles of discussion that reinforce the centrality of African ideas and values as a valid frame of reference for acquiring and examining data." Afro-centricity is a standpoint perspective, viewing historical development and social change from "the standpoint of the agency of African people and the centrality of Africa in its own story," with the view that "African Americans should be viewed not as objects or victims, but as actors and subjects of history" (quoted in Marable 2000:16–17).

22. Williams was granted asylum by Fidel Castro, and from Cuba he broadcast "weekly encouragements to armed resistance over 'Radio Free Dixie'" (Van Deburg 1997a:93).

23. Just after the war there had been an attempt by the newly arrived radio network ABC to broadcast "The Jackie Robinson Show," but public support had not yet arrived and the show was "short-lived" (Barlow 1999:76).

24. In 1933, Carter Woodson wrote: "The word *Negro* or *black* is used in referring to this (skin color) particular element because most persons of African descent approach this color. The term does not imply that every Negro is black; and the word white does not mean that every white man is actually white ... We are not all Africans ... because many of us were not born in Africa; and we are not all Afro-Americans, because few of us are natives of Africa transplanted to America" (Woodson 1933:192).

25. According to Lischer (1995:200), "the African-American tradition of (biblical) interpretation ... did not pass through the Enlightenment, never enjoyed the leisure of disinterested moral applications. The cruelties of slavery made it imperative that African Americans not step *back* but step *into* the Book and its storied world of God's personal relations with those in trouble."

26. Lischer contrasts this to Franz Fanon's call to "use different symbols, myths, and sounds from those of the established order" (1995:148). This needed to be because "the oppressed ... can never use the language of the established order with as much skill as the oppressor" (1995:148).

27. Gardner Taylor, one of King's mentors in the preaching traditions of the black church and minister of a large Brooklyn Baptist congregation, recalled for Richard Lischer (1995:143) that, "there was never more than a 'core' of the black church that made an active commitment to civil rights."

28. Lischer (1995:33) describes Richard Allen, the founder of the AME Baptist Church, in this way: "In doctrine Allen remained a loyal Methodist and a Sustainer of his people, encouraging them to loyalty and affection for their masters. In his church

policy, Allen pursued a more aggressive line. He was a bold Reformer who shrewdly manipulated his white Methodist antagonists and attacked slaveholding Christians on the basis of the Christian's Bible."

29. In 1959, the folklorist and musicologist Alan Lomax made a return trip through the delta region of Mississippi collecting new material in areas he had been to in the 1940s. Musically there was much that had remained the same and in the music he recorded one can experience the living memory of both slavery and Africa. Lomax's (Rounder Records) recording of the work songs, field hollers, and back porch blues of everyday people recalls the sounds of the past. Lomax (1993) adds the complementary field notes and commentary.

30. For the more instrumental aspects of this demand and engagement, see Ward (1998), where it is shown how organizers within the movement actively pressured entertainers for their support.

31. Such developments of course are not unique to the civil rights movement or to black Americans. They are rather common to modern social movements. The institutionalism of the modern women's movement can be similarly traced.

32. Although Asante does not mention it, there is a distinct reference here to the "emancipatory interest" that Habermas identified in his discussion of the three distinct "knowledge interests" underlying the development of scientific thought. The aim of Afrocentric theory is "the use of knowledge for the cultural, social, political, and economic liberation of African people by first recentering African minds" (Marable 2000:196). This way of linking theory and practice is clearly in line with Habermas' notion of "emancipatory science" and can be compared with his paradigm case of Freudian psychoanalysis, especially in the work of Franz Fanon, which Asante draws upon.

33. Henry Louis Gates, Jr. (1991:164) makes the provocative comment that the film "Guess Who's Coming to Dinner" "did more to fuel the death of the civil rights movement and the birth of black nationalism than did any other film because it suggested that the movement would achieve its fulfillment in the creation of a new middle class – assimilated, desexualized and safe."

34. "Blues for Mister Charlie" inspired Amiri Baraka, who had earlier been one of Baldwin's harshest critics. Baraka, whose "Dutchman" would open a few months after *Blues*, called the latter "a deeply touching 'dangerous' play . . . it not only questioned nonviolence, it had a gutsy – but doomed – black hero and his father go at each other's values, echoing the class struggle that raged between Dr. King and Malcolm X . . ." (cited in Hay 1994:95).

35. They have played a role in stimulating social as well as cultural change, as in this case. Tape-recorded messages capable of being played on inexpensive and thus readily available portable cassette players, played an important role in the Iranian revolution, where cassette recordings of Khomeni's sermons were easily smuggled into the country and secretly distributed.

36. On the links between rap and the Nation of Islam, see Gardell (1996). Gardell defines religious nationalism as postulating "that nations are divine creations with specific God-given purposes and features" (1996:8). A nation, on the other hand, is "an

imagined community of people founded on selected criteria as language, history, culture, destiny, religion, to which sentiments of belonging, loyalty, solidarity are attached, together with a theory, if not a practice, of legitimate political authority" (1996). Nationalism is "an ideology that gives priority to the *nation* over other imagined communities such as class and gender" (1996).

37. Lee Baker (2000) explains the popularity of Afrocentrism amongst the newly expanded black middle class, which according to the standard views of integration should reject it and embrace the "American dream," by seeing it as a typical American form of ethnic politics. "The rise of Afrocentricity is as American as hamburgers" (2000:231). Leith Mullings (2000), on the other hand, interprets this popularity as part of what I have called cultural trauma, the limited success of the civil rights movement and the continuation of racism, especially in the academy. Viewing Afrocentricity as part of the cultural turn, she writes "the resurgent turn toward culture is in part a reaction to the failures of liberal integration, in part a consequence of the state-sponsored destruction of the left, and in part a challenge to apologists for inequality who attribute the cause of increasing poverty to the culture of African Americans" (2000:211).

References

Alexander, Jeffrey, Ron Eyerman, Bernhard Giesen, Neil Smelser, and Piotr Sztompka (2001) *Cultural Trauma Theory and Applications*, Berkeley: University of California Press.

Allen, Robert (1970) *Black Awakening in Capitalist America*, New York: Doubleday.

Allen, William, Charles Ware, and Lucy Garrison (1867) *Slave Songs of the United States*, Bedford: Applewood Books.

Anderson, Benedict (1991) *Imagined Communities*, London: Verso.

Andrews, William (1992) "Introduction," *The African American Novel in the Age of Reaction*, New York: Mentor Books.

Angelou, Maya (1969) *I Know Why the Caged Bird Sings*, New York: Bantam Books.

  (1974) *Gather Together in My Name*, New York: Bantam Books.

  (1976) *Singin' and Swingin' and Gettin' Merry Like Christmas*, New York: Bantam Books.

Appiah, Anthony (1985) "The Uncompleted Argument: Du Bois and the Illusion of Race," in Gates (ed.), *"Race," Writing, and Difference*.

Arendt, Hannah (1978) *The Life of the Mind*, vol. I *Thinking*. New York: Harcourt Brace Jovanovich.

Asante, Molefi (2000) "Afrocentricity, Race, and Reason," in Manning Marable (ed.), *Dispatches from the Ebony Tower*.

Baker, Lee (1999) *From Savage To Negro Anthropology and the Construction of Race 1896–1954*, Berkeley: University of California Press.

  (2000) "Afrocentricity and the American Dream" in Manning Marable (ed.), *Dispatches from the Ebony Tower*.

Banks, William (1996) *Black Intellectuals*, New York: Norton.

Barlow, William (1989) *Looking Up At Down*, Philadelphia: Temple University Press.

(1999) *Voice Over, The Making of Black Radio*, Philadelphia: Temple University Press.

Barton, Craig (ed.) (2001) *Sites of Memory*, New York: Princeton Architectural Press.

Benhabib, Seyla (1996) *The Reluctant Modernism of Hannah Arendt*. London: Sage.

Bergmann, Martin and Milton Jucovy (eds.) (1982) *Generations of the Holocaust*, New York: Basic Books.

Berlin, Ira (1974) *Slaves Without Masters*, New York: Vintage.

(1998) *Many Thousands Gone*, Cambridge, MA: Harvard University Press.

Berlin, Ira, Mark Favrean, Steven Miller (eds.) (1998) *Remembering Slavery*, New York: The New Press.

Blight, David (1995) "W. E. B. Du Bois and the Struggle for American Historical Memory" in G. Fabre and R. O'Meally (eds.), *History and Memory in African-American Culture*, New York: Oxford University Press.

(1997) "Reunion and Race," in D. Blight and B. Simpson (eds.), *Union and Emancipation*, Kent: Kent State University Press.

Boime, Albert (1990) *The Art of Exclusion*, Washington: Smithsonian Institution Press.

Bontemps, Arna and Jack Conroy (1945) *They Seek a City*, New York: Doubleday, Doran and Company.

(1969) "Introduction," in A. Bontemps (ed.), *Great Slave Narratives*, Boston: Beacon Press.

Bordelon, Pamela (ed.) (1999) *Writings by Zora Neale Hurston*, New York: Norton.

Bowser, Pearl (1999) "Pioneers of Black Documentary Film," in P. Klotman and J. Cutler (eds.), *Struggles for Representation*.

Bronz, Stephen (1964) *Roots of Negro Racial Consciousness*, New York: Libra.

Broude, Norma and Mary Garrard (1994) *The Power of Feminist Art*, New York: Harry Abrams.

Brown, Elsa (1995) "Negotiating and Transforming the Public Sphere: African American Political Life in the Transition from Slavery to Freedom," *The Black Public Sphere*, Chicago: The University of Chicago Press.

Carby, Hazel (1998) *Race Men*, Cambridge, MA: Harvard University Press.

Caruth, Cathy (1996) *Unclaimed Experience*, Baltimore: Johns Hopkins.

Caruth, Cathy (ed.) (1995) *Trauma Exploration in Memory*, Baltimore: Johns Hopkins.

Cash, Stephanie (2000) "Jacob Lawrence, 1917–2000," *Art in America*, Sept.: 166.

Cashmore, Ellis (1997) *The Black Culture Industry*, London: Routledge.

Cassidy, Donna (1997) *Painting the Musical City*, Washington: Smithsonian Institution Press.

Charters, Ann (1992) *The Portable Beat Reader*, New York: Viking.

Chesnutt, Charles (1995) *The Wife of His Youth and Other Stories*. Ann Arbor: University of Michigan Press.

Christian, Charles (1995) *Black Saga*, Boston: Houghton Mifflin.

Chuck, D. (1997) *Fight The Power*, Edinburgh: Payback Press.

Clark, Kathleen (1999) "History is No Fossil Remains: Race, Gender, and the Politics of Memory in the American South, 1863–1913," unpublished dissertation, Yale University.

Cleaver, Eldridge (1968) *Soul on Ice*, New York: Dell.

Clegg, Claude (1997) *An Original Man*, New York: St. Martin's Press.

Connerton, Paul (1989) *How Societies Remember*, Cambridge: Cambridge University Press.

Cruse, Harold (1984) *The Crisis of the Negro Intellectual*, New York: Quill.

Cruz, Jon (1999) *Culture on the Margins*, Princeton: Princeton University Press.

Darden, Norma Jean and Carole Darden (1994) *Spoonbread and Strawberry Wine*, New York: Doubleday.

Davis, Angela (1981) *Women, Race and Class*, New York: Vintage.

(1998) *Blues Legacies and Black Feminism*, New York: Pantheon.

Davis, David (1999) "Jew and Blacks in America," *New York Review of Books*, Dec. 2: 57–63.

Davis, Thulani (1992) *1959*, London: Hamish Hamilton.

Denning, Michael (1997) *The Cultural Front*, London: Verso.

Deveaux, Scott (1997) *The Birth of BeBop*. London: Picador.

Dictionary of Literary Biography (1983) "Amiri Baraka," vol. 16, Detroit: Gale Research Company, pp. 3–24.

Dillon, Merton (1974) *The Abolitionists*, De Kalb: Northern Illinois University Press.

Douglas, Aaron (1994) "Aaron Douglas Chats about the Harlem Renaissance," in David Lewis (ed.), (1994) *The Portable Harlem Renaissance Reader*.

Douglass, Frederick [1873] (1991) *The Frederick Douglass Papers*, 1st ser. vol. IV (*1964–80*), John Blassingame and John McKivigan (eds.), New Haven: Yale University Press.

(1969) *My Bondage and My Freedom*, New York: Arno Press.

Drake, St. Clair and Horace Cayton (1945) *Black Metropolis*, New York: Harper and Row.

Du Bois, W. E. B. [1897] (1999) "The Conservation of Races," a speech before the American Negro Academy, in *The Oxford Du Bois Reader*, Eric Sundquist (ed.), New York: Oxford.

(1903) *The Souls of Black Folk*, New York: Bantham Books.

[1920] (1999) *Darkwater: Voices From Within the Veil*, New York: Dover Books.

[1926] (1999) reprinted in *The Crisis Reader: Stories, Poetry, and Essays from the NAACP's Crisis* Magazine, Sondra Wilson (ed.), New York: Modern Library 1999

(1935/1973) *Black Reconstruction in America 1860–1880*, New York: Atheneum.

(1971) *W.E.B. Du Bois Reader*, A. Paschal (ed.) New York: Macmillan.

(1986) *Writings*, Nathan Huggins (ed.) New York: Library of America.

(1997) *John Brown*, Armonk, New York: M.E. Sharpe.

Duberman, Martin (1989) *Paul Robeson*, London: Bodley Head.

Ellison, Ralph (1953/ 1990) *Invisible Man*, New York: Vintage.

(1953a) *Shadow and Act*, New York: Vintage.

Erikson, Kai (1978) *Everything in its Path*, New York: Simon and Schuster.

Essien-Udom, E. U. (1962) *Black Nationalism*, Chicago: University of Chicago Press.

Eyerman, Ron (1994) *Between Culture and Politics*, Cambridge: Polity Press.

Eyerman, Ron and Andrew Jamison (1991) *Social Movements: A Cognitive Approach*, Cambridge: Polity Press.

(1998) *Music and Social Movements*, Cambridge: Cambridge University Press.

Eyerman, Ron and Bryan Turner (1998) "An Outline of a Theory of Generations," *European Journal of Social Theory*, vol. 1, no. 1.

Fanon, Frantz (1994) *The Wretched of the Earth*, New York: Grove Press.

Floyd, Samuel (ed.) (1994) *Black Music in the Harlem Renaissance*, Knoxville: University of Tennessee Press.

Foster, Gaines (1987) *Ghosts of the Confederacy*, New York: Oxford.

Frazier, E. Franklin (1932) *The Negro Family in Chicago*, Chicago: University of Chicago Press.

(1957) *Black Bourgeoisie*, New York: Free Press.

(1974) *The Negro Church in America*, New York: Schocken Books.

Fredrickson, George (1971) *The Black Image in the White Mind: the Debate on Afro-American Character and Destiny, 1817–1914*, New York: Harper and Row.

(2000) "The Skeleton in the Closet," *New York Review of Books*, vol. 47, no. 17: 61–66.

Fuller, Hoyt (1968/1994) "Towards a Black Aesthetic," in Angelyn Mitchell (ed.), (1994) *Within the Circle*.

Gaines, Ernest (1997) *A Lesson Before Dying*, New York: Vintage.

Gaines, Kevin (1996) *Uplifting the Race*, Chapel Hill: University of North Carolina Press.

Gardell, Mattias (1996) *In the Name of Elijah Muhammad*, Durham: Duke University Press.

Garvey, Marcus (1994) "Africa for Africans," in David Lewis (ed.) (1994) *The Portable Harlem Renaissance Reader.*

Garwood, Willard (1990) *Aristocrats of Color The Black Elite, 1880–1920*, Bloomington: Indiana.

Gates, Henry Louis, Jr. (1991) "Jungle Fever; Or, Guess Who's Not Coming to Dinner," in *The Films of Spike Lee: Five For Five*, David Lee and Spike Lee (eds.), New York: Stewart, Tabori & Chang.

Gates, Henry Louis, Jr. (ed.) (1985) *Race, Writing, and Difference*, Chicago: University of Chicago Press.

Gates, Henry Louis, Jr. and Manning Marable (2000) "A Debate on Activism in Black Studies," in Manning Marable (ed.) (2000) *Dispatches from the Ebony Tower.*

Gayle Jr., Addison (ed.) (1972) *The Black Aesthetic*, New York: Doubleday.

Gibson, Ann (1997) *Abstract Expressionism and Other Politics*, New Haven: Yale University Press.

Gilmore, Glenda (1995) *Gender and Jim Crow* Ph.D. diss., University of North Carolina Chapel Hill 1992, UMI Disseration Service Ann Arbor.

Gleason, William (1999) "Chesnutt's Piazza Tales: Architecture, Race, and Memory in the Conjure Stories," *American Quarterly*, vol. 51, no. 1, pp. 33–77.

Goffman, Erving (1974) *Frame Analysis: A Essay on the Organization of Experience*, New York: Penguin.

Goldfarb, Jeffrey (1998) *Civility and Subversion*, Cambridge: Cambridge University Press.

Grant, Joanne (1998) *Ella Baker*, New York: John Wiley & Sons.

Griffin, Farah (1995) *"Who set you flowin'?" The African-American Migration Narrative*, New York: Oxford.

Gutman, Herbert (1987) *Power and Culture*, in Ira Berlin *et al.* (eds.) (1998) *Remembering Slavery*, New York: Pantheon.

Halbwachs, Maurice (1992) *On Collective Memory*, Chicago: University of Chicago Press.

Hale, Grace (1998) *Making Whiteness*, New York: Vintage.

Haley, Alex (1965) *The Autobiography of Malcolm X*, New York: Ballantine Books.

Hamilton, Carl (1991) *Adam Clayton Powell, Jr.*, New York: Atheneum.

Handy, W. C. (1941) *Father of the Blues*, New York: Macmillan; Collier Books, 1970.

Harris, Jessica (1995) *The Welcome Table: African American Heritage Cooking*, New York: Simon and Schuster.

Harris, Michael (1992) *The Rise of Gospel Blues*, New York: Oxford University Press.

Hay, Samuel (1994) *African American Theatre*, Cambridge: Cambridge University Press.

Haywood, Harry (1978) *Black Bolshevik*, Chicago: Liberator Press.

Higginbotham, Evelyn (1993) *Righteous Discontent*, Cambridge, MA: Harvard University Press.

Hill, Patricia (1993) "Jacob Lawrence's *Migration* Series: Weavings of Pictures and Texts," in Elizabeth Turner (ed.), (1993) *Jacob Lawrence: The Migration Series*.

Himes, Chester (1947/1997) *Lonely Crusade*, Edinburgh: Payback Press.

Hoffman, Eva (2000) "Review of *The Holocaust in American Life*," *New York Review of Books*, vol. 47, no. 4: 19; vol. 47, no. 10: 78–79.

hooks, bell (1992) *Black Looks*, Boston: South End Press.

Howe, Stephen (1998) *Afrocentrism*, London: Verso.

Huggins, Nathan (ed.) (1995) *Voices from the Harlem Renaissance*, New York: Oxford.

Hughes, Langston (1990) *The Ways of White Folks*, New York: Vintage.

Hurston, Zora (1928) "How it Feels To Be Colored Me," in Steven Watson (ed.) (1995), *The Harlem Renaissance*.

—— (1942) *Dust Tracks on the Road*, Urbana: University of Illinois Press.

—— (1981) *The Sanctified Church*, New York: Marlowe & Company.

—— (1999) *Writings From the Federal Writer's Project*, New York: Norton.

Hutchinson, George (1995) *The Harlem Renaissance in Black and White*, Cambridge, MA: Harvard University Press.

Huyssen, Andreas (2000) "Present Pasts: Media, Politics, Amnesia," *Public Culture* vol. 2, no. 30: 21–8.

Igartua, H. and Paez, I. (1997) "Art and Remembering Collective Events," in James Pennebaker *et al.* (eds.), *Collective Memory of Political Events*, Mahwah, NJ: Lawrence Erlbaum Associates.

Jackson, Walter (1990) *Gunnar Myrdal and America's Conscience*, Chapel Hill: University of North Carolina Press.

James, Joy (1997) *Transcending the Talented Tenth*, London: Routledge.

The James Weldon Johnson Collection, Bienecke Library, Yale University

Johnson, Charles (1941) *Growing Up in the Black Belt*, Washington, DC: American Council on Education.

Johnson, James Weldon [1927] (1989) *The Autobiography of an Ex-Colored Man*, New York: Vintage.

—— (1934) *Along This Way*, New York: Viking Press.

Johnson, Sargent (1998) "Sargent Claude Johnson and Modernism," in *Sargent Johnson: African American Modernist*, Catalogue, San Francisco Museum of Modern Art.

Jones, Hattie (1990) *How I Became Hattie Jones*, New York: Penguin.

Jones, Jacqueline (1985) *Labor of Love, Labor of Sorrow*, New York: Basic Books.

Jones, LeRoi (Amari Baraka) (1963) *Blues People*, New York: William Morrow and Company.

   (1966/1994) "The Myth of 'Negro Literature,'" in Angelyn Mitchell (ed.), *Within the Circle*, Durham: Duke University Press.

   (1993) *The LeRoi Jones/Amiri Barak Reader*, William Harris (ed.), New York: Thunder's Mouth Press.

Kirschke, Amy (1995) *Aaron Douglas*, Jackson: University Press of Mississippi.

Klein, Joe (1980) *Woody Guthrie*, New York: Knopf.

Klotman, Phyllis (1999) "Military Rites and Wrongs," in P. Klotman and J. Cutler (eds.) (1999) *Struggles for Representation*.

Klotman, Phyllis and Janet Cutler (eds.) (1999) *Struggles for Representation*, Bloomington: Indiana University Press.

Kolchin, Peter (1993) *American Slavery 1619–1877*, New York: Hill and Wang.

Krasner, David (1997) *Resistance, Parody, and Double Consciousness in African American Theatre, 1895–1910*, New York: St. Martin's Press.

LaCapra, Dominick (1994) *Representing the Holocaust*, Ithaca: Cornell University Press.

Larsen, Nella (1986) *Quicksand and Passing*, New Brunswick, NJ: Rutgers University Press.

Lee, Spike (1993) *By Any Means Necessary*, New York: Vintage.

LeFalle-Collins, Lizzetta (1998) "Sargent Claude Johnson and Modernism: An Investigation of Context, Representation and Identity," in Sargent Johnson (1998) *Sargent Johnson: African American Modernist*.

Lehmann, Nicolas (1991) *The Promised Land*, New York: Knopf.

Levine, Lawrence (1978) *Black Culture, Black Consciousness*, New York: Oxford.

Lewis, David (1993) *W.E.B. Du Bois*, New York: Henry Holt.

   (2000) *W.E.B. Du Bois* (vol. 2), New York: Henry Holt.

Lewis, David (ed.) (1994) *The Portable Harlem Renaissance Reader*, New York: Penguin Books.

Lewis, Samella (1990) *African American Art and Artists*, Berkeley: University of California Press.

Lincoln, C. Eric (1974) *The Black Church Since Frazier*, New York: Schocken Books.

   (1994) *The Black Muslims in America*, Trenton, NJ: Africa World Press.

Lischer, Robert (1995) *The Preacher King*, New York: Oxford University Press.

Litwack, Leon (1979) *Been in the Storm so Long*, New York: Vintage.
(1998) *Trouble in Mind*, New York: Vintage.
Locke, Alain [1936] (1969) *The Negro and His Music, Negro Art: Past and Present*, New York: Arno Press.
Locke, Alain (ed.) [1925] (1997) *The New Negro*, New York: Simon and Schuster.
Logan, Rayford (1965) *The Negro in American Life and Thought: The Nadir, 1877–1901* later reissued as *The Betrayal of the Negro* (1954), New York: Collier Books.
Lomax, Alan (1993) *The Land Where the Blues Began*, New York: Pantheon.
Lovell, John, Jr. (1972) *Black Song: The Forge and the Flame*, New York: Paragon House.
Maier, August (1963) *Negro Thought in American 1880–1915*, Ann Arbor: University of Michigan.
Mannheim, Karl (1952) *Essays in the Sociology of Culture*, London: Routledge.
Marable, Manning (ed.) (2000) *Dispatches from the Ebony Tower*, New York: Columbia University Press.
Margolick, David (2000) *Strange Fruit*, Philadelphia: Running Press.
Marqusee, Mike (1999) *Redemption Song*, London: Verso.
Martin, Tony (1983) *Literary Garveyism*, Dover, MA: The Majority Press.
(1986) *Race First*, Dover, MA: The Majority Press.
Melosh, Barbara (1991) *Engendering Culture*, Washington, DC: Smithsonian Institution Press.
Melucci, Alberto (1995) "The Process of Collective Identity," in Johnson and Klandermans (eds.), *Social Movements and Culture* London: UCL Press.
McAdam, Doug (1982) *Political Process and the Development of Black Insurgency, 1930–1970*, Chicago: University of Chicago Press.
McDowell, Deborah and Arnold Rampersad (eds.) (1989) *Slavery and the Literary Imagination*, Baltimore: Johns Hopkins University Press.
McKay, Claude (1940) *Harlem: Negro Metropolis*, New York: E.P. Dutton and Company.
McMurry, Linda (1999) *To Keep the Waters Troubled*, New York: Oxford University Press.
Meier, August (1962) "Negro Class Structure and Ideology in the Age of Booker T. Washington," *Phylon*, vol. 23: 258–66.
Miers, Earl (1969) "Introduction" in *Charles W. Chesnutt: The Wife of His Youth and other Stories of the Color Line*, Ann Arbor: University of Michigan Press.
Miskin, Tracy (1998) *The Harlem and Irish Renaissances*, Gainsville: The University Press of Florida.
Mitchell, Angelyn (ed.) (1994) *Within the Circle*, Durham: Duke University Press.

Molyneaux, Sandra (1994) "Expanding the Collective Memory: Charles Chesnutt's *The Conjure Woman* Tales," in Singh *et al.* (eds.) (1994) *Memory, Narrative and Identity*.

Morrison, Toni (1977) *Song of Salomon*, London: Grafton Books.

(1997) *Paradise*, New York: Plume.

Moses, Wilson (1978) *The Golden Age of Black Nationalism*, Hamden, CT: Archon Books.

(1998) *Afrotopia: The Roots of African American Popular History*, Cambridge: Cambridge University Press.

Mullins, Leith (2000) "Reclaiming Culture: The Dialectics of Identity," in Manning Marable (ed.) (2000) *Disparches from the Ebony Tower*.

Musser, Charles (1999) "Troubled Relations," in Jeffrey Stewart (ed.), *Paul Robeson, Artist and Citizen*, New Brunswick: Rutgers University Press.

Myrdal, Gunnar (1944) *An American Dilemma*, New York: Harper & Brothers Publishers.

Naison, Mark (1983) *Communists in Harlem During the Depression*, New York: Grove Press.

Neal, Arthur (1998) *National Trauma and Collective Memory*, Armonk, New York: M.E. Sharpe.

Newton, Huey (1973) *To Die For The People*, New York: Writers and Readers Publishing.

Novick, Peter (1999) *The Holocaust in American Life*, Boston: Houghton Mifflin.

The Oxford Douglass Reader (1996) William Andrews (ed.), New York: Oxford University Press.

Painter, Nell (1976) *Exodusters*, New York: Norton; new edn 1979.

Patterson, Orlando (1998) *Rituals of Blood*, Washington, DC: Civitas.

Payne, Charles (1995) *I've Got the Light of Freedom*, Berkeley: University of California Press.

Pennebaker James, and Becky Banasik (1997) "On the Creation and Maintenance of Collective Memories: History as Social Psychology," in Pennebaker *et al.* (eds.) (1997), *Collective Memory of Political Events*.

Peterson, Richard (1997) *Creating Country Music: Fabricating Authenticity*, Chicago: University of Chicago Press.

Pinckney, Darryl (2000) "James Baldwin: The Risks of Love," *New York Review of Books*, vol. 47, no. 6.

Powdermaker, Hortense (1968) *After Freedom*, New York: Antheneum.

Powell, Richard (1997) *Black Art and Culture in the 20th Century*, London: Thames and Hudson.

Powell, Richard and Jock Reynolds (1999) *To Conserve A Legacy*, Addison Gallery of American Art and The Studio Museum in Harlem.

Radley, Allan (1990) "Artefacts, Memory and a Sense of the Past," in David Middleton and Derek Edwards (eds.), *Collective Remembering*, London: Sage.

Rampersad, Arnold (1976) *The Art and Imagination of W.E.B. Du Bois*, Cambridge, MA: Harvard University Press.

(1989) "Slavery and the Literary Imagination," in D. McDowell and A. Rampersad (eds.) (1989) *Slavery and the Literary Imagination*, Baltimore: Johns Hopkins University Press.

Rauch, Esther (1993) "Paul Laurence Dunbar," in Valerie Smith *et al.* (eds.), *African American Writers*, New York: Collier Books.

Redkey, Edwin (1969) *Black Exodus*, New Haven: Yale University Press.

Reid, Mark (1998) "Race, Working Class Consciousness, and Dreaming of Africa: *Song of Freedom* and *Jericho*" in *Paul Robeson*, J. Stewart (ed.) New Brunswick, NJ: Rutgers University Press.

Ripley, C. Peter (ed.) (1993) *Witness for Freedom*, Chapel Hill: University of North Carolina Press.

Rodgers, Lawrence (1991) "Paul Laurence Dunbar's *The Sport of the Gods*: The Doubly Conscious World of Plantation Fiction, Migration and Ascent," *American Literary Realism*, vol. 24, no. 3: 42–57.

Rose, Tricia (1994) *Black Noise*, Hanover: University Press of New England.

Rosenstone, Robert (1995) "Walker," in Robert Rosenstone (ed.), *Revisioning History*, Princeton: Princeton University Press.

Sampson, Harry (1977) *Blacks in Black and White*, Metuchen, NJ: Scarecrow Press.

Sandler, Irving (1996) *Art of the Postmodern Era*, Boulder: Westview.

(no date) *The Triumph of American Painting*, New York: Harper and Row.

Savage, Barbara (1999) *Broadcasting Freedom*, Chapel Hill: University of North Carolina Press.

Savage, Kirk (1994) "The Politics of Memory: Black Emancipation and the Civil War Monument," in *Commemorations*, John Gillis (ed.), Princeton: Princeton University Press.

Schoener, A. (ed.) (1995) *Harlem On My Mind*, New York: The New Press.

Schomburg, Arthur (1994) "The Negro Digs Up His Past," in David Lewis (ed.), *The Portable Harlem Renaissance Reader*.

Schudson, Michael (1989) "The Present in the Past versus the Past in the Present," *Communication*, vol. 11: 105–13.

Schuman, Howard and Jacqueline Scott (1989) "Generations and Collective Memory," *American Sociological Review*, vol. 54: 359–81.

Schwartz, Barry (1982) "The Social Context of Commemoration: A Study in Collective Memory," *Social Forces*, vol. 61, no. 2: 374–97.

Semprun, Jorge (1997) *Literature or Life*, New York: Penguin

Simmons, Charles (1998) *The African American Press*, Jefferson, NC: McFarland.

Singh, Amritjit, Joseph Skerrett, Jr., and Robert Hogan (eds.) (1994) *Memory, Narrative and Identity*, Boston: Northeastern University Press.
  (1996) *Memory and Cultural Politics*, Boston: Northeastern University Press.

Siraganian, Lisa (1997) "Is This My Mother's Grave? Genocide and Diaspora in Atom Egoyan's *Family Viewing," Diaspora*, vol. 6, no. 2.

Sitkoff, Harvard (1978) *A New Deal for Blacks*, New York: Oxford.

Skrentny, John (1998) "The Effect of the Cold War on African-American Civil Rights," *Theory and Society*, vol. 27, no. 2: 237–85.

Smelser, Neil (1962) *The Theory of Collective Behavior*, New York: Free Press.

Snow, David *et al.*, (1986) "Frame Alignment Processes, Micromobilization, and Movement Participation," *American Sociological Review*, vol. 51: 464–81.

Southern, Eileen (1983) *The Music of Black Americans*, New York: Norton.

Spenser, Jon (1993) *Blues and Evil*, Knoxville: University of Tennessee Press.
  (1997) *The New Negroes and Their Music*, Knoxville: University of Tennessee Press.

Stein, Judith (1986) *The World of Marcus Garvey*, Baton Rouge: LSU Press.
  (1989) "Defining the Race," in Werner Sollors (ed.), *The Invention of Ethnicity*, New York: Oxford University Press.

Stepto, Robert (1991) *From Behind the Veil*, Urbana: University of Illinois Press.

Stewart, James (1976) *Holy Warriors*, New York: Hill and Wang.

Stewart, J. (ed.) (1998) *Paul Robeson*, New Brunswick, NJ: Rutgers University Press.

Stewart, Jeffrey (1989) *To Color America*, Washington: Smithsonian Institution Press.

Stocking, George (1993) "The Turn-of-the-Century Concept of Race," *Modernism/Modernity*, vol. 1, no. 1: 4–16.

Stovall, Tyler (1996) *Paris Noir: African Americans in the City of Light*, Boston: Houghton Mifflin.

Stuckey, Sterling (1987) *Slave Culture*, New York: Oxford University Press.

Suggs, Henry (ed.) (1983) *The Black Press in the South 1865–1979*, Westport, CN: Greenwood Press.

Sundquist, Eric (1993) *To Wake Nations*, Cambridge, MA: Harvard.

Survey Graphic (1925) "Harlem Mecca of the New Negro," reprint Balto, MD: Black Classic Press.

Tepfer, Diane (1993) "Edith Gregor Halpert: Impresario of Jacob Lawrence's *Migration* Series," in Elizabeth Turner (ed.) (1993) *Jacob Lawrence: The Migration Series*.

Thompson, Daniel (1974) *Sociology of Black Experience*, Westport: Greenwood Press.

Thurman, Wallace [1929] (1997) *The Blacker the Berry*, London: The X Press.

Tillery, Tyrone (1992) *Claude McKay*, Amherst: University of Massachusetts Press.

Tocqueville, Alexis de (1981) *Democracy in America*, New York: Mentor Books.

Tracy, Steven (1988) *Langston Hughes and the Blues*, Urbana: University of Illinois Press.

Turner, Elizabeth (ed.) (1993) *Jacob Lawrence; The Migration Series*, Washington, DC: The Rappahannock Press.

Turner, H. M. (1917) *The Life and Times of Henry M. Turner*, Atlanta.

Van Deburg, William (1997a) *New Day in Babylon and Black Camelot*, Chicago: University of Chicago Press.

Van Deburg, William (ed.) (1997b) *Modern Black Nationalism*, New York: New York University Press.

Walker, Alice (1976) *Meridian*, New York: Pocket Books.

(1983) *In Search of Our Mothers' Gardens*, London: The Women's Press.

(1996) *The Same River Twice*, New York: Washington Square Press.

Wallace, Anthony (1956) "Revitalisation Movements," *American Anthropologist*, vol. 58.

Walzer, Michael (1985) *Exodus and Revolution*, New York: Basic Books.

Ward, Brian (1998) *Just My Soul Responding*, Berkeley: University of California Press.

Washington, Booker (1986) *Up From Slavery*, New York: Penguin.

Watkins, Mel (1994) *On The Real Side*, New York: Simon and Schuster.

Watson, Steven (1995) *The Harlem Renaissance*, New York: Pantheon.

Werner, Craig (1994) *Playing the Changes*, Urbana: University of Illinois Press.

White, Deborah (1999) *Too Heavy A Load*, New York: Norton.

White, Hayden (1987) *The Content of the Form*, Baltimore: Johns Hopkins, University Press.

Williams, G. W. (1882) *History of the Negro Race in America*, New York: Putnam's Sons.

Willis-Braithwaite, Deborah and Rodger Birt (1998) *VanDerZee Photographer 1886–1983*, New York: Harry Abrams.

Wilson, William Julius (1978) *The Declining Significance of Race*, Chicago: University of Chicago Press.

(1987) *The Truly Disadvantaged*, Chicago: University of Chicago Press.

Wintz, Cary (1988) *Black Culture and the Harlem Renaissance*, Houston: Rice University Press.

Woodson, Carter (1915) *The Education of the Negro Prior to 1861*, New York.
  (1933) *The Mis-Education of the Negro*, n.p.
  (1994) "The Migration of the Talented Tenth," in David Lewis (ed.), *The Portable Harlem Renaissance Reader*, New York: Penguin.
Woodard, Komozi (1999) *A Nation Within A Nation*, Chapel Hill: University of North Carolina Press.
Wright, Richard (1940/1991) *Uncle Tom's Children*, New York: Harper-Perennial.
  (1941/1988) *12 Million Black Voices*, New York: Thunder's Mouth Press.
  (1954) *Black Power*, New York.
Young, Allan (1995) *The Harmony of Illusions: Inventing Post-Traumatic Stress Disorder*, Princeton: Princeton University Press.
Zamir, Shamoon (1995) *Dark Voices*, Chicago: University of Chicago Press.

Index

Morrison, Toni, 176, 180, 190, 216
Moses, Bob, 200
Muhammad, Elijah, 162, 167–73, 184, 187, 215
Muhammad Ali, 190
Murray, Freeman, 43
Myrdal, Gunnar, 138

narrative, 4, 6, 21, 26, 42, 43, 44, 174, 182, 189, 199, 208, 221–2
Nation of Islam, 168–73, 190, 194
National Association for the Advancement of Colored People (NAACP), 2, 19, 72, 79, 82, 98–99, 111, 135, 166, 177, 201
National Association of Colored Women, 73
Neal, Arthur, 2, 7
Neal, Larry, 198
Negro World, 99–100, 103
New Deal, 130–34
New Negro, 60, 61, 69, 84–87, 96, 101–4, 110–11
Newton, Huey, 183
Niagara Movement, 71–72

O'Neill, Eugene, 104–5, 107
Opportunity, 97, 101–2
Ottley, Roy, 143

Painter, Nell, 32, 35, 36
Park, Robert, 51
Parks, Rosa, 206
Patterson, Orlando, 2, 214, 221
Payne, Charles, 201
Powell, A. C., 135, 138, 144
Powell, Richard, 60

race, 36, 37, 39, 53, 59, 62–67, 105, 140
race memory, 37, 119
radio, 141–48
Radley, Allen, 5, 8
Rainey, Ma, 119–20, 122
Rampersad, Arnold, 69
Randolph, A. P., 96, 99, 134, 162–63
rap, 219–21
Reconstruction, 5, 13, 32, 33, 35, 36, 58, 68, 130–31
Reiss, W., 110, 123, 125
representation, 1, 2, 13, 14, 21, 46, 56, 70, 81, 115–17, 156
Robeson, Paul, 98, 105, 110, 116, 123, 144, 145, 164
Robinson, Jackie, 164, 202
Rodgers, J. A., 121–22
Roosevelt, Franklin, 130, 132
Rooskam, Edwin, 156–57

Rustin, B., 164
Ryder, Chuck D, 217–19

Sampson, H., 85
Savage, Augusta, 131
Savage, Barbara, 147
Schomberg, Arthur, 97
Schudson, Michael, 7
Schwartz, Barry, 7
Scottsboro, 134
Simmons, Charles, 163
slavery, 1, 9, 14–17, 24, 28–30, 33, 36, 39, 40, 42, 45, 57, 59, 61, 65, 74–75, 87, 90, 119, 148, 157, 171–73, 180, 188, 194, 209–10, 221
Smelser, Neil, 2
Smith, Bessie, 119–20, 122
social movements, 10, 20
   revitalization, 101, 164–65, 179–80
Sorrow Songs, 59, 76–78, 118
Spelman College, 28
Steinbeck, John, 156
Steinberg, M., 150–52
Stepto, Robert, 43
Stowe, Harriet B., 42, 106
Survey Graphic, 110–13, 123, 166
Synge, John M., 49, 58
Sztompka, Piotr, 3

talented tenth, 60, 64, 82
Thurman, Wallace, 37, 125
Trotter, William, 71
Tubman, Harriet, 23
Turner, Henry, 40–41
Tuskegee Institute, 99

United Negro Improvement Association (UNIA), 99, 165–66

VanDerZee, James, 100, 159–61
Van Vechten, Carl, 107–8

Walker, Alice, 153, 215–17
Walker, Margaret, 155
Ward, Brian, 151
Washington, A., 41
Washington, Booker T., 14, 34, 43, 44, 46, 54, 64, 67–69, 71, 82, 99, 137
Waters, Muddy, 149
Watkins, Mel, 76–77
Wells, Ida, 34, 45, 51–54, 73, 96
White, Deborah, 132
White, W., 95, 137
Williams, G. W., 23, 24, 28
Williams, Robert, 196
Wilson, William J, 214–15

MICHAEL MULKAY, *The Embryo Research Debate*
0 521 57180 4 hardback 0 521 57683 0 paperback

LYNN RAPAPORT, *Jews in Germany after the Holocaust*
0 521 58219 9 hardback 0 521 58809 X paperback

CHANDRA MUKERJI, *Territorial Ambitions and the Gardens of Versailles* 0 521 49675 6 hardback 0 521 59959 8 paperback

LEON H. MAYHEW, *The New Public* 0 521 48146 5 hardback
0 521 48493 6 paperback

VERA L. ZOLBERG AND JONI M. CHERBO (eds.), *Outsider Art*
0 521 58111 7 hardback 0 521 58921 5 paperback

SCOTT BRAVMANN, *Queer Fictions of the Past* 0 521 59101 5
hardback 0 521 59907 5 paperback

STEVEN SEIDMAN, *Difference Troubles* 0 521 59043 4 hardback
0 521 59970 9 paperback

RON EYERMAN AND ANDREW JAMISON, *Music and Social Movements* 0 521 62045 7 hardback 0 521 62966 7 paperback

MEYDA YEGENOGLU, *Colonial Fantasies* 0 521 48233 X hardback
0 521 62658 7 paperback

LAURA DESFOR EDLES, *Symbol and Ritual in the New Spain*
0 521 62140 2 hardback 0 521 62885 7 paperback

NINA ELIASOPH, *Avoiding Politics* 0 521 58293 8 hardback
0 521 58759 X paperback

BERNHARD GIESEN, *Intellectuals and the German Nation*
0 521 62161 5 hardback 0 521 63996 4 paperback

PHILIP SMITH (ed.), *The New American Cultural Sociology*
0 521 58415 9 hardback 0 521 58634 8 paperback

S. N. EISENSTADT, *Fundamentalism, Sectarianism and Revolution*
0 521 64184 5 hardback 0 521 64586 7 paperback

MARIAM FRASER, *Identity without Selfhood* 0 521 62357 X
hardback 0 521 62579 3 paperback

LUC BOLTANSKI, *Distant Suffering* 0 521 57389 0 hardback
0 521 65953 1 paperback

PYOTR SZTOMPKA, *Trust* 0 521 59144 9 hardback
0 521 59850 8 paperback

SIMON J. CHARLESWORTH, *A Phenomenology of Working Class
Culture* 0 521 65066 6 hardback 0 521 65915 9 paperback

ROBIN WAGNER-PACIFICI, *Theorizing the Standoff*
0 521 65244 8 hardback 0 521 65479 3 paperback

RONALD R. JACOBS, *Race, Media and the Crisis of Civil Society*
0 521 62360 X hardback 0 521 62578 5 paperback

ALI MIRSEPASSI, *Intellectual Discourse and the Politics
of Modernization* 0 521 65000 3 hardback 0 521 65997 3 paperback

RON LEMBO, *Thinking Through Television* 0 521 58465 5 hardback
0 521 58577 5 paperback

MICHÈLE LAMONT AND LAURENT THÉVENOT (eds.),
Rethinking Comparative Cultural Sociology 0 521 78263 5
hardback 0 521 78794 7 paperback

STEPHEN M. ENGEL, *The Unfinished Revolution: Social Movement
Theory and the Gay and Lesbian Movement* 0 521 80287 3 hardback
0 521 00377 6 paperback